PROFESSIONAL SECRETARIES INTERNATIONAL® COMPLETE OFFICE HANDBOOK

**PROFESSIONAL
SECRETARIES
INTERNATIONAL** ®

COMPLETE OFFICE HANDBOOK

The Secretary's Guide to
Today's Electronic Office

Susan Jaderstrom, Leonard Kruk, and
Joanne Miller

General Editor   Susan W. Fenner

RANDOM HOUSE
NEW YORK

Copyright © 1992 by Professional Secretaries International®

All rights reserved under International and Pan-American Copyright Conventions. No part of this publication may be reproduced in any form or by any means, electronic or mechanical, including photocopying, without permission in writing from the publisher. All inquiries should be addressed to Reference Department, Random House, Inc., 201 East 50th Street, New York, NY 10022. Published in the United States by Random House, Inc., New York, and simultaneously in Canada by Random House of Canada Limited, Toronto.

Library of Congress Cataloging-in-Publication Data
Jaderstrom, Susan.
    Professional Secretaries International® complete office handbook :
  the definitive reference for today's electronic office / by Susan
  Jaderstrom, Leonard Kruk, and Joanne Miller.
     p.   cm.
  Includes index.
  ISBN 0-679-74611-0
  1. Office practice—Automation. I. Kruk, Leonard B. II. Miller,
Joanne. III. Professional Secretaries International. IV. Title.
HF5548.J34 1992
651.8—dc20   91-43208   CIP

Paperback edition ISBN: 0-679-74611-0

Manufactured in the United States of America

  2   3   4   5   6   7   8   9 P

    3   4   5   6   7   8   9 H

New York, Toronto, London, Sydney, Auckland

CONTENTS

ILLUSTRATIONS

FIGURES

TABLES

PART I

PROFESSIONAL DEVELOPMENT AND HUMAN RELATIONS

CHAPTER 1

GROWING PROFESSIONALLY

Career options for office professionals at all levels are rapidly expanding as a result of automation of office tasks. Technology has created an information age that has changed the way offices operate and the way information is handled, affording new opportunities for professional growth.

By the year 2000, it is predicted that nearly 90 percent of all personnel will be working in offices. These professionals will be required to have strong technical and interpersonal skills and function as integral parts of the management team. In addition, office-support positions will require the lifelong education and retraining of workers for them to keep pace with changing office technology and to be responsive to marketplace demands.

CHANGING ROLES: FROM SECRETARY TO EXECUTIVE ASSISTANT

The position of secretary has its earliest recorded mention in the 16th century. Then a secretary was usually a man with the ability to read, write, and calculate; he wrote all manuscripts, letters, and records by hand.

Not until the late nineteenth and early twentieth centuries did the mechanized office come into being. The invention of the typewriter, telephone, duplicating equipment, and calculating machine helped to speed up information processing within business. As a result, the male secretary's support role evolved into management as he became an understudy for the executive and the executive's successor in managing the business. With that change, more and more women were hired and trained to perform clerical support tasks for this male-dominated management.

The office today, however, is very different from the one that existed earlier in the twentieth century. Several important factors have contributed to this change.

One factor is technology. The computer is replacing the typewriter. The ease of having facts and figures available and able to be manipulated by electronic tools makes computer literacy essential for everyone in business.

Business is also increasing in size and complexity. The economic need to reduce office costs through greater productivity has made the secretarial role emerge as a major responsible position within the office.

No longer is the secretary necessarily a woman, nor is the secretary viewed as a lowly clerk. Both men and women are opting for administrative support careers. These office positions are recognized as a significant factor in the efficient operation of an organization, especially given the rising costs of information processing. The position of office professional has thus become a management apprenticeship with nearly unlimited opportunities.

The recent evolution of the secretary to administrative or executive assistant is significant. Although expert keyboarding and language skills are still critical, the role is evolving to one of a paraprofessional who supports management in the processing and organizing of information.

The job market for office professionals is exceptionally strong. A secretarial shortage exists due to changing career goals, retirement of an older work force, and creation of more and more jobs within this field by advances in technology.

Among the findings of a recent study of secretarial help wanted ads conducted by Dartnell Corporations Institute of Business Research and From Nine to Five, the demand for secretarial computer skills is greater than ever. Nearly two-thirds of the want ads required some type of computer experience. Word processing is the most frequently requested skill in secretaries, appearing in 56 percent of the ads.

Professional Secretaries International® defines today's secretary as "an executive assistant who possesses a mastery of office skills, who demonstrates the ability to assume responsibility without direct supervision, who exercises initiative and judgment and who makes decisions within the scope of assigned authority."

Job titles and responsibilities vary dramatically from organization to organization. The title "secretary" is rapidly being replaced by other terms, such as "office professional," to reflect the changing office environment and responsibilities of today's office support staff.

ENTRY-LEVEL OPPORTUNITIES

As more positions are evolving, the term "secretary" is now increasingly applied to entry-level or clerical positions. There is no standardization within this field, nor is there a single, clear definition for different job titles. However, a number of entry-level opportunities exist for office professionals to begin their careers in the office-support field.

It is relatively easy to enter this profession. At least a high school education with an emphasis on keyboarding, effective written and oral communication, and information management is necessary. Knowledge of office procedures and familiarity with word processing and computer equipment and software packages are additional assets.

Professional Secretaries International® (PSI®) recently conducted an entry-level competency study and found that beginning office workers should know how to manage records; handle telephone calls, mail, and appointments; keyboard; prepare correspondence; and use language skills. In addition, the ability to use word processing and financial software packages is important, as is projecting a professional image and self-direction in learning.

A number of entry-level positions exist. Persons in entry-level positions must be prepared to perform a variety of office functions, with broad emphasis on professional attitudes, behaviors, and skills rather than on particular job titles or stereotyped roles. Since each organization is different, job titles may vary.

Administrative support (AS) generally includes most of the nonclerical functions previously performed by the traditional secretary. Skills and characteristics needed within the area of administrative support include ability to work as part of a team, good communication and organization skills, and initiative.

Beginning positions include the following:

Switchboard operator: Handles incoming calls and processes outgoing calls, has a good telephone voice, takes messages, answers inquiries, and handles fax transmissions.

Receptionist: Welcomes, orients, and directs visitors, handles phone system or switchboard, does some filing and correspondence, handles fax transmissions, controls petty cash, uses office equipment, distributes mail, and controls courier and messenger dispatch.

Secretary: Handles routine functions in the office, such as processing the mail and answering telephones.

With new technology being used in business almost as quickly as it is introduced, nearly 90 percent of all medium- to large-sized businesses use integrated office systems, that is, office equipment, including computers, connected via a communications network. These systems require specially trained personnel with traditional basic skills as well as new skills to manage and operate the office.

Word processing positions are excellent starting points for office careers, since they offer valuable training for people at the entry level and exceptional advancement potential for those who gain experience. The demand nationwide for word processing skills has increased.

Entry-level positions within the word processing field include:

Word processing operator/trainee: Keys simple correspondence and reports and applies various word processing software applications.

Word processing specialist: Keys and produces dictated work; keys assignments submitted in writing, in printed form, or in other forms.

Skills and characteristics needed for those interested in a career in word processing include the ability to work independently, a technical orientation, computer skills, a knowledge of word processing software, a team consciousness, accuracy, language arts and grammatical skills, audio acuity for transcription, and the ability to proofread, edit, and prioritize tasks.

Records management has become a technically specialized field, but it offers entry-level opportunities in three major areas: filing and micrographics; archiving; and destruction of records. Micrographics is the process of recording information in a reduced form through microfilming.

Entry-level job opportunities in records.management include: .

Records clerk/trainee: Performs simple sorting and retrieving of information.

Junior file clerk: Processes material already classified by a senior clerk.

Micrographics technician: Operates technology in the preparation of microforms under close supervision.

Skills and characteristics needed for this field include having a team consciousness and being detail-minded, logical, systematic, and security conscious.

Several other entry-level opportunities exist in office services. Among them is:

Travel services clerk: Delivers tickets, car keys, and communications related to travel; uses data processing and telecommunications to provide travel services.

ADVANCED-LEVEL OPPORTUNITIES

Advancement from an entry-level position within an organization largely depends on the perseverance and hard work of the entry-level professional. Each organization varies in how far it will advance its office-support personnel. Titles such as administrative assistant, executive assistant, and executive secretary are often used interchangeably to describe secretaries performing higher-level office tasks or working for higher-level executives.

Entry-level professionals often advance into administrative support, which generally involves the following:

- Providing support services to executives
- Performing general office duties in addition to typing
- Carrying out administrative assistance tasks

Other important skills and abilities for office administrators to have include:

- English skills
- Human relations skills
- Problem-solving abilities
- Analytical and decision-making abilities
- Computer literacy
- Supervisory and managerial techniques
- Communication skills, including speaking, listening, and writing
- Research skills

These skills may also qualify office professionals for first-line managerial positions. Within word processing, this could mean advancement to the following jobs:

Word processing supervisor: Guides and directs administrative and word processing personnel; makes sure that work in the department is completed correctly, efficiently, and on time.

Administrative support supervisor: Hires, evaluates, and trains new personnel; delegates and assigns work; coordinates work schedules; keeps attendance and payroll records; tracks new office technology; develops, writes, and implements office procedures; establishes and maintains work production standards; supervises and motivates personnel.

Word processing coordinator: Coordinates work flow, determines priorities, and monitors work distribution.

Word processing supervisor: Supervises word processing staff.

Word processing manager: Manages, budgets, and controls the word processing operation.

Advancement in records management follows paths similar to advancement in word processing. Advanced positions include:

Records supervisor: Supervises the records center clerks; assumes responsibility for record protection and security; and evaluates records staff performance.

Records coordinator: Coordinates work flow, determines priorities, and monitors work distribution.

Records manager: Manages, budgets, and controls the records department.

SPECIALIZED OFFICE CAREER OPPORTUNITIES

Just as in any career, office professionals have an opportunity to specialize in many fields. In the fields of law, medicine, education, government, and technology, numerous career opportunities exist for the office professional.

Although the basic duties within each specialized field may be similar and the use of office technology the same, terminology, applications, and procedures vary greatly from field to field. A quick look at each field will help to clarify some of the differences.

THE LEGAL OFFICE PROFESSIONAL

Accuracy and speed are important requirements for a career in the legal field. Whether in a one-lawyer office or a large firm, the work of a law office is detailed and exacting. Terminology is precise; timing, organization, and confidentiality are essential in this field.

Duties include keying and transcription. A knowledge of legal documents and legal terminology as well as good oral and writing skills are important. The work is highly varied, ranging from managing the office to preparing legal documents and court papers; it also includes extensive contact with clients.

Many kinds of positions are available within the legal profession. They include opportunities in single-attorney offices, in partnerships, in large law firms, in the legal departments of major corporations, and in the local, state, and federal court systems. Legal firms' practices vary from general law to specialization in such areas as real estate, corporate law, tax law, criminal law, estate planning, marital law, or labor law.

THE MEDICAL OFFICE PROFESSIONAL

The medical office professional's special duties include managing the office, scheduling patients, quoting and collecting fees, preparing and processing insurance claim forms, ordering and maintaining supplies and equipment, transcribing dictation, maintaining patients' records, assisting and supporting patients, and assisting in clinical duties if trained to do so by attending physicians. Confidentiality of patient records must always be maintained.

Opportunities within the medical profession exist in physicians' offices, medical clinics, public health facilities, hospitals, health maintenance organizations, nursing homes, research centers, medical centers, foundations, laboratories, insurance agencies, private agencies, medical departments of large companies, educational institutions, companies that manufacture medical supplies and equipment, and medical transcription service companies.

THE EDUCATIONAL OFFICE PROFESSIONAL

A career in the educational field can be multifaceted regardless of the educational level. This office professional must have excellent communication skills and the ability to work under established policies and practices as well as to plan and organize work schedules. Computer skills and transcription are important, as is familiarity with other office machines. The educational office professional must serve as liaison between students, teachers, administrators, coworkers, parents, and the local community, so interpersonal skills are essential.

The duties of educational office professionals vary from institution to institution. Opportunities for such personnel exist from the preschool to the graduate level and can be in public, private, or church-affiliated schools, large or small. Specialized schools for special need students, vocational schools, and correctional schools also need office professionals. Many not-for-profit organizations, such as the National Education Association and the American Association of School Administrators offer job opportunities.

THE GOVERNMENT OFFICE PROFESSIONAL

The largest employer in the United States is the federal government, which offers numerous opportunities both here and abroad for office professionals. To become eligible for most government positions, you must take a written civil service examination. Promotions are usually made from within based on the availability, demonstrated skills, and seniority of those applying.

Other positions are available in state, county, and municipal governments as well as in quasi-governmental agencies. Contact the Office of Personnel Management in the region in which you desire employment; it is the best source for checking available jobs in the public sector.

THE TECHNICAL OFFICE PROFESSIONAL

Aerospace, agriculture, engineering, environmental protection, chemistry, life sciences, mathematics, and the physical sciences are just some of the career fields available to the technical office professional.

Knowledge of electronic office equipment is essential for the technical office professional. Technical documents such as scientific reports and abstracts, require proper formatting. Technical office professionals must have the ability to key technical data accurately and to proofread text that includes mathematical equations, symbols, and technical data. A strong background in mathematics or science and a knowledge of technical terminology are definite assets. Confidentiality is also a critical element for this field.

The growth of research and technology, within both government and private companies, has created many opportunities for office professionals who have the ability to deal with technical terms and symbols. Because these offices deal with technology, most such offices use modern electronic equipment that can provide additional experience.

PART-TIME, TEMPORARY, AND HOME OFFICE CAREERS

Changes in the demographics of the work force, labor shortages, and the advancement of technology have made the options for office professionals more flexible. While most are employed on a full-time basis in a particular office, today's office professional also works part-time, as a temporary, or even from home.

Some businesses prefer hiring on a part-time rather than a full-time basis. An individual or firm may require only a few hours of work each day or a few days of work per week in order to fulfill necessary work requirements. For some companies, dividing a full-time job between two part-time employees has proven to be a plus and has added to job flexibility. Part-time work enables individuals to maintain important career skills while at the same time allowing them to pursue other responsibilities and interests.

TEMPORARY CAREER OPTIONS

More than a million temporary workers are used by businesses every day, according to the National Association of Temporary Services (NATS), a trade group based in Alexandria, Virginia. Businesses use temporary workers, or temps, for a variety of reasons. Many firms use temps to handle seasonal peak workloads better. Some companies use temporary agencies to avoid the problems of recruiting and training permanent workers or as a way to maintain lean permanent staffs. For various reasons, the temp career is a viable option for today's office professional.

Two economic trends are also contributing to the use of temps. The first is a shortage of qualified workers. According to *The Occupational Outlook Handbook,* an annual publication from the U.S. Department of Labor, the demand for skilled clerical and technical help is forecasted to grow significantly faster than the demand for the work force as a whole.

The second trend is the changing lifestyles of the work force itself. Factors such as the women's movement, the aging of the work force, and increased labor-force mobility have created a labor shortage.

As a result of these trends, a temporary office career fits with many workers' career goals. Temps come in all ages, both genders, and are highly trained. To keep pace with the growing demand for computer-literate office workers, temp services usually provide training to sharpen computer skills and to provide knowledge of current hardware and software. This not only helps the employer, but can also provide temps with skills that might otherwise never be learned or upgraded.

THE HOME OFFICE CAREER

For at least 34 million Americans, modern technology has allowed the world of work to remain at home part-time or full-time. The trend toward working at home is driven by the personal computer, which can be connected to a phone in order to "telecommute" to the office. Increasingly, clerical workers use this option to do tasks formerly performed in offices, as do home-based entrepreneurs who provide services to numerous organizations. A home office career allows professionals to maintain skills and pursue a career. They can contribute to the organization while following other interests or while managing the household, all without having to leave home.

PREPARATION FOR OTHER CAREERS

Unlike many other professions, the office professional field offers many career options. Neither extensive preparation nor a degree in business administration or a technical or scientific field is necessary.

For example, a secretary who is interested in a career in the communications industry might take a position at a television station or public relations firm to gain firsthand experience. With that experience, an office worker could advance to being an account executive or a salesperson. A secretary interested in law might train as a legal secretary, obtain a position in a law firm, and then advance to a paralegal position.

With the increased knowledge needed to use office technology, office professionals have found positions as word processing equipment salespersons and as marketing support representatives. They have also become customer service representatives, who provide training and backup services for word processing customers.

Traditional furniture vendors are expanding and diversifying their marketing horizons to include office furniture that is especially designed to meet the needs of the electronic office. Managers of such vendors often seek marketing representatives who are knowledgeable about the furniture required by the integrated office, its effects on personnel, and the expectations of users.

Other advanced office career options in the computer field include training directors, who train personnel in user companies on word processing and related equipment; programmers, who write the software that tells computers what operations to perform; systems analysts, who develop appropriate programs, systems, and applications for users; and equipment technicians, who repair and service word processing equipment. Another option is to become an independent word processing contractor, who word processes at home for firms that have no word processing equipment or that need additional support during peak periods.

The likelihood for an entry-level secretary in today's office to advance to an operational or managerial job is great, thanks to automation. Automation has freed the office professional to make more decisions and receive more recognition. Within this profession, you can guide your career in a direction that will be in harmony with your own talents. Growing numbers of office professionals find their careers following a path into computers, finance, desktop publishing, administration, personnel, and management.

PROFESSIONAL DEVELOPMENT AND GROWTH

To advance in your career, it is important to continue education in your field. Reading is the best and easiest way to grow professionally. Current news magazines, business-oriented publications, and trade publications can help keep you informed about events, trends, policies, and procedures.

If you can, enroll in a local college or in continuing education courses. Colleges offer evening and weekend courses; many give credit for life experiences. Take advantage of company-sponsored workshops and seminars. In addition, many professional organizations offer seminars to help office professionals understand and perform better in their jobs.

Another good step is to join professional organizations, such as the Professional Secretaries International® (PSI®); the National Association of Legal Secretaries (NALS); the Association of Word Processors; the American Association for Medical Assistants (AAMA); the American Association for Medical Transcription (AAMT); and many others. These groups provide a wealth of information on word and information processing and office automation. Most offer newsletters, magazines, seminars, workshops, and equipment exhibits.

Other groups, such as consultants, retailers, and manufacturers, offer seminars and information on such topics as how to integrate word and data processing and how to increase office productivity as well as training in time management, office organization, and filing techniques.

See About Professional Secretaries International® on page 573.

PROFESSIONAL DEVELOPMENT THROUGH CERTIFICATION

Professional Secretaries International® administers two business-oriented certification programs in the office professional field. Receiving these certifications is indicative of meeting the highest professional standards. The registered service mark for the rating that measures secretarial proficiency is Certified Professional Secretary® (CPS®). The rating is obtained by (1) completing and verifying educational and secretarial employment experience requirements and (2) passing a six-part, two-day examination administered each May and November by the Institute for Certifying Secretaries, a department of PSI.

Working secretaries, students, and business educators are eligible to take the CPS examination. Many colleges and universities grant credit hours to people with the CPS rating who are enrolled in a degree program.

The examination is divided into the following six parts:

1. *Behavioral Science in Business:* This part tests for knowledge of the principles of human relations and organizational dynamics in the workplace. It focuses on needs, motivation, the nature of conflict, problem-solving techniques, essentials of supervision and communication, leadership style, and understanding of the informal organization.

2. *Business Law:* This part measures knowledge of the principles of business law and of the effect of governmental controls on business.

3. *Economics and Management:* This part consists of 35 percent economics and 65 percent management. Emphasis is placed on understanding the basic concepts underlying business operations.

4. *Accounting:* This part measures knowledge of the elements of the accounting cycle, the ability to analyze financial statements and accounts, the ability to perform arithmetical operations associated with accounting, and the ability to summarize and interpret financial data.

5. *Office Administration and Communication:* This part measures proficiency in subjects unique to the secretary's position, such as office management, records management and reprographics, preparing communications, and editing.

6. *Office Technology:* This part covers knowledge of data processing, communications media, advances in office management, technological applications, records management technology, and office systems.

PSI also has an entry-level certification assessment program. The Office Proficiency Assessment and Certification™ (OPAC™) Program is a $3\frac{1}{2}$-hour, PC-based program administered by educational institutions and corporations. Areas covered by this program include: keyboarding and word processing; communications; handling mail, telephone, and appointments; and technical and financial records management. It also provides diagnostic information to allow the user to assess his or her skills and abilities.

Certification is also possible in certain specialized fields. A legal secretary may become a Professional Legal Secretary (PLS). This is the only certification program for legal secretaries; it provides a standard measurement of legal secretarial knowledge and skills.

In order to qualify to take the two-day certification exam, a person must have three years' experience as a legal secretary. A partial waiver of the three-year experience requirement may be granted if the applicant has a bachelor's or associate's degree. Seven areas of legal secretarial practice and procedures are included in the exam: written communication skills and knowledge; ethics; legal secretarial procedures; legal secretarial accounting; exercise of judgment; legal secretarial skills; and legal terminology, techniques, and procedures. Additional information can be obtained by contacting the National Association of Legal Secretaries.

Medical assistants are eligible to join the American Association of Medical Assistants (AAMA). The AAMA offers a certifying examination that upon successful passing leads to certification as a Certified Medical Assistant (CMA). The exam is given twice a year on the last Friday in January and June, at designated centers. Recertification is mandatory every five years. This can be achieved through continuing education or through reexamination. For more information contact the American Association of Medical Assistants.

Certification as a medical transcriptionist can be obtained through the American Association for Medical Transcription (AAMT). Their examination leads to certification as a Certified Medical Transcriptionist (CMT). Certification is valid for three years. It may be renewed by paying the annual certification administration fee and earning a minimum of 30 continuing education credits in each three-year period of certification, or by passing the certification examination every three years. Additional information can be obtained by contacting the American Association for Medical Transcription.

Office personnel in the educational field can obtain certification through the National

Association of Educational Office Personnel (NAEOP). Their Professional Standards Program leads to the distinction of a Certified Educational Office Employee. This is awarded to those who meet established criteria.

Organizations for office professionals include:

General
Professional Secretaries International
10502 NW Ambassador Drive
PO Box 20404
Kansas City, MO 64195
(816) 891-6600

Legal
National Association of Legal Secretaries
2250 East 73 Street, Suite 550
Tulsa, OK 74136
(918) 493-3540

Educational
National Association of Educational Office Personnel
7223 Lee Highway, Suite 301
Falls Church, VA 22046
(703) 533-0810

Medical
American Association of Medical Assistants
20 North Wacker, Suite 1575
Chicago, IL 60606
(312) 899-1500
(800) 228-2262

American Association for Medical Transcription
PO Box 6187
Modesto, CA 95355
(800) 982-2182

SEMINARS, WORKSHOPS, AND TRAINING

In addition to certification, office professionals today must rely on seminars, workshops, and other training programs to achieve ongoing career development and to keep up with changing technology in the automated office. Many professional associations sponsor seminars on professional development. Other organizations train businesspeople through other workshops and seminars.

Many companies provide in-house training programs to their employees as a means of keeping their work force's skills at optimum levels. Some programs are taught by instructors from within the organization. Others are hired from outside the company for their expertise in particular topics.

Other training programs are self-taught. They may use manuals, which may be combined with a computer software program; tutorials; audiotapes; videotapes; or interactive video instruction. Interactive video instruction allows the trainee to become actively involved with the computer screen and keyboard. The trainee in effect directs the lesson by "dialoguing" with the computer.

SETTING PERSONAL GOALS

The growth in jobs for office professionals represents 50 percent of the total growth in jobs for white-collar workers. The office and all its related support areas offer some of the greatest growth potential ever known. As an office professional you have a better chance to achieve your personal goals if you know your own goals as well as the goals of your organization.

In order to set personal goals, you must know what you want out of life and how hard you are willing to work for it. Goals define where you want to go and how you want to get there. They are benchmarks by which you can measure your progress. By setting goals, high achievers are able to seize opportunities to make those goals realities.

Every job you hold is a critical step in the development of your career. A career requires long-term planning and commitment to help you reach your professional potential. A master career plan should consist of long-range goals and short-range, more immediate objectives. An inventory of the skills you have—the things you do well and enjoy—is the very core of a plan for your career.

To build a successful career, you also must know the basic skills and components of your career. For example, if your goal is to become a word processing trainer, you must know word processing, the equipment used, and the procedures involved in order to be an effective teacher. Such knowledge is usually gained through work experience.

The development of job and career objectives is a continuous process. Each day, month, and year you know more about yourself. At the same time, you deepen and broaden your knowledge of the world of work and continue to work toward meeting your goals—whatever they may be.

When planning goals for your career, you need to decide what role you want to pursue in the offices of both today and tomorrow. You must be open-minded in order to maintain the flexibility needed to work within this ever-changing environment.

CAREER PATHS AND CAREER LADDERS

The average American today will work for 10 different employers, keep each job only 3.6 years, and change entire careers three times before retirement. These statistics may sound somewhat astonishing, but they show that career paths and career ladders are important elements in this process. A **career path** is a course of action in a career and the various steps taken to achieve an end result. A **career ladder** is a list of the promotions achieved during one's career.

A career path addresses goals that have been established. For instance, suppose an office professional determined that her desired career is to be a lawyer specializing in the medical field. Initially, she took a job as a secretary at a medical office. Then she spent time getting a law degree at night from a local university. Her career path showed her the steps to take to achieve her career goal.

Climbing the career ladder, on the other hand, begins when one has determined one's career path and is advancing up the "rungs" through promotion. In any career, several career ladders exist. Within an office, a career ladder for word processing may exist as well as one for administrative services. Only you can determine which ladder you want to climb and only you can create opportunities in order to climb the ladder.

THE FUTURE

Technology is creating a new information age that will forever change the way offices operate and the way information is handled. High technology is proliferating in the office environment. It is estimated that 90 percent of all medium to large businesses will have integrated office systems by the year 2000. Eventually, almost everyone in the office will have a personal computer sitting on his or her desk, from the executives down to the clerks.

Keyboards, video screens, satellite communications, telephone lines, fiber optics, and computers are all being integrated into the electronic environment. Within the next few years, computers may take voice dictation, transcribe and type letters, take edited phone calls, correct one's vocabulary and syntax, and do filing.

One thing is certain—machines are not replacing the secretary in the office. If anything, they are enhancing and expanding the position to one of greater importance than ever. The future will be dominated by a new discipline, termed "knowledge management." As the office environment becomes electronic, the key to the office professional's career success lies in his or her ability to connect—to connect phone calls, messages, schedules, information, reports, and data—and to put information together for a particular use. Administrative support personnel are the gatekeepers of the electronic channels. As these channels become more prevalent and more developed, the role of controlling and making sense of all this electronic traffic will become even more important.

Most executives do not have the basic skills or interest to deal with all information management. As a result, the office professional will be increasingly called upon to organize information and to do research using electronic media, thus increasing opportunities for professional growth.

The future for office professionals is focused on electronically aided management of information. Lifelong education and retraining must be an integral part of the office professional's career in order to keep pace with changing office technology and to respond to marketplace demands for office professionals with keyboarding skills, computer savvy, communication skills, and team spirit.

CHAPTER 2

CAREER ADVANCEMENT

Career advancement can be a job promotion or new job within your present company or a new position with another firm. In order to prepare for career opportunities, you must be able to:

- Prepare a resume
- Write a cover letter
- Fill out an employment application
- Interview successfully
- Follow up on the interview
- Complete employment tests
- Determine when to use employment agencies or other support networks

THE RESUME

A resume is a written summary of abilities, accomplishments, and work history. The purpose of the resume is to get an interview, not a job. Employers do not hire on the basis of a resume alone, but the resume should motivate an employer to meet you. The resume should have the following qualities:

❏ It should be well organized, so it can be read in six to eight seconds. The preferred length is one or two pages of $8\frac{1}{2}$-by-11-inch paper, no matter how many previous jobs or how much experience and education a candidate has.

❏ It should emphasize strengths and accomplishments and show that the candidate is qualified for the available job. It should demonstrate excellent writing skills, with perfect grammar, spelling, and punctuation. A well-written resume is tailored to the available job, showing a knowledge of the necessary skills, talents, and background. A resume is not a life history, lengthy job description, or detailed listing of irrelevant earlier jobs.

❏ It should be attractive to the eye. The best way to ensure this is to use a computer. Word-processed resumes may be easily and quickly accessed in order to make changes and corrections. Many word processing packages have graphics capabilities that include options for different typefaces and type sizes, which can produce a highly professional-looking resume.

The resume should be printed with a laser printer or comparable high-quality printer on 16- to 20-pound bond paper. If a copy machine is used to copy an original, the quality of the copy should be excellent. If the copy machine cannot copy on bond paper, have the resume printed at a print shop. Design the resume so that the information does not look crowded on the page by using wide margins, double spacing, or indentations. White, beige, gray, or pale blue paper may used.

Your resume should have the following components:

- Heading
- Job objective
- Work experience
- Education

HEADING

The heading includes your name, address (including ZIP Code), and home and/or work telephone numbers (including area codes). If a home telephone answering machine is used, the recording should be professional and to the point. If your present employer is aware of your job search, then include your work number. If it is impossible to talk with a prospective employer at a work phone, then omit it.

Some suggested styles for resume headings are shown in the sample resumes. (See Figures 2-1 and 2-2, for example.)

JOB OBJECTIVE

The job objective may be included, although if you have only a little experience you may find a job objective limiting. A candidate with experience should have a clear idea of a career area. The job objective lets the employer know that you have gone through a thorough self-analysis and know what you want in your career.

The job objective immediately follows the heading and states a job title or specific occupational field. Unless the job objective is general, it should be restated to reflect each different position you apply for. This rewriting is easy to do if the resume is on a computer.

Here are some possible job objectives:

- Administrative assistant to the director of sales
- Legal secretary for a law firm specializing in litigation
- Word processing specialist in the insurance industry
- Medical transcriptionist in a metropolitan hospital
- Records management specialist for a manufacturing firm

WORK EXPERIENCE

This is the core of the resume. Experience should be listed in reverse chronological order or according to job functions. Reverse chronological order is preferable if you are staying in the same field, especially if your job history shows growth and development. Reverse chronological resumes list the most recent job first. (See Figures 2-1 and 2-2.) If there are many jobs to list, select the last four or five.

Listing experience by job functions can be useful if you are changing careers, entering the job market for the first time, reentering the job market after an absence, or have an irregular work history. This type of resume describes your responsibilities over the years, starting with the most important work-related tasks. Your employers are listed separately.

Any major accomplishment can be included under the job function without stating the name of the employer. (See Figure 2-3.) Separating the job functions from employer names is particularly useful when changing from one type of business to another (for example, applying for a job in a nonprofit association after working for a manufacturer).

Whether the resume lists jobs reverse chronologically or by job functions, all descriptions should be clear. Phrases such as "worked as acting administrative assistant" or "worked as accountant" are too vague and will not give employers an idea of the work performed. Even the phrase "responsible for" does not give a good idea of job duties.

Employers want to know what you accomplished on the job, not just what your job description was. You should use action verbs, which are verbs that help create a well-defined image of contributions and accomplishments. Listed below are some action verbs you could use to describe your accomplishments:

Analyzed	Evaluated	Presented
Assisted	Examined	Processed
Calculated	Generated	Produced
Collected	Implemented	Purchased
Composed	Instructed	Recommended
Conducted	Interpreted	Represented
Consulted	Maintained	Researched
Coordinated	Managed	Reviewed
Created	Ordered	Saved
Designed	Organized	Scheduled
Developed	Performed	Supervised
Diagnosed	Planned	Trained
Directed	Prepared	Wrote

Numbers and figures should be included whenever possible. Money-saving techniques should be stated. "Managed yearly operation budget of $170,000" is more impressive than "managed budget." Supervisory experience should be emphasized, stating how many people were hired, trained, and supervised.

The following are additional suggestions for writing about your experience:

Carol Garcia
87 Wilmington Drive
San Rafael, CA 94903
415-975-4975

Objective

To secure a position of office manager offering responsibility, growth, and interaction with people.

Experience

1981–present

Resvail Office Equipment, San Rafael, CA
Regional Sales Support Manager
- Hire, train, supervise, and evaluate an office staff of six.
- Monitor and control regional expense budget.
- Develop marketing plans and activities designed to generate new business.
- Direct the development of promotional mailings and telemarketing campaigns.
- Assist in planning and organizing sales meetings, workshops, and conferences.
- Research and recommend systems, equipment, and supplies to maintain office productivity.
- Conduct training sessions on new products, equipment, and software.
- Develop and maintain excellent customer relations with key customers.

1973–1981

Statistical Specialist
- Analyzed sales figures and reported trends to regional manager.
- Prepared monthly sales reports by region, district, and representative.
- Computed end-of-year sales figures for bonus plan.
- Trained sales representatives on the sales information systems.
- Monitored and reported out-of-stock problems.

Education

San Francisco City College, San Francisco, CA
Degree: Associate in Arts and Science
Major: Accounting and Business Administration

Special courses: Customer-Oriented Selling, Supervision, and Management

Attended Certified Professional Secretary Seminar, Savannah, GA, 1990

Figure 2-1 A reverse chronological resume for a person with many years of experience in one firm.

Marcia Hernandez _____
38 South Hawthorne Way • Washington, DC 20009
202-998-7236

Job Objective   Administrative assistant with sales firm

QUALIFICATIONS AND SKILLS

- Fourteen years of office support experience, including customer relations
- Excellent time management and organizational skills
- Self-motivated, dependable, and goal-oriented employee
- Skilled in written and verbal communications
- Professional appearance and high professional standards

PROFESSIONAL EXPERIENCE

1985–present   SENIOR SALES ASSISTANT
Bigelow Publishing Co., Washington, D.C.

Primary focus of this position was marketing and technical support for six sales representatives in Florida, West Virginia, Virginia, North Carolina, South Carolina, and Pennsylvania.

- Develop specialized education materials.
- Coordinate regional sales exhibits and conferences.
- Serve as liaison between central office, editorial staff, customers, and sales representatives.
- Research and compose correspondence for representatives.
- Coordinate city and county textbook adoptions, and develop and maintain production information.
- Access computerized inventory and customer database.

1980–1985   DISPATCHER
3M Business Products Sales, Inc., Reston, VA

Routed and dispatched 20 service representatives for copy machines in the greater Washington, D.C., area

1975–1980   ORDER CLERK
3M Business Products Sales, Inc., Reston, VA

Received orders for 300 businesses over the telephone for office and school supplies in the greater Washington, D.C., area.

Figure 2-2 A reverse chronological resume for a person looking for work in the same field.

Joanne Jacobson
3948 Grove Street • Kansas City, MO 64112
816-473-4930

Objective: Position as an executive secretary involving information services with a high degree of public contact.

HIGHLIGHTS OF QUALIFICATIONS

- Ten years of experience as an administrative assistant.
- Familiar with both PC-DOS and Macintosh operating systems plus a variety of word processing, database, and spreadsheet software.
- Learns new computer systems quickly.
- Consistently earned outstanding performance evaluations.
- Attained Certified Professional Secretary (CPS) rating, 1989.

PROFESSIONAL EXPERIENCE

Organizational and Planning Skills
- Conducted in-house systems training on the computer network for 200 employees.
- Developed office procedures, including office manuals.
- Planned and supervised yearly national sales meetings for 200 employees, including choosing the meeting site, confirming speakers, and arranging for support services.
- Prepared all reports for the Board of Directors' monthly meetings.

Interpersonal/Communication Skills
- Served as a liaison with data-processing manager and outside consulting firm to coordinate personal computers with the mainframe.
- Coordinated payroll preparation with outside processing firm.
- Wrote press releases.
- Took dictation and prepared correspondence.

Computer Skills
- Researched, proposed, and supervised the installation of a $55,000 purchase of telecommunications and computer equipment.
- Prepared income and expense spreadsheets using Lotus 1-2-3 on the IBM PC.
- Designed company newsletter on the Macintosh computer using Word and PageMaker software.

–Continued–

Figure 2-3 A resume highlighting job duties for a person with similar work experience in a variety of firms.

JOANNE JACOBSON
Page two

EMPLOYMENT HISTORY

1989–present	Administrative Assistant	First Interstate Bank Kansas City, MO
1987–1989	Administrative Assistant	Valley Bank Overland Park, KS
1985–1987	Secretary	Kellogg and Sons Blue Springs, KS
1984–1985	Secretary	Borden Foods Company East Point, GA

EDUCATION

Enrolled in Administrative Management program at Mission College, Kansas City, MO.

Member of Professional Secretaries International.

Figure 2-3 *(cont'd)*

❏ Avoid long sentences. A description of a job or job duty should be ten lines long or less.

❏ Avoid using "I," for example, "I was responsible for supervising five employees. In this position I did . . ." Instead, use action verbs without a pronoun: "Managed and maintained local area network of 15 office computers. Recommended selection and purchase of new database software."

❏ Use years instead of months and days: 1985–present or 1988–1990.

❏ Write "continued" on the bottom of the first page of a two-page resume and your full name and "page 2" on the second page.

❏ Omit jobs that go back 10 or 15 years if space is limited. It is not necessary to list every position ever held. Jobs can be summarized with a statement such as "1970–80   A variety of secretarial positions."

❏ Describe duties in detail only once if several jobs involved similar responsibilities. Avoid giving several examples of work performed when one is adequate.

❏ Omit company addresses; the name and location of the company are adequate.

❏ Include home and volunteer work if job experience is limited. (See Figure 2-4 for an example of how to include volunteer work on a resume.) Volunteer work and part-time jobs should not be included if work experience is extensive.

EDUCATION

If your education occurred within the last five years and is related to the job, it can be emphasized by placing the information about it (including the years) immediately after the job objective. If you have been out of school for some time or your education is not related to the job, you may decide to deemphasize it by placing this information at the bottom of the resume and omitting the years.

Providing graduation years will give an employer an idea of your age, which could be used to eliminate qualified candidates. Omit reference to high school if you hold post–high school degrees. List each associate, bachelor's, or master's degree separately unless they were earned from the same institution. The date should be included if a degree was earned recently.

If an associate, bachelor's, or master's degree has been earned, list the degrees as follows:

Santa Rosa Junior College, Santa Rosa, CA
Associate Degree in Business Office Technology

Dana College, Blair, NE
Bachelor's Degree in Business Administration

University of Wyoming, Laramie, WY
Master of Business Administration

If you have taken classes beyond high school but have not earned a degree, list the institution and courses relevant to the prospective job. Include seminars or other job training. It is also appropriate to list professional certification such as the Certified Professional Secretary (CPS) rating. The following are examples:

KATHLEEN GLENN
102 Rancho Coati Drive
White Plains, NY 10604
914-843-4905

Objective   Office Assistant

QUALIFICATIONS

- Five years' experience in office environment; familiar with office procedures.
- Experience on the Macintosh computer using word processing, spreadsheet, and desktop publishing software.
- Knowledge of the IBM computer.
- Understanding of alphabetic and numeric filing systems.
- Well-developed telephone communication skills; patient, personable, and receptive.
- Ability to work independently and as a cooperative team member.

EXPERIENCE

1989–present   GABLER SALES COMPANY, White Plains, NY
Secretary: Duties include communicating with customers by telephone and scheduling appointments, creating and maintaining a database of customers, organizing an accurate alphabetic filing system, typing correspondence and generating price lists and brochures, processing mail and shipping, preparing bank deposits, and maintaining records for taxes.

VOLUNTEER EXPERIENCE

1988–1989   THE PRACTICAL PRESS, White Plains, NY
Office assistant: Duties included answering marketing questions for telephone customers. Handled mail order of books, processed invoices, implemented bookkeeping procedures.

EDUCATION

Currently attending White Plains Community College, White Plains, NY
Working toward Administrative Assistant Certificate.

Figure 2-4 A resume highlighting qualifications and accomplishments for a person with recent work experience.

College of Marin, Kentfield, CA
Completed courses include: Business Math, Typing, Accounting I and II, Microcomputer Accounting, WordPerfect, and Lotus 1-2-3.

Findlay University, Findlay, OH
Will receive a Bachelor of Science degree in Accounting, August 19—
Achieved a 3.8 grade point (out of a possible 4.0).

San Francisco State University, San Francisco, CA
Completed 10 hours graduate work in Business Administration.

Achieved the Certified Professional Secretary (CPS) rating, 19—.

Attended Certified Professional Secretary (CPS) Seminar, June 19—, Savannah, GA
Received 2.1 CEU for the Local Area Network courses.

If you have completed no education beyond high school, high school can be either included or omitted. The year of graduation is not necessary unless it was recent. The following is an example:

Graduated from Petaluma High School, Petaluma, CA

Here are some other resume preparation techniques:

❏ Include academic awards and grade-point average if they are impressive.
❏ Include major awards if they are relevant to your profession. For example, "Won a national award for designing a computerized loan amortization program."
❏ Include leadership roles, such as holding an office in a professional association or an important club. This information is stated under a "Professional Associations" heading. For example, "President of the Dallas chapter, Professional Secretaries International, 1990–92."
❏ Omit hobbies unless they are relevant to the job.
❏ Do not include references. They can be given when the employer is serious about a candidate. It is not necessary to say "References provided upon request."
❏ Avoid buzzwords unless they are related to the industry to which you are applying.
❏ Omit salary requirements; they will be discussed during the interview.
❏ Do not give reasons for leaving previous jobs. This information will come up either on the employment application or during the interview.
❏ Never include personal information such as height, age, weight, sex, health, and marital status. It is illegal for a job interviewer to ask you about such matters.

CHECKLIST FOR RESUMES

Is it on one or two pages?
Is it printed on good-quality bond paper?
Is the layout (organization) attractive?
Is it easy to scan?
Are there any spelling, grammar, or punctuation errors?

Are the following items in the heading?
   Name
   Address (including ZIP Code)
   Phone numbers (including area code)
Is the job objective clearly stated (if included)?
Is your experience presented effectively?
   Included necessary information?
   Omitted days and months?
   Omitted employer addresses?
   Used action words?
   Limited descriptions to fewer than ten lines?
   Avoided use of "I"?
   Listed previous jobs relevant to the position?
Is your education presented effectively?
   Included necessary information?
   Placed at the top of the page if recent?
   Provided dates if recent?
   Included special courses, certificates, and leadership roles that apply to the job?

THE COVER LETTER

A cover letter is sent to a prospective employer with the resume. A personalized cover letter gives applicants an additional opportunity to sell themselves. It usually describes how the qualifications and skills listed on the resume correspond with those required for the job. A three-paragraph letter will be sufficient in most cases. Your cover letter should have the following qualities:

❏ It should be readable, to the point, and refer to the specific job. Some job openings attract hundreds of responses, so the cover letter should be so well-written as to place it in the category of applicants the firm "definitely will interview."

❏ It should be keyed, no longer than one page ($8\frac{1}{2}$ by 11 inches), and printed on paper that matches the paper used for the resume. Good spelling, grammar, and punctuation are necessary, because they show the care you put into your work.

❏ It should be addressed to a specific individual. If an individual's name is not listed in an advertisement or job announcement, phone the company to find out the name of the person making the hiring decision, the correct spelling of the name, and the person's title. If there is no company name or phone number listed in an advertisement, address your letter "Dear Manager" or "Dear Selection Committee."

❏ Do not use an envelope from your current company to mail in your letter. You are using office supplies for personal use.

FIRST PARAGRAPH

The first paragraph is the introduction and answers the following questions:

- Why are you writing?
- Where or how did you learn about the job?
- What is your most important qualification for the job?

Avoid starting out in an unconventional or annoying way. A direct statement is more positive and professional than a question, such as "Are you looking for a dynamic, young, and talented administrative assistant?" The following is an example of an opening for a job advertised in a newspaper. It is not necessary to repeat the exact words of an advertisement.

I am applying for the bookkeeping position you advertised in the May 10 edition of the *San Francisco Chronicle.*

If an instructor, friend, or employee of the firm told you of a job opening, state that fact also.

Carol Starnes, instructor at Glendale College, suggested I contact you about the word processing specialist position available at XYZ Company.

Richard Kerry of Interstate Bank told me a new branch bank was opening in Fremont.

The second part of the first paragraph indicates your main qualifications for the job. Select one fact that justifies suitability for the job.

I have ten years' experience as an office manager for the national headquarters of an insurance agency.

I have been an administrative assistant to the president for the last five years.

I am a recent graduate of San Jose State University, with a degree in Accounting.

SECOND PARAGRAPH

The second paragraph emphasizes education and work background and creates interest in you as an applicant. It may be six or seven sentences long and it must relate your education and experience directly to the available job. It should describe exactly how schoolwork and job experience qualify you to function in the job advertised. Your goal is to create interest in you as an applicant. State your knowledge about the company in the opening sentence to show your interest in a job with that firm. The following is an example of an opening statement about the company:

Because Company X is well known for its technical expertise, you are looking for employees who are experienced in handling technical information.

The work experience description indicates how your experience will be valuable to an employer and does not describe your desire for a job. (See Figures 2-5 and 2-6.) For example, avoid this kind of sentence when replying to an advertisement for a position requiring word processing skills: "I have worked with WordPerfect software before, and this experience will give me the edge in operating it. I can adjust quickly to any working environment." The following sentence is more meaningful to an employer, because it describes what you can do for him or her:

I am a highly motivated self-starter with five years' experience using WordPerfect software on an IBM computer. My work experience includes writing and editing customer reply letters, keying and formatting the company newsletter, developing promotional brochures and flyers, and producing the company's annual report.

THIRD PARAGRAPH

The third paragraph asks for an interview and indicates your availability for one. This paragraph is usually only two or three sentences long. The following is an example:

I would like to schedule an interview to discuss further the possibilities of our working together. I can be reached at 415-555-3994 after 4 p.m. during the week.

Some people recommend stating that you will call in a week to ten days to set up a meeting. This tactic may or may not work. Depending on the size of the company and the number of applications received, employers might not accept calls from a prospective employee. Employers who travel may not be available at the time the call is made.

CHECKLIST FOR COVER LETTERS

Is it on one page?
Is it printed on good-quality bond paper?
Is the layout attractive?
Are spelling, grammar, and punctuation correct?
Is it addressed to an individual?
Does the first paragraph
   state why you are writing?
   tell where you heard about the job?
   mention your major qualification for the job?
   italicize or underline the newspaper name?
Does the second paragraph
   show that you know something about the company?
   relate educational accomplishments to the job?
   relate experience to the job?
   match your qualifications with the needs of the company?
Does the third paragraph
   ask for an interview?
   include a phone number where you can be reached?
   indicate the best times to call?
Does it make an employer want to meet you?

394 East Forest Avenue
Sonoma CA 95476
May 7, 19--

Mr. Richard Herndon, Director
Valley of the Moon Hospital
384 Oak Leaf Lane
Sonoma CA 95476

Dear Mr. Herndon:

I am applying for the administrative assistant position
advertised on May 7 in the <u>Press Democrat</u>. I am skilled on IBM-
compatible computers, detail-oriented, and able to work under
pressure.

With five years of experience as an administrative assistant in
the advertising department of a Fortune 500 firm, I know the
importance of meeting deadlines and following through on
details. I am exceptionally well organized with a wide range of
experience, including supervising and training a staff of twenty.
My computer skills include expertise in Lotus 1-2-3, Microsoft
Word, WordPerfect, PageMaker, and dBASE IV software.

I feel I have much to offer Valley of the Moon Hospital, and I
would enjoy discussing my qualifications and your needs in
person. Please contact me at 707-555-4883 after 3:00 p.m. to
schedule an appointment.

Sincerely,

Maralee Shadle

Figure 2-5 Cover letter showing work experience correlating closely with the job opening.

4390 Westwood Road
Pasadena CA 91104
June 23, 19--

Ms. Christine Rummler
Personnel Manager
Lifetime, Inc.
Department 2093, Box 24
Pasadena CA 91109-7237

Dear Ms. Rummler:

I am applying for the administrative assistant position advertised on June 22 in the <u>Los Angeles Times</u>. I have extensive experience in office procedures and secretarial functions and have been trained in the use of computers and word processing and spreadsheet software.

My last five years have been spent as an administrative assistant to an executive vice president. Some of my accomplishments have included complete organization and management of office procedures for our division of fifty support staff. I have designed brochures and flyers on WordPerfect 5.1. Although the enclosed resume states some of my skills, it does not take into consideration my willingness to take on new tasks, ability to learn quickly, and desire to succeed.

I welcome the opportunity to talk with you about the position and my interest in working for Lifetime. I can be reached at 818-555-9938 after 5:00 p.m.

Sincerely,

Peggy Giradi

Figure 2-6 Cover letter showing a willingness to take on new responsibilities.

THE EMPLOYMENT APPLICATION

Many employers ask a prospective employee to complete an employment application. It is important that the employment application be filled out neatly and accurately. If the application can be filled out at home, where there are fewer distractions, there will be less possibility of error. Make a copy of the application to fill out as practice before completing the actual application. Answer all questions truthfully and as accurately as possible.

Read the directions carefully. If it says to print or type all responses, a typed copy will make the most favorable impression, assuming corrections can easily be made. If a typewriter is not available, use a pen with dark ink that will not smear to print the responses. Do not use a pencil.

Fill in all blanks. If an item does not apply, write in "N/A," which means "not applicable." Usually an application requires more information than is on a resume. There may be questions about salary, your reason for leaving your last job, and references.

Personal Information

Your name, address (including ZIP Code), and home phone number will always be requested. Other items may include work telephone number, Social Security number, and driver's license number. (See Figure 2-7.)

Unless height and weight directly relate to a job requirement (police officer, for example), these questions are illegal. Nor should an employer ask about marital status, number and ages of children, or date of birth. Asking for proof of age after hiring is acceptable. (For other illegal questions that should not be asked on an application form, see under the heading *Illegal Questions* in the section on The Job Interview later in this chapter.)

Candidates for civic appointments or government positions may be asked to waive the privilege of confidentiality of information on file at federal, state, or city agencies. To know ahead of time what is in those records, contact the Federal Information Center in the nearest city.

Education

Most applications have a section for education. Unless the application states otherwise, list the most recent education first and work backwards. Information requested often includes dates attended, grade-point average, credits completed, and the full address of the educational institution. (See Figure 2-8.)

Job Experience

This will ask for the names and addresses (including ZIP Codes) of current and previous employers and dates employed. Usually the current job is listed first. The application may ask the name of the supervisor, phone number, and job title. (See Figure 2-9.)

If a job description is asked for, use action verbs. There will probably only be room for

NAME	McClintock	Sheila	M	DATE	10/7/--
	Last	First	Middle		

POSITION SOUGHT	Administrative Assistant

I can accept FULL-TIME ☒. PART-TIME ❑ employment. Date I will be available   10/30/--

MAILING ADDRESS	2790 Western Ave.	Ames	IA	50010
	No. and Street	City	State	ZIP

ADDRESS	same as above			
	No. and Street	City	State	ZIP

HOME PHONE	515-293-4039	SOC. SEC. NUMBER	481-49-4834

BUSINESS PHONE	515-292-4837	DRIVER'S LIC. NUMBER	47893

Have you ever been convicted of a crime other than a minor traffic violation?
Yes ❑   No ☒   If so please explain. _____

Figure 2-7 An example of completed personal information on an application blank.

a few words, so use the ones most relevant to the job. If you prefer the interviewer not contact your present employer, a note can be placed in the margin asking that the company not contact your present employer without your permission.

You may be asked your reason for leaving past jobs. If the reason is that you received a promotion, make certain the next job listed actually is a promotion. Try to avoid using the term "fired"; reword to "looking for a more responsible position."

If the application has a blank for "salary requested," you can either list a salary range or write "negotiable" or "open." It is also appropriate to leave this item blank if you wish. If you fill in an amount, however, be sure it is accurate.

REFERENCES

The best references are former employers or teachers who can relate positive information about you. Friends and relatives are not appropriate. All references should be contacted ahead of time so they are not surprised by phone calls. Their names, addresses, phone numbers, and occupations will probably be requested. (See Figure 2-10.)

EDUCATION

HIGH SCHOOL OF GRADUATION	Ames High School			Ames	Iowa
	Name			City	State

COLLEGES ATTENDED	LOCATION (CITY, STATE)	DATE (MO., YR.)	DEGREES RECEIVED	MAJOR(S)	MINOR(S)
Iowa State University	Ames, IA	FROM 9/78 TO 12/82	B.S.	Business	English
		FROM TO			
		FROM TO			

CHECK SKILLS & TRAINING ACQUIRED

☒ TYPING–WPM __65__ Errors __3__   ☐ Statistics   ☐ Shorthand Dictation_____ WPM

☒ Dictaphone   ☒ Adding Machine   ☒ Keyboard Skills   ☐ Duplicating Machine

☒ Filing   ☒ Bookkeeping   ☐ Accounting   ☒ Mathematics

☐ Other __IBM PC computer; WordPerfect, Lotus, dBASE III+ software__

Figure 2-8 An example of completed educational information on an application blank.

CHECKLIST FOR EMPLOYMENT APPLICATIONS

Is every blank completed with information or N/A?

Is the application typewritten or printed in dark ink?

Is it neat?

Is it free of spelling, grammar, and punctuation errors?

Is all personal information given as requested?

Is all education information complete?

Is all work experience information complete?

Are references listed?

Is the application signed and dated?

THE JOB INTERVIEW

A job interview is an opportunity for you to learn more about a company and a job and for the employer to see if you will match the needs of the company. Some positions may require two or three interviews. The higher the job level and the more bureaucratic the organization, the more interviews there will be.

JOB EXPERIENCE

COMPLETE ALL ITEMS FULLY

PERIOD OF EMPLOYMENT (Month, Year) FROM: 1/83 TO: present FULL–TIME: ☒ PART–TIME ❏	EMPLOYER'S NAME Dr. Robert Hibbald
	ADDRESS 1126 Burnett Ave., Ames IA 50010
	PHONE 515-232-8899 SUPERVISOR Dr. Robert Hibbald
	JOB TITLE Office Manager
	TYPICAL DUTIES AND RESPONSIBILITIES Scheduled appointments, supervised a staff of three, billed patients and insurance, answered telephone.
	REASON FOR LEAVING Dr. Hibbald is retiring.
PERIOD OF EMPLOYMENT (Month, Year) FROM: 9/80 TO: 12/82 FULL–TIME: ❏ PART–TIME ☒	EMPLOYER'S NAME Central Stores, Iowa State University
	ADDRESS 3789 East Russell, Ames IA 50010
	PHONE 515-399-3892 SUPERVISOR Sharon Zickefoose
	JOB TITLE Clerk
	TYPICAL DUTIES AND RESPONSIBILITIES Typed correspondence, answered telephone inquiries, prepared report for yearly inventory.
	REASON FOR LEAVING Wanted to work full-time.

Figure 2-9 An example of completed experience information on an application blank.

A successful job interview calls for a candidate to do the following:

- Dress conservatively and appropriately
- Arrive on time
- Maintain eye contact
- Greet interviewer with a firm handshake
- Demonstrate enthusiasm and initiative
- Use good speech and grammar and the same kind of action verbs used in the resume
- Indicate specific job goals
- Bring samples of work, educational transcripts, or performance reviews
- Listen carefully to questions
- Think before you answer
- Act naturally
- Be informed about the company
- Have questions to ask about the position
- Be realistic about salary

PERSONAL REFERENCES

List 3 references excluding relatives who can comment on your work experience (i.e., past supervisors, employers, work associates, etc.)

NAME (RELATIONSHIP)	ADDRESS	PHONE
Martin Miller, Supervisor	Evert's Florist 7394 Main, Ames IA 50010	515-232-4839
Cathy Rivers, Teacher	Meeker School 998 Crinella Dr., Ames IA 50010	515-232-4988
Lee Simon, Associate	Simon Brothers 805 Middlefield, Ames IA 50010	515-334-3290

Under what circumstances may we contact your previous employers?
You have my permission to contact all references.

Figure 2-10 An example of completed reference information on an application blank.

APPEARANCE AND BEHAVIOR

Research shows that most interviewers decide whether to hire someone in the first 10 to 30 seconds of the interview. The goal of a prospective employee is to make that first impression positive.

One of the ways to make a good first impression is to be well-groomed and appropriately dressed. Your clothes must be clean, pressed, and in good condition. When interviewing, you should wear the kinds of clothes that would be worn in the office. When in doubt, dress conservatively and avoid both overdressing and dressing too casually.

Good manners require eye contact and a firm handshake. Eye contact is absolutely essential, and a lack of it may cost you the job. A firm handshake is also important. If you get nervous, hold a cotton handkerchief in your hands to absorb any moisture before shaking hands.

It is best to act self-confident, rather than shy. An employer is looking for someone who is assertive, self-assured, and competent. Even if you desperately need or want the job, you should not convey this during the interview.

RESEARCHING THE COMPANY

If you learn as much as possible about the company, its products, and the interviewer prior to the interview, you will show the interviewer how interested you are in the job. The reference librarian at a public library is a good source of information. Newspaper articles also provide information about the company.

Before going to the job interview, you should:

❏ Secure a copy of the company's annual report, if possible, through the company, the public library, or the Chamber of Commerce.

❏ Know the company's major products and services.

❏ Be aware of the company's competition.

❏ Find out about the company's reputation.

❏ Ask others about the organization and the interviewer. Try to find someone who works for the company and talk with them. Try to find someone who has been interviewed by the person who will be interviewing you.

❏ Know the supervisory role of the person doing the interviewing.

INTERVIEW QUESTIONS

An effective interviewer evaluates skills, ability, and experience. At the same time, the interviewer makes judgments about a candidate's motivation, enthusiasm, and ability to fit into the organization. Keep your answers on a professional, not a personal, level. Some possible interview questions include:

Q: Tell me something about yourself.

Hint: Outline several strong work-related points and accomplishments; make a summary statement and then stop talking.

Q: Tell me about your professional experience. What are your most important achievements?

Hint: Mention the most impressive achievement first; prepare success stories ahead of time.

Q: What are your goals?

Hint: Be general and mention that you see yourself gaining increased responsibility, if the firm has opportunities for advancement.

Q: What are your major strengths?

Hint: Highlight qualities that will help you succeed in the job available (for example, you work hard, learn quickly, and are conscientious).

Q: What are your major weaknesses? What areas do you need to improve?

Hint: Disguise weaknesses as strengths (for example, "I like to stick with a problem until I solve it"; "Sometimes I have ignored my family to finish a project"); select a problem you solved early in your career and describe how you overcame it.

Q: Why are you looking for a new position? Why did you leave Company X?

Hint: Indicate a desire for greater responsibility and challenge or an opportunity to use talents not used in the present position; avoid mentioning money, personality conflicts, or anything that is not a major component of the job. Never deride a former employer.

Q: Why do you want to work for this company?

Hint: Show familiarity with the company; draw on the research you did.

By asking open-ended questions such as these, the employer can learn about a prospective employee's communication skills and thought processes.

The following are some suggestions for answering open-ended questions:

❏ Listen to the question and answer all parts of it.

❏ Show that the question has been anticipated by answering questions directly.

❏ Describe education and work experience in a clear, concise way.

❏ Describe the most important results and accomplishments of your career or experiences.

❏ Ask the interviewer to clarify the question if you are in doubt about its meaning.

❏ Let the interviewer set the pace of the discussion. An interviewer should be in control.

❏ Avoid giving either lengthy answers or simple "yes" or "no" answers. Keep your answers to the point.

❏ Discuss problem areas briefly and honestly.

❏ Do not criticize former employers. Avoid displaying bitterness and a negative attitude.

ILLEGAL QUESTIONS

When applying for a job, a person cannot be discriminated against because of race, color, national origin, religion, sex, age, or, in many cases, physical or mental handicaps. The following questions are illegal:

- Are you married (single, divorced)?
- Do you have children? How old are they? What are your childcare arrangements?
- Are you planning a family?
- How old are you?
- Do you have any handicaps?
- Have you ever received psychiatric or psychological treatment?
- What race are you?
- Where were you born? Where were your parents (spouse) born?
- Of what country are you a citizen?
- Have you ever been arrested?
- What is your credit rating?
- What is your religion?
- You went to St. Michael's College. What kind of school is that?
- Do you belong to any union?

If an illegal question is asked, there are several options available:

❏ If the job is interesting and the answer will help rather than hurt your chances, answer the question. After you are hired, bring the illegal question to the attention of the interviewer.

❏ Do not answer immediately. After a long pause, quietly ask, "Why did you ask that question?"

❑ Ask politely what the question has to do with job performance. Explain that the question does not pertain to the ability to do the job.

❑ State that you would like to discuss the job to see whether you are interested and that after that discussion, you would be willing to talk about other things.

Advice and assistance on job discrimination issues are available from state labor and human rights agencies or from an office of the Equal Employment Opportunity Commission.

PROBLEM AREAS

Several problem areas may come up in the interview. However, they can be neutralized with the right strategy. Major problem areas are discussed below.

Being fired, although problematic, is not the worst thing that can happen. The reason for being fired is important. If you were fired because you were unqualified for a job, you have a serious problem to overcome. A response might be: "I realized after I took the job it was wrong for me. I tried to stay with it, but they asked me to leave. Now I have a better idea of the kind of job that would be best for me."

If the firing resulted from a personality conflict, indicate that to the interviewer. Give the employer names of people who can describe the work you did and the circumstances of the dismissal. Do not go into lengthy details but do offer an honest perspective.

If the firing was a part of a major change in the company, explain that. Mergers and acquisitions have made layoffs common.

Emotional problems can be another area of concern. You need to use your own judgment before discussing emotional, alcohol, or drug problems. Some companies may understand, but others may hold these problems against job candidates. Unless such a problem became an issue in a previous job, it may be better to refrain from discussing it.

Health problems can also raise questions. An employer may ask whether applicants have any health problems or handicaps that may affect work performance. If you do have physical limitations (such as the inability to lift more than 20 pounds) which will affect your ability to do the job, mention this during the interview. If your limitation does not affect your work performance, do not discuss it during the interview.

Past criminal activity can present difficulties. Some employers will ask whether you have been convicted of a crime other than a minor traffic violation. The key word is "conviction." If you were arrested but not convicted, then the arrest requires no further discussion.

It is illegal for an employer to check a person's arrest, court, or conviction record if it does not substantially relate to the responsibilities of the prospective job. Any lawful questions about past encounters with the law should be answered truthfully. If a record has been sealed, a conviction has been reversed, or you have been pardoned, it is legal to answer any questions about the conviction in the negative.

Gaps in work history may raise a few eyebrows. Do not be defensive. Explain that the job market was tight or that you took time off to go back to school, travel, take care of your children, or define career objectives.

Job hopping, too, can be an issue. Explain that it was necessary to change jobs frequently because of factors beyond your control, such as company layoffs or company moves. Mention your eagerness to make a long-term commitment to the next employer.

QUESTIONS TO ASK THE INTERVIEWER

An important goal of the job interview is to discover whether you are interested in the job. Here are some questions to ask the prospective employer:

- Why is this job open?
- Would you describe a typical day?
- Why did the person who previously held this job leave?
- What are your expectations for this job?
- To whom would I be reporting?
- What are the promotional and career opportunities in the organization?
- With what kind of team will I work?
- Does the company promote or sponsor advanced education for its employees?
- Are my background and experience a good match?
- When do you expect to make a decision on this position?
- When can I expect to hear from you?
- Please show me where my work area will be. (This gives you an idea of whether the work space is comfortable and attractive and a chance to see what the other workers are like.)

SALARY NEGOTIATION

You should know the salary range for the open position or for similar jobs before going to the interview. Researching the company and the job often reveals this type of information. If your research shows that the salary is significantly below what you are willing to accept, it is best to decline the interview.

Here are some ways to negotiate salary:

❑ Let the interviewer introduce the subject of money.

❑ Avoid disclosing your present salary until it looks like the company is serious about hiring you.

❑ Turn a direct question to you about salary into a question to the interviewer, such as, "What kind of range does this position pay?"

❑ Be prepared to answer any questions about salary. Be honest about previous salaries.

❑ Start negotiating as high in the range as possible, preferably toward the top of the range.

❑ Never react with anger or surprise. Pause to think.

❑ Take 24 hours to think about every job offer.

❑ If the salary is lower than you are willing to accept, look for other areas for negotiation, such as vacation time, shorter working hours, or tuition for additional school or training. It may also be possible to negotiate a performance review and salary increase in three months.

THE FOLLOW-UP LETTER

Follow up on every job interview. A follow-up letter is usually more effective than a telephone call because the employer can review the letter during the decision-making process. The letter can also bring up any additional information you may have omitted during the interview, although there is no need to restate information already on the resume or in the cover letter. In the follow-up letter, you can express interest in the job or indicate otherwise. (See Figure 2-11.)

Here are some tips for the follow-up letter:

❏ Keyboard it on good-quality bond paper. The envelope should not be handwritten.
❏ Send it within 48 hours of the interview.
❏ Keep it short and to the point.
❏ Proofread it carefully so there are no errors in grammar, spelling, or punctuation. Spell the interviewer's name and company name correctly and use the exact title of the interviewer. Call the company to get this information if necessary.
❏ Thank the interviewer for taking the time to interview you and to explain the job.
❏ Express your interest in the position (or explain why you are no longer interested).
❏ Reemphasize why your skills match the job.
❏ Give a phone number where you can be reached.

EMPLOYMENT TESTING

Some companies use employment tests to screen applicants further. If the applicant wants a job, taking the tests is necessary. When the interview is arranged, ask whether any tests will be given. Tests may analyze personality, determine skill level, assess knowledge about a subject, or test for illegal drug use. If a skill or subject-matter test is to be given, studying and practice can help increase test scores.

PERSONALITY TESTS

Some employers test personality in order to determine whether the applicant's personal and behavioral preferences match the job. Some companies use standardized tests such as the Minnesota Multiphasic Personality Inventory (MMPI) and others use ones they have developed themselves. Sometimes companies administer personality tests to current employees as one factor in making promotion decisions.

There is no way to prepare for this kind of test. It may be possible to guess what an employer is looking for, but then you might have to act that way on the job. When taking a personality test, it is best to be honest and mark the first reaction to the question. A possible question on a personality test might be, "What would you prefer? (a) stay home and read a book; (b) go to a party; (c) don't know."

638 Sixth Street
Petaluma CA 94952
June 1, 19--

Ms. Mona Garza
Personnel Director
Transamerica Insurance
384 Sutter Street
San Francisco CA 94132

Dear Ms. Garza:

Thank you for the opportunity to discuss the administrative
assistant position with Transamerica. It seems to be a very challenging position requiring flexibility, initiative, and imagination.
I am very interested in the position and would welcome the
opportunity to discuss my qualifications further with you.

After talking with you, I feel my skills and abilities would help
you meet the goals you are trying to accomplish in your department. When you mentioned the purchase of a new network system, I starting thinking of all the preparations that could be done
ahead of time to make the transition smooth, including the development of manuals and procedures.

Again, thank you for your time. I look forward to hearing from
you soon.

Sincerely,

Marilyn Meyer

Figure 2-11 A follow-up letter should be sent after every interview.

SKILL TESTS

The purpose of skill testing is to determine whether the applicant has the skill level needed to perform the job. Skill tests may test the following:

- Proofreading
- Spelling
- Grammar
- Punctuation
- Using adding machines or calculators
- Keyboarding speed and accuracy
- Record keeping
- Filing
- Transcription of dictated material
- Composition and transcription of correspondence
- Shorthand dictation and transcription
- Knowledge of computer software
- General math, including fractions, percentages, and decimals

If the skill being tested is something used every day on your present job, little review is necessary. If, however, you feel insecure about any skill area, it is best to postpone the test for a few days and spend that time preparing for it.

To review, go to a library or bookstore and find a current book on the subject. General reference books review the rules of grammar, spelling, punctuation, and letter styles. Computer software is available that tests and analyzes keyboarding skill. College and other bookstores have workbooks with math problems and explanations on how to solve them. Self-help books are available at bookstores and computer stores.

In order to feel confident about taking a skill test, you need to know details of the testing procedure. Some questions to ask before the interview are:

❏ What kind of test is it—multiple choice? true/false? problem? fill in the blank?
❏ How much time does each test take?
❏ Will there be an opportunity to repeat any test?
❏ Will the testing be on a typewriter, electronic typewriter, or computer? What is the brand name of the equipment?
❏ For computers and software: Is the computer a Mac or an IBM compatible system? Is it a hard disk or floppy disk system? What is the software? What version is the software? Is spell-checker software allowed? Can the software reference manual be used during the testing?
❏ Are dictionaries or reference manuals allowed?

SUBJECT-MATTER TESTS

Some professional positions require either oral or written tests or a combination of both. The purpose of the tests is to find out how much you know about a subject or how well you can analyze and solve hypothetical cases in a subject area, such as management, sales, personnel, or training.

Try to get as many details as possible about the test from the interviewer or others who have taken the test. Often it is difficult to review or prepare ahead of time, but it builds confidence to know what to anticipate. If the questions are written ones about a specific subject, practice writing out answers. Review important aspects of the particular field. Find out how long the test takes to complete.

DRUG TESTS

Some employers test prospective employees for the use of illegal drugs. Civil libertarians have expressed concern about drug testing because, among other issues, the tests may not be accurate. Unless you are willing to go to court, you will probably have to submit to drug testing in order to get a job at a company that has a policy of testing new employees.

LOCATING JOB OPPORTUNITIES THROUGH EMPLOYMENT AGENCIES

Employment agencies, or placement firms, as they are now often called, work as intermediaries between employers and prospective employees. Their job is to match the talents and interests of the prospective employee with the company and the job. Most placement firms prefer to work with candidates who have solid job experience or training.

Agencies may deal with permanent or temporary positions, or both, and usually specialize in specific fields, such as accounting, marketing, secretarial, engineering, chemical, heavy industry, or technology. If an agency does not specialize in one particular field, it may employ counselors who do.

PLACEMENT FIRMS

A placement firm is useful only when you have a good idea of the career area you are interested in, although some agencies provide career information and counseling. As a part of their service, agencies usually provide help with interviewing techniques, resumes, and salary negotiations. They also conduct appropriate skill testing.

Placement firms depend on the premise that they can get you a better job than you can get on your own. Often the jobs are listed only with the firm. A fee is charged for this service. In most cases, the company doing the hiring pays the fee. In some cases, however, the new employee and the company split the fee or the employee pays the entire fee. The fee varies and may be a percentage of salary. Sometimes the employee may pay the fee on an installment basis.

The placement firm arranges all interviews. A prospective employee may interview at several companies before accepting a job. To increase job opportunities, some people use more than one placement firm. Even if you use a placement firm, you should still watch the want ads and network with your coworkers and friends.

The following questions may assist you in deciding whether to use placement firms:

❏ In what areas does the firm specialize?
❏ Does the office look well organized?
❏ Is the placement firm well known? Does it have a good reputation? Do you know of anyone who has used its service?

> **Hint:** Phone the personnel departments of major employers and ask with which agencies they work and which ones have a good reputation. Check with the Better Business Bureau to see whether there have been any complaints against them.

❏ How many people work for the firm? How long have they worked there?

> **Hint:** If a counselor has no business cards, assume he or she is new. Ask the agency manager to switch you to another counselor.

❏ Does the counselor seem really interested in your background and career goals? Is the counselor familiar with the job market?
❏ Does the firm do career counseling and testing? Does it help with resumes? Does it help with interviewing skills?
❏ Is there a fee involved? If so, who pays? If you pay, could you get the job on your own? If you quit the job after a short period, will any part of the fee be refunded?

> **Hint:** Never pay a fee unless an employer has offered you a job and you have accepted. Get all promises in writing.

Other types of firms also provide services to job-hunters. Headhunters, executive search firms, and consultants are paid to find people to fill positions that may or may not be open. They usually deal with high-level executive secretaries and executives. Headhunters typically contact job candidates themselves, although people looking for jobs also contact headhunters.

Resume services help write and print resumes. For an additional fee, they will send out resumes to a list of companies they have compiled.

Career counselors charge a fee to provide testing and career counseling. They also give advice on a job search. They do not make job placements, and they charge a fee whether a job is secured or not. Career counselors can be located in the Yellow Pages under "Career and Vocational Counseling." Free career counseling may be offered through college and business schools to students and graduates. Some schools have a lifetime commitment to counsel and/or place graduates.

TEMPORARY EMPLOYMENT AGENCIES

Temporary employment agencies quickly find jobs for people on a temporary basis. These jobs may range in length from one day to several months or even years.

The temporary agency serves as your employer. It interviews and evaluates the skills and preferences of temporary employees, tests employees' skills, and finds prospective employers. A company would then use temporary employees for peak work periods, temporary replacements, one-time projects, specialized work, or vacation replacements.

The skills, capabilities, and requirements requested by the company determine the level of pay. Temporary employees submit timecards each week and receive paychecks from the temporary agency. The agency bills the company for salary and fees. There are no fees or deductions from wages other than legally required payroll taxes that all employees must pay. Usually temporary employees receive no paid vacation or sick leave, nor are they paid at a higher rate for overtime. Some temporary agencies make health benefits available to their workers.

Ask the following questions when deciding whether to choose temporary work:

❑ In what areas does the temporary agency specialize?

❑ Is it well known? Does it have a good reputation? Do you know of anyone who has been a temporary for this firm?

❑ How often will you be called for work?

❑ Do you have enough financial security to go without work if you are not called?

❑ Are there enough jobs available that you can work as much as you want?

❑ How often can you turn down jobs if they do not interest you?

❑ What is the pay period? Can the check be mailed? How promptly will you receive it?

❑ Are insurance benefits available? If not, where can you get insurance and what will it cost?

❑ Can you accept a full-time position if one is offered?

❑ Is workmen's compensation available if you are injured on the job?

❑ Are there any bonus incentives, such as holiday pay, for working for a temporary agency for a long period of time?

TIME MANAGEMENT AND PROBLEM SOLVING

Businesses view time as an extremely valuable resource. Office professionals have a major role in helping business meet the demands of productivity and customer service. Applying effective time management principles to office tasks is crucial for office professionals.

Effective time management requires that important tasks and projects be identified and completed in the time available and that they be done well. Ineffective use of time results in unnecessary confusion and last-minute upheavals, personnel misunderstandings, disgruntled customers, and stress. To avoid these pitfalls, office professionals must *analyze, plan, schedule,* and *control* the use of their time.

ANALYZING CURRENT USE OF WORK TIME

Analyzing your current use of work time allows you to adopt more realistic approaches to planning time use and to find alternative ways to do certain tasks. To begin, make a list of all the tasks you do each day and record the amount of time you spend on each task. You may wish to indicate the priority status (Rush [R], Same Day [SD], Next Day [ND], Later [L]) of these tasks. You will also find it helpful to record the interruptions that occur. It is important to keep a log for each day. (A sample log appears in Figure 3-1.)

Maintain this log for two weeks; then review the answers to the following questions. Your responses may provide you with valuable insights about the current use of your time.

❏ What time period or time periods during the day were the most productive? the least productive? Why?
❏ During what hours of the day did the most interruptions occur? Who caused the interruptions? Supervisors, coworkers, or outside visitors?
❏ How much time was spent on crises that materialized during the day?
❏ How much of the day was spent handling personal concerns?

TASK

TIME	Typing/Entering Information on Computer	Proofreading/Editing Copy	Copying Documents	Transcribing Dictated Material	Filing Records	Greeting Clients/Making Appointments	Handling Incoming/Outgoing Mail	Attending Meetings	Composing Communications	Answering the Phone	Placing Outgoing Calls	Conferring with Supervisor	Conferring with Coworkers	Arranging Meetings/Travel	Supervising Personnel	Handling Personal Requirements	Other
A.M. 7:45–8:00																	
8:00–8:15																	
8:15–8:30																	
8:30–8:45																	
8:45–9:00																	
9:00–9:15																	
9:15–9:30																	
9:30–9:45																	
9:45–10:00																	
10:00–10:15																	
10:15–10:30																	
10:30–10:45																	
10:45–11:00																	
11:00–11:15																	
11:15–11:30																	
11:30–11:45																	
11:45–12:00																	
P.M. 12:00–12:15																	
12:15–12:30																	
12:30–12:45																	
12:45–1:00																	
1:00–1:15																	
1:15–1:30																	
1:30–1:45																	
1:45–2:00																	
2:00–2:15																	
2:15–2:30																	
2:30–2:45																	
2:45–3:00																	
3:00–3:15																	
3:15–3:30																	
3:30–3:45																	
3:45–4:00																	
4:00–4:15																	
4:15–4:30																	
4:30–4:45																	
4:45–5:00																	
5:00–5:15																	
5:15–5:30																	
5:30–5:45																	
5:45–6:00																	

EVALUATION

Tasks to eliminate _____

Tasks to simplify _____

Tasks to modify _____

Tasks to group _____

Tasks to delegate _____

Comments _____

Figure 3-1 Sample daily log.

❏ Were there any daily routines or tasks that could have been streamlined, combined with other tasks, delegated, or eliminated?

❏ Were the tasks requiring 15 minutes (or less) priority tasks or were these tasks to fill time? When are you most productive?

❏ Could the "Rush" tasks have been started sooner? Could large tasks be broken down into smaller daily segments?

❏ Were there times in the day when the pace was slow? Were there specific times when the stress level was particularly high? Were there specific times when you needed extra assistance?

It is important to analyze, evaluate, and make comments about your use of time on *each* day's log. The task of improving time management will become overwhelming if you try to solve too many problems immediately. Attempt to solve only one problem at a time, but set a realistic deadline for solving it.

Your supervisors may be able to recommend suggestions for more effective use of your time. Share the time-log you have completed with them. In addition to asking for their input, present a tentative list of suggestions for improvement. If other workers are part of the problem, make them part of the solution.

The time logs may indicate there are slow- and fast-paced time periods. Determine if these periods are predictable. Use the analyses to request extra assistance or overtime during peak periods. Include the request as a part of the normal budgetary process so you are not caught unprepared during a peak period.

TAKING TIME TO PLAN

A written plan can assist you in directing your efforts to reach predetermined goals. Doing random tasks without a plan can be expensive and inefficient. On the other hand, adhering to a plan so rigidly that it does not allow for interruptions or special requests can also be self-defeating.

A simple planning technique that most time management experts recommend is the "to do" list. Tasks that need to be accomplished that day or week as well as the priority of each task are listed on this form. (A sample daily "to do" list is found in Figure 3-2.)

PLANNING "TO DO" LISTS

Although there is no one right way to prepare "to do" lists, several suggestions include:

❏ List all tasks that need to be completed for a week. Use these weekly lists as the basis for preparing the daily "to do" lists. The daily lists may be prepared at the end of each day or the first thing each morning.

❏ Prioritize each task; label each task A (must do), B (should do), or C (nice to do). Category A tasks are important and must be done without delay; category B tasks should be completed as soon as possible, preferably the same day; and category C tasks may be completed later, if there is time.

Things to Do	
Task	Priority

Telephone Calls to Make		
Number	Name	Purpose

Figure 3-2 Sample daily "to do" list.

❏ Highlight the top three A items on the "to do" list to signify that these tasks should take precedence over the other A tasks. This is especially useful when there are numerous A tasks on the "to do" list.

❏ Keep the list visible. Cross out tasks that are completed; add tasks to the list when necessary. Show the tasks that have been delegated or that are in progress.

❏ Rewrite the list at the end of the day by carrying forward those tasks that were not completed to the next day's "to do" list. Reorder the priorities of the tasks.

❏ Include names of people to contact and their phone numbers on your "to do" list. Highlighting the names of the people who cannot be reached serves as your reminder to try them again at a later time.

❏ Use a calendar to record monthly and yearly events; e.g., dates for payroll reports, staff meetings, sales conferences, and budget deadlines. These reminders can then be worked into the planning of the daily "to do" lists.

❏ Analyze the "to do" lists periodically; establish backup plans for major tasks so that if one plan goes awry, there will be another plan to take its place.

❏ Divide a project, such as planning a conference, into many subparts. Prioritize these subparts; keep a project notebook with a page for each subpart; list all contacts, phone numbers, and sources of information associated with that subpart; establish feasible deadlines for each subpart; check the notebook regularly and include the appropriate subtasks on the daily "to do" list.

SPECIAL CONCERNS ABOUT PLANNING TIME

All items listed on a "to do" list are not of equal value; therefore treat each task individually.

Interruptions happen, so be flexible when listing tasks and their priorities. Adopt a realistic attitude toward planning. Do not list *all* the long-range projects in need of completion. The result will be too overwhelming, and you will only get frustrated. Instead, list the subtasks involved with a long-range project and include the subtasks as part of the daily "to do" lists. This will help you *get started* on complicated or lengthy tasks.

When you do not complete all the tasks on the list, there is no need for you to admonish yourself. If the tasks are identified realistically, the process will work. However, if a task appears on a list three or four times, try to determine why. If you are avoiding the task because it is too difficult or uninteresting, handle it immediately rather than take the time to transfer it to the next day's list.

Planning *how* to do a task requires time. Be sure to include sufficient time for organizing the materials and collecting the resources you will need. Allow at least half an hour of planning time for new projects.

MAKING A REALISTIC SCHEDULE

A plan requires action in order for it to be useful. If you schedule tasks realistically, you can expect to accomplish the *important* things within the time available. Before determining your schedule, you need to consider several questions:

❑ Who is requesting the work? The more important or senior the person, the higher the priority of the task to be completed as soon as possible.
❑ When must each task be completed?
❑ What types of materials must be available before starting each task? Do you need someone's approval?
❑ Where does the work go after it is completed? If it goes to another department, how much time must be allowed for completion there?
❑ What tasks require service outside the company; e.g., typesetting?
❑ What tasks can best be accomplished by others?
❑ Which of the tasks will take the longest to complete? Are there subtasks that can be identified and started immediately?
❑ Are there similar activities in any of the tasks that may be subgrouped and done at the same time?

SCHEDULING TIME TO SPEND ON EACH TASK

Here are some ways to schedule the time you need to spend on each task:

❑ Estimate the time it takes to complete a task; then compare the estimated time to the actual time. Revise your estimate in the future to better reflect the actual time. For example, if a 40-page proposal needs to be keyed into the computer, estimate normal input time based on the number of pages you can input per hour.

❑ Set more specific, self-imposed deadlines. Instead of deciding to finish a task "today," set a deadline of late morning or early afternoon.

❑ Determine the best time of your day to do creative work or work that requires concentration. Many people prefer early in the morning, for instance. Use "your best" time for thinking and planning or for tackling your most difficult task.

❑ Try to complete routine tasks such as opening mail or doing data entry at the same time each day.

❑ Try to play games with unpleasant or routine tasks. For example, set aside 15 minutes before a break or before lunch to file, so you will get a reward at the end. Try to complete routine tasks five minutes before the self-imposed deadline. This leaves you with an extra five minutes of time and also sharpens your basic skills.

❑ Group similar tasks together. For example, it is more efficient to return and place calls during a single block of time than to make them periodically throughout the day.

❑ Place work with the highest priority in a brightly colored folder in the center of your desk before you leave the office.

❑ Collect ideas of things to do to keep busy during slow days or hours. Examples of such tasks include purging files from the hard disk, ordering supplies, reviewing infrequently used word processing procedures, and showing a new procedure to a subordinate.

❑ Schedule time for self-improvement. Review career goals to determine if you are making progress in reaching these goals. Inquire about company-paid tuition plans, or check the possibility of getting time off from work to take additional coursework.

Here are some special considerations:

It is more efficient to start a long, complex project than to concentrate on tasks that are simple and quick to complete. Also, it is important to perform high-priority tasks—those in category A on your "to do" list—first.

Without a plan, it is easy to get sidetracked. Concentrate on one task at a time. Finish a task rather than place it aside, thinking it will just take 15 minutes to finish and so can be done later. Unfinished tasks can create chaos on days that suddenly become filled with crises.

There is no one right way to get started. Some people begin a project by doing the most difficult parts first. Others begin with the easiest parts and work into the project. Use the technique that is comfortable, *but get started*.

CONTROLLING WORK TIME

There are two important steps to take to make your work time efficient and productive: organize your work and minimize interruptions.

PROCEDURES FOR ORGANIZING WORK

The following are a few ways to organize work in order to make the best use of your time. Additional suggestions may be found in each of the chapters covering specific tasks.

❑ Arrange your working environment so it is more efficient. Keep frequently used supplies within close reach. Clear the working area of distractions and clutter. Arrange equipment, such as the computer and printer, so that each piece can be comfortably reached.

❑ Handle each piece of paper as few times as possible. When handling a piece of paper, try to take at least one step in moving it to its appropriate destination. Sort materials into action folders such as "Urgent," "To Read," "To Sign," and "To Check Later."

❑ Prepare form letters, form paragraphs, frequently used phrases, and formats for computer storage. Use macros to minimize keystrokes and prevent irritating errors from occurring.

❑ Keep samples of previously completed forms as references. Attach a description of how the data were obtained, what sources were used, and who should receive copies.

❑ Prepare a notebook of facts for future reference that includes:

- Temporary agencies—contact persons; fee schedules; and, if applicable, the names of individuals who have done excellent work on previous assignments.
- Bank names—account numbers, hours, and names of people to contact.
- Organizations—dues and meeting dates, times, and locations.
- Available community information sources; e.g., the library, Chamber of Commerce, and state employment department.
- Credit card names and numbers, expiration dates, and telephone numbers to call in case the cards are lost or stolen.
- Supervisor's preferences for rental cars, hotels, restaurants, airline carriers, airline seating, and flight times. Include telephone numbers and addresses where appropriate.
- Conference or meeting room availability, contact person, and room capacity.
- Computer network hotline sources—numbers to call and hours of operation.
- Equipment repair contacts—numbers to call, hours, notes on repairs already made, and signatures required to authorize repairs.

❑ Know your organization. Identify sources of assistance; express your appreciation to those who have helped you. Most people will willingly assist someone in a crisis who has taken the time to recognize another's previous efforts.

❑ Organize a tickler file to avoid missing deadlines. Label 12 folders with the months of the year, 31 folders for the days of the month, and one folder for the next year. Decide on what day a document should be handled and place the item in that day's tickler folder. If a document needs to be handled in a future month, place it in that month's folder; then at the end of the current month, remove the items and place them in the appropriate daily tickler folders. Check the files daily and place tasks that need to be completed on your "to do" list.

❏ Plan outgoing calls carefully. Have the information needed for each call and a checklist of questions available. For the people you call frequently, make a list of the things you want to ask or tell them. When the list is a few items long, make the call.

MINIMIZING INTERRUPTIONS

Interruptions are a part of a normal day; however, the effects of interruptions may be minimized by taking some of the following steps:

❏ Block a period of "quiet time" when you ask a coworker to cover your telephone and greet clients. Reciprocate by doing the same for your coworker. Schedule activities that require concentration for this uninterrupted time.

❏ Listen attentively to telephone calls and take complete notes so additional time will not be wasted making another call.

❏ Keep a telephone message pad, pencil, and notebook within reach at all times for telephone messages, directions, or notes. If your supervisor is not available to speak with a caller, ask the caller the best time for your supervisor to return the call.

❏ Discourage lengthy telephone conversations and excessive socializing with coworkers, personal friends, and clients. Suggest that the discussions be continued during break or lunch periods, or indicate it is necessary to complete your present task within the hour to meet a deadline.

SPECIAL CONCERNS ABOUT CONTROLLING TIME

It is more impressive to do a task right the first time than to use overtime to redo it. Listen attentively to instructions and think through the strategies for completing tasks. Ask questions when instructions are not clear or discrepancies exist in the materials. Take enough time to understand the assignment. Being too hasty often results in more serious problems later.

If you cannot complete work by the time requested, communicate this to the person making the request. It is more prudent to say "no" and suggest an alternative solution than to accept an impossible deadline. Refrain from mediating disputes about whose work has priority.

SCHEDULING A SUPERVISOR'S TIME

Office professionals not only have their own time to manage, they often must schedule and control the time of their supervisors. Having more than one supervisor makes the task even more difficult. Here are some ways to schedule the time of your supervisor:

❏ Understand thoroughly the goals of your organization and your supervisor. Find out how the office staff can assist in meeting those goals.

❏ Determine how your supervisor prefers you to schedule appointments, handle interruptions, and take messages. Ask about these matters the first week you are in a new position.

❏ Organize a system for telephone messages. Place all messages in a special message box on your desk; arrange the messages in the order of their importance or by the time of the call. Color-code the message slips by person if you work for more than one supervisor.

❏ Design a work request form that may be completed by supervisors. It should indicate the current date and time, specific job instructions, the date and time the work is needed, the signature of the person requesting the work, and the account or accounts to be charged.

❏ Try to discuss goals, priorities, and changes with your supervisor for a few minutes each day. Ask for instructions so you will not have to interrupt your supervisor throughout the day. Write your questions, ideas, and suggestions in a notebook so you can refer to them the next time you meet.

❏ Share potential time-saving ideas with your supervisor; outline specific reasons for any changes you wish to make.

❏ Use an electronic calendar to remind your supervisor of things to do, meetings, and appointments. If software is not available or appropriate, prepare an appointment reminder form that highlights important events scheduled for the next day and give it to your supervisor before you leave the office.

❏ If you and your supervisor agree to do so, underline, circle, highlight, or summarize information in documents that may be of interest to your supervisor. If the material is to be read at a later time, identify it by topic and prepare a file for each.

❏ Keep track of where your supervisor is throughout the day in case you need to contact him or her on an urgent matter. Also, inform your supervisor when you leave your desk area. Forward your telephone calls if you will be away from your desk for 15 minutes or longer.

SPECIAL CONCERNS ABOUT SCHEDULING

Your assumptions about what items have high priority may be incorrect, so check with your supervisor to determine the relative importance of your projects.

Several warning signs may indicate impending time crises—a supervisor's procrastination, equipment malfunctions, or missed intermediate deadlines by people to whom work has been delegated. When you notice such warning signs, stay ahead of your own schedule so these last-minute crises can be handled with a minimum of frustration.

If you have delegated work to the people you supervise, set intermediate deadlines and monitor the progress of the tasks. Prepare a backup plan you can place in action if there is a delay in the completion of a project.

Request assistance before a rush period occurs. Monitor work schedules and check for assignments to other departments so you can estimate more accurately the amount of assistance and the amount of time you will need.

TECHNOLOGY FOR SCHEDULING

Software and devices exist for appointment scheduling, appointment reminders, telephone number lists, idea organization, task prioritization, and project management. These include time management software, electronic organizers, and personal information managers. Beware of using software or devices so complicated that they waste more time than they save.

TIME MANAGEMENT SOFTWARE

Time management software programs, sometimes referred to as desktop organizers, usually include such features as appointment scheduling, expense tracking, and note taking, as well as a database for telephone numbers and messages. Regular standing appointments for a year may be entered in the calendar. Schedules may be printed out, so you can keep appointment calendars up to date for yourself and your supervisor. The program can be directed to remind you of a scheduled event; a beep will sound on the computer or a reminder will flash on the screen.

ELECTRONIC ORGANIZERS

Electronic organizers are portable minicomputers the size of a paperback book that can track appointments and project due dates. Organizers also have the capability of storing phone numbers and messages, creating multiple lists, and recording notes. Most electronic organizers can be linked to microcomputers, which allows notes and calculations to be easily transferred, updated, and printed. If confidential information is involved, you can select a personal password.

References such as dictionaries, thesauruses, foreign-language phrase books, and worldwide timetables are available in electronic form. Sound chips that allow the machine to give correct pronunciations of words are also available.

PERSONAL INFORMATION MANAGERS (PIMs)

Personal information managers (PIMs) incorporate features of word processing, spreadsheets, and databases. Personal information management software includes features found in desktop organizers and electronic organizers. This software aids in decision making by recognizing patterns, pointing out relationships, and assigning priorities. Based on a user's guidelines and preestablished categories, some PIM programs can even make a decision automatically. Since personal information management software is complex, it requires time to learn its features. Do not expect to become a knowledgeable user in a day or two.

A PROCESS FOR SOLVING PROBLEMS

Problems can result in an office from uncertainty, disagreement, and unanswered questions; they require solutions that will bring about change. Bringing about change requires special skills, and office professionals with effective problem-solving skills are valuable employees.

One systematic process for solving problems involves the following steps:

1. Define and analyze the problem.
2. Consider possible solutions.
3. Select the best solution and defend it.
4. Evaluate the results.

DEFINE AND ANALYZE THE PROBLEM

To define and analyze a problem may be the most difficult step in solving it. The symptoms of a problem are often more evident than its causes. To define the underlying problem accurately, answers to several questions may be helpful.

❑ From your perspective, is there really a problem?
❑ Has this problem happened before? If so, were the conditions similar and were the same personnel involved? How was the problem solved before? Did that solution work or is a new approach needed?
❑ How can you learn more about the problem?
❑ With whom can the problem be discussed? Are there other viewpoints?
❑ What are the specific circumstances surrounding this problem?
❑ What company policies and procedures are involved?

CONSIDER POSSIBLE SOLUTIONS

The second step is to explore numerous possible approaches to solving the problem. Brainstorming is one effective technique for seeking creative solutions to problems. It is a technique that does not restrict or judge any suggestions so that as many ideas as possible are generated. Several questions that will assist you in generating alternative solutions include:

- What is the first solution that you considered?
- What would be the easiest solution?
- What are the conventional approaches to solving the problem?
- What other ideas (workable or not) can be used as alternative solutions?

SELECT THE BEST SOLUTION AND DEFEND IT

After identifying all the possible solutions, the next step is to list the likely consequences of each solution, select the best solution, and prepare to defend it. In most situations, some factors will have an impact on those decisions, such as time, money, convenience, and impact on personnel. Although each solution will have strengths and weaknesses, the best solution should be selected on the basis of all the factors that you have identified and ranked. Here are some questions to help you select the best solution:

❏ What individual department or company limitations must be considered? What solutions are eliminated because of these restraints?
❏ What are the weaknesses and strengths of each solution?
❏ What factors are used to judge all solutions? Rank the factors by importance.
❏ What justification can be made for a decision? How will it solve the problem? What will be the outcome if applied?

EVALUATE THE RESULTS

After you have identified the best solution, try out the solution and evaluate the results. If successful, the solution will be helpful in solving similar problems and eliminating a recurrence of the same problem. The answers to the following questions may be helpful in evaluating the problem-solving process:

❏ What step-by-step tasks were involved in trying out the solution? Were all the subtasks identified and approved?
❏ Was the solution successful? Was it necessary to put a second solution into effect? What were the positive and negative consequences? What improvements were needed?
❏ What experiences with this process could be applied to other problems? What changes would be recommended if these solution procedures were used again?

SPECIAL CONCERNS ABOUT PROBLEM SOLVING

Frustration with a problem may cause it to be blown out of proportion. Focus your attention on a solution and do not imagine every horrible consequence that may result.

Some problems are difficult to solve and may need input from your supervisor. Ask for assistance if the authority to solve a problem rests with another department or a colleague. Do whatever is necessary to handle a problem, but if it becomes too complex, consult with your supervisor before the situation becomes unmanageable.

ORGANIZATIONAL STRUCTURES AND OFFICE RELATIONSHIPS

Organizational structures vary widely from company to company, even in the same industry. Within any given company, especially a large one, the relationships between functions and subfunctions undergo continual change, reflecting external changes in market demands, corporate objectives, and employee needs. Organizations usually develop a chart indicating what positions exist and how these positions are related to each other. The authority and responsibilities of personnel are also shown. Understanding the office professional's place, authority, and responsibilities in an organization can contribute to your overall effectiveness in the company.

ORGANIZATIONAL PRINCIPLES

All organizations are built on a number of principles. Among them are:

1. *Lines of authority:* An organization plan makes one person responsible for each worker and/or group of workers in an organization.

2. *Responsibility and authority:* Each position must be clearly defined through job descriptions.

3. *Equating responsibility and authority:* Responsibility is coupled with corresponding authority.

4. *Delegation:* Authority needs to be delegated as far down as possible. However, the delegator remains fully responsible and accountable for what has been delegated.

5. *Simple structure:* An organizational structure should be kept as simple as possible, with minimal levels of authority.

ORGANIZATIONAL STRUCTURES

Based on these principles, businesses develop an organizational structure and an organization chart to depict it graphically. In an organization with a **line structure**, management has direct authority over, and is responsible for, the performance of all workers reporting to them. This is the most common structure. A line organization chart usually takes the form of a pyramid, with the president at the apex. (See Figure 4-1.)

In a **line and staff** organization, assistants are assigned to executives. These assistants handle specific advisory responsibilities, such as research, planning, accounting, distribution, public relations, and industrial relations. Staff personnel have advisory or support positions with no direct authority over workers down the line. Staff positions are usually designated by a dotted line on the organization chart. (See Figure 4-2.)

CHARTING ACTIVITIES WITHIN AN ORGANIZATION

Office professionals are occasionally called upon to chart an organization's structure. There are four general ways to chart the activities of an organization:

1. *By function, activity, or process:* An organization chart arranged by function breaks the enterprise into groups involved in a single class of activity, such as finance or sales. (See Figure 4-3.) Such a chart can use either broad categories, such as sales, or a specific activity, such as sales promotion.

2. *By customer or type of customer:* In this kind of chart, workers can be listed alphabeti-

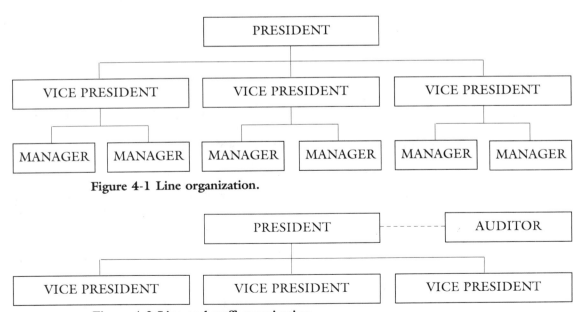

Figure 4-1 Line organization.

Figure 4-2 Line and staff organization.

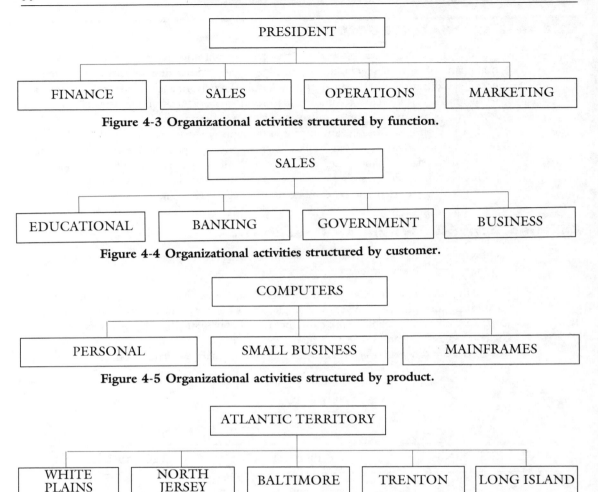

Figure 4-3 Organizational activities structured by function.

Figure 4-4 Organizational activities structured by customer.

Figure 4-5 Organizational activities structured by product.

Figure 4-6 Organizational activities structured by geography.

cally by customer name or by the customer's type of business, e.g., insurance, banking, transportation, or government. (See Figure 4-4.) Such an organization fits products more closely with customer needs.

3. *By product:* A chart in which activities are grouped by product is useful for an organization that focuses on a specialized product and has experts about that product. (See Figure 4-5.)

4. *By geography:* A chart structured by geographical location permits special attention to local conditions and requirements. It is particularly important in sales and marketing, where local traditions and habits have great influence on success. However, such an organization may duplicate common activities, such as accounting and marketing. (See Figure 4-6.)

THE MATRIX STRUCTURE

An alternative to these four structures is the matrix structure. In a matrix structure, each person reports to two executives: the person in charge of the particular project or product on which the employee is working, and the person in charge of the particular area in which the employee works. For example, in a high-tech company, a software design specialist may report to both the manager of the product on which the specialist is working and the manager of software for the organization. (See Figure 4-7.)

This structure is complex. It often works best when employees and management are well educated and professionally oriented, and the company is small and entrepreneurial. Many companies use a matrix structure as a transition between being functionally organized and being organized by product or market.

THE MODERN OFFICE STRUCTURE

Because each organization is different, there is no ideal way to place administrative support personnel in the organizational structure. In fact, many businesses are restructuring to better suit their needs and to maximize productivity. Business costs have also increased, partly because white-collar workers now comprise more than 60 percent of the total work force. As a result, the office is now viewed as a professional environment where skilled people perform functions vital to the smooth operation of an organization. Businesses are placing more emphasis on the management of office support, and in the process they are creating new career opportunities.

TRADITIONAL OFFICE SUPPORT

Traditionally, offices have been organized so that upper-level managers have private or personal secretaries or executive assistants. Moving down in the organization, middle- and lower-level managers have often shared secretaries. Within the traditional structure, execu-

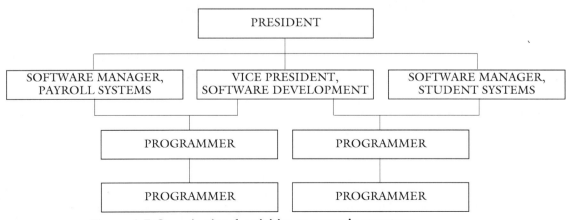

Figure 4-7 Organizational activities as a matrix structure.

tives have immediate access to secretarial support. There is more flexibility in scheduling and prioritizing managerial work. The executive assistant works with his or her boss on a one-to-one basis and does a variety of tasks.

The disadvantage of a traditional secretarial structure is that there is often an uneven workload, with some periods when the work is overwhelming and others when there may be little or nothing to do. Interruptions may cause priorities to change, which could result in poor-quality work and lowered productivity. (See Figure 4-8.)

CENTRALIZED ADMINISTRATIVE SUPPORT

A **centralized word processing (WP) center** can be an effective use of technology and people. All document preparation—memos, reports, proposals, and letters—is completed by word processing specialists on text-editing equipment in one central location. (See Figure 4-9.) The advantage of this type of structure is that it consolidates all word processing equipment and personnel into one central location. A centralized word processing center provides sophisticated equipment for complex documents. The disadvantage is that there may be delays in producing documents if many departments all demand that work be done at the same time.

In some organizations, administrative support specialists are also located in a centralized location. These specialists perform all tasks other than producing documents, such as scheduling meetings, customer relations, making travel arrangements, and research. Work in an organization with this structure comes to the administrative group from each department as well as from the word processing center.

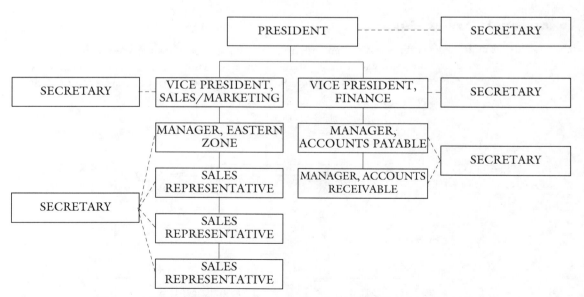

Figure 4-8 Traditional office secretarial support organization structure.

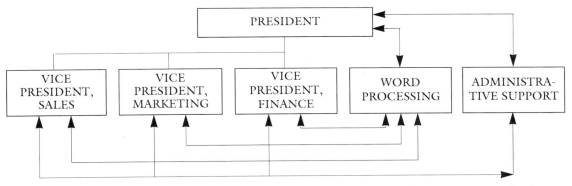

Figure 4-9 Centralized word processing and administrative support organization.

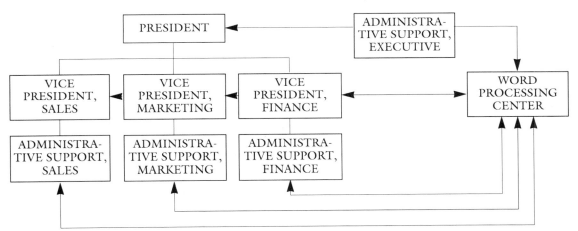

Figure 4-10 Centralized word processing with decentralized administrative support organization.

DECENTRALIZED ADMINISTRATIVE SUPPORT

In other organizations, the word processing center may be centralized, but the administrative support staff is **decentralized**. Staff may be located in several locations near users. For example, departments such as sales, marketing, or personnel may each have an administrative secretary. The word processing center, however, remains centralized for all departments to use for document-producing tasks. The advantage of this structure is that there is a cost-effective word processing center, but managers have easier access to administrative support personnel. The disadvantage is that the work flow may be inconsistent. (See Figure 4-10.)

Finally, both word processing and administrative support may be **decentralized**, in which case word processing and administrative support staff are assigned to each department. However, most organizations use a combination of centralized and decentralized structures. In that case, a main word processing center can store data for the departmental word processing centers, which are known as **satellite centers**.

ORGANIZATIONAL CHARTS

An organization chart is a schematic representation of an organizational structure, showing lines of authority and the relationships among employees. A properly constructed chart:

- Provides a view of the general structure of the company's work by showing relationships and areas of responsibilities
- Serves as a historical record of organizational changes
- Serves as information for orienting new employees
- Can be a work plan for expanding a business and an information piece for the general public or special groups

The design of an organization chart can range from a simple line chart of job titles to a more detailed chart that includes titles, job responsibilities, and photos of the top company executives.

Computer programs are available for use in creating organization charts. Lines can be automatically drawn with the use of the cursor or mouse, and boxes can be formatted with the use of a menu. Charts can be created with an unlimited number of levels. In most cases, changes can be made easily by modifying the chart onscreen before printing.

After creating an organization chart, whether it is done via a software program or manually, the following questions should be answered:

- Are titles correct and up to date?
- Are names spelled correctly?
- Is the reporting structure correct?
- Is the organization chart dated?
- Has management reviewed the chart and approved its distribution?
- Has the organization chart been revised according to an established schedule, e.g., semiannually or annually?

OFFICE RELATIONSHIPS

Another important aspect of any organization is the way its informal working relationships operate. Understanding those relationships contributes to better communications and greater overall productivity. Human resources are vital in today's work environment.

As today's companies merge, downsize, and invest in technology to meet the changing demands of business, team management is emphasized more than ever before. The team approach allows management to share responsibility for implementation of corporate goals. The team approach also helps office professionals to build a framework for professional equity and greater efficiency.

A team has the following characteristics:

Results: A team's purpose is to accomplish something.

Goals: A team must have a common purpose that is understood and pursued by the whole group.

Energy: An extra dimension of energy is created as a team works together to achieve an end result.

Structure: An organization should be orderly and members should respond to pressures in a uniform way. However, the structure should be flexible as the team tries to accomplish its goals.

Spirit: Team spirit reflects the quality of the team's work.

Identity: Having a sense of belonging is important.

Collective learning: Because teams learn together as they answer difficult questions and solve hard problems, their collective knowledge will become part of the team as well as part of each individual member.

The relationship between manager and administrative assistant is the most common team within the office. This unit is motivated by the goal of making the workplace more efficient. Managers and administrative assistants must address face to face such issues as trust, joint problem solving, giving and receiving feedback, time management, and behavioral styles. Team building commands the presence of all the players.

Everyone in an office works together in a team effort, whether formally or informally, at some level. Acting as a team member:

- Maximizes work distribution for the organization
- Allows an interchange of office professionals when one person is out ill or on vacation
- Provides a career path and opportunities for career development for the office professional
- Maximizes productivity through full utilization of human resources and technology

To be an effective team member, you must:

❏ Understand the group's objective. What is the group expected to achieve? Is the purpose of a particular meeting to exchange information or to solve a conflict? Ask questions to help clarify the purpose, but do so in a nonthreatening way. For example, you might ask, "Am I correct in my understanding of our goal? As I see it we are . . ." "As I see it" is a useful phrase because it implies that you are receptive to other viewpoints.

❏ Focus on the objective. Keep to the subject and try not to deviate.

❏ Be economical with words. Do not ramble. Try to use strong nouns and active verbs.

❏ Listen carefully. Concentrate on ideas, not just facts. Watch for nonverbal cues from the speaker. Reserve judgment until the speaker has finished. Be open-minded.

❏ Interact informally. Important information exchanges are often made in informal settings. Informal interactions offer opportunities to express opinions, influence others, compare information, and learn about decisions that have not yet been made.

To work effectively in a team-managed organization and enhance your opportunities for career advancement, you should:

1. Assess the needs of each member of the team for computer skills, education, experience, and certification. Such an assessment will pinpoint the technical, administrative, and interpersonal skills needed by members of the team.

2. Focus on developing and improving communication skills such as writing, speaking, and listening.

3. Understand and keep informed about the organization's goals, products, and competition. Be aware of changes within the company and industry.

4. Develop self-initiative.

5. Learn to delegate.

6. Be organized and manage your time well, not only for yourself but for others in the team.

---

1. Communicate clearly; describe what is expected and when the job is to be completed.
2. Do not limit the delegation to the jobs you do not want to do.
3. Explain the importance of assignments.
4. Share power with other office professionals.
5. Know your fellow office professionals, their aptitudes, and their interests.
6. Delegate work evenly among all office professionals.
7. Schedule program checks of delegated tasks.
8. Define responsibilities for each office professional and make this information known to others.
9. Establish reasonable deadlines.
10. Reinforce good performance; offer suggestions to improve unsatisfactory performance.

Figure 4-11 Ten rules for effective delegation.

COMMUNICATION IN THE OFFICE

Effective communication helps create a desirable work climate in which individuals can cooperate to accomplish personal, group, and organizational goals. In organizations, communication occurs between overlapping and interdependent groups as well as individuals. Organizations rely on communication in order to work effectively. For that reason, they develop communication networks to facilitate the flow of messages. An administrative assistant is often the controller of the communication network and therefore must have good communication skills.

Finally, keep in mind that office professionals also communicate and interact with clients, customers, stockholders, financial institutions, and civic and community groups. How an office professional responds to people outside the organization reflects on the organization's image.

CHAPTER 5

SUPERVISION AND TRAINING

As a supervisor, overseeing, assisting, and monitoring the work of those reporting to you is only one aspect of your job. Other responsibilities include interviewing and hiring, training new and temporary employees, conducting performance appraisals, and administering discipline.

THE HIRING PROCESS

Hiring good people can be a long and difficult process or a short and simple one. There are many steps involved, from writing the job description to interviewing potential candidates to checking references. As today's office professionals advance to supervisory positions, they are increasingly involved in hiring others to work for them.

WRITING A JOB DESCRIPTION

Organizations require division of responsibilities. As more and more people are added to the organization, this division becomes greater. Job descriptions have several important advantages. They help the manager analyze and improve organization structure and determine whether all company responsibilities are fully covered. They can also help in the reallocation of responsibilities to achieve a better balance, if necessary.

An effective job description does more than simply list specific duties and responsibilities. It also indicates the relative importance of each duty and responsibility.

A job description serves multiple purposes:

- It explains and clarifies an employee's responsibilities within the organization.
- It helps an employee understand his or her accountabilities.
- It is used by human resources personnel for information about the knowledge, training, educational skills, and aptitudes needed for each job.

Blind ad (no listing of company's name, only post office box number):

> Educational organization needs organized, outgoing person with strong word processing and interpersonal skills to coordinate production and planning of public presentations and management seminars. Desktop publishing and graphic arts a plus. Send resume to this newspaper, P.O. Box 1011.

Open company ad:

> Detail-oriented individual needed with minimum 2 yrs. exp. to handle work analysis. Write job descriptions, conduct surveys, and assist in personnel screening. Send resume to the XYZ Corp., 91 Victor St., Scotch Plains, NJ 07091

Figure 5-1 Sample job advertisements.

- It plays a role in personal development and performance appraisal.
- It serves as an objective checklist during performance reviews.
- It is part of a wage and salary program, helping clarify the nature of a particular position for job grading, compensation, and possible upgrading.

(See Chapter 11, Office Manuals and Publications.)

WRITING A JOB ADVERTISEMENT

Once the decision has been made to create a new job, a job advertisement may have to be written for the newspaper or for posting within the company. The human resources department (if one exists in the organization) is the best source of assistance in writing the ad. (See Figure 5-1.) However, if it is left to you or your supervisor, the following considerations should be noted:

❑ An advertisement should explain as succinctly as possible what the job is.

❑ Job requirements or prerequisites should be stated to screen out unsuitable applicants.

❑ The advertisement should reflect the legal issues in hiring, such as stating that your organization is an equal employment opportunity employer.

❑ Being creative in the advertisement can help attract a higher quality of applicant.

❑ The advertisement should not misrepresent the job but rather explain it, indicating the most important points of the job. Beware of the ad that promises too much.

❑ Use a post office box if the company wants to protect its identity, or avoid a possible flood of applicants.

❑ The ad can be placed in trade magazines and newsletters as well as in the classified section of local newspapers (usually placed on Sunday and running for three to five days), business newspapers, and professional association publications.

INTERVIEWING

Conducting a successful interview involves a number of steps. First, screen the written applications. The basic screening device is the application form or resume. Once you have done this, talking to candidates by phone is also a good way to narrow the field further. Try to turn such conversations into mini-interviews.

Before each interview, familiarize yourself with the candidate's application form or resume. Jot down some questions that you want to ask to make sure you control the conversation. The eight most common questions asked during an interview are:

1. What are your major strengths?
2. What are your major weaknesses?
3. How is your previous experience applicable to the work we do here?
4. Why are you changing jobs?
5. Is there someone we can contact who is familiar with your work activities?
6. Where do you see yourself in this company ten years from now?
7. What kind of work are you looking for?
8. What kind of compensation do you expect?

During the initial interview, which should last about 30 minutes, you should acquaint the applicant with the company and position(s) available and try to learn as much as possible about his or her background. A good rule of thumb is for the interviewer to talk about 20 percent of the time and the applicant 80 percent.

Write down your impressions during and after the interview. This can help you begin further to narrow down the list of applicants. An initial interview helps in gathering factual information about the applicant's background, attitudes, reasoning process, motives, and personal goals.

Certain questions that are illegal to ask during the interview are shown in Table 5-1.

Here are some additional interviewing techniques:

❏ Create a proper interview environment by holding the interview in a place free from interruptions.
❏ Put the candidate at ease. This helps to generate a useful flow of information; it also indicates to the candidate this could be a good place to work.
❏ Perfect your questioning techniques. Vary your use of questions that require a simple "yes" or "no" and those that require more explanation so that the end result is a conversation, not a grilling session.
❏ Give the applicant feedback to his or her responses; this encourages more in-depth answers.
❏ Keep your reactions to yourself; stay in control and maintain a professional rapport.
❏ Be honest. Conclude the interview by letting the candidate know whether he or she is being considered for the position and will be called for additional interviews.

If you know after the interview that this is not the candidate for the job, write to the applicant of your decision to hire someone else and thank him or her for applying. If the applicant calls, this information should be conveyed orally.

Table 5-1 Acceptable and Unacceptable Questions to Ask in an Interview

Category	Unacceptable	Acceptable
Name	The fact of a change of name or the original name of an applicant whose name has been legally changed	Maiden name of a married woman
Birthplace	Birthplace of applicant Birthplace of applicant's parents Requirement that applicant submit birth certificate or naturalization or baptismal record	Applicant's place of residence Length of applicant's residence there
Religion	Applicant's religious affiliation Church, parish, or religious holidays observed	
Race/color	Applicant's race Color of applicant's skin, eyes, hair, etc.	
Age	Date of birth, *except* when information is needed for: 1. Apprenticeship requirements based on a reasonable minimum age 2. Satisfying the provisions of either state or federal minimum age statutes 3. Verifying that applicant is above the minimum legal age 4. Avoiding interference with the operation of the terms and conditions and administration of any bona fide retirement, pension, or employee benefit program	
Citizenship	Any inquiries concerning citizenship	Can applicant produce documentation of eligibility to work in this country
National origin/ancestry	Applicant's lineage, ancestry, etc. Nationality of applicant's parents or spouse	

Table 5-1 *(con't)*

Category	Unacceptable	Acceptable
Language	Applicant's mother tongue Language used at home How the ability to read, write, or speak a foreign language was acquired	Language(s) the applicant speaks fluently
Relatives	Name and address of any relative	Names of relatives employed by company Person to be notified in case of emergency Whether the applicant has ever worked for the employer under a different name
Military experience	Applicant's military experience, other than 1. U.S. National Guard or Reserve 2. Draft classification 3. Dates and conditions of discharge	Military experience in U.S. Whether applicant has received any notice to report for duty
Organizations	Membership in any club, social fraternity, society, or lodge	Membership in any union or professional, trade, or service organization
References	Name of pastor or religious leader	Names of persons willing to provide professional and/or character references
Sex and marital status	Sex of applicant Marital status Dependents	Maiden name
Arrest	Number and kinds of arrests	
Height	Only if it is a bona fide occupational requirement	

Finally, when choosing one candidate over another ask yourself the following questions:

1. Does this candidate fit in with the people already here? Does this person have compatible perspectives, integrity, and a desire to work as part of the team?

2. Does this candidate show enthusiasm for this particular job?

3. Does this candidate project a good image?

4. Would this candidate go the extra distance to get the work done?

5. Does this candidate have a genuine enthusiasm for this organization and its goals?

In the hiring process you should give serious considerations to candidates who

- Demonstrate ability to do the job
- Show achievements
- Have a definite interest in the job
- Show enthusiasm
- Ask logical questions
- Get to the interview on time
- Dress properly
- Have good manners

Following the initial screening and interview process, the top candidates can be invited back for further interviews with other members of the staff. If the position requires certain skills, such as keyboarding or dictation proficiency, tests may be given.

HIRING TEMPORARY HELP

Temporary help is used to fill in for unplanned absences (such as illness), planned leaves, vacations, and seasonal or short-term workloads. Before you can effectively use temporaries, however, you must:

❏ Identify what positions can be filled by temporaries and specific duties the temporaries will be performing.
❏ Summarize skills needed for each position, being as specific as possible.
❏ Compile a short outline of company-specific procedures, based on job descriptions. Give copies to the agency for its reference and be sure they are available to temporaries when they arrive for work.

In selecting a temporary agency, make appointments with several firms. Evaluate according to:

Prompt and accurate response: The agency should confirm requests quickly and provide the names of other qualified agencies should it not be able to accommodate your request.

Feedback and quality control: The agency should monitor the temporary the first day to ensure that the temporary has the proper skills and should be ready to respond if problems occur.

Adequate insurance coverage: The agency should provide insurance in several areas to protect both the employee and your employer. Bonded personnel should be available if required.

Solid references: An agency should provide references from both other clients and employees.

The key to working with temporary agencies is to develop a long-term relationship. The better you know each other, the better the employees you will receive.

CHECKING THE RESUME AND REFERENCES

In the process of selecting a candidate, you should thoroughly review the resume and check the candidate's references. According to national personnel surveys, 33 percent of the resumes submitted contain false information. Employment dates, salary levels, job responsibilities and titles, and reasons for termination are the most frequent areas where the truth gets stretched.

A starting point for detecting dishonest resumes is to question such things as omissions, abbreviations, peculiar wording, and ambiguous information. Copies of transcripts, W-2 forms, and letters of reference in conjunction with thorough interviews are also common means to counter resume fraud. However, heavy workloads compounded by understaffing may not give you enough time to check resumes. The best alternative, to make sure you hire the right person for the job, is to use a professional resume checking service. A good background checking service has the expertise to spot areas that should be questioned and the resources to check them out.

GIVING REFERENCES

As a supervisor or as a colleague, you may be called on to give potential employers references on people you have worked with or trained. In today's litigious society, this is not always as easy as it seems.

Because of the threat of lawsuits, many companies refuse to give references unless they are positive. Often employers will have employees sign a waiver granting the company permission to give references. Despite these seemingly careful measures, companies that refuse to give references or give them with employees' permission may still end up being sued.

The best way to approach references is to assume your information will be heard in court and be prepared to defend what you say as fact. Consult your company's legal representative to determine the best policy in providing references.

Some guidelines to follow in giving references:

If you give a telephone reference, maintain a written record of who called you, when they called, and what you said. If you provide a letter of reference, keep a copy for your files.

Check your company policy to find out what information you may provide. This policy should be stated in writing as part of any waiver that employees sign granting the company permission to give information to potential new employers.

Provide only information regarding verified and documented job performance. References are not the place to advertise a *personal* grudge against a past employee.

If you do make a personal statement, it should begin with the phrase ''in my opinion'' or ''I believe'' to make it clear it is your personal opinion and not an objective fact. Trying to prove objectively that a person lacks motivation or has a difficult personality is extremely hard.

Provide only the information asked of you. If you give information beyond that requested by the caller, make it clear that this information should be treated as confidential. One way to convey that the information you are providing is not intended to damage an employee's reputation is to qualify it. Use phrases such as, "This information is for professional use only."

TRAINING EMPLOYEES

Because today's office professional has become the main interface between management and computer-based office systems, a sound knowledge of office automation is imperative. The office professional is expected to be able to access a database, manipulate financial models, output to graphic displays, and integrate the applications into a comprehensive word processing document. She or he is also expected to apply conceptual and human relations skills within this fast-paced environment. Effective training fills gaps in an individual's skills and knowledge.

To determine the areas of training, a needs assessment should be done among office staff. Separate training topics can be implemented after a needs assessment. Surveying management and office professionals will pinpoint the technical, administrative, and interpersonal skills in need of improvement. Assessments may reveal needs in the areas of self-esteem, dealing with organizational politics, career development, conflict resolution, assertiveness, stress and time management, and dealing with change.

Professional Secretaries International recently introduced the Office Proficiency Assessment and Certification™ program (OPAC™), a three-and-a-half-hour computerized assessment tool to help entry-level students, business teachers, job applicants, and employers determine proficiency in five areas: word and information processing, keyboarding, administrative support skills, records management, and language skills. Data can be used to verify skills or identify areas needing skill development.

Training can be handled through several methods:

- Classroom training
- Self-study manuals, audiotapes, and videotapes
- Seminars, workshops, or structured on-the-job training
- Videodisk training packages
- Computer-assisted instruction (CAI)

Training can be done by the organization's own personnel or supplied by outside vendors either on-site or at off-site locations.

CLASSROOM TRAINING

Despite a new focus on self-paced training, instructor-led training is still the most popular form. Instructor-led training has the following advantages:

- Trainees receive immediate feedback from an acknowledged leader.
- It is scheduled training with a specific time set aside.
- It is less expensive than one-on-one tutoring.

On-site training is more convenient and eliminates the cost of travel. Off-site training is more concentrated and eliminates office interference and having equipment tied up for training purposes. Electronic materials are also available to supplement classroom instruction.

AUDIOTAPES

Through the use of a cassette, a voice prompts the learner through a series of programmed segments. An accompanying diskette controlled from the computer keyboard works along with the tape, displaying additional course materials on the screen and illustrating particular points.

VIDEOTAPES

Trainees can also watch a training videotape on a TV screen and may also perform exercises on a microcomputer.

INTERACTIVE VIDEO INSTRUCTION

Considered the state-of-the-art in self-paced instruction, interactive video instruction (IVI) allows the user to control the pace and content of a video. It takes advantage of the educational precept that people retain only about 25 percent of what they hear, 45 percent of what they see and hear, and 70 percent of what they see, hear, and do. IVI lets the user see, hear, and do.

COMPUTER-AIDED INSTRUCTION

Computer-aided instruction (CAI) uses a program encoded onto a diskette along with courseware that introduces features of the program frame by frame. The learner turns on the computer, inserts the disk, and hits the proper start-up keys; the system then takes over, showing and telling the student what to do next.

TRAINING TEMPORARY HELP

If a position needs to be filled by temporary help, you must effectively organize the temp's time. Here are some pointers for using temporary help:

- Arrange the work to be done in sequence. Prioritize.
- Set aside a specific place for the temp to work.
- Provide all equipment and supplies needed.
- Prepare instructions and write them out.
- Furnish samples of company brochures, letters, forms, etc.
- Assign a full-time person to assist the temp. Let that person monitor the temp's performance.
- Keep your expectations reasonable.
- Introduce the temp to other office personnel. Make the temp welcome as a team member.

- Keep a list of temps who work out well, and ask the agency to send one of these temps the next time you need one.

SUPERVISING EMPLOYEES

How effectively work is accomplished depends a great deal on the supervision people receive. Good supervision encompasses motivation, performance review, the ability to make decisions and communicate expectations and disappointments, and ordinary common sense.

MOTIVATING EMPLOYEES

Motivation comes from the Latin word meaning "to move." Thus motivation is the internal process that moves or energizes you to fulfill various goals. Motivation techniques are important to your job of supervising others. Such techniques include the following:

Set objectives: Help employees establish challenging, measurable objectives that will motivate them. Supervisors with little experience frequently fail to motivate workers because they are afraid to demand too much. Once you have helped set the objectives, you must follow through to see that the objectives are achieved.

Give recognition: Recognition should be given through verbal praise, a thank-you letter, the company newsletter, etc.

Enrich the job: Give employees a greater variety of duties to perform, though only if the employee wants them and has the time to do them. By making the job more challenging, you help prepare the employee for advancement. Job enrichment can also be achieved through additional education. Seminars, workshops, or classes can provide a greater understanding of the jobs and duties of office professionals. Additional responsibility has been shown to increase the employee's sense of satisfaction. It also contributes to promotional possibilities, since new skills will be acquired by performing additional duties.

Develop a team: Productivity can increase when each person in the group contributes to the effectiveness of the team. Motivation starts when you give your undivided attention to the people you supervise.

Compensate the job appropriately: Yearly or semiannual performance reviews that reward good work can help motivate individuals. A pay increase should be the result of a good review. It not only motivates; it helps to develop loyalty and dedication to the organization.

Delegate: Delegation is the process of entrusting the performance of a specific job to another person. Delegation is one of the keys to effective supervision, but it is also one of the hardest things for most supervisors to do. Some supervisors may not understand their role and therefore cannot delegate what they do not understand. Some believe that the work will not be done properly unless they do it themselves. Some fear competition or loss of credit and recognition. Delegation is important, however, to distribute work fairly and to motivate employees and give them an opportunity to grow.

Conducting Job Evaluations

A job evaluation or performance **review** is a private meeting between an employee and his or her immediate supervisor to discuss the employee's past and present performance. Through a systematic rating procedure, management should maintain a record of the performance of its personnel and make decisions regarding employment, placement, transfers, promotions, dismissals, and individual salary rewards.

Evaluations answer the basic question, "How am I doing?" A formal evaluation is scheduled at least once a year. Informal evaluations occur on a continuous basis.

Here are a number of suggestions for conducting formal and informal evaluations:

1. Prepare the employee: Do not evaluate without letting the employee know why the appraisal is required.

2. Evaluate on the basis of current behavior and performance.

3. Assess all the facts objectively. Be fair.

4. Be consistent. Do not say one thing in the evaluation and write something else on the evaluation form.

5. Appraisal information should be given only to those who need it. Such information should be kept confidential.

6. Be clear, concise, and accurate in writing the evaluation report.

7. Allow adequate time for the evaluation.

8. Listen to what the employee says in the meeting.

9. Establish attainable objectives. Set down in writing a plan of action for improvement, with dates for achieving each objective.

10. Support these objectives by providing opportunities for professional development such as internal training programs, outside seminars, or classes to build skills and promote career advancement.

The evaluation should be constructive. The main objective of such a process is to improve performance. Keep in mind that you should evaluate an employee as if you were the person being evaluated.

A performance appraisal should include the following elements:

- Quality of work
- Quantity of work, or productivity under normal daily requirements
- Performance under stress
- Knowledge of work, e.g., utilization of training and experience and understanding of the job in the organization
- Initiative
- Adaptability and flexibility
- Judgment
- Resourcefulness
- Cooperation or teamwork
- Job presence, e.g., lateness, absenteeism
- Administrative ability
- Professional appearance and behavior

For those personnel involved in word processing, the performance appraisal would also encompass such skills as typing, dictation, and telephone manners.

GIVING AND RECEIVING CRITICISM

Learning to give and take criticism is an important skill for supervisors. Since no one is perfect, criticism should be expected. The way in which you deliver criticism, however, determines whether its effect will be productive or disastrous. Whether you are receiving or giving criticism, some important points should be remembered and practiced.

If you must criticize, keep the following points in mind:

❑ Stay calm. Anger creates a physical reaction that can make you tense and unreasonable. Walk away. Sit at your desk or some quiet place and relax. Uncross your legs and arms and close your eyes and think of a peaceful scene. Holding your body in this fashion helps to relieve the anger.

❑ The best times to criticize someone are early in the morning and at midday. This gives you a chance to speak to your coworker again during the day in a casual manner, reassuring the person that you have found fault with the behavior, not the person.

❑ Listen to what the other person has to say. Create an open environment for discussion. Use body language and a tone of voice to let the person being criticized know that you are on his or her side. Criticize the person's actions or behavior only.

❑ Criticize in private but compliment in public. Criticizing in public alienates the person you are criticizing and may lower the opinion of you held by people overhearing your remarks.

❑ Be specific. Say exactly what the person is doing wrong, such as, "This is what I don't like and here's why."

❑ Be supportive. Give the sense that the criticism is meant to help the person do better.

❑ Help solve the problem. Suggest a solution or offer to help find a way to improve things.

❑ Be timely. Give the message soon after the problem occurs.

These destructive ways to give criticism should be avoided:

- Being vague by offering no specifics, merely making a blanket statement, such as "That was a lousy job."
- Blaming the person by attributing the problem to personality or some other unchangeable trait.
- Being threatening, and making the person feel attacked, by saying things such as, "Next time, you're fired."
- Being pessimistic by offering no hope for change or suggestions for doing better.

If you are being criticized:

❑ Listen without becoming defensive.

❑ Remain calm. Remind yourself that you can learn from criticism.

❑ Take notes and repeat the main points to make sure you understand correctly. Doing so allows you time to calm down and shows the other person that you are considering his or her statements.

❑ Thank the other person if it is a justified and helpful criticism. But if you feel it is unjustified, present your side.

❑ Tell the person you would like to consider the criticism and discuss it later.

❑ Outline your responses to the criticism. Explain why you think the criticism is unjustified (if that is the case) and try to end the discussion on a firm and friendly note.

Not all criticism is negative, however. Criticism can also suggest a better method of doing an assignment or a different approach to handling a situation. Such criticism should be viewed as a growth and learning experience.

FINDING A BALANCE

As in most things, finding a balance for effective supervision is important. There is no "best" way to supervise, but certain elements are central for good supervision. They include leadership, ability to communicate, respect for self and others, giving the incentive and the opportunity to grow, fairness, providing educational opportunities, allowing relative independence and freedom to accomplish useful work, and having the ability to change.

EMPLOYEE DISCIPLINE

Experts indicate that over the course of a management or supervisory career, there is a 90 percent chance of being confronted with a problem employee. Problem employees can be, among other things, chronic complainers, constant talkers, rumormongers, incompetents, habitual latecomers, persistent arguers, or practical jokers.

Dealing with such employees requires a systematic, legal-awareness approach, particularly with today's lawsuits for discrimination and unfair treatment.

Several elements are involved in determining how to discipline an employee:

Facts: The supervisor must seek to discover the facts—the who, what, when, where, why, and how of the incident.

Reason: The supervisor must act as a counselor and listen directly to the employee's account of the incident. This may mean allowing the employee to give the reasons for his or her absence, explain poor performance, or deny an accusation of theft. If an employer fails to give an opportunity for the employee to give his or her side of the story, an arbitrator can reverse the disciplinary action.

Audit: A review of the employee's personnel file must be made as a means of gathering data. The audit should review past performance evaluations and any disciplinary actions that may have been taken. Not all infractions are documented, however, which can make it difficult to support an allegation. By documenting the infraction, support for the disciplinary action can be upheld later in court, if necessary.

Consequences: The supervisor must analyze the impact of the infraction. An employee's behavior can result, for example, in loss of productivity or delay in getting work done.

Type of infraction: The supervisor must define which policy or procedure has been violated. Some offenses are more serious, resulting in more severe discipline or termination.

IMPROVING THE PROBLEM EMPLOYEE'S PERFORMANCE

The first thing to do when you are having problems with an employee is to find out the cause of the problem. Personal problems as well as work-related ones often result in poor performance. Personal problems that affect work performance range from car trouble to divorce, mortgage problems to the death of a close friend or family member. Work-related problems range from poor lighting to insufficient training, from smoke in the office to a poor relationship with the manager.

Personal problems often manifest themselves at work through mood swings or attendance problems. A supervisor's involvement in personal problems should be kept at a minimum. It is not your role to act as a therapist; rather, you should counsel the employee on job performance and help resolve the problem, using your authority and leverage to encourage and persuade people to do things they might not be interested in doing on their own.

In dealing with work-related problems, several steps need to be taken:

1. Analyze the employee's performance, taking positive and negative behaviors into account.

2. Develop specific goals for improvement.

3. Meet with the employee for a performance improvement interview. Find out from the employee how things are going on the job, if there are any problems, and what you can do to help.

4. Ask the employee to do a self-analysis in order to identify concrete examples of effective performance and areas needing improvement.

5. Present your own analysis to the employee and negotiate a performance agreement that assigns both of you specific tasks designed to improve the employee's work performance within a three- to six-week period.

6. Follow up with a formal interview within a month to evaluate progress.

Firing is only one of several options at the time of the follow-up. The employee's behavior may have worsened, remained the same, or changed only minimally. Before considering firing, a supervisor should explore the possibility of restructuring the employee's job to take advantage of strengths or transfer the employee to another, more suitable position in the organization. Firing may be the only alternative if these options are not feasible, as well as in cases of dishonesty, absenteeism, substance abuse, insubordination, and general lack of productivity. However, thorough documentation of the entire performance improvement process should be made to avoid legal difficulties, and other types of disciplinary action can be taken.

TYPES OF DISCIPLINARY ACTION

When all else fails with problem employees, disciplinary action generally is taken. Based on the infraction and a review of the steps outlined, the following types of discipline can be selected:

Oral warning: This is used for minor infractions and as a first step in progressive discipline. Documentation of a verbal warning is usually not placed in the employee's personnel file, but the supervisor should keep a record of the discussion.

Written warning: A written warning is given by the employee's supervisor as documentation of an infraction. It clearly states future expectations for the employee and indicates what future action will take place if further infractions occur.

Suspension: Suspension is used when the seriousness of either the present infraction alone or a combination of the employee's past and present behavior warrants a more severe form of discipline. Loss of pay highlights the seriousness and the fact the employee is in jeopardy of losing his or her job.

Sending an employee home: If an infraction is dangerous to the employee or to others, the best course of action is to have the employee leave work for the day. The employee should be told that he or she is to report to work the next day and that management will then inform him or her of the discipline that will be administered.

Discharge: Discharge, or firing, should happen only when it is no longer possible to correct the employee's behavior. The rationale for discharging is that the employee's actions gave management no other alternative.

CHAPTER 6

BUSINESS ETHICS AND ETIQUETTE

BUSINESS ETHICS

The most successful people and companies are those who behave ethically. The leaders of a corporation set the tone for ethical behavior, and this determines how employees, customers, and competitors are treated. Ethical problems in business are not just a matter of knowing right from wrong, but involve looking at business questions from a reasonable, responsible, and consistent point of view.

LEGALITY VERSUS MORALITY

The legality of an action is determined by law. The morality of an action is determined by ethical rules of right and wrong. Ethical behavior requires following the spirit as well as the letter of the law. An ethical business follows rules and trusts that other businesses and their employees will do the same, despite the fact that some unscrupulous businesspeople take advantage of this trust.

Employees may behave unethically because they do what they are told to do without considering the consequences. They may be afraid of losing their jobs, or they may not understand management expectations. The corporate climate often determines employee behavior. For example, when there are slack internal controls, employees may feel free to take home office supplies or to make an excessive number of personal telephone calls. On the other hand, when management treats employees as trustworthy adults, employees are more likely to act responsibly.

CORPORATE IMAGE

The reputation of a company is judged by its image in the public eye. One factor of a corporation's image is the care and upkeep of its building, grounds, and offices. Its logo and letterhead also communicate a message about the company. One of the most important factors in a company's image is the way its employees treat its customers and clients as well as the general public. Finally, the way a company treats its own employees is another important factor in corporate image.

A positive corporate image creates respect and confidence in the company and its product or service. Every employee can contribute to a positive image by wearing appropriate business attire, by being courteous in telephone calls and written correspondence, by treating visitors well, and by participating in community activities.

More and more people determine where they want to work and with whom they wish to do business based on corporate ethics. Here are some questions to ask in determining whether or not to work for or do business with a company:

- Does the company make quality products or offer superior service?
- Is the company trusted by customers and employees?
- Is the company comfortable and personal, no matter what the size?
- Does the company sacrifice quality for profit?
- Do employees feel that unethical behavior "goes on all the time"?
- Has the company been involved in any sexual harassment or civil rights lawsuits, or in any coverups?
- Does the company contribute to the community through public service, charity, youth activities, or the like?

HANDLING ETHICAL PROBLEMS

As an employee, you may be faced with a situation that is unethical or illegal or both. You will have to decide how best to handle the problem. For example, you might be asked to prepare expense reports for trips never taken or to underreport state sales tax. Such a situation calls for a choice of action. All choices have consequences. When making a choice, you must define the problem and weigh the potential consequences. You need to assess the risks of stepping forward and of keeping silent, and to calculate your chances of being fired, reprimanded, demoted, or of having a promotion withheld. You must also live with the possible stress the situation causes.

In order to help you best solve such borderline ethical problems, it is helpful to answer the following questions:

- What is the problem?
- Is there a law against it? Is there a company policy against it?
- Who is affected by your decision? How are they affected?
- What are the alternatives? What are the consequences of the alternatives?

Hint: Try to come up with two or three possible solutions.

- Who can be consulted for help?

Hint: Discuss the problem with several of your peers.

- How will your decision make you feel? How does it relate to your personal values? Does it reflect the kind of company/person you are or want to be?

If your personal ethics and those of your manager or company do not match, you will not be comfortable in the position. It may be best to find a new position that matches your personal ethics.

COPYING PRINTED MATERIALS AND SOFTWARE

An important issue of legality in today's office involves copyright law. Copyright law defines the rights of copyright owners to authorize others to use their work. Copyright protection applies to published material, software, musical works, pictures, sound recordings, and motion pictures. Reproducing, displaying, or performing copyrighted work without permission is a copyright infringement.

The courts permit "fair use" in copying protected works. Therefore, copying printed documents for purposes such as criticism, comment, news reporting, teaching, or research usually does not violate copyright laws. For example, an article in a newspaper or magazine can be legally copied and distributed to employees. However, copying an article and using it in a seminar where enrollment fees are charged is illegal.

It is illegal to copy software if it is copyrighted. Although licenses vary, software should be treated as if it were a single item, like a book, and should not be used by more than one individual at a time. Software can be moved from computer to computer, but installing copies of the same program on more than one computer is illegal. The copyright law applies to both copy-protected and non-copy-protected software. (See Chapter 8, Office Computer Software, for a discussion of other sorts of programs, such as shareware.)

In order to help firms with many users, most software producers have reasonable pricing for multiple copies. Advantages to purchasing rather than copying software include free customer support, usually via an 800 number, and notification of price breaks on software upgrades.

Violators of copy protection laws can be charged with a misdemeanor. If a person calls the software company for support and the name of the caller does not match the name registered with the serial number of the program given, the software manufacturer may threaten to sue.

Many companies have policies against illegal software copying, which, if violated, can result in the firing of the violator. When management treats unauthorized duplication of software as a serious violation of company policy, employees are more aware of copyright laws.

The following questions will help to determine whether software has been legally obtained:

- Is there a preprinted, professional-looking label?
- Is the name of the software company on the label with copyright information?
- Is there a printed manual (not a photocopy)?
- Is there a registration number or a registration card to complete and send to the software company?

Many businesses have scanners (optical computer input devices for graphics and text), but it is not legal to copy and scan all graphics. For example, most cartoons are copyrighted and should not be scanned without getting prior permission in writing from the publisher or copyright holder. Clip art is the term for graphics that can be purchased and legally scanned.

BUSINESS VERSUS PERSONAL PHONE CALLS

Each company sets its own policy, either formally in writing or informally by example, regarding personal phone calls at work. Charging personal long-distance calls to the company or tying up company phones with personal calls are commonly unacceptable practices. Some companies scrutinize phone bills more closely than others and confront employees about questionable calls.

It is best to ask about the company policy when you are hired to avoid embarrassment or questions about your personal integrity. Just because "everybody else is doing it" does not make it right.

BUSINESS VERSUS PERSONAL OFFICE SUPPLIES

Is it permissible to take home paper, pens, and staplers? These questions should be asked at the time of hiring. Employees who travel or do company business at home may have permission to take supplies out of the office. Employees who take company supplies for their personal use, however, may be accused of stealing. Some businesses have tighter controls than others over the supply area and are able to monitor how many supplies are taken and by whom. If the company uses an honor system for supplies, it is a violation of trust to use supplies for personal use.

SEXUAL HARASSMENT

In 1980 the Equal Employment Opportunity Commission (EEOC) declared harassment such as offensive jokes, leering, ogling, unwanted touches, and outright propositions to be a form of sexual discrimination that is forbidden by law. The victim of sexual harassment has a responsibility to complain, and the employer must establish a procedure to handle such complaints.

Corporations are held responsible for sexual harassment by their employees (even if top management was not aware of the problem) and could be forced to pay damages. An employer is legally responsible for preventing sexual harassment and providing a harassment-free environment.

Sometimes men are harassed by women and sometimes a person is harassed by someone of the same sex, but most frequently women are harassed by men. There are no objective criteria for determining what is or is not sexual harassment. Some situations are more obvious than others (e.g., "If you don't have sex with me, you don't get the promotion or get to keep your job").

Legally there are two kinds of sexual harassment: (1) unwelcome verbal or physical conduct of a sexual nature that implies having sex is a condition for advancement or employment and (2) a hostile or intimidating work environment created by sexual jokes, teasing, comments, or suggestive posters.

To determine whether you are being sexually harassed, ask the following questions:

- Is the action unwelcome?
- Does the behavior continue on a regular basis?
- Is your job at stake if you do not go along with propositions?
- Does it affect your ability to function at work?

If you feel that your answers indicate you are being harassed, here is a series of steps to take:

1. Tell the harasser that the behavior is offensive and that you want it to stop. Be specific about the behavior.

2. Keep a record of the behavior with dates, times, and detailed circumstances, including names of witnesses.

3. Write a letter to the harasser specifying what is objectionable and why. Keep a copy.

4. Keep copies of positive work evaluations and memos or letters of praise. These records can refute allegations by the harasser that your work was poor.

5. If the behavior does not stop, discuss the harassment with another colleague.

6. Follow the company's complaint procedure, which usually means reporting the problem to your supervisor. If the person is your supervisor, go to the harasser's supervisor.

7. If these steps fail, file a formal complaint with the state's department of labor or human resources, the local human rights commission, or the local EEOC office. It is illegal for the harasser to retaliate by firing or demoting you for these actions.

8. Consider conciliation, such as a transfer to another department. If you have a solid case, you may deserve financial compensation.

9. If conciliation fails, decide whether it is worth suing. The court case may take years to settle, though, so this should be only a final step.

BUSINESS ETIQUETTE

Proper business etiquette is essential for good human relations in the office. Good etiquette sets a high standard for handling daily encounters and situations. Treating others with respect and courtesy increases cooperation and enhances working relationships. Most business etiquette is based on common sense and sensitivity.

INTRODUCTIONS

When introducing yourself, extend your hand and give your name. In social settings, the woman is traditionally introduced first. In business, however, decisions on who is introduced to whom depend on the ranks of the individuals, not their gender. The higher-ranking person should be named first (e.g., "Ms. Higher Rank, I would like you to meet Ms. Lower Rank").

When making introductions, always use both names in a sentence (e.g., "Ms. Jones, I'd like you to meet Ms. Smith"). It is not necessary to repeat the introduction in reverse (e.g., "Ms. Smith, I'd like you to meet Mr. Jones; Mr. Jones, this is Ms. Smith").

When being introduced, always stand if you are sitting and extend your hand. It is appropriate for both men and women to shake hands. When someone is introduced to you, stand up, maintain eye contact, and shake hands firmly. The handshake should communicate sincere enthusiasm.

An older man introduced to a woman may not extend his hand unless the woman extends hers. If the other party does not extend a hand, withdraw yours and do not worry about it. Having arthritis or other health problems may make shaking hands uncomfortable. If someone is handicapped, take the lead from them on their preferred manner of greeting.

In foreign countries, a handshake is not always the accepted means of greeting. In Japan, the preferred form of greeting is a bow from the waist. Most Japanese businesspeople visiting the United States will bow slightly from the waist and then shake hands. In India and South Asia, one form of greeting is placing the palms together at chest level or higher and giving a slight bow. Indian customs discourage a man from touching a woman or talking with her alone in public. In Europe, a handshake is used, but it is not as firm as the American handshake. In Northern Africa and Central Europe, greetings may be an embrace and a kiss on one or both cheeks.

The following are general guidelines for introductions:

❏ The person making the introduction should give a little information about each person to make small talk easier. This information might include title and areas of responsibility.

❏ Whether or not to use first names depends on the location and size of the company. Some cities and companies are more formal than others. Generally a lower-ranking person should not use the first name of a higher-ranking person unless asked to do so.

❏ After being introduced, repeat the other person's name and say something like, "I am pleased to meet you, Ms. Senior Executive."

❏ When introducing a company employee to a client, always name the client first: "Mr. Client, I would like you to meet Bob Green, assistant to the president. Mr. Client is with Jones, Inc."

❏ Introduce a person individually to each member of a group and leave time to shake hands before going on to the next person in the group. Always name the new person first unless the people in the group outrank the new person: "Jim, I would like to introduce my colleagues—June Cortez, John Baker, and Doris Hing. This is Jim Hernandez, manager of information services."

❏ When introducing people of equal rank, titles (Mr., Ms., Dr.) are not necessary.

❏ If you forget a name, introduce the person to those whose names you remember. This should be a cue to the omitted person to give his or her name. If this does not happen, admit lapse of memory and say something like, "I'm sorry I've forgotten your name," or "Your name is—?"

❏ Present a spouse to someone who outranks you. Always name the higher-ranking person first: "Ms. Senior Executive, I'd like you to meet my husband, Mark."

RESPONDING TO INVITATIONS

Any invitation, whether to a cocktail party introducing a new product line or from a client celebrating a tenth anniversary, should be responded to promptly, to the person named on the invitation. If an invitation was accepted and at the last minute something prevents attendance, it is important to notify the host immediately. If someone other than the person who received the invitation will attend, the host should be notified of this substitution.

INTERRUPTING A CONFERENCE

Occasionally an important client or manager asks to talk with another manager who is in a meeting or conference. It is the role of the administrative assistant to determine whether or not to interrupt the conference.

If the decision is made to interrupt the meeting, the most unobtrusive method is to wait for a break in the meeting to speak with the manager. If the administrative assistant does not know when the next break will occur, a folded note can be given to the manager. The administrative assistant waits for a response, typically a nod of the head, before leaving the room.

BUSINESS CARDS

Business cards have become an important part of every business occasion, and all office professionals should have them. The purpose of the business card is to identify you and give the recipient information about you and your company. The business card can be attached when sending someone a magazine article or the company annual report and even used when sending someone a present or flowers.

The typical business card is $3\frac{1}{2}$ inches long and 2 inches high. Most businesses have designed their business cards to match their corporate image, including the company logo and the placement of information on the card.

The following information should appear on the business card:

- Company logo
- Company name, exactly as the official name is written (e.g., if the word "company" is abbreviated it must be abbreviated on the card)
- Company business address, including city, state, and ZIP Code (including all nine digits)

Hint: If a company uses a post office box number and a street address, both are included. The U.S. Postal Service prefers that the street address be listed before the post office box number.

- Company business phone number and car phone, including area code and extension

Hint: Some businesspeople also list their home phone number on their cards.

- Incoming 800 number or Telex number
- Name in full

Hint: Omit the middle name if it is not used (the initial could be included). Any nicknames should be in parentheses after the first name or in quotation marks (e.g., Margaret "Peggy" Martin). Avoid Mr. or Ms. unless the name could be mistaken for either sex (e.g., Chris or Marion). Titles such as Ph.D. are placed after the name (e.g., Jennifer E. Ubarra, Ph.D.).

• Title

Hint: Put the title in smaller type under the name.

• Department (if appropriate)
• Office hours (if unusual, such as evening or weekend hours)

Hint: Office hours are helpful for the medical profession.

Suggestions for printing the business card:

Paper: Thicker paper gives a higher quality look and feel. The card should be strong enough to withstand a certain amount of wear and still look attractive.
Printing: Engraved cards, where the letters can be felt, are usually reserved for senior management. Offset or letterpress printing is less expensive than engraving, but can produce an effective card with the proper choice of paper and design.
Type Style: The style of type should be legible, and it should be the same style as that used in the logo.
Color: The color should match company stationery.

When enclosing your business card with a business gift, write a message on the back and sign your first name. When using the business card for forwarding material, clip the card on the upper left side of the material. When exchanging cards, let senior management make the first move.

It generally is not appropriate to give a business card out socially. Business cards should not be wrinkled or soiled, nor should they include handwritten information (such as a new phone number or address). If business is done internationally, the cards should be in English on one side and in the other country's language on the other.

Usually it is the responsibility of the office professional to order business cards. It is extremely important to proofread any business card order carefully before it is given to the printer and to proofread it again after it has been printed. It may take several weeks to receive an order.

THE BUSINESS LUNCH

A popular way of entertaining employees or clients is the business lunch, which gives people an opportunity to relax and get to know one another away from the office. When a guest is invited to lunch, careful planning and a caring attitude are important.

Here are some tips on inviting guests to lunch:

❑ Let guests choose the best time.
❑ Ask for culinary preferences (Italian, Chinese, vegetarian, etc.).

❑ Decide on the restaurant. Ask coworkers for suggestions, check on the price range, and make certain the location is convenient for the guest.

❑ Make a reservation, even though one may not be required. Avoid tables near the kitchen, waiters' station, or door. If the location is unacceptable, request another table before sitting down.

❑ Check for credit card or cash before leaving for the restaurant. If using a credit card, make certain the restaurant accepts that card.

❑ Arrive earlier than the guest (you may be seated or wait just inside the restaurant door).

Here are some suggestions for dining with a business associate:

❑ Sit opposite each other for best eye contact. Guests should have the best seat.

❑ Decide what beverage is appropriate. If the other person has ordered an alcoholic beverage, it is acceptable (but not necessary) also to drink alcohol.

❑ Avoid eating anything that will distract you from the conversation.

❑ Wait at least ten minutes before discussing business. Do not expect anyone to do a great deal of reading or note taking during the meal.

❑ Start with the utensil farthest from the plate and work inward.

❑ Ask the guest whether there is time for dessert and coffee before ordering them.

Here are some suggestions for handling the check:

❑ Pick it up quickly and do not make a scene. Notify the waiter during the meal that you are picking up the check. If the check is presented to your guest, let the guest know the company is paying and ask for the check back.

❑ Leave a 15 percent tip before tax at a moderate restaurant, 20 percent if the restaurant is expensive. Tip even if the service was not good; bring the problem to the attention of the restaurant's management later.

SMOKING

Smokers should always be aware of federal, state, and local laws regarding smoking in public places. Many businesses regulate smoking in the office. If smoking is only allowed in designated areas, it is important to abide by all rules, including not smoking in rest rooms.

When dining with a group and no one is smoking at the table, assume that you may not. If smoking is permissible, do not light up until everyone has finished eating. When visiting someone's office or conference room where there are no ashtrays, ask permission to smoke.

THE CHANGING ROLES OF MEN AND WOMEN IN THE OFFICE

Traditional social etiquette suggested that a man should always let women leave elevators first, stand up when a woman enters a room, open doors for women, and walk next to the curb. These rules are considerate, but they no longer apply in today's office.

Office etiquette is now based on rank in the company. Never automatically assume that one person (usually a man) ranks higher than another. The following etiquette is appropriate:

❑ The person closest to an elevator door should exit first.

❑ The first person to a door should open it and hold it open until all have passed through. If the door is heavy or if a person is carrying something, it is courteous to help no matter what his or her gender is. A visitor to an office should be treated like a guest and be allowed to go through a door first.

❑ Men and women should help each other with coats.

❑ A person of either gender can hail a taxi.

❑ When riding with several people in a car (especially if the car belongs to a person of higher rank), it is best to ask where to sit.

❑ All staff should rise when a visitor of either sex comes into the office from the outside. Staff should also rise for a higher-ranking executive unless that executive is frequently in the office, in which case the lower-ranking person should stop work and acknowledge the presence of the senior person. It is not necessary to stand when a colleague (man or woman) enters or leaves a room.

OFFICE POLITICS

In any job it is important to know who has the power, who will be inheriting the power, and how to assimilate into the organization. Balance is important in office politics. Being overly political and not concentrating on your work will cause people to notice, and not being politically savvy may mean you get overlooked for promotions. Managers in every organization periodically change; the key to surviving office politics is being respectful to everyone.

Be careful of office gossip. People gossip out of boredom or jealousy. Office gossip can give early warnings about corporate reorganizations, the effect of a competitor's product on corporate sales, or the loss of a major client. However, gossiping about personal or work problems of coworkers is counterproductive and dangerous and should be avoided.

Here are some suggestions for dealing with office politics:

❑ Avoid sharing confidential information unless you are prepared to have the rest of the office know.

❑ Treat all coworkers with respect and interest. Give everyone a chance to express his or her opinion. If you avoid negative remarks, coworkers are more likely to treat you with the same respect.

❑ Avoid criticizing a subordinate in front of others.

❑ Counteract untruths by mentioning the truth when the subject comes up in a conversation. Avoid arguing or losing your temper.

❑ Ignore harmless gossip and do not pass it on.

It is important for administrative assistants to be discreet and not to talk about company business inside or outside the business. An executive must feel secure that all information will be confidential, including any knowledge about financial matters or private life.

Holiday and Birthday Gifts

Many companies have a standard gift or a set amount of money to give to employees during the holidays, a standard gift for customers or clients, and inexpensive promotional items to give away. Companies vary widely in their holiday gift giving, ranging from none at all to giving a turkey or to having or sponsoring a company party.

Employees are usually not expected to give gifts to their employers during the holidays unless the relationship is longstanding and close. A simple gift of homemade cookies or flowers from the garden that can be shared with others is best. Other possibilities are a bottle of wine or a book. Follow the lead of other employees or rely on tradition.

Many businesses send out holiday greeting cards to clients or customers with an imprinted company name. Use a card with "Season's Greetings" to avoid the problem of sending religious cards. Each card should be personalized with a signature and a short message.

Some businesspeople send holiday greetings to employees and their families at their home address. This is a nice gesture but not expected or necessary. Office professionals may wish to remember those who have done them favors throughout the year, such as maintenance or security employees.

It is often the responsibility of the administrative assistant to keep an up-to-date holiday mailing list each year. This mailing list is best kept on a computerized database program for easy updating and printing of address labels, and to avoid duplication of gifts from one year to the next.

Holiday cards should be ordered at least two months in advance, particularly if cards are sent abroad. If company gifts are given to clients and customers, they should also be ordered in advance. When giving a gift to someone from another country, make certain it cannot be interpreted as a bribe under the definition of the 1977 Foreign Corrupt Practices Act. If uncertain about the proper gift to give someone from another country, ask a colleague who is familiar with that country. In Argentina, for example, giving a set of knives is interpreted as a desire to cut off the business relationship. In China a clock is a symbol of death.

Many businesses keep a list of employee birthdays and celebrate by bringing in a cake and having employees sign a card. Donations for a gift may be requested from coworkers, but it is perfectly acceptable to politely say "no" when asked to contribute.

Procedures for an Employee Illness or Death

If an employee or client has been injured, is seriously ill, or is in the hospital, a card is usually sent. Depending on office policy, flowers may also be sent. Some offices have a special fund for purchasing cards and flowers, or donations may be solicited as needed. Other offices have written procedures describing when cards or flowers are to be sent.

Flowers can be ordered through a local florist, who will either make the delivery or contact another florist. For illness, plants are appropriate because they can be brought home or to the office.

In the case of death, a letter of sympathy should be sent to the family. Flowers may also be sent, if appropriate. Some families prefer that donations be made to charities or other organizations. The family should be consulted to determine their wishes.

If a manager dies, the administrative assistant may be asked to notify other employees, clients, and associates. Depending on the family circumstances, a company employee may be responsible for helping make the funeral arrangements as well as acknowledging all flowers and memorials. Writing an obituary notice for the newspaper may also be necessary. The obituary notice should include the following information:

- Name
- Address
- Age
- Education, including degrees and honorary degrees
- Current title and important past career information, including any major awards received
- Date, place, and cause of death
- Names and relationships of survivors (spouse, children, parents, brothers, sisters)
- Details about the funeral

The administrative assistant may also be asked to gather all personal effects for the family. Someone in the company should be designated to receive and place all calls about the death.

PART II

EQUIPMENT AND SUPPLIES

CHAPTER 7

OFFICE EQUIPMENT

The last half of the twentieth century has seen vast changes in office tasks. In the 1960s, data processing significantly changed the way information was handled in the office; in the 1970s, word processing, or automated text editing, was introduced as a substitute for repetitive typing; and in the 1980s, information processing, the integration of data and text, became a reality through the widespread use of the personal computer. As a result, the role of the administrative assistant has changed dramatically.

Personal computers (PCs), copiers, fax machines, and other products now make information handling easier. Thanks to these new types of equipment, the office workers of the 1980s are becoming the "knowledge workers" of the 1990s. This chapter provides an overview of the office equipment now available.

THE COMPUTER

A computer is an electromechanical, programmable machine that accepts, processes, interrelates, and displays data. All digital computers have the following components:

- A *central processing unit (CPU),* the device that contains the central control and arithmetic units used for controlling the system
- *Memory* for temporary storage of programs and data
- *Mass storage* for permanent storage of programs and files
- A *visual display monitor,* usually a cathode-ray tube (CRT), for viewing text, graphics, and numerical data
- An *input device* for entering data
- *Software* to give instructions to the computer. (See Chapter 8, Office Computer Software.)
- An *output device,* usually a printer. See below under the heading *Printers* for more information.

CENTRAL PROCESSING UNIT (CPU)

This is the "brain" of a computer. The CPU accepts data, manipulates it according to programmed instructions, and then can direct storage and output of the data. The CPU consists of a control unit and arithmetic logic unit. The control unit is like a telephone switchboard, controlling and coordinating the parts of the computer system as directed by a set of instructions called a **program**. The arithmetic logic unit does the actual calculating or data processing.

MEMORY

Memory enables a computer to store program instructions, data to be processed, and the intermediate results of the mathematical and logical operations it has performed. The size of a computer's memory is given in bytes. A **byte** is roughly the size of one character (single letter, number, or graphics symbol) and is equal to eight bits. A **bit** is the smallest electrical unit of data and is represented as either 1 or 0 in the electronic circuits making up the computer. Two other frequently used terms are **kilobyte**, which is 1,024 bytes of information, and **megabyte**, which is 1,084,576 bytes. Kilobyte is abbreviated as K (or KB), so a 640K computer has approximately 640,000 bytes of memory, while megabyte is abbreviated as M (or MB), so a 2M computer has approximately 2 million bytes.

A computer has two types of memory, read-only memory **(ROM)** and random-access memory **(RAM).** Measurements of a computer's memory normally refer to RAM.

READ-ONLY MEMORY (ROM)

ROM is the permanent internal memory of a computer. It contains the computer's instructions for starting up (or "booting") the system and for reading the **operating system** instructions. An operating system controls the input, processing, storage, and output of the computer's operations, by managing the interaction between the computer and its peripheral devices, such as the keyboard, printer, and disk drives. (See the section on Systems Software in Chapter 8.)

ROM instructions are generally nonprogramable, that is, their contents cannot be altered by the user. The CPU can only access instructions in ROM; it cannot write instructions to ROM.

RANDOM-ACCESS MEMORY (RAM)

RAM is the computer's temporary memory; its contents are erased when the power is turned off. It is used to store programs and information only while the computer is operating. The size of the program and amount of data you are working with are limited by the amount of RAM memory installed in your computer. For example, if your computer has 512K of RAM and the software program you want to use requires 640K of RAM, you will have to purchase additional RAM memory chips.

Mass Storage

A variety of magnetically coated materials are used for data and program storage. The main types include:

Floppy disk (or *diskette*). This is a magnetically coated disk that comes in two basic sizes: 5 1/4-inch disks (minifloppies) are flexible and come enclosed in a protective envelope. They commonly store either 360K (double-density disks) or 1.2M (high-density disks) of information; 3 1/2-inch disks (microfloppies) are encased in rigid plastic and commonly store 720K (double-density disks) or 1.44M (high-density disks) of information. A disk drive with a higher capacity can read from and write to a lower-capacity disk. However, the reverse is not possible. For example, if your system has a 1.2M minifloppy drive, you can read and write to a 360K disk in that drive. You cannot read a 1.2M disk in a 360K drive.

Hard disk. This is a rigid, random-access, high-capacity magnetic storage medium. Disks may be removable, providing off-line archival storage, or nonremovable. Capacities range from 1M bytes (1MB) to well over 300MB per disk. The major advantages of a hard disk over a floppy disk are speed and permanent storage. You can retrieve and store information almost 100 times faster with a hard disk system. Also, you do not have to continually insert floppy disks when using a hard drive.

Cartridge. This is a magnetic tape loaded into a cartridge (such as a single reel or reel-to-reel) that holds multiple pages of text.

Cassette. This is a magnetic tape loaded into reel-to-reel cassette with a capacity of approximately 30 text pages.

Other storage options include:

Magneto (rewritable) optical disk. This uses a laser beam to store and read data on a magneto-optical substrate over a layer of aluminum. These disks are erasable and perform similarly to hard disks, but they are removable and the entire system is more powerful.

WORM disk. This stands for "write once, read many" times. A WORM disk is generally used to store items that are going to be retrieved many times but do not need to be updated. It is available in several sizes—$5\frac{1}{4}$, 8, 12, and 14 inches in diameter. It is used primarily to store correspondence, invoices, and other business documents. It can be read thousands of times without degradation, and the information cannot be changed. Since they are slow, in comparison to magnetic hard disks, WORM disks are primarily used for data archival purposes.

CD-ROM. This stands for "compact disk read-only memory." CD-ROMs are similar to music CDs. They are 4.71 inches in diameter, capable of storing digitized text, data, images, and sound. Capacity generally is up to 650M per disk. CD-ROM disks have data stored on them when a user receives them and cannot be changed. Typical applications include large databases of information, such as encyclopedias, catalogs, or other reference information.

DISPLAY MONITORS

A monitor is an output device that provides a temporary image of information on a video screen. When combined with a keyboard it is called a **video display terminal** (**VDT**). A display screen can be like a television or can be a flat panel. Monitors vary in size, type, and quality of resolution.

The television-like display screen is called a **cathode-ray tube** (**CRT**) and typically comes in sizes of 12, 13, 14, and 19 inches. They can be monochrome (one background color and one foreground color) or multicolor. Monochrome screens are available in green or amber on black and in black on white.

The 19-inch display screens are suitable for such applications as **presentation graphics**, which generate, display, and print line drawings, organization charts, bar graphs, and pie charts; **computer-aided design**, which generates, displays, and prints standard engineering drawings to assist engineers and designers; and **desktop publishing**, which creates a document of typeset quality using personal computers and appropriate software.

The following are among the common display standards:

Color Graphics Adapter (CGA). This offers a resolution of 320 by 200 pixels (picture elements) in 4 colors selected from a palette of 16 colors. (A pixel is one or more dots treated as a unit. The pixel can represent as little as one dot for monochrome screens or three dots—red, green, blue—for color screens.)

Enhanced Graphics Adapter (EGA). This offers a resolution of 640 by 360 pixels, with 16 colors that can be selected from a palette of 64 colors.

Video Graphics Array (VGA). This offers greater resolution than EGA—up to 720 by 400 pixels in text mode and, in graphics mode, up to 640 by 480 pixels, in 16 colors that can be selected from a palette of 256.

Super VGA (SVGA). Compatible with the older VGA standard, SVGA also offers even greater resolution, usually 800 by 600 pixels but, in some instances, as high as 1024 by 768 pixels. Although SVGA has no clearcut standards for colors, the graphics cards that support it offer a much wider choice than VGA does, with 256 available colors not uncommon.

New video standards, with increasingly high resolution and wide arrays of colors, are constantly evolving.

Some monitors can be used with only one display adapter. Multisync monitors, however, can be used with more than one adapter. The additional cost may be well worth it for the greater flexibility.

Flat panel displays are usually 5 inches or 9 inches in diameter and are classified as follows:

Liquid crystal display (LCD). An LCD forms characters by subjecting a liquid crystal solution to an electrical charge. The readout is either dark characters on a dull white background or the reverse. A backlight option can enhance the quality of the image.

Light-emitting diode (LED). An LED is a semiconductor device that emits light when electrical current passes through. The colors emitted are red, yellow, or green.

Gas plasma display (GASP). A GASP is characterized by an exceptionally clear, flicker-free image. It has a sharper image than the LCD and does not depend on any external light source.

INPUT DEVICES

An input device is a means through which a user can enter data and instructions into the computer. The most common device is a **keyboard**. Computer keyboards are similar to standard typewriter keyboards. When a key is pressed down, an electrical pulse is emitted that translates the symbol represented by that key into a digital code that the computer can interpret. The code most often used is **ASCII** (American Standard Code for Information Interchange). This code enables one computer to communicate with other computers.

Most keyboards are arranged in a QWERTY layout, which is the same as for the typewriter and is named after the left portion of the top row of alphabetic keys. An alternative to the QWERTY keyboard is the Dvorak keyboard, named after its designer, August Dvorak. The layout is based on the frequency of use of the letters of the alphabet. Both keyboards are available from many manufacturers.

In addition to alphabetic and numeric characters, keyboards have other special purpose keys:

Function keys are programmable, changeable keys, switches, or buttons that initiate predetermined instructions when depressed, such as storage, insertion, or deletion of characters.

Cursor control keys are used to position the **cursor**, the marker that shows the exact location on the screen where one is working. These keys are usually labeled with arrows, one each pointing up, down, left, and right.

Designated-purpose keys include ctrl, alt, caps-lock, and shift keys and special software program command keys. Some keyboards also have a separate numeric keypad similar to an adding machine.

Other input devices or techniques include:

Touchscreen: A video terminal input device using a clear panel overlaid on the CRT screen. The user simply touches the screen with a finger to select available options.

Mouse: A handheld input device that when rolled across a flat surface moves the cursor to a corresponding location on the display.

Voice input: A means of recognizing spoken words and converting them into digital signals that are then changed into characters.

Light pen: A pen-shaped light-sensitive device that when touched to the display screen can create or change images on the display.

Digitizer or *scanner:* A device used to transform a graphic image into signals that can be accepted for processing by the computer.

Optical character reader (OCR): A device that can read printed or typed characters and then digitally convert them into text and/or numeric data.

Pen-based computer: Characters are written by hand on an LCD display and converted into text or saved as images.

Desktop computer (Courtesy of Digital Equipment Corporation)

TYPES OF COMPUTERS

There are three types of computers: the mainframe, the minicomputer, and the microcomputer.

MAINFRAME COMPUTERS

The earliest computers were **mainframes**, developed in the late 1940s. Mainframe computers have CPUs that can process millions of bytes of information at extremely fast speeds. These systems can support hundreds of input terminals tied directly into the computer. Mainframes are used to manipulate large databases and for payroll, inventory, and other large-volume applications in business and science.

MINICOMPUTERS

The **minicomputer** was developed in the 1960s. It uses the integrated circuit, in which hundreds of electronic components are formed chemically on a piece of semiconductor material, or "chip." Minicomputers are midsized computers, smaller than a mainframe and

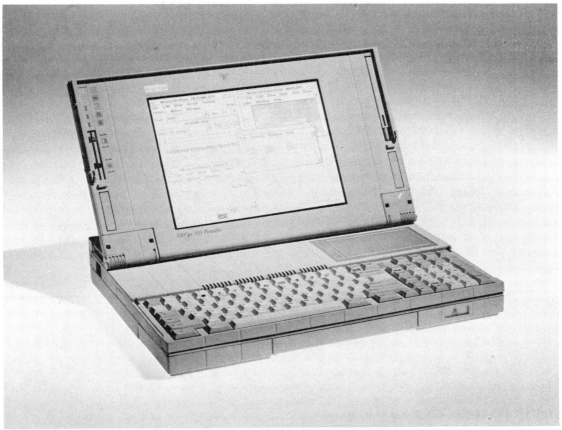

Laptop computer (Courtesy of Digital Equipment Corporation)

usually with much more memory than a microcomputer. They are sometimes referred to as small business computers. Minicomputers are frequently used at the department level to perform functions such as accounting or word processing. They can share peripheral devices and can support multiple users.

MICROCOMPUTERS

Microcomputers are also known as **personal computers (PCs)**. Developed in the mid-1970s, they are reprogrammable electronic devices that process information. A microcomputer uses a microprocessor, a single chip containing all the elements of a computer's CPU. These computers are meant for a single user and generally have a smaller CPU than the minicomputer. They usually fit on the top of a desk. More and more offices are networking microcomputers together to provide capabilities similar to those of minicomputers.

Personal computers are available in portable versions. These units use the same basic components as their desktop counterparts. Portables are classified into two broad categories: **transportables** and **laptops**. Transportables come in a case called a "suitcase," "lunchbox," or "sewing machine." They weigh more than 15 pounds, require AC power, and can be transported from one location to another. Laptop computers come in a case called a "clamshell" or "briefcase." They weigh from 4 to 14 pounds and can be powered by electricity or by batteries. The smaller, lighter laptops are called "notebooks."

Portables provide a wide range of computing power, although they do not always have the memory capacity of a desktop. They may include a flat panel display using LCD, LED, or GASP. Most can be used with the monitor and printer of a compatible PC.

Handheld microcomputers make extensive use of memory and storage innovations known as ROM and RAM "cards." These removable cards may contain the operating system, utilities, and customized applications that obviate the need for heavy and power-hungry disk drives. Handhelds are generally used for task-specific purposes such as inventory accounting, research, and industrial or military data gathering.

Utilizing the notebook technology of the portable computer, pen-based computers, such as the GRiDPAD®, lets users write directly on the screen with an attached electronic pen. This type of computer can be used with form applications, word processing, and schedulers.

WORD PROCESSING EQUIPMENT

Word processing is the automated production of documents and correspondence using electronic equipment. It encompasses a cycle of inputting (keyboarding), processing (editing), outputting (printing), distribution/communication (mailing/calling), and storage and retrieval (filing). Several categories of word processing equipment exist.

COMPUTERIZED WORD PROCESSING

The first category is software-driven word processing on mainframes, minicomputers, and personal computers. Computers with word processing software provide for extensive and powerful capabilities. They have the ability to add graphics and to integrate documents with spreadsheet, database, and communications software without having to retype the documents.

ELECTRONIC TYPEWRITERS

Another category of word processing equipment is the electronic typewriter. Electronic typewriters (ETs) are found at traditional secretarial workstations and are used for limited-volume document production. Typical applications best suited for the electronic typewriter include letters, memos, short documents, forms, labels, index cards, and envelopes.

ETs are noted for their durability. They operate with electronic circuit boards and microchips, using few mechanical parts. The downtime is so low that some users forgo the purchase of service contracts.

There are six categories of ETs:

1. Portable or compact ETs are lightweight, transportable, and may include internal memory and a display. They are intended for light typing jobs. They are sometimes referred to as personal word processors.

2. Standard-level ETs have a memory that ranges from automatic error correction only to text storage up to 4KB. They do not have a display but provide basic electronic typing features and limited text editing features.

3. Mid-level ETs provide standard-level features as well as phrase/format storage, a text storage area of 4KB to 8KB, automated typing features, and more advanced text processing features. Some have a one-line display for viewing text.

4. High-level ETs incorporate the features of the standard and mid-level with text storage of 8KB or more. They offer external text storage media as an option, a line display with one or more lines, text search, block/move/copy/delete, document assembly, pagination, and headers and footers.

5. Video ETs have a display screen to view and manipulate text. Screen capacities range from 10 to 25 text lines. They include external text storage, PC compatibility, calendar and scheduling, name/address files, sort capability, spreadsheets with math calculation, full-page image, and an undo function.

6. Add-on word processors consist of a system unit, a monitor, and/or diskette drive that are cable-connected to a basic ET.

High-end ETs are capable of processing long documents (as many as 350 pages on a 720K diskette) and are equipped with advanced text processing capabilities that rival a low-end word processing application.

Some ET vendors offer a combination electronic typewriter/word processor/personal computer housed in one unit and referred to as an ET/PC. This product combines the text processing capability of a word processing program with the data processing power of a low-end personal computer and a direct key-to-paper typewriter mode.

With the addition of appropriate connections, ETs can serve as letter-quality printers and remote input terminals for the micro or personal computer, word processing systems, and local area networks. This feature enhances the usefulness of both pieces; however, the machine cannot be used as a typewriter and as a printer at the same time.

Voice-activated typewriters (VATs) are currently being developed. Combining voice processing boards, microphones, and an array of electronics, they can interpret a speaker's voice with 95 percent accuracy.

COMPONENTS OF THE ELECTRONIC TYPEWRITER

Memory. The electronic typewriter has both internal and external memory. The internal memory can store phrases (datelines, standard closings, signature lines, line lengths, and tab settings) or information for later retrieval or printing. Internal memory capacity can be a few hundred to 64,000 (64K) characters. Capacity can be increased by purchasing additional memory. The external memory requires some form of magnetic media, usually disks. Some disks can provide additional memory capacity of up to 300,000 characters.

Visual Display. The display can be a cathode-ray tube (CRT) or liquid crystal display (LCD). If the electronic typewriter has a display, the display window may show from 16 characters up to 25 lines of text. (A normal computer monitor shows 25 lines.)

Hint: Information displayed on a cathode-ray tube tends to be easier to read, but CRT machines take up more space than a standard electronic typewriter. LCD displays are more compact but are more difficult to read.

Keyboards. A full-sized typewriter keyboard is typical. Some keyboards do not have dedicated function keys as on a computer keyboard; certain standard keys double as function keys. Special keys include the following:

- Directional keys are used to move the cursor up, down, left, or right.
- Operation keys are used to send keyboarded information to the storage unit, to retrieve information for viewing, or to instruct the printer to print.
- Function keys instruct the processor to perform certain functions automatically, such as delete or search.
- Format keys are used to direct the overall placement or layout of the information in a document.

Disks. Most ETs come with a single disk drive that takes a microfloppy disk, usually $3\frac{1}{2}$ inches, for storing until retrieval at a later date. It is important to be aware that the disks used with electronic typewriters usually cannot be read by other manufacturers' machines.

Printer. Almost every ET is its own printer, although some newer ET/PCs operate with remote printers. The print speed of most ETs averages 20 characters per second. Most typewriters use daisywheel impact print mechanisms. However, some models operate with thermal print mechanisms. The daisywheel models provide letter-quality printouts and can print carbons and multicopy forms, but they are not as quiet as thermal print models.

It is virtually impossible to detect the corrections made by a thermal print ET. Because of this capability, it is possible to forge legal documents using these models. Users who type legal documents should be aware of this and elect not to purchase such a machine.

FEATURES OF THE ELECTRONIC TYPEWRITER

Automated text features vary with each model. The following features are found on many ETs, depending on their category.

Automatic carriage return (word wrap): Print carriage automatically returns without the typist depressing the carriage return key.

Automatic indentation: Causes text to be temporarily indented at the left margin for as many lines as necessary.

Automatic widow/orphan adjust feature: Prevents a paragraph's last line appearing at the top of the following page (a widow) or a paragraph's first line appearing by itself at the bottom of the preceding page (an orphan).

Block move/copy/delete/print: The move function marks the beginning and end of a block of text and moves it to another location within the document or another document.

The copy function is used to mark a block of text and copy it to another location within the document or another document, without erasing the original. The delete function is used to mark a block of text and delete it from the document. The print function is used to mark a block of text and print only that block.

Centering: Automatic centering of text between margins, over columns, or at any position on the typing line.

Column layout: Automatically calculates the placement of columns between the margins.

Default format: Consists of the most commonly used settings for margins, tab position, line spacing, and pitch selection.

Decimal tabulation: Aligns columns of numbers automatically on the decimal point as the numbers are typed.

Document assembly/merge: Assembles new documents from previously stored text that can be merged to create a whole new document.

Dual column typing: Prints a document in two or more columns with equal margins in each column.

Forms mapping: Used to program the stop positions of standard, preprinted forms into the memory so the print carriage can automatically move from position to position on the form when filling it in.

Global search and replace: Searches through stored text for the location of each occurrence of a word or phrase and automatically replaces it with another word or phrase.

Headers and footers: Automatically inserts one or more lines of information at the top of the page (header) or at the bottom of the page (footer) on designated pages of hard copy.

Hyphenation: Allows for a uniform right margin by hyphenating words that go beyond the margin.

Mail merge: Prints multiple copies of a standard letter and merges the letters with a list of names and addresses.

Pagination and numbering: Divides a multipage document into pages of a specified number of lines before printout and prints the number of the page on the printout.

Relocation: Automatically returns to the typing position after going back in text to correct an error.

Right justification: Aligns text flush with left and right margins by automatically adding extra white space between words and/or characters.

Search and replace: Searches for a word of group of words in the text and allows optional replacement.

Underlining: Underlines text as needed.

The following features are usually available as options:

Dictionaries/spell check: Used to flag misspelled words either while keying or while scanning a stored document before printing or to create a user dictionary to prevent the system from flagging words that are spelled correctly or missing from the dictionary.

Grammar check: Identifies wordy, vague, misused, and overused phrases.

Thesaurus: Provides synonyms for words.

DEDICATED WORD PROCESSING

A dedicated word processor is a microcomputer that is programmed specifically to do word processing. It is designed to do more sophisticated applications than typically found with most personal computer software, such as electronic mail, electronic calendars, list processing, security, records processing, math, form design, split-screen editing, and integration of files from spreadsheet programs. However, the capabilities of dedicated word processors are often matched by increasingly sophisticated word processing software. These machines are available in stand-alone and shared versions. Stand-alones have independent computing capability and may be connected to other stand-alones so they can share peripheral devices, such as a printer or an optical character reader. Shared word processors have a CPU to which numerous terminals are connected via a network. The terminals cannot independently process information. They are dependent upon the CPU to do so. When problems occur with the CPU in a shared system, the entire system can go down, whereas a problem at an individual terminal does not affect the rest of the system.

DICTATION EQUIPMENT

Dictation equipment records spoken dictation so that the office professional may type the material later while listening to the playback. Dictating systems use either an endless loop or discrete media. An endless loop system uses a loop of tape that records the dictation and erases it after it has been transcribed, allowing new dictation to be recorded. It resembles a reel-to-reel tape recorder. The tape fits within a case called a "tank." A discrete media dictation system is one in which the recording medium can be removed. It uses cassettes (mini, micro, or standard), magnetic disks, or magnetic belts.

These tapes, disks, and belts are reusable and semipermanent. They may be stored for some time but will eventually deteriorate. Therefore, it is important to have critical information filed on paper or stored on a computer disk.

Dictating systems use analog recording, the same as magnetic audiotapes, or digital recording, which translates the spoken word into the 1s and 0s of binary machine language to interface with a computer. Users of analog systems, the older of the two technologies, can retrieve a document only by fast-forwarding through previous documents on the tape. A cue tone or electronic signal is used to mark the beginning of a document or to alert the transcriber to editing instructions.

Digital systems can store more information in less space, and they offer random access to documents. They also include more efficient editing functions as well as computer compatibility. Insert and delete functions allow the user to dictate changes within the document itself so that the transcriber can work with one continuous document.

Central Dictation System

A central dictation system provides a telephone-like handset for dictation from each executive's office; it can also be accessed from elsewhere by a touch-tone telephone. A central system permits more than one person to record simultaneously.

The following features are found in most central dictation systems:

Digital or analog recording.

Immediate access to transcription.

Automatic job identification.

Display status of job.

Priority coding: Allows the user to designate to the word processing center or transcriber which recording has priority.

Productivity tracking: Provides a printed summary of activity and data to analyze the performance and productivity of the word processing department.

Editing capabilities: Allows corrections to be put on a separate track on the tape from the body of the dictation. Where insertions are indicated, the tape automatically switches to the correction track as it is played back and returns to the right spot on the main track at the end of the insertions.

Programmability to suit the specific needs of a business.

Random access.

Built-in telephone recording.

Voice mail.

Intercom.

Desktop Dictation System

A desktop dictation system is about the size of a desktop telephone and may include a conventional handheld microphone or a telephone-like handset. Desktop systems store and record on tape inside the desktop unit. When the document is ready for transcription, the author must remove the tape from the machine and deliver it to the transcriber. The transcriber unit is usually controlled by a foot pedal so the transcriber's hands need not leave the keyboard while typing.

Hint: A desktop system is useful for offices where two to four people each dictate several hours daily.

The following features are found in most desktop dictation systems:

Analog recording.

Voice-activated recording: Begins recording when the user begins to speak into the microphone without turning on the machine.

Cue tones: Allows an author to alert the transcriber to the end of a document, beginning of a new document, or special instruction.

Conference recording: Records conversations of two or more people without losing the voices farthest from the microphone.

Pitch and speed control: Automatically corrects for variations in speed and keeps the recorder's voice intelligible at any speed.

Instant review: Allows the user to listen to what has been recorded without rewinding. Push-button control.

Dual speed recording: Allows user to run the tape at two speeds, with the lower speed doubling the capacity of storage.

Audible fast-forward: Allows user to locate a specific portion on a tape.

Tape counter or liquid crystal display (LCD).

Clocks, alarms, and appointment reminders.

Record meter: Alerts user when voice becomes too soft or too loud for quality recording.

Electrical pause control.

Fail-safe warning: Alerts user to cassette malfunction or approach of end of tape.

Intercom.

Ability to double as answering machine.

PORTABLE DICTATION MACHINES

A portable dictation machine is battery operated and fits in the palm of one's hand. It is about the size of a midsized calculator and has a built-in microphone. The transcriber unit is often controlled by a foot pedal so the transcriber's hands need not leave the keyboard while typing.

The following features are found in most portable dictation machines:

Portability
Analog recording
Voice-activated recording
Cue tones
Push-button control
Dual speed recording
Audible fast-forward
Tape counter or liquid crystal display (LCD)
Clocks, alarms, and appointment reminders
Record meter
Electrical pause control
Fail-safe warning

REPROGRAPHICS

Repographics is the reproduction of documents by any process that uses light or photography. A wide variety of reprographics equipment is available. The choice of which process to use depends on the quality and quantity of copies needed, cost, and the time factor involved.

Photocopier (Courtesy of Xerox Corporation)

PHOTOCOPIERS

Photocopiers are the most commonly used office machines for reproducing documents. Two imaging technologies are used: analog and digital. An analog system reflects light through a series of mirrors and lenses directly to a drum, creating a latent image. The drum is applied to the paper, leaving a pattern created by static electricity. Black powder called *toner* then adheres to the statically charged places, creating a copy.

Digital copier technology, based upon the same binary logic as computers and CDs, allows for higher-quality prints. It also gives the user the ability to manipulate images, making digital copies superior to analog copies. However, digital technology is more expensive and slower.

Digital copiers can serve as both a printer and a copier, and many can electronically transmit copies by fax. The two main components are the scanner and the printer. Images can be scanned into a computer, where the image is converted into digital signals. Software makes it possible to manipulate and create changes to stretch, condense, reverse, or shade images. Future models will combine into one unit a copier, fax, scanner, phone, printer, and computer.

There are three categories of copier, based on their speed. High-volume units can produce 50,000 to more than 100,000 copies per month at a speed of 50 to 100 copies per minute (CPM). Medium-volume units can produce 20,000 to 50,000 copies per month at a speed of 20 to 50 CPM. Low-volume units come in three types: low-high units that can produce 10,000 to 20,000 copies per month at a speed of 20 to 30 CPM, low-medium units that can produce 3,000 to 10,000 copies per month at a speed of 15 to 20 CPM, and low-low units that can produce up to 3,000 copies per month at a speed of 10 to 15 CPM.

> **Hint:** Low-volume copiers are called **convenience copiers** and are suitable for small
> offices or departments where most jobs are only a few pages in length. Most are small
> enough to fit on a desktop. Others come with their own stand, which can also be used
> to store paper and supplies. Few special features are available for low-volume copiers.

Machines that use one or more toner colors are available. They give users a choice of copy color other than the traditional black. More expensive **color copiers** use a photographic process to produce an exact color reproduction of the original. There are also dual-purpose machines that function as either full-color or as black-and-white copiers.

Some copiers can interface directly with a computer. This feature allows color images on the CRT screen to be immediately captured in the copier. This process provides copies of near-photographic quality.

Many features are available on copiers as options. They are often standard features on high-volume machines. They include:

Automatic document feed (ADF): Multiple originals can be placed in the ADF bin without having to feed one original at a time.

Automatic duplexing: Two-sided copying is done automatically.

Electronic editing: Allows users to manipulate the image of the original document in a cut-and-paste approach to produce modified versions.

Multifunction memory: Preset instructions related to specific types of copying jobs can be set into memory for future recall on frequently run jobs.

Reduction/zoom: Reduces or enlarges a version of the original in order to fit the image on a standard sheet or concentrate on a blown-up section of the original document.

Sorters: A bin sorter can collate copy sets by feeding the output into individual racks or slots on a peripheral device attached to the main copier.

Stapler: Automatically staples the corner of each sorted set of papers at the end of a run.

Three-hole punch: Punches each copy as it exits the copier.

Multiple paper trays: Trays are available in several sizes so that when a different size of paper is needed, one tray can be removed and replaced with the desired size.

Some copiers include built-in electronic information displays to help the user. Some allow for restricted access. Another feature is automatic copy-quality adjustment. Standard serial and parallel interfaces permit the use of copiers with PCs. Other options permit access to local area networks (LANs).

PRINTERS

Printers provide the printed output, or hard copy, from a computer. They vary widely in speed, quality of output, available printing fonts, and cost. When selecting a printer, it is necessary to relate one's office tasks and budget to the available printing hardware. Two categories of printers exist—**impact** and **nonimpact**. Impact printers strike a ribbon, similar to typewriters, whereas nonimpact printers create characters through the use of heat or light or by spraying ink on a page.

Word processing equipment and desktop computers use two types of impact printers: **letter-quality printers** and **dot matrix printers**.

LETTER-QUALITY PRINTERS

A letter-quality printer produces a document that has the same quality as an original typed on an electric typewriter. Most have various styles and pitches. **Daisywheel printers** use a flexible disk or wheel with letters attached to the edge, similar to a many-petaled daisy. A hammer or printhead pushes the letter onto the ribbon and against the page.

DOT MATRIX PRINTERS

Dot matrix printers strike the ribbon with a series of tiny dots to form a character. They are relatively inexpensive and used when the emphasis is on information and not on the visual quality of the output. A top-line dot matrix printer, often called a near-letter-quality (NLQ) printer, has a larger number of pins in its printhead than the average dot matrix printer, typically 24 rather than 9.

> **Hint:** Impact printers can handle multipart forms and produce up to five or six copies. Dot matrix printers print at a higher speed than letter-quality ones and are good for draft output.

NONIMPACT PRINTERS

Nonimpact printers are noiseless but cannot make carbons. There are four types of nonimpact printers: ink jet printers, thermal-transfer printers, laser printers (of which there are several varieties), and plotters.

Ink jet printers spray ink onto the paper in the shape of the character intended. Printer speeds range from 1,000 to 2,200 words per minute.

Thermal-transfer printers create characters and images by melting a wax-based ink off the printer ribbon and onto the paper. These printers are quiet and produce high-quality output. Their speed is about 4 to 8 pages a minute.

Laser printers use a laser beam to form images on a light-sensitive drum. These images are then transferred onto the paper a page at a time; thus they are sometimes called page printers. These machines print at a rate of 4 to 8 pages per minute for low-end desktop models and 10 to 17 pages per minute for high-end equipment. Copies are of the highest quality, approaching typeset quality. Laser printers can use a variety of fonts. They can also produce forms, letterheads, and signatures.

PostScript printers are laser printers that use a page description language, or page-formatting program, called PostScript, which facilitates the printer's communicating with the computer. High-resolution graphics can be printed on PostScript printers. They also have a wide range of available typefaces that can be scaled to various sizes.

Desktop publishing laser printers are essentially business-quality typesetters. They can handle any amount of graphics and include a range of built-in, high-quality typefaces.

Intelligent printer/copiers combine the technology of the microprocessor, laser, and photocopier, so they have features of both printers and copiers. They print a page at a time at a rate of 50 to 100 pages per minute. A microprocessor allows them to accept text, graphics, and instructions from computers, word processors, or magnetic media. They produce hard copy directly from the digitized information received.

Hint: Depending on the number and types of fonts available with your laser printer, you may wish to purchase optional font cartridges. These contain the instructions and memory your printer will need to print the fonts. Soft fonts, on the other hand, are fonts that can be loaded from your computer into your printer's memory; they can be used when your printer has adequate internal memory.

Plotters are used for printing computer graphics and are used in computer-aided design (CAD). High-quality output is created by the movement of ink pens over the paper. A variety of color pens are available.

MIMEOGRAPH MACHINES

Mimeographing or stencil duplication requires the use of an absorbent or sulfite paper to cut a master, called a stencil. Various weights, colors, and sizes can be used. Between 3,000 and 5,000 copies can be run from an ordinary stencil. Stencils are frequently used by schools, churches, and organizations.

SPIRIT DUPLICATING

In this method of reproduction, spirit masters are prepared by typing or drawing on a glazed paper that is backed by a special carbon paper. Short-run masters produce about 100 clear copies; long-run masters, 300 to 400. Because of its simplicity and low cost, this method is popular for internal use in schools and small organizations.

Hint: Purple carbon masters reproduce best.

OFFSET PRINTING

Offset printing is of high quality and is used for large-volume production. Usually offset printing is done by a printer or a copy shop, not by someone in the office. Paper, aluminum, or plastic (electrostatic) masters are used for offset printing. Paper masters are good for 25 to 3,000 copies, the plastic for up to 5,000 copies, and the aluminum for up to 50,000 copies.

PHOTOTYPESETTING

Phototypesetting is a photographic printing process that produces high-quality documents. Characters are formed at high speeds on photosensitive paper or film. This film is then developed and proofread. Material can be input directly through the phototypesetting equipment or on a personal computer and sent to the phototypesetter on a disk. Many varieties of type sizes and fonts are available. Brochures, newspapers, promotional materials, and books are generally prepared with this process.

Hint: One typeset page is often the equivalent of two typed pages.

MICROGRAPHICS

The paper bottleneck in many offices can be efficiently handled with micrographic systems. Micrographics is the process of recording and reducing paper documents or computer-generated information onto film for long-term storage and archival. Records are photographed and reduced so that many small images in color or black and white will appear on a reel or sheet of film. The micrographic media used to store file information are known as **microforms**. A reader is needed to enlarge the microform image and display it for viewing. Microfilm and microfiche are the best-known types of microform.

Micrographics are usually filmed and developed by micrographics service bureaus. These companies can also provide for document pickup, inspection and quality control, duplication of microforms, and the sale or lease of micrographics equipment.

MICROGRAPHICS FORMATS

Roll film, the least expensive form of microfilm, is usually found in 16mm, 35mm, or 105mm sizes. The 16mm roll is used for storing $8\frac{1}{2}$-by-11-inch or $8\frac{1}{2}$-by-14-inch records, such as correspondence and legal documents. The 35mm film is used for large records such as engineering drawings, newspaper pages, and blueprints. Roll film can be stored in cartons or cabinets.

Cartridges use a plastic collar snapped over the film roll, becoming a magazine that self-threads to film readers. Cartridges are used extensively with automated readers, cameras, and automated retrieval systems.

Aperture cards contain a microfilm image or images mounted on a small card. Information about the microfilm record or records is printed on or punched into the remainder of the card. Aperture cards are used to store large documents such as maps or engineering drawings.

Film jackets are clear, plastic carriers with one or more sleeves or channels designed to hold 16mm or 35mm filmstrips, or a combination of the two. Jackets are available in a variety of sizes, the most common being 4 inches by 6 inches. Jackets allow the user to update film files easily and quickly by removing outdated strips and inserting newer material.

Microfiche is suitable for filming reports, periodicals, catalogs, parts lists, and other collections of pages on a permanent, unitized microform. It contains rows of document on a sheet of film about 4 inches by 6 inches. Full-color or black-and-white images can appear on microfiche. A 4-by-6-inch fiche produced with a 24-times reduction ratio can hold up to 98 document images. One produced with a 48-times reduction ratio can hold up to 270 images.

Hint: About 200 fiche can be filed per inch of space in a file drawer.

Ultrafiche is an extension of microfiche; it allows more images per inch than any other type of microform. It is possible to store up to 1,000 pages on a 3-by-5-inch sheet of film.

Film folios are aperture cards the size of microfiche inserted into jackets.

METHODS TO PRODUCE MICROFORMS

Three methods exist for producing microforms:

1. Photography by micrographics cameras, either rotary or planetary is one method. Rotary photography produces roll microfilm; planetary photography produces fiche.

2. Computer output microfilm (COM) is a method of microfilming in which computer data are printed on film, processed, and duplicated. The use of computer printouts can be minimized or eliminated with this process.

3. Computer-assisted retrieval (CAR) uses a computer to retrieve documents stored on microfilm. CAR systems can utilize bar coding or optical character recognition for indexing. Records can be accessed in various combinations; for example, accounts with an outstanding balance or clients in a specific geographic location could be accessed.

READERS, READER/PRINTERS, AND RETRIEVAL TERMINALS

Microform readers are categorized as follows:

Handheld or *projection readers:* Simple, inexpensive image magnifiers that are held to the eye for viewing or projecting images onto external screens.

Portable readers: Lightweight, briefcase, or smaller-sized full-screen readers powered by a conventional outlet or rechargeable batteries.

Desk or *console reader/printers:* Stationary readers that are also capable of producing full-sized paper copies of microform originals.

Desk or *console retrieval terminals* and *retrieval terminal/printers:* Stationary reading units with automatic image-seeking capabilities. Retrieval terminal/printers produce full-sized paper copies of microform originals. On some reader/printers, the printer is an integral part of the reader; in others it is a modular unit that attaches to the reader.

Computer screens or *facsimile:* Sophisticated microfilm readers can be tied in with computer systems using a device called a "jukebox." The user calls up a file on the PC, then the computer searches for the document and directs the jukebox to select the proper microfilm cassette for loading into the reader. The image is automatically called up, digitized, and output into the user's PC.

OPTICAL DISK SYSTEMS

Optical disk storage systems are state-of-the-art devices based on laser beams and precision optics. An optical disk system is made up of a number of components. Scanners are the major input source for optical disk–based systems. Drives record documents in digital form onto WORM (write once, read many times) disks and retrieve documents from all types of disks. Jukeboxes are automated disk libraries. The control computer manages the system by cross-referencing data, keeping audit trails, and providing necessary reports. Software is used for image enhancement, database management, and operating systems. Monitors give high-resolution images, and laser printers give printed output.

The major differences from micrographics systems are the following:

Packing density: Some optical disk systems can hold up to 400,000 pages of text.
Retrieval: Documents can be retrieved in seconds.
Transmission speed: Optical disks store documents in a digital form, which means they can be transmitted on a local area network (LAN) or telephone line in two or three seconds.
Paperwork flow: Optical disk systems manage the paperwork flow and control the pacing and sequencing of paperwork by automatically prompting individuals to the next step.
Integration with other systems: Optical systems can interface with other electronic systems. Different users can simultaneously access data on the same file or document.

An optical disk system performs the following functions:

- It scans images from either paper or microfilm.
- It stores documents containing letters and numbers as well as graphics.
- It displays documents on a CRT terminal.
- It searches and retrieves documents.
- It prints documents on paper and/or microfilm.
- It copies documents to and from computer hard disks and optical disks.

OPTICAL CHARACTER SCANNING

An **optical character reader (OCR)** is a computer device combined with software that can copy graphics or read text in a variety of typefaces and styles. The copy is stored in the computer and is reproduced immediately on a CRT for correction and revisions. The accuracy rate for text recognition is about 95 percent, and the technology is constantly improving. Photographs, drawings, and charts can be scanned for use in desktop publishing or electronic filing.

TYPES OF SCANNERS

There are two primary types of scanners. A **handheld scanner** may be held in the hand and manually swept across the document or image. These have a scan width 2 to 5 inches. A **page** or **desktop scanner** can handle a full page at a time.

Page scanners are further divided into three categories:

❑ *Sheet-feed:* These operate by automatically moving the document to be scanned via rollers in much the same manner as a fax machine.

❑ *Flatbed:* These have a flat top upon which the document to be scanned is placed face-down, in much the same manner as on a photocopier. Typically, they offer the best scan results and are the most expensive.

❑ *Overhead* or *copyboard:* These look like overhead projectors. They scan documents and objects from above. Documents are placed face-up on the scanner's flat scanning surface.

SCANNER RESOLUTION

A scanner's **resolution** is the number of dots it can sample for each linear inch of the document. Common resolutions are 75, 100, 150, 200, 300 and 400 dots per inch (dpi). By comparison, most laser printers have a 300 dpi resolution.

Scanners are either *bilevel* or *gray scale.* Bilevel scanners output only black-and-white dots or pixels. They are used for simple drawings and other line art. Gray scale scanners are capable of determining a numeric value for the darkness of each pixel scanned, allowing for shades of gray. The more shades supported, the more accurately the digitized image is represented. These scanners are used for professional publishing.

APPLICATIONS

Scanners have various uses in the office. Among the most important are the following:

- Desktop publishing uses scanners to incorporate images into a computer or onto paper as well as for character recognition of typewritten manuscripts.
- Scanners are used with databases to incorporate price lists, tabular data, and other text as well as for image databases such as those used by real estate companies and police departments.
- Scanners are used in information storage to store documents in organizations with intensive paperwork operations, such as banks, hospitals, and government agencies.
- Paper documents can be scanned into a personal computer and transmitted via a facsimile board to a fax machine.

TELECOMMUNICATIONS EQUIPMENT

Telecommunications uses telephone and computer technology to transmit voice, image, data, and textual information from one place to another. The most used telecommunications device today, outside of the telephone, is the facsimile machine, or fax.

TELEPHONES

A variety of telephone equipment is available that can efficiently meet the needs of any organization.

The conventional *rotary dial telephone* with a 10-hole dial is being replaced by the touch-tone telephone. A *touch-tone phone* uses a 12-button keypad arrangement. It has ten buttons with the digits 0–9, plus two special buttons, * (star) and # (pound), that activate automatic electronic features, permitting a phone call to be placed in half the time it takes a rotary-type phone. A *touch-a-matic* telephone is a touch-tone phone that is equipped with an automatic telephone dialer that can store from 15 to 31 numbers. It can dial one of these numbers at the touch of a button.

A *call director* is a desktop switchboard allowing a receptionist or executive assistant to pick up calls that come in on 18, 30, or as many as 60 extensions. One receptionist or assistant can be responsible for the phones of a number of people who may not be at their desks. Call directors usually connect to larger switching system devices in the telephone system.

A *speakerphone set* consists of a microphone and loudspeaker and permits the user to carry on a telephone conversation from anywhere in an office without lifting the receiver from its rest. The microphone picks up the user's voice and the loudspeakers broadcast the voice of the party at the other end of the line. A speakerphone also allows a group of people to talk through one phone.

Cordless *portable telephones* are also available as well as *cellular phones* for use in cars or airplanes.

VOICE MAIL

Voice mail, or *store-and-forward messaging,* combines the technology of a telephone, computer, and recording device. It stores messages for immediate or later delivery. Access to the system is gained by entering a code on a rotary or touch-tone telephone. A recording tells the user to speak the message into the phone and then to dial the voice-mail number of the recipient. The system codes the message into digital data and attempts to deliver it immediately. If the system cannot deliver the message, it is filed in the computer's memory for later delivery. When the recipient dials into the system to get his or her messages, the caller's voice is reconstructed and the message is repeated.

SWITCHING SYSTEMS

Single line telephones are ordinarily used in homes and small offices. They have only a single line available, so it is not possible for two or more people to place calls at the same time.

For larger businesses, however, the routing of calls to and from the public lines of the telephone company to the private lines within an organization is handled through a *switching system.* These systems include key systems, PBX systems, and Centrex.

Multiline telephones, or *key phones,* allow one person to handle several lines, each with a separate button on the phone. These telephones may be equipped with up to 30 buttons placed above, below, or beside the dial. If a line is in use, a light by the button is lit. To place a call, the caller pushes an unlit line button and dials the number. A flashing light signals an incoming call; to answer it, an individual pushes the flashing line's button and picks up the receiver. If a call comes in on one line while an individual is on another, the second line can be answered after the first caller is put on hold by pressing the hold button. The person on hold cannot hear the other conversation.

PBX systems (*p*rivate *b*ranch e*x*change) are used by large companies to channel calls through a central switchboard. A PBX requires a full-time operator to connect incoming calls with company extensions. Internal and outgoing calls, however, are made without operator assistance. Outgoing calls can be made directly, usually by dialing "9" to make a connection to an outside line.

A *PABX system* (*p*rivate *a*utomatic *b*ranch e*x*change) has more automated features than a PBX system. It may be attended by an operator or may work unattended. An unattended, cordless switchboard distributes calls automatically to the proper extensions in the order in which the calls are received. Lighted buttons indicate when lines are engaged. These models have replaced older switching systems that required the attendant to manipulate a series of jacks and plugs.

Most PBX and PABX systems feature voice mail. Some systems feature voice recognition, which allows a caller to choose among various options within the voice mail by simply saying a number. For example, a user may speak the personal identification number of the mailbox. The system would then transfer the caller to the correct mailbox and offer a list of options, such as to hear, send, or delete messages. The caller says the number of the option and the system responds with the appropriate function.

Some systems feature *automatic number identification* (ANI), which logs the caller's phone number for the recipient the moment a call is received. This lets a caller record a callback message without having to leave a phone number.

A *Centrex system* allows a call from the outside or a call from one extension to another to be made without an operator. Centrex systems provide direct internal dialing, so that all calls go directly to the number dialed without use of a switchboard. Every telephone extension in the system usually has the same three-digit prefix as the company's main number, and the last four digits are different. If a caller does not know a particular Centrex extension number, he or she can dial the company's principal number and ask the operator to make the connection.

A *Computerized Branch Exchange* (CBX) uses microcomputer technology to add a variety of features to the Centrex system. Program features include automatic callback, call forwarding, call hold, call backup, call waiting signal, three-way conference calls, and call transfer.

FAX MACHINES

A fax machine, also called a facsimile machine, instantaneously transmits a copy (or facsimile) of a document from one location to another. Pages of the document are fed into the transmitting machine, electronically digitized, and sent via phone lines to the designated receiving fax machine. The receiving machine converts the digital transmission back into characters and prints it out on paper.

TYPES OF FAX MACHINES

There are two types of fax technology available: thermal-paper, which uses specially coated paper, and plain paper, which uses regular $8\frac{1}{2}$-by-11-inch copy paper. Thermal paper comes in continuous rolls that are useful for receiving documents of nonstandard lengths.

Faxes can be:

- Stand-alone, desktop units
- Personal fax units sized to fit into a briefcase and designed for use at home or when traveling
- Public fax machines, much like a public phone booth, that are available in such places as hotels, shopping malls, airports, and post offices
- Units that double as desktop copiers, answering machines, and regular telephones
- Machines that are compatible with cellular phones
- Color fax units that transmit and receive color photographs, color slides, video images, color images, color documents, and transparencies
- Voice-to-fax units that allow users to call a fax machine and leave a voice message that will be converted by the machine into a printed document

Advantages of fax machines include the following:

Speed: An $8\frac{1}{2}$-by-11-inch page takes an average of 17 seconds to transmit; no rekeying or document preparation is necessary.

Ease of installation: It can be located at any site where power and a telephone outlet are available.

Input flexibility: Sketches, charts, maps, and photographs can be transmitted or received.

Automatic operation: The operator merely needs to insert the copy; the machine handles the rest.

Fax machines range from low-end to middle-range to high-end units. Capabilities and features in each category vary. A low-end unit differs from a middle-range facsimile machine in type of receiving and transmitting paper used; paper roll size; and receiving tray, automatic cutter, and autodial features. High-end fax machines use plain paper. They also include the capability to restrict unsolicited transmissions to and from the units, increased memory capacity for additional automatic features, and faster transmission speeds.

The majority of units installed since 1981 are fully digital and capable of transmitting a page in less than a minute. They are also usually compatible with older, slower machines. Advances in technology now allow the latest machines to send a document in less than five seconds. However, the actual printing can take longer.

FAX FEATURES AND FUNCTIONS

The following are some of the major features and functions of fax machines:

Autodial: Recalls preset numbers from internal memory and automatically dials the destination number of the receiving facsimile unit.

Automatic reduction: The size of the incoming document can be changed to fit the available paper size. This is important because plain paper fax machines must print on standard $8\frac{1}{2}$-by-11-inch paper.

Delayed timer transmission: Documents can be placed into the fax machine, which is then programmed to send the information at a preset time. Newer units have the capability to send to multiple locations at different times.

Fall-back speed: Allows the sending unit automatically to reduce the transmission speed when it senses a problem with the telephone line quality. Note that reducing the speed helps to ensure a better copy quality on the receiving end.

Interfaces: Allow the fax unit to be connected with other equipment to meet special communications needs. It can receive from TWX/Telex, send and receive from personal computers, and send and receive encrypted messages. (Encryption is the conversion of text into code.)

Sender I.D./time date stamp: Prints the telephone number of the sending fax unit on top of each page received. It also prints the time and date.

Transmission log: Records and prints out a list of all transmissions received. It lists the number of pages of each batch of transmitted documents received, date and time, and sending unit telephone number.

APPLICATIONS

Fax machines are especially useful for these applications:

Business communications: To transmit documents or photos. Faxes are cheaper and faster than overnight mail or private messenger.

Financial accounting: To handle customer credit information requests, process invoices, and forward ledger or statistical data cheaply and accurately.

Sales: To transmit order notices, delivery schedules, spec sheets, drawings, proposals, and price quotes.

Purchasing: To expedite quotations and orders and to speed order confirmations.

Retailing: To speed delivery information, inventory status, and price change notices.

Advertising and public relations: To meet media deadlines and to forward publicity releases, product photographs, and drafts for approval.

Manufacturing and engineering operations: To transmit design and drawing changes or new procedures.

Law enforcement, news services, weather map communications, and medical data transmission are also areas in which fax transmissions are highly useful and highly used.

PC-FAX

The PC-fax is a combination of hardware and software that enables a personal computer to mimic the operations of a fax machine. The hardware is usually comprised of an expansion board or external unit that plugs into the personal computer, a modem, a scanner, and a printer.

A PC-fax has the following features:

Background modes: Users continue to perform other tasks while the system is operating.

Automatic date/time: Documents are printed with date and time.

Autodialing: Allows users to begin transmission by selecting a fax number stored in the system's directory.

Autoanswer: Receives messages without the sender and receiver establishing a voice telephone call.

Unattended or delayed timer: Allows users to preprogram a transmission to occur at a specific time and date.

Automatic polling: Allows users to contact remote units and request transmission of their documents.

Mailbox capabilities: Allows multiple users access to a single local PC-fax system. Users check their individual mailboxes for messages.

Multiple transmissions: Allows users to transmit to various sites in a predefined order.

FAX DIRECTORIES

As the use of the fax as a primary form of communication has grown, fax directories have been published. They offer a comprehensive listing of companies and private individuals using fax machines to send and receive correspondence. The directories include the company name, fax number, and other pertinent information, such as office hours or street address. Such directories also offer on-line databases with similar listings.

Hint: An on-line data base is useful for PC-fax users, who can use their PCs to review the directory listings.

PUBLIC FAX SERVICES

Public fax services are available to companies without their own fax machine. Senders must pay a telephone charge, a basic transmittal fee with additional charges for additional pages, and a delivery charge if applicable. The costs and transmission times vary. Recipients may pick up the documents or have them delivered. Delivery in foreign countries is to a business center or designated post office.

Hint: To locate addresses and telephone or fax numbers of public fax services, use the *Public Fax Directory.* This directory lists public fax service. Directory and fax referral assistance is also available from the toll-free number 800-USA-FAX1.

TELETYPEWRITERS

Another telecommunications device is the teletypewriter; however, it is being replaced by the fax machine. Teletypewriters transmit and receive only alphanumeric information over phone lines; they cannot transmit graphics. Some companies have their own teletypewriter networks. Many companies use one of Western Union's teletypewriter networks, Telex or TWX. "Telex" stands for teleprinter exchange and is generally used for international transmissions. "TWX" stands for teletypewriter exchange. Both systems permit a user to keyboard information and then send it to another Telex or TWX unit over standard telephone lines. The system provides the immediacy of a phone message as well as the documentation of a letter.

Major disadvantages are the following:

- Information must be keyed into the teletypewriter.
- Graphics cannot be sent via Telex.
- The cost is about four times that of a fax.

OTHER ELECTRIC AND ELECTRONIC EQUIPMENT

In addition to the major office equipment outlined in the preceding sections, other equipment includes:

Shredder: Used to shred documents containing sensitive information. Some fit on a desktop while others are large, free-standing units that can handle up to 140,000 sheets of paper an hour.

Electronic copy board: Electronically copies ideas, diagrams, or charts written on the copy board and prints them onto paper for distribution. Used especially for meetings.

Electric copyholder: Allows a line guide to advance down printed copy as a foot pedal or hand switch is operated by a typist. Generally made in four sizes to accommodate letter size, legal size, and two sizes of ledger paper.

Electric letter opener: Opens envelopes automatically.

Electric collator: Collates pages of material automatically.

Electric pencil sharpener: Automatically sharpens lead pencils.

SELECTING OFFICE EQUIPMENT

Rapidly evolving technology, the multitude of vendors in the market, technical jargon, announcements of new products nearly every day, and the threat of companies going out of business make selection of office equipment a difficult task. What is brand new today can be obsolete next year.

The following guidelines will help you evaluate prospective equipment for your office:

1. Analyze your office's needs. A thorough needs analysis helps to determine equipment applications, the number of users, frequency of use, and types of documents produced.

Hint: In selecting electronic typewriters, a good rule of thumb is to double the size of the memory you think you will need. Also, fax usage is often underestimated. To figure usage, take a projected usage number and multiply by 3.

2. Identify available products. Match the available products to the information gathered in the needs analysis. Determine the available products by talking to equipment dealers, reviewing sales literature, and reading office-related trade magazines. Ask the following:

❏ What are the benefits that differentiate one brand from another?
❏ Will the features meet your departmental needs?
❏ Is the equipment easy to use?
❏ Is the equipment compatible with other equipment in the office?
❏ What software is available?
❏ Is service available after the sale? By whom? Is there an 800 phone number for trouble-shooting problems? What are the terms of the warranty?
❏ Are the costs of installing the equipment included in the price?
❏ Is training free or is there a charge? What type of training is available?

3. Create a comparative chart of available products. Make a list of the information you have gathered by categories in the first column and put the products you have studied across the other columns. In each column, list the comparative information you have gathered on that product. You may wish to assign both a weight and a score, from a low of 1 to a high of 10, for each item. The weight is an estimate of how important each item is. Multiply the weight by the score for each item and then total the weighted scores. In this way you can quantitatively compare the prospective equipment choices.

Hint: Consider using a spreadsheet program for this purpose. This will allow you to adjust the size of the rows and columns as needed to accommodate available information. The scores assigned to each item can also be automatically totaled for you.

4. Ask for a demonstration of the equipment and/or a trial use. A thorough demonstration, or preferably trial use, is important before making a final decision. Some dealers will allow prospective customers to use the equipment for one or two weeks at no cost. Both the demonstration and the trial use will provide valuable insights that are not possible through any other form of evaluation.

5. Make a dealer or vendor comparison. A thorough review of the dealer or vendor is needed to avoid problems after the sale. Ask the following questions:

❏ How many service technicians are employed?
❏ What is the average tenure of technicians and number of placements serviced by the firm?
❏ What is the average response time to a service call?
❏ Are parts and supplies readily available?
❏ Is a list of references available that can be randomly called? Ask the references the same questions you are asking the dealer and compare the answers. Ask if the service was as good six or more months after the sale as it was in the beginning. Also ask the reference to identify any major service problems, along with how they were resolved. Are there any patterns to the answers received from the various references you called?

INVENTORY AND MAINTENANCE OF EQUIPMENT

With more electronic equipment entering the office, the responsibility for maintaining it is increasing. Some recommended procedures will help you do this.

1. Make a card record for each piece of equipment. The record should contain the name, address, and phone number of the vendor or dealer; date of purchase; model number; serial number; and basic information regarding the warranty and/or service contract. These cards should be filed alphabetically and periodically updated as the equipment is serviced. A yearly inventory of each piece of equipment should also be done and noted on the card.

Hint: A database software program can facilitate this process. You can use one that is part of a spreadsheet program or use a stand-alone program.

2. Consider purchasing a service or maintenance contract. These are available for an additional monthly or annual fee. A service or maintenance contract extends the warranty on the equipment for a longer period of time. Most contracts include options for either mail-in or carry-in service. Others will offer a pick-up and delivery service or on-site repair. Some will also provide a temporary replacement.

Hint: Electronic typewriters need little maintenance, and users usually do not purchase a maintenance contract. The same is not true of office copiers. With copiers, maintenance contracts are recommended.

3. Establish a maintenance schedule. Have the equipment serviced on a regular basis. Prevention through proper servicing can help to avoid unnecessary downtime. The maintenance schedule should be maintained by the equipment operator or, in the case of executives, by their administrative assistants. Service contracts are available that include periodic cleaning and/or testing of equipment components.

4. Use cleaning products on a regular basis. These products include cleaning kits for personal computers, glass-cleaning products for copiers and CRT screens, and dusters for electronic typewriters.

Hint: Weekly cleaning of personal computers is recommended, focusing on the screen, keyboard, disk drive, printer, and housing to remove dust and dirt.

CHAPTER 8

OFFICE COMPUTER SOFTWARE

Computer software consists of programmed instructions that direct and control a computer's operations. Mainframes, minicomputers, and personal computers all use software. Software programs can be purchased from equipment manufacturers, vendors whose specialty is designing software, or retail software stores.

Software falls into two categories: systems software and applications software. Systems software governs the operation of the computer. Applications software includes programs that perform specific applications, such as word processing.

SYSTEMS SOFTWARE

Systems software includes operating systems, programming languages, and utilities. An **operating system** is a group of programs that act as an interpreter and manager for the computer, display monitor, and any peripherals, such as a printer. The operating system also directs and interprets information moving to and from disk drives. Some operating systems are multitasking systems, that is, they can process more than one task at a time.

Microsoft Corporation's MS-DOS is the most popular operating system. Others include OS/2 by IBM, a multitasking system that works for single users as well as within networks; UNIX by AT&T, a multiuser, multitasking operating system as well as several variants such as Ultrix and Xenix; and Macintosh by Apple Corporation, an operating system with a graphical user interface.

Programming languages are special languages that allow users to communicate with computers. The most frequently used are C, a general-purpose programming language; FORTRAN, which was developed by IBM for scientific, engineering, and mathematical operations; COBOL, which was developed especially for business applications and in which English-like statements are used; Pascal, a flexible language useful for scientific programming; RPG (Report Program Generator), which is used on many small computers to generate reports; and BASIC, an interactive language that allows communication directly with the computer. Microprocessors as well as many small, business-oriented computers use BASIC.

Utilities are special programs that perform such tasks as copying files or transferring files from one storage medium to another.

APPLICATIONS SOFTWARE

Applications software consists of programs that enable the computer to perform specific office applications. Applications include word processing, spreadsheets, graphics, desktop publishing, accounting, database management, personal information management, desktop management, project management, and records management. Other software used in offices includes integrated software, groupware, shareware, communications, local area network (LAN), and linking software.

WORD PROCESSING

Word processing is the single most commonly used PC application. A word processing program allows the user to enter, edit and print text documents, such as letters and reports. The functions available in a word processing program will vary, depending on the brand and cost of the software as well as the size of the machine's memory. They also depend on whether the program is stored on hard or floppy disks.

Hint: Selection of a word processing system should be based on the functions needed to create typical office documents. Software limitations can be found only by testing it. (See the section below, Selecting Software, for more advice.)

Word processors can be menu-driven, command-driven, coded, or what-you-see-is-what-you-get (WYSIWYG). A menu-driven program supports the performance of all major operations, presenting them as a multiple-choice menu. The main menu includes choices such as create a new document, edit an existing document, or print a document. (See Figure 8-1.)

Command-driven programs consist of functional units that perform tasks in a logical order chosen by the operator. Functions are entered by one or two keystrokes or by command words that are typed into text but not printed. (See Figure 8-2.)

```
Select function with  →  or  ↓  then press

File      Edit        Spell       Options       Disk       Quit


H=Help
```

Figure 8-1 Menu-driven word processing software.

```
01/15/91   15:08      Directory B:\*.*

Document size:  0          Free Disk Space:   294912

.<CURRENT> <DIR>                  ..<PARENT>    <DIR>

01110          .1   133    01/21/91
ACCOUNTS       .4   657    11/03/90
CBS1           .7 15909    06/12/91


1 Retrieve;  2 Delete;  3 Rename;  4 Print;  5 Text In;
6 Look;  7 Change Directory;  8 Copy;  9 Word Search;
0 Exit: 6
```

Figure 8-2 Sample menu in a command-driven program.

Coded systems do not display onscreen the necessary codes for such functions as margins, spacing, or page length. Instead, codes are embedded in the computer file.

WYSIWYG programs display text styles, margins, page breaks, line spacing, fonts, and graphics onscreen close to or exactly as the final document will look when printed.

Basic features of word processing systems include:

Margin set
Tab set
Page set
Strikeover
Delete characters
Delete words, phrases
Delete sentences, paragraphs
Insert characters, words, phrases
Center text
Caps-lock
Automatic underscore
Move text
Search and replace techniques
Boldface
Header: prints the same information at the top of every page of a document
Footer: prints the same information at the bottom of every page of the document
Store and recall documents
Ability to merge mailings with mailing lists
Printer support: allows the printer to work with the program to print out documents
Integrated graphics
Automatic reformatting
Document/file retrieval
Text retrieval
DOS file management

Network support
File conversions from other word processors
File imports from spreadsheets; graphics programs
Macro capabilities: Permits the operator to record a series of keystrokes, assigning the entire series to a single key or pair of keys; thus an entire string of text can be recalled with one or two keystrokes
Spelling dictionary
Thesaurus

SPREADSHEET SOFTWARE

A spreadsheet program is an electronic replacement for an accountant's columnar ledger, pencil, and calculator. Spreadsheets can be used to calculate budgets, track sales and budgets, prepare financial statements, and analyze financial problems. They may be used as journals or ledgers and to generate data for management information reports.

Spreadsheets permit data to be moved, changed, inserted, deleted, and formatted without rekeying. Spreadsheets automate calculations so that the user enters only a set of numbers and appropriate formulas in order to find totals, averages, percentages, or the like.

There are four basic categories of spreadsheets: traditional, linked, three-dimensional, and relational spreadsheets.

❏ **Traditional:** The simplest form of spreadsheet is the traditional spreadsheet. It is a grid of cells identified by a column letter and a row number. Each cell may contain a number, a label, a formula, or a function. A label is a piece of text that usually functions as a title or the heading for a column or row. A formula is an equation used to calculate an answer given the numbers in the spreadsheet. A function is a common computation that can be invoked with a brief command; for example, many spreadsheets have a function to sum the numbers in a column or row and another function to calculate the average of the numbers in a column or row. Examples include the original VisiCalc, Lotus 1-2-3 (release 2.01), and Quattro.

❏ **Linked:** Linked spreadsheet programs use data from separate spreadsheets without having to copy values or build giant models. Linked spreadsheet programs have the ability to coordinate information in different spreadsheets. Any changes made in one spreadsheet will be automatically changed in the corresponding cells of each of the connected spreadsheets. Examples include Multiplan, PC Excel, and Surpass.

❏ **Three-dimensional:** A three-dimensional (or 3-D) spreadsheet program adds depth by providing a third axis. Each cell has three coordinates that identify it: row, column, and page. Examples include SuperCalc and Lotus 1-2-3 (release 3).

❏ **Relational:** A relational spreadsheet program separates data files from the spreadsheets themselves. Data identification is by name, supports more than three dimensions, and provides automatic consolidation. Examples are VP-Planner and TM/1.

Determining which spreadsheet design is best in a particular office requires taking a look at the nature of the information to be processed. Adaptability, flexibility, and ease of operation are also important factors to consider. A key consideration in choosing a spreadsheet program is hardware. Some programs run on 64K of RAM while later versions need as much as 1MB (megabyte) of memory to operate.

Basic features of any spreadsheet program include the following:

Format option: Indicates how the numbers should be printed, including currency, percent, fixed, and scientific notations

Variable column widths

Move or copy cells and ranges

Insert or delete columns or rows

Functions: Shortcut formulas to make calculations, e.g., SUM (@SUM) to add a series of numbers, AVG (@AVG) to find the average of a series, MAX (@MAX) to find the largest number in a series

Extract and consolidate data

Edit a cell

Store, print, and edit

What-if table creation: Allows the user to evaluate the alternatives in calculations by changing figures

Solver function: Allows users to choose a desired result and suggests the best way for them to get it.

Outlining: Allows the user to view only the most important parts of a worksheet

Supports add-ins, which are software programs that work with spreadsheets to increase capabilities such as word processing, desktop publishing, better two- or three-dimensional graphics, or more cells per screen

Windows: Splits the screen into two or more sections horizontally or vertically to enable the user to see two sections of a long or wide spreadsheet on one screen

Graphics: Modules that turn numeric data into line, bar, or pie charts

ACCOUNTING SOFTWARE

Accounting software is used to manage financial data. It serves as a vehicle for inputting information about business transactions and organizing that information into meaningful management reports.

Accounting software packages can be broken into modules, or they can be fully integrated to include any or all of the following: accounts payable, accounts receivable, general ledger, order entry, sales analysis, invoicing, inventory control, job costing, purchasing, payroll, fixed assets, and report writing.

Features of accounting software include the following:

Production of reports

File export: can exchange data with spreadsheets and databases

Audit trail

Multi-user operation

Network support

Security

Customization of system for the business

GRAPHICS SOFTWARE

Graphics software permits the display of graphs, charts, and other line art work whether on screen or on paper. It adds visual interest to reports and presentations.

Presentation graphics are images generated by computer that can be printed on overhead transparency film or photographed for 35mm slides. Graphic images can also be printed on paper, with varying degrees of quality, using computer printers or plotters. Some software packages allow the user to project the images electronically through a liquid crystal display (LCD) panel or show them directly on a PC screen. (Additional information on graphics software can be found in Chapter 19, Office Publishing.)

Common graphics programs include the following:

Paint programs: A series of dots are "painted" on the screen from a palette of available colors. Paint programs are the easiest graphics programs to use. However, they do not allow the degree of editing that other graphics programs offer.

Tagged image file format (TIFF): Through the process of scanning, photographs, artwork, and letters are captured and saved as a tagged image file that can be manipulated by any program that works with TIFF files.

Computer graphics metafile (CGM): CGM, or drawing, programs produce objects that can be manipulated at any time. Such programs, also known as vector graphics or object-oriented programs, are composed of rectangles, ovals, lines, and text that can be arranged and edited. Such programs are suitable for business graphics because corrections and revisions are easy to do and printouts generally look better than those done with paint programs.

Spreadsheet graphics files: These are graphics modules within spreadsheet programs that turn numeric data into bar, line, pie, or X-Y charts. There are also a number of separate charting programs that permit charts to be generated from worksheet data.

PICT (Macintosh draw format): Such programs work like CGM programs to generate objects.

Before investing in graphics software the following factors should be taken into consideration:

1. Most graphics software will run better on newer, more advanced computers with faster processors.

2. Most packages are more productive on a hard disk machine.

3. A video graphics array (VGA) graphics card is the most helpful in running graphics programs. (See the *Display Monitors* section of Chapter 7.)

4. Some software programs require a windowing environment, such as that on a Macintosh computer or on an IBM PC-compatible using Microsoft Windows.

5. A pointing device such as a mouse or light pen is needed if the software runs under a windowing environment or if the user intends to make illustrations that resemble freehand drawings.

6. Access to an ink jet or thermal transfer printer will increase one's options in producing color visuals with graphics software.

7. The ability to import or export files from or to other programs is an important feature.

Major features of graphics software include the following:

Graph, text chart, and drawing tools
Ability to crop, rotate, re-size drawings
Templates
Macros
Ability to import and export various files to and from other programs
Standard symbols

DESKTOP PUBLISHING SOFTWARE

Desktop publishing is defined as the writing, assembling, and designing of publications, such as business reports, newsletters, brochures, and trade journals, with the use of a personal computer. Through the use of desktop publishing software (DTP), pictures or graphics are combined electronically with words on the same page. DTP software includes draw or paint programs, clip-art programs, and page layout programs. (See Chapter 19, Office Publishing, for more details on desktop publishing software.)

The design of DTP software follows two approaches: programs with command-driven user interfaces and programs with menu-driven interfaces. As a general rule, command-driven programs are geared toward those users with typographic experience. Menu-driven programs appeal to nontechnical users. It is critical that the word processing program, page makeup program, and output devices be compatible.

Features of desktop publishing software include the following:

Text creation and editing
Graphics creation and editing
Different fonts and character sizes
Interactive page layout (usually utilizing a mouse) and a graphic display of the page
Output devices support
Batch composition: All pages are automatically composed according to preset page and typographic specifications
Ability to import text and graphics from other programs
Control over hyphenation, justification, leading (line spacing), kerning (intercharacter spacing), etc.
Automatic page numbering
Automatic repagination once a document has been edited

DATABASE MANAGEMENT SOFTWARE

A database is a collection of information. Database management software is the set of instructions used with a computer to organize, store, and retrieve data.

Data are placed into "files" relating to a particular subject, such as customer lists, accounts receivable, and inventory or personnel records. Within the files are individual records pertaining to individuals or groups. Information in each record is broken down into different blocks, such as name and address, which are called fields.

Database programs are used by businesses to maintain inventories and process customer orders. Banks use databases to handle checking and savings accounts. The use and purpose of databases is limited only by your imagination.

Database management software can be placed into four categories: flat-file, relational, programmable, and library.

❏ **Flat-file** databases are menu-driven programs that work with only one data file at a time. They are designed for people who need to organize facts in a very simple manner. These are the easiest databases to use.

❏ **Relational** databases use multiple forms and multiple disk files to store information. Information that appears on different forms is entered only once into the computer.

❏ **Programmable** databases are designed for computer programmers who need to construct large and complex systems.

❏ **Library** databases employ routines that allow a user to manipulate data files and maintain records and keys in stored order. These are intended for sophisticated users.

Features of database management software include the following:

Multiple-file access and consolidation
Report generation
Onscreen creation of forms
Rearrangement of files without destroying existing data
Security mechanisms
Math capability
Menu-driven operations
Documentation
Onscreen interactive tutorials
Onscreen help
Networking capability
Record locking: Allows only one user at a time to make changes to a record in a database file.
Multiuser capability

PERSONAL INFORMATION MANAGEMENT SOFTWARE

Personal information management (PIM) software allows users to enter, retrieve, analyze, and cross-reference personal information. Personal information includes various kinds of information that are needed daily, such as phone messages, management information, addresses, dates, and meeting times.

Applications of personal information management software include: appointment calendars and time managers; text retrieval and text-base databases; outline managers; contact managers; and hypermedia, which links information in different media, whether text, graphics, video, or audio.

Features of personal information management software include the ability to do the following:

Handle structured data and freeform text
Maintain multiple types of data in the same information base
Make relationships between multiple types of data
Perform cross-referencing both on demand and automatically
Understand time
Provide ad hoc grouping of information
Customize the PIM application to organize, file, and retrieve information according to individual preferences
Enter new information

DESKTOP MANAGEMENT SOFTWARE

Along the same lines as personal information manager software, desktop management software is designed to help manage the details of daily life for users with electronic calendars, onscreen lists of things to do, and pop-up directories for names, addresses, and telephone numbers. Unlike PIM software, it does not cross-reference the data between categories. Desktop management software uses a flat-file rather than a relational database structure.

Desktop management software is of two basic sorts: memory-resident programs and stand-alone programs. However, some stand-alone programs have optional memory-resident modules, giving the user the ability to choose whichever mode is suitable.

❏ **Memory-resident** programs can be accessed, usually with a **hot key,** allowing a user to update a calendar, use an onscreen calculator, or access MS-DOS without leaving the main program the user is working in, such as a word processor.

❏ **Stand-alone** programs perform the full range of desktop functions, but the user must exit from the main program, such as a word processor, in order to access them.

Hint: If a modem, which converts computerized digital information to analog information used in telephone communications, is attached to the computer, the software can automatically dial numbers selected from the phone directory.

Features of desktop management software include the following:

Arithmetic and financial calculator
Daily and monthly calendar
Electronic file system for text and graphics
Alarm clock
Telephone directory with automatic dialer
"Notepad" for composing letters or lists
Text editor
Electronic mail function for network applications

PROJECT MANAGEMENT SOFTWARE

The object of project management software is to keep track of project schedules and costs. Such programs can be as simple or as complex as the projects they are used to manage. Project management software allows the user electronically to monitor and evaluate tasks in order to finish on time and within budget. Such tasks include keeping track of the resources needed, coordinating and allocating resources, and monitoring deadlines and budgets. It also helps to identify potential conflicts and to determine the effects of schedule delays on deadlines and budgets.

Features of project management software give the ability to do the following:

Produce charts, including Program Evaluation and Review Technique (PERT) charts
Assign costs according to such categories as fixed costs, cost-per-time-unit, and cost-per-resource-unit
Create customized monthly calendars
Create schedules
Automatically update all project information

RECORDS MANAGEMENT SOFTWARE

Records management involves managing and controlling office information. Typical applications include maintaining a records center, tracking active and inactive records, making note of vital records, creating archives or historical records, and developing a record retention schedule.

No one system is right for all users. Criteria for judging all records management software, however, are: support, vendor stability, quality of documentation, ease of use, error handling ability, and value (how well a package addresses user needs).

Features of records management software include the following:

Keyword search: searches for and selects a word for retrieval
File management
Retention maintenance: a system for purging inactive files according to a schedule
Destruction notification: supplies a form notifying the user of erasure of a document
Request processing
Records retrieval and inventory
File tracking
Generation of reports
Space allocation: the assignment of a given amount of characters
Bar coding
Mixed media: allows more than one type of device for storage of records, e.g., microfilm, microfiche, or floppy disk.
Computer-assisted retrieval (CAR): used with micrographics

INTEGRATED SOFTWARE

Integrated software is software that can do more than one function. Functions work together so that information can be transferred from files of one application to another. Integrated software can consist of word processing, database management, spreadsheet, graphics, and telecommunications.

Multiuser integrated software operates in a network environment. Such software includes inter-workstation electronic mail, shared file storage, and many business applications.

The following are the two types of integrated software:

All-in-one: These allow users to move between applications without leaving the program.

Modular: These provide a "family" of programs produced by the same software house and sharing similar commands. They permit the sharing of information among individual stand-alone programs. When selecting integrated software, it is important to know how the product integrates applications. A file-conversion utility is less desirable than a cut-and-paste approach, because with the latter, the application usually must be abandoned when the utility is activated.

Features of integrated software include the following:

Applications for spreadsheet, word processing, database, communications, and graphics
Integration between applications—can be file conversion or cut-and-paste where users "cut" data from a file in one application and "paste" it to a file in another.
Documentation
Programmability
Automatic updating
Mail merge
Multiple open files
Networking capability
Ease of use and learning
Error handling

GROUPWARE

Groupware is the term for the combination of software needed to support the work of a group. It is built on three major functions: document formatting, information management, and wide-area communication.

Groupware includes an electronic calendar to help keep a group organized and on schedule. It tracks management objectives and goals, arranges meetings, sends reminders, and warns when a project falls behind schedule. Groupware also runs an electronic mail network that links the work group with remote operations. It also includes an information system to handle all data relevant to the business and to make this data instantly available throughout the organization.

SHAREWARE

Shareware programs are software programs that can be distributed and copied at little or no cost without breaking copyright laws. Shareware is distributed through electronic bulletin boards, on-line information services, user groups, and shareware catalogs from a mail-order company that specializes in shareware programs.

A user who decides to keep a shareware program is expected to register with and pay a fee to the software company that created the program. After registering and paying the fee, the shareware user will receive support and manuals for the shareware.

Companies that copy and distribute shareware include:

People's Choice
P.O. Box 171134
Memphis, TN 38187
(901) 753-2828

Quicksoft Inc.
219 First Ave., N No. 224
Seattle, WA 98109
(206) 282-0452

Public Brand Software
P.O. Box 51478
Indianapolis, IN 46251
(800) IBM-Disk

Sofsource
P.O. Box 838
East Lansing, MI 48826
(517) 349-3560

Hint: The Public Software Library in Houston maintains one of the largest collections of public domain software and shareware for IBM PC and Macintosh computers. For a free copy of the library's PC newsletter, call (800) 242-4775.

COMMUNICATIONS, NETWORK, AND LINKING SOFTWARE

Communications, network, and linking software programs enable a computer to transmit and receive information from another computer over telephone lines. They can also link a PC to a mainframe, minicomputer, or other PCs, and transfer files from one application program to another.

In order to transmit and receive information, a *modem* (Modulator-DeModulator) is needed. A modem is a device that is used to convert digital signals into analog (voice-like) signals for transmission over a telephone line. At the other end of the line, another modem converts the analog signals back into digital form. A modem is also known as a data set.

Local area networks (LANs) are used to distribute information throughout an office via different terminals (called nodes) connected to a central information repository (called a server). The server allows people to share peripherals and data files. The server functions like a traffic cop, managing the flow of information between the computers hooked together on the LAN. Thus, a LAN allows people in a department to share information with each other electronically as well as to share common resources like printers and large hard disks. A LAN electronically ties functions together for better communications among individuals, departments within the office and/or satellite offices or locations, and it reduces equipment costs, since different PC users can share expensive peripherals, such as laser printers.

SELECTING SOFTWARE

The following general guidelines will help you evaluate prospective software:

1. Perform a needs analysis, either through a survey, questionnaire, or interviews of other users. A thorough needs analysis helps to determine the software applications needed, who the users are, frequency of use, types of documents produced, the operating system currently in use (if applicable), the computer hardware available, and the printer requirements. It can also indicate what your future needs are likely to be.

2. Identify available packages. Determine the available packages by talking to software manufacturers, software dealers, reviewing sales literature, and reading office related trade magazines. Ask the following questions:

What are the benefits that differentiate one brand from another?

What tasks need to be done?

Will the features meet the needs of the end-user?

How easy are the package's features to learn in relationship to performing the task?

What is the availability and compatibility to other equipment and software already being used? Will the software interface with existing hardware and software?

Is support available after the sale? By whom? Is an 800 phone number available for troubleshooting problems? Is there a user group that you can join? Are there others within the organization who have knowledge of the software to assist when problems occur? What kind of maintenance or upgrading is available for software? Are there add-on packages for the software available?

Is training free or is there a charge? What type of training is available?

Hint: Software decisions drive hardware decisions. Match available packages to the information gathered in the needs analysis.

3. Establish a comparative grid, or matrix, of available packages. Make a list of the information gathered by categories in the first column and put the packages studied across the tops of the other columns. Fill in the comparative information at the appropriate cell intersections. You may wish to assign both a weight for each category and a score for each package, from a low of 1 to a high of 10. Multiply the weight by the score in each cell and then total the scores in each column. In this way you can quantitatively compare the prospective software package choices.

4. Request a demonstration of the software and/or a trial use. A thorough demonstration, preferably with trial use, is necessary before making a final decision. Both the demonstration and the trial usage will provide valuable insights that are not possible through any other form of evaluation, helping you to determine if the software is easy to use.

Hint: Small organizations with limited budgets should consider integrated software, which can combine a few categories of tasks. The larger the organization, the more specialized the software usually needs to be.

- Ask questions.
- Start the search process at least 90 days before use.
- Perform a methodical software selection process.
- Remember good software recognizes the importance of people in processing while poor software only tolerates people.
- Comparison shop.
- Consult current users of the software for references.
- Know your needs.
- Determine if after-purchase support is available.
- Purchase on facts.
- Keep asking "Does the software fit my needs?"

Figure 8-3 Guidelines for buying software.

ASSORTED SOFTWARE ISSUES

INDEXING AND MAINTAINING SOFTWARE FILES

Information stored on floppy or hard disks demands a conscious effort to maintain and organize files. Considerable time can be lost searching for files, particularly when using hard disks.

The following are three strategies for indexing software files:

Simplify the search: Create space on the disk by eliminating unnecessary files. Archive inactive files on removable media such as floppy disks, cartridges, and tapes to free up hard disk space. Adopt a file-naming system by establishing a consistent method of naming files.

Divide and conquer: Use subdirectories to divide files into meaningful segments. For example, make a separate subdirectory for each application.

Use a utility program: A utility program helps organize files (for example, by indexing them) as a means to find disk-based files. Such programs include Norton Commander, Worksheet Utilities, PC Tools Deluxe, XTreePro, Lotus Magellan, Viewlink, ReTreeve, and GOfer. Other utility programs can read floppy disks and print a label listing all the files on it. The label shows the filenames, the date the label was created, and the amount of disk space remaining.

ESTABLISHING A SOFTWARE INVENTORY

Managing software is an important function of the administrative assistant. With the addition of more and more personal computers into the office and home, maintaining an inventory of software has become important. Such an inventory not only shows what software is available but also provides a degree of consistency and standardization in the software used.

A software inventory can be done manually or electronically through a database management system. An inventory sheet (or file, if maintained on the computer) for each software package should be completed. An inventory sheet contains important information concerning the software: name of the software, version number, number of copies, serial number, users' names, and vendor information.

By maintaining an inventory sheet, upgrades in the software by the manufacturer can be easily made. Notification of these changes can be quickly incorporated into the appropriate departments. Security and copyright issues can be better managed, protected, and documented.

BACKING UP SOFTWARE

The magnetically stored information on diskettes can be destroyed by exposure to a magnetic field, by improper use, or by mishandling. Several backup copies of important diskettes should be made prior to use. If anything happens to a backup diskette, another copy should be made. The original software disks should be stored in a safe place to avoid damage. Just as with software, data files should also be backed up. A regular schedule should be maintained for backing up files—once a week, every other week—in case of computer or user errors, power failures, or "head crashes" (the landing of the drive's read/write head on the surface of the hard disk, making the disk useless).

The two most common backups for a hard disk are floppies and tape cartridges. Tape cartridges should be used when a backup of everything is needed. Since tape cartridges have a storage capacity equal to that of hard disks, data access from tape is slow. Floppies, on the other hand, should be used for data files only.

Backing up files is also a good idea if security is an issue. Keeping crucial files on floppies, which can be removed from the computer while not in use, is the most common method of maintaining security. Other security methods include key locks, which interrupt power to the display and keyboard until the key is turned on; personal identification codes and passwords; and encryption, the changing of intelligible data into unintelligible data so that any unauthorized person will not be able to access the data.

SAFEKEEPING OF SOFTWARE

Software disks should be kept in a protective sleeve and stored in a box especially designed for diskette storage when not in use. (See the section on *Disk Storage* in Chapter 9.)

COMPUTER VIRUSES

Computer viruses are self-replicating blocks of computer code that enter a computer through a modem or network, or locally through a contaminated diskette. By replicating themselves thousands or millions of times, viruses may tie up the computer's processor and block other functions. Virus "infections" spread just as biological viruses do—by contact. As healthy diskettes and programs come in contact with an infected system, the virus merges into healthy programs or disks, causing an infection. The insertion process takes only a fraction of a second.

A virus may destroy data, reformat a disk, wear out its drive, or flash a harmless message on the screen. A virus not only affects PCs, but it can also attack mainframes and minicomputers.

A number of things can indicate that a virus has infected or attempted to infect a system. Unexplained system "crashes," programs that suddenly don't work right, data files or programs that are mysteriously erased, and disks that become unreadable are all possible signs of a virus.

Products are available to help a system recover from a virus attack. There are three categories of antiviral programs:

- Infection prevention products, which stop the virus from repeating and infecting the system.
- Infection detection products, which detect an infection soon after the infection occurs. These products identify the area of the system that has been infected. Such products check the program when it is run for any changes. If a change from the original is detected, the user is notified of the affected area.
- Infection identification products, which identify specific virus strains in systems that are already infected and usually remove the virus and restore the system to its correct state, prior to the infection.

To help prevent the risk of viral contamination, companies should have a data backup procedure scheduled, at least once a week for moderate users and one or more times a day for heavy users. Access to backups should be controlled so their availability and integrity are guaranteed. The backups should be carefully dated and kept for several months, at least. Access to programs and data should be restricted to an "as needed" basis.

Some additional steps to follow to help keep a good system from becoming infected include the following:

1. Floppy-disk–based systems should be started only with a specific, clearly labeled boot, or startup, diskette. Only one boot diskette should be assigned to each PC. It should be clearly marked as the boot diskette.

2. Never boot a hard disk system from a diskette. If an infected floppy is used to boot the system, it can infect the hard disk system.

3. Never put shareware programs into a hard disk's root directory. This protects the root directory, which serves as the base for other subdirectories within the system. Most viruses can affect only the directory from which they are executed. In a LAN, avoid placing shareware in a common file-server directory that makes it accessible to any PC in the network. Viruses can also be downloaded into the system through bulletin boards or via disks from traveling executives who use other computer systems. Disks that have been used elsewhere should be checked prior to use (through the use of an antiviral program).

4. In a shared resource system, where data is transported between PCs or printers, the output data should be put on a floppy disk. No other files including system files should be on the floppy disk.

5. Software should be tested before it is used on the system. Backing up an infected disk will create a second infected disk.

6. There should be strict policies regulating the downloading of software from other systems, since a virus can be transferred from the originating computer.

SOFTWARE COPYRIGHT ISSUES

Copyright infringement is on the rise, primarily because employees do not know the scope of the laws against it. According to the law, an author or creator of a work owns all the rights to any form of it, including the right to copy and distribute it. Title 17 of the U.S. Code states that "it is illegal to make or distribute copies of the copyrighted material without authorization." The only exception is the user's right to make a backup copy for archival purposes.

An employee who makes duplicates of a copyrighted story, book, or report and distributes them to fellow employees is violating the law. Unauthorized duplication of software is a federal crime. Penalties include fines of as much as $100,000 and jail terms of up to five years. In addition, the material in question can be impounded or destroyed.

Major PC-software companies as well as many smaller ones are bringing suits in court

---

1. (Company/Agency) licenses the use of computer software from a variety of outside companies. (Company/Agency) does not own this software or its related documentation, and unless authorized by the software developer, does not have the right to reproduce it.

2. With regard to use on local area networks or on multiple machines, (Company/Agency) employees shall use the software only in accordance with the license agreement.

3. (Company/Agency) employees learning of any misuse of software or related documentation within the company shall notify the department manager or (Company's/Agency's) legal counsel.

4. According to the U.S. Copyright law, persons involved in the illegal reproduction of software can be subject to civil damages of as much as $50,000, and criminal penalties, including fines and imprisonment. (Company/Agency) does not condone the illegal duplication of software. (Company/Agency) employees who make, acquire, or use unauthorized copies of computer software shall be disciplined as appropriate under the circumstances. Such discipline may include termination.

I am fully aware of the software use policies of (Company/Agency) and agree to uphold these policies.

_____

Employee Signature and Date

Figure 8-4 Sample corporate employee agreement: company/agency policy regarding the use of personal computer software.

that will hash out just what constitutes legal copying of a computer program. Eventually, laws may change as computer networks become more widely used. Companies may end up charging for organizing, adapting, and updating the products instead of charging by the copy.

Management should work with the company's legal department to develop policies related to copyright issues. These policies should be discussed with employees to educate and remind them of the consequences. (See Figure 8-4.) The simplest and best policy is to have one authorized copy of a software product for every computer upon which it is run.

The Software Publishers Association produces a self-Audit Kit that describes procedures appropriate for ensuring that a business or organization is "software-legal." SPA is located at 1101 Connecticut Avenue NW, Suite 901, Washington, DC 20036; (202) 452-1600.

CHAPTER 9

OFFICE SUPPLIES

Office supplies such as pens and pencils, file folders, and paper are consumable, disposable, and easily replaced. Changes in technology and an increased variety of machines found in contemporary offices, however, have resulted in an increase in the number and type of supplies. Knowledge of supply control, suppliers, and the different types of supplies helps in organizing supplies for efficient office use, in identifying the best source of supplies, and in purchasing supplies with the qualities and features needed in a particular office.

PURCHASING OFFICE SUPPLIES

Office supplies can be purchased through a variety of sources, including office supply stores, salespeople representing dealers and stationers, mail-order firms, warehouse stores, and discount merchants. Some manufacturers also sell directly to large customers.

SOURCES OF OFFICE SUPPLIES

The following are important sources of office supplies:

Wholesalers: Wholesalers buy finished products from manufacturers and store, market, and deliver the products to dealers; they rarely sell directly to the consumer.

Retail stores: These are office supply stores with walk-in and phone customers; their inventories are generally limited. Because their customers buy in smaller volumes, product cost is relatively high. However, they are convenient for most customers and a good source for rush orders in emergencies.

Contract stationers: These firms have sales representatives who call on customers; some have retail stores; some limit their selling to medium or large accounts in metropolitan areas. They carry large inventories and thus can offer better prices. They offer discounts based on the size of the account and negotiations with the customer.

Mail-order firms: These firms sell through catalogs; customers order by phone, mail, or fax. They range from firms with small, specialized inventories to ones with a large variety of products. They are the best source of supplies for small and medium-sized businesses and home offices. Most emphasize speedy shipping.

Specialty stores: Such firms specialize in one type of product, such as computer or copy supplies; they offer hard-to-find supplies.

Discount merchants: These are warehouse stores with floor-to-ceiling shelves; they buy products directly from manufacturers and offer good discounts. They are good for the small- and medium-sized business used to buying supplies at retail price through dealers. Some charge a membership fee; many have catalogs for customers to look at before coming to the store; and some may deliver orders for a fee.

Warehouse stores: These stores carry office supplies in addition to general merchandise; they are very competitive in price. They are usually cash-and-carry and their offerings may be limited. They buy from the best price sources, so they use various sources and buy from manufacturer's close-out sales.

CHOOSING THE BEST SOURCE

It is best to choose one source for most supplies instead of buying from a variety of dealers. Your main supply source might not carry every item needed, but a specialty supplier or mail-order firm can fill those orders if necessary. Every company should have a local emergency source that has a delivery service available for rush orders.

Retail prices shown in catalogs (except mail-order ones) are a starting point for choosing a supplier. Businesses can negotiate discounts of up to 20 percent from some dealers. Some catalogs have multiple-column price charts for quantity discounts; but even if there is no quantity discount chart, you should always ask for a discount quote. Another way to save money on large-volume purchases is by asking several companies to bid on merchandise. Although this takes time and paperwork, it may be worth the effort to get a low price.

A large part of the cost of buying office supplies is the cost of placing and receiving orders. Businesses that shop with discount and wholesale stores need to determine whether the time and expense involved in this process is worthwhile, whether it is more cost-effective to order from a catalog, or whether it is best to order from a sales representative who might make recommendations that improve efficiency and productivity.

The following factors should be considered when choosing a source for office supplies:

Price
- Is the price full retail or discounted?
- Are prices guaranteed?
- Are prices published or is it necessary to call each time an order is placed?

Hint: Good values and competitive prices should be available on most of the items needed.

Hint: Occasionally compare dealer net prices to make certain you are getting the best price.

Hint: Choose a supplier based on overall price levels rather than by price shopping on one item.

Placing an order
- Is it convenient, whether by phone, by mail, or in person?
- Does the sales representative suggest alternative products to save money or suggest quantity discounts?
- Is the catalog index easy to locate and use?
- Are prices clearly marked?

Hint: When calling in an order, ask if the items you are ordering are on sale.

Receiving an order
- How quickly are orders shipped?
- Are rush deliveries available?
- Do the freight charges increase if the order is partially shipped?
- Is the order consistently accurate?
- Are you notified of substitutions ahead of time?

Hint: Most orders should be shipped within 48 hours.

Hint: Do not accept unordered quantities or extra merchandise.

Billing
- How long does it take to receive the bill?

Hint: A bill should be sent within a week of delivery.

Hint: Become familiar with credit policies in order to maintain a good credit standing and to take advantage of discounts.

Returns
- How many days do you have to return merchandise without penalty?
- Is there a simple return policy?
- Are warranties honored?
- Is there a guarantee of 100 percent satisfaction?

Hint: A good supplier may allow up to 90 days to return merchandise with no penalty.

BUYING IN BULK

Offices may buy large quantities of products and receive volume discounts. This works well if there is enough storage area. The shelf life of the product may determine the quantity to order.

Generic Supplies

Buying generic supplies is one way of saving money. Some good generic products are available, but some generic products that appear to be the same as name brands do not have the same quality.

The cost savings realized by purchasing a generic product often may be offset by the lack of a guarantee or a major manufacturer backing the product. The only way to tell whether or not to use a generic product is by trial and error and having a willingness to take a risk.

Freight Charges

Unless supplies are purchased locally, the customer pays freight charges. Dealers may give free delivery, free delivery on selected items, or only customer-paid delivery. For lightweight items, freight is 2 to 5 percent of the cost; for heavy items, it can be as much as 20 percent.

Listed below are freight terms that office supply dealers use:

F.O.B. (Free on Board): Customer pays freight from the location mentioned after the letters.

F.O.B. Dealer: Customer pays freight from dealer to customer.

F.O.B. Factory: Customer pays freight from the factory where the product is made to customer.

F.O.B. Point of Origin: Customer pays freight from where the item is loaded onto the truck to the customer.

F.O.B. Destination or F.O.B. Delivered: Freight is paid by the dealer.

Prepaid: Freight is paid by the shipper.

Prepaid and Add: Freight is paid by the shipper but the price is added to the customer's bill.

Freight Collect: Customer pays freight to the trucker when the shipment arrives.

CONTROLLING OFFICE SUPPLIES

Every organization needs a method for controlling office supplies. If individuals or individual departments order their own supplies, the company may miss out on preferred pricing or extra services it would otherwise receive. Inventory and usage tracking are essential to manage supplies.

The following are some steps to take in establishing a system for controlling office supplies:

Designate a specific area for storage of all office supplies and lock the area. Note, however, that one person besides yourself should have a key in case of an emergency. Frequently used, inexpensive items such as paper clips or staples, however, can be located in an unlocked closet or drawer that is readily accessible by all office workers.

Appoint a supplies supervisor to set procedures to prevent waste. Typically this is the office manager.

Determine typical usage of supplies. Estimate monthly, bimonthly, and annual usage so that you know how often to order each item.

Establish a budget. Break the budget down into product categories to determine whether too much money is being allocated to certain items. The budget will help in future planning.

Hint: Breaking down the budget into items is also a way to compare costs. Printer ribbons, for example, can be itemized and yields determined for different brands.

Hint: If you know how much is spent on individual items each year, you can negotiate prices with dealers.

Store office supplies with in-house labeling of categories. Here are some suggested categories: *Paper products*—writing paper, forms, file folders, envelopes, labels, computer paper, and copy paper. *Writing instruments*—wood pencils, mechanical pencils, all types of pens, and markers/highlighters. *Computer/copy supplies*—disks, printwheels, toners, and tapes. *Ribbons*—ribbons for all office machines. *Miscellaneous supplies*—rubber bands, staples, paper clips, and other small items.

Hint: Label products in stock according to the machines they fit.

Keep the supply storage area in order. Arrange supplies so the most often used ones are easily accessible—and do not pile supplies so high that stacks of items have to be moved to obtain what is needed. Small items should be stored in labeled boxes.

Keep a minimum number of supply items on the shelves to avoid stockpiling. But be sure you know when to reorder. Put a rubber band and a reorder slip around the "last batch" of stock to indicate that it is time to reorder. Note that reordering time must reflect the time necessary to process the order, obtain the supplies, unpack them, and place them on the shelves.

Be sure that supplies are labeled with expiration dates when applicable.

Store materials by location numbers giving the drawer, shelf, bin, and/or slot. Label each location with the cabinet number (if more than one), location number, and brief description of the supply. For example, the label "II-3 Env. 10" could be used for Cabinet II, shelf 3, No. 10 envelopes.

Hint: A supply area can look messy if items do not have designated storage locations.

Distribute a master inventory list of available supplies with location designations to everyone who has access to the supply area.

Develop an inventory sheet describing supply types and quantities. Post the sheet in the supply area. The person in charge notes reductions in or additions to supplies.

Develop a supply requisition form. Preprint commonly used items on the sheet. Circulate periodically (perhaps as often as once a week) and purchase only what appears on the sheet. (See Figure 9-1.)

Hint: The form should help remind users to request any items they will be using for special projects in their departments.

Hint: Check the supply area at least once a week.

Date_____								REQUISITION FORM		
Department	Ordered by	Name of Item (include Item #)	Brand Name (if required)	Catalog Name	Page #	Model or size	Quantity	Color	List price

Figure 9-1 Sample supply requisition form.

When a supply is low, prepare either a stock requisition, if the supply is carried in-house, or a purchase requisition, if it must be ordered elsewhere. If you are authorized to do so, call or fax the order and prepare the necessary paperwork for the accounting department.

Before placing an order, look for items on sale. Low-cost and quickly used products are the most likely to be on sale. Order a one- or two-month supply.

Establish a schedule for ordering, which may be weekly or monthly. Random buying wastes time and money. Know delivery schedules. For low-value or low-volume items, order as much as a year's supply (as long as it will not deteriorate on the shelf).

Hint: If you have a schedule for ordering, you will avoid handling charges for small orders and you may save on freight charges.

Have current office supply catalogs available for employees.

Check each incoming order to be certain the items received are the ones that were ordered. Place the new supplies behind or beneath the other supplies. Inform the purchasing department that the supplies have been received.

Buy case lots or cartons to save money and avoid partial shipments.

Order by phone, Telex, or fax for faster service. Ask for "rush" service and plan an emergency shipping method.

Hint: Preplanning avoids costly rush orders.

SPECIAL STORAGE REQUIREMENTS

Paper, ribbons, and copier and laser printer cartridges all have special storage requirements.

PAPER

Paper is very susceptible to atmospheric conditions. Paper has a shelf life of over a year. Forms and printed products have shelf lives of six months to a year. These storage suggestions for paper will help increase its shelf life:

❑ Immediately replace the lid after removing reams from a packing box.

❑ Keep paper sealed in its original, moisture-resistant wrapper.

❑ Never store more than one partially unwrapped ream on an open shelf, since fading can occur. Color stock fades more easily than white.

❑ Avoid cold, damp rooms, areas of high heat or humidity, and exposure to direct sunlight.

❑ If the paper storage area is not climate-controlled, keep a relatively low inventory for infrequently used sizes and colors. Extreme changes in the environment can cause paper to warp.

❑ Keep stocks of paper on pallets, off the floor. Stack no more than six cartons high, with each carton upright. Improper stacking of cartons or dropping a carton on its corner can damage paper.

❑ Move paper from storage to user areas at least 48 hours before it is needed to allow the paper to adjust to the temperature in the operating environment. The greater the temperature difference, the longer this adjustment period will be. Some paper manufacturers recommend stabilizing unopened cartons one hour for every degree of difference between the storage and user areas.

❑ Use older paper first.

❑ Do not place other objects on top of paper, whether it is packaged or unpackaged.

RIBBONS

Ribbons should be stored at normal room temperature, away from heat, light, and humidity. Most ribbons have an estimated average shelf life of up to two years, although some dry out in six months.

LASER PRINTER AND COPIER CARTRIDGES

Laser printer and copier cartridges should be stored in the aluminum bag in which they were originally packaged. Keep them in a dark cabinet away from direct sunlight and rest them in a horizontal position, not vertically. Room temperature should be between 32 and 95 degrees Fahrenheit, and they should be protected from high humidity.

PAPER

Paper accounts for a major part of most company supply budgets. There are many types of papers for different purposes, including paper for copiers, fax machines, computers, and special printers, and letterhead for correspondence. Purchasing paper that can be used on more than one kind of equipment, such as paper that can be used for copy machines and laser printers, simplifies ordering, handling, and stocking of paper. It can also save your company a significant amount of money. Below are some considerations to bear in mind when selecting paper.

GRADES

Paper can be purchased in economy, standard, or premium grades. Better grades provide increased brightness and greater contrast between copy and paper, an important paper characteristic for laser and ink jet printers. Table 9-1 describes paper grades, their brightness and their uses.

CONTENT

The content of paper is the amount of wood pulp, which affects durability and appearance. Office paper is either cotton fiber bond or sulphite bond.

Cotton fiber bond (or "rag") is made of cotton pulp combined with chemically treated wood pulp. It is available in grades indicating the amount of cotton pulp combined with the wood pulp: 25 percent, 50 percent, 75 percent, 100 percent, and extra 100 percent. Cotton bonds have a watermark, which is an impression, pattern, or symbol on the paper that signifies its quality. The higher the cotton content, the more durable the paper. Table 9-2 describes the uses of different types of cotton fiber bond.

Note that cotton bond may not perform well on electronic printers and copiers, although some manufacturers make a 25% cotton paper specifically designed for ink jet, dot matrix, and laser printers.

Sulphite bond is made from chemically treated wood pulp. This paper is also known as xerographic paper, because it is typically used for copiers and laser printers. It is smoother and less expensive than cotton-content bond, so it has less of a tendency to curl up and jam in a copy machine or laser printer.

Although sulphite bond comes in five grades, numbered 1 through 5, only #1 and #4 are recommended for general office use. Table 9-3 gives the characteristics of these two commonly used paper types.

FINISH

Paper comes in a variety of finishes, which determine the paper's look and feel. Smoother finishes are less expensive and work better with most office machines. However, the choice of finish is often based on personal preference. Table 9-4 describes three commonly used finishes.

Table 9-1 Paper Grades

Grade	Brightness	Uses
Economy	81	Suitable for everyday use and internal correspondence; used when appearance is less important than economy.
Standard	84	Gives a professional but not a formal look; suitable for interoffice communications.
Premium	$86\frac{1}{2}$	Company letterheads; good for laser printers or copiers.

Table 9-2 Uses of Cotton Fiber Bond

Content	Uses
100% cotton	Legal documents, certificates, prestige stationery, and vital records.
75% cotton	Permanent records, prestige letterhead, and executive correspondence.
50% cotton	Semipermanent records and letterhead.
25% cotton	Most popular letterhead bond; also used for price lists, report forms, circulars, and bulletins.

Table 9-3 Grades of Sulphite Bond

Grade	Characteristics
#1	Has a watermark; looks so good it is difficult to distinguish from a more expensive cotton bond; cost-effective for letterheads, especially if the letterheads are used in a copier or a laser printer, where permanence is not essential.
#4	Most popular for copying and laser printing; only available in a smooth finish; least expensive since it is made from lower quality pulp and has a very white appearance.

Table 9-4 Paper Finishes

Finish	Description	Uses
Smooth	Few irregularities.	Works well with copiers and laser printers; most popular for letterhead.
Linen laid	Embossed with a linen design, with a fairly rough feel and appearance.	High-quality letterhead.
Ripple	Wavy, glossy finish, with the indentations darker than the higher spots.	Document papers, certificates.

Table 9-5 Paper Weights for Common Office Uses

Use	Weight (lb.)	Description
Adding machine rolls	12–16	Standard size is $2\frac{1}{4}$ by $3\frac{1}{8}$ inches but is usually expressed as $2\frac{1}{4}$ inches by 165 feet. Rolls specify inner (ID) and outer (OD) diameters of the core. This measurement is crucial to fitting the roll on the machine.
Cash register rolls	12–16	Same as for Adding machines.
Carbon copies	4–9	Check manufacturer's specifications for estimates on numbers of copies recommended.
Dot matrix printers and daisywheel printers		Recommended: Xerographic (#4 sulphite); 84 brightness, smooth. The higher the groundwood, the lower the price.
		Available in continuous fanfold sheets as well as cut sheets.
		Sizes: $9\frac{1}{2}$ by 11 inches ($8\frac{1}{2}$ by 11 inches when perforated edges are removed); $14\frac{7}{8}$ by 11 inches.
		Green bars: Used for statistical work where easy reading of data is important.
		Blue bars: Used when printouts are to be copied, since the blue bars do not show.
		Higher grades of paper, such as 25 percent cotton bond, are available for letterhead paper.
	10–12	Short-term use.
	15	Average use; lighter handling and less permanence.
	18–20	For reports to be stored for several years, where appearance is important, or for high-speed printers.
Copier paper	20	Recommended: Xerographic (#4 sulphite). Refer to the heading in this chapter on *Copier Problems Caused by Paper.*

Table 9-5 *(con't)*

Use	Weight (lb.)	Description
Envelopes	24	Opaque; heavier weight than letterhead paper; check user's manual for compatibility with postage meters, mailing machines, and laser printers. Refer to the section in this chapter on Envelopes for additional details.
Ink jet printer	20	Use special smooth paper capable of ink absorption and quick drying. Ordinary bond paper absorbs ink too quickly and allows characters to "feather" on the page.
Laser printer	16–28	Refer to user's manual for weight specifications. Most laser printers cannot accept extremely heavy paper stocks and work best with a very smooth sheet of paper such as xerographic or specially formulated laser printer paper. Colors and cotton bond are available.
Letterhead		Recommended: 25 percent cotton bond; $86\frac{1}{2}$ brightness. Note: Not all letterhead works well with laser printers.
	20	Most popular weight.
	24	More body; generally used for special purposes.

Paper with a textured surface typically does not work well in laser printers or copiers because of its greater potential for misfeeding and paper jams. Smoother paper avoids these problems and also ensures sharper resolution of details. Laser printer paper specifically designed for certificates and documents is available that has the look and feel of parchment.

WEIGHT

Paper weight is the weight of one ream (500 sheets) of paper, which is called the basis weight. The weight is a measure of the thickness and density of paper. In English units, the basis weight is the weight of 500 sheets of 17-by-22-inch paper. Measured in metric units it is the weight in grams of one square meter of paper. Office paper weights range from 9 to 28 pounds. In general, paper specifications should follow the recommendations of the equipment or paper manufacturer. Table 9-5 gives paper weights for common office uses.

Color

Many companies now prefer neutral colors such as ivory, off-white, gray, and blue for important correspondence. Firms that use colored paper or letterhead with color want their message to stand out from others. Research has shown that direct mail on colored paper increases readership, retention of detail, and response from readers.

Colored paper can make the following materials more effective:

- Annual reports
- Brochures
- Color-coded documents
- Direct-mail pieces
- Dividers for reports
- Letterhead
- Memos
- Product information
- Sales materials

Colored paper can also improve interoffice communication by using it to:

❑ Distinguish department correspondence (e.g., green for accounting, yellow for personnel, etc.)

❑ Avoid wasting time; this can be done by color-coding documents that look similar (e.g., color-code legal documents that look alike but have different contents).

❑ Call attention to information. Use a bright, visible color for information that must be read immediately, such as companywide information posted on bulletin boards. Reserve tan or gray for confidential information; such a document will stand out if it is in the hands of the wrong person.

❑ Add a festive mood to holiday announcements or party flyers.

Bear these points in mind when using colored paper:

Equipment compatibility: Check the user's manual for specifications to be sure the paper is compatible with the equipment. Colored paper is available in continuous form for dot matrix printers.

Laser printers: Not all colored paper can withstand the heat of laser printers. Avoid paper with a colored coating that has been added after the paper is produced. The paper should be of the same quality as white paper used in the laser printer.

Letterhead: Use light-colored paper for letterhead because it has the best contrast and readability.

Photocopying: Try photocopying any document on colored paper before ordering large quantities to see if the result is a shadowed copy.

Multipart Forms

Carbonless paper produces copies without the use of carbon paper. Chemical coatings in the paper form an image when pressed with a pen, typewriter, or printer. It is used especially for forms needed by several departments.

Multipart continuous carbonless paper is available for computers. Chemical carbonless paper will produce up to five legible copies if handwritten and seven if computer generated or typewritten. Mated mechanical carbonless paper should produce 9 handwritten copies or 12 to 20 if machine imaged.

FAX PAPER

Most fax machines use rolls of thermal paper, although some accept plain paper. (See the heading *Fax Machines* in Chapter 7 for more information.) Different machines use different degrees of heat, so consult the user's manual and purchase the recommended type of thermal paper. Typical ink colors are blue and black, but red and green inks are also available.

COPIER PROBLEMS CAUSED BY PAPER

Copy paper should be properly placed in paper trays. Most paper manufacturers provide loading instructions on their packages (usually an arrow indicating which surface is to be printed on). Some copiers discharge the sheet the same way it is placed in the tray, while others turn it over.

Hint: To test how a copier works, mark one side of a sheet and run it through to determine the imaging side.

Hint: When purchasing a copier, it is important to have a demonstration on the various thicknesses of paper to determine the minimum and maximum possible.

Table 9-6 provides a quick reference for solutions to copier problems.

RECYCLED PAPER

More people are becoming aware of the limited supply of natural resources and have begun to recycle office paper. To facilitate recycling, offices have recycling containers for used white and sometimes colored paper next to wastepaper baskets and near copiers. Building maintenance staff collect the paper for recycling.

On the other side, recycled paper is available for copiers and computers, as well as for writing and memo pads. File folders and mailers may also be made from recycled fibers. Recycled paper may be white or colored, and it may have some cotton content. Offices that use recycled paper will frequently have that information printed on correspondence.

ENVELOPES

Envelopes come in hundreds of styles and sizes to accommodate all mailing purposes. Although other sizes are available, Table 9-7 shows the most common types and sizes of envelopes. Listed below are the characteristics and typical uses of business envelopes.

Table 9-6 Solutions to Copier Problems

Problem	Cause	Solution
Feed difficulties	Heavy-stock paper, such as letterhead, may cause static buildup.	Use lighter-weight paper.
Misfeeding	Uneven edges or excessive curl; mixing different paper weights in the same tray or cassette.	Turn the paper over or use another ream.
Jamming in the finish bins or sheets sticking together	Excessive curl.	Turn the paper over.
	Moisture.	Check storage conditions.
	Low humidity.	Ask vendor to check static eliminator.
Wrinkling	High moisture content resulting when the paper is incorrectly wrapped or stored in a damp location; paper has been left too long in the copy machine.	Check storage conditions; use another ream.

Table 9-7 Common Envelopes

Type	Size	Description
No. $6\frac{3}{4}$	$3\frac{5}{8}$ by $6\frac{1}{2}$ inches	Commercial
No. 9	$3\frac{7}{8}$ by $8\frac{7}{8}$ inches	Official
*No. 10	$4\frac{1}{8}$ by $9\frac{1}{2}$ inches	Official
No. 11	$4\frac{1}{2}$ by $9\frac{1}{2}$ inches	Document/policy
No. 12	5 by $11\frac{1}{2}$ inches	Document/policy
No. 14	9 by 12 inches	First-class mailer
	10 by 13 inches	
	10 by 15 inches	
	12 by $15\frac{1}{2}$ inches	

*The envelope used most often for correspondence.

Commercial and official envelopes (also called business or regular)
- Usually 24 lb. bond for first-class, airmail, or bulk-rate mail handling.
- A No. 9 envelope fits into a No. 10 envelope.
- Available with an inside blue tint for confidentiality.

- Cotton fiber bond envelopes should always match letterhead stationery.
- May have a window to use for invoices, statements, addressed documents, or payroll checks. A window eliminates retyping, reducing errors and saving time.

Kraft envelopes
- Durable, thick, heavyweight stock (up to 50 lb.).
- Bleached or unbleached paper (a dark tan color).
- Available in a full range of sizes.
- Closures may be string and button, clasp, gummed, or self-stick. String and button and clasp envelopes can be reused. Clasp envelopes have gummed flaps for extra strength and security.
- Have wide usage, from storing small coins to mailing large catalogs.

Tyvek™ envelopes
- Available in No. 14 size.
- Made of polyolefin fibers bonded together by heat and pressure, making the envelopes rip-proof, puncture-proof, and water resistant.
- Because they weigh about half as much as paper, they can save postage.
- May incorporate a seal in the closure to reveal tampering, and a window on the flap changes to the word "opened" if the flap is lifted.

Interdepartment delivery envelopes
- May have either a string and button tie or resealable adhesive.
- Some have drilled holes to make contents visible.
- Available in Tyvek™.
- Available in colors such as red, yellow, blue, or orange.
- Transmittal information can be printed on one or both sides.

Dot matrix printer envelopes
- Available as continuous-form No. 10 envelopes; specially designed to stay closed when used on a dot matrix printer.

Laser printer envelopes
- Check the user's manual for envelope use.
- Must be of good construction, with a well-creased fold and no more than two thicknesses of paper.
- Should not have a paper weight greater than 24 lbs.
- Adhesives must not scorch, melt, offset, or release hazardous emissions when going through the laser printer.
- Most laser printers cannot accept window, string and button, or clasp envelopes.
- Usually, larger envelopes are more difficult to feed into the printer.

- Poorly constructed envelopes may result in a jammed printer or a wrinkled envelope.

See the following section on Labels for an alternative to envelope use with laser printers.

LABELS

Labels are available in many sizes and widths, ranging from one to four labels across a page. Labels have been developed specifically for laser and dot matrix printers, copiers, and typewriters. White labels are common; however, clear labels are available to blend into white, patterned, or colored envelopes to look neater and more personalized.

Table 9-8 Basic Label Formats

Format	Description	Use
Sheets	Sizes range up to $8\frac{1}{2}$ by 11 inches; may have a single label or many labels.	Laser printers, copiers, typewriters, handwriting.
Rolls	One label wide.	Typewriters.
Continuous (or fanfold)	Pin holes on the outer edge to drive the labels through the print mechanism; folded and perforated every 11 inches; may be one to four labels wide; sold by the carton.	Computer printers.

Table 9-9 Basic Label Types

Type	Description	Uses
Dry back	Must be moistened to activate the glue.	Addresses.
Permanent self-adhesive or pressure sensitive	Premoistened; has a backing paper that peels off; difficult to remove once affixed.	Addresses.
Removable	Holds firmly yet removes easily without leaving a mark; available in sheets and a variety of sizes and colors; not recommended for laser printers or copiers; not recommended for address labels.	Changing, updating, or covering incorrect information; labeling for a short period of time.

Table 9-10 Equipment and Labels

Type of Equipment	*Type of Labels*
Laser printers	Self-adhesive labels specially designed to prevent edge-lift and paper curl; sheet size is $8\frac{1}{2}$ by 11 inches, with a variety of sizes on the sheet. The adhesive should be an acrylic-based emulsion, which is more stable than other adhesives during the printer's fusing printer process. They should be specifically guaranteed not to jam, melt, or predispense inside the machine. To test label stock for adhesive strength, press a sheet of plain paper against a sheet of label stock. The plain paper should not stick to the label stock.
Dot matrix printers	Self-adhesive address labels used for computer-generated mailings; available in white, clear, or colors such as green, blue, or pink; designed to be heat-resistant to prevent a separation from the backing and to allow high-speed printing; typical size is $3\frac{1}{2}$ by $\frac{15}{16}$ inches with one label across, accommodating a four-line address; also available four across; can be pin-fed, perforated, and fanfolded.
Copiers	Self-adhesive for use in sheet-fed or plain paper copiers; available in a variety of label sizes with sheet sizes of $8\frac{1}{2}$ by 11 inches; available for liquid toner copiers, although there are not as many sizes to choose from. By using copier labels, a keyboarded master list may be used over and over again.
Typewriters, stencil, mimeo, and Verifax	White self-adhesive address labels are available; sizes are limited; typewriter labels (that can also be written on) are available in $8\frac{1}{2}$-by-11-inch sheets or in rolls.

Labels are available in three basic formats, as described in Table 9-8. Table 9-9 describes the three basic types of labels.

Office equipment should use labels specially designed to work best with that equipment. Table 9-10 lists some of the products available.

TRANSPARENCIES

A wide variety of overhead transparency film is specially developed to work on the types of office machines shown in Table 9-11.

Table 9-11 Transparencies for Use with Office Equipment

Equipment	Description	Colors
Plain paper copier	Uses special transparency film that is loaded into the paper tray; copies can be made of line art, graphics, handwritten text, and typed or printed copy; some machines require a sensing strip to activate the machine; others work with or without the sensing strip.	Black image on clear or colored background.
Infrared and thermal transparency makers	Uses special transparency film; heavy thicknesses can be used for active use or handling without a mounting frame.	Black image on clear or colored background; color image on clear or colored background.
Printers	Check the user's manual for specifications and use only the film recommended. Separate transparency film is available to use on each of the following types of machines: pen plotters; ink jet, dot matrix, laser, and daisywheel printers; typewriters; and word processors.	Black image on clear or colored background; color image varies according to the type of equipment.

FILING AND RECORDS MANAGEMENT SUPPLIES

Most manual filing systems use file folders, labels, and guides. These products are available in a variety of sizes, shapes, colors, and styles. Filing supply choices depend on individual preferences and needs.

FILE FOLDERS

There are two basic types of file folders. (1) Manila file folders are made of heavyweight stock that resists tearing, folding, and bursting. They are typically a light creamy color but are also available in a variety of colors. (2) Kraft file folders are made of unbleached sulfite stock in a dark tan color and are preferable when strength and rigidity are required. They look clean longer than manila folders, but they are more expensive.

File folders hold either letter- or legal-size documents. Letter-size file folders are $9\frac{1}{2}$ by $11\frac{3}{4}$ inches while legal-size folders are $9\frac{1}{2}$ by $14\frac{3}{4}$ inches. The $9\frac{1}{2}$-inch height includes the tab.

Table 9-12 File Folder Sizes

Weight	Point	Use
Medium	$9\frac{1}{2}$	Two or three times a week (semiactive) or less (inactive).
Heavy	11	Several times a day (active).
Extraheavy	17	Numerous times a day (very active); a common weight for guides.
Superior rigidity	25	Guides; available in pressboard (a hard, dense stock).

Both manila and kraft folders are described by the thickness of the folder, measured in points. One point is equivalent to 0.001 inch. As the point size increases, so does the durability and price of the folder. Typical weights for manila folders are $9\frac{1}{2}$- and 11-point stock. Typical kraft folders weights are 11- and 17-point. Table 9-12 lists the various sizes and uses of file folders.

In order to be cost-effective, the minimum weight for a task should be used. When transferring files for storage, information should be transferred to lighter-weight, less expensive folders. The heavier folders should be reused for active files.

TAB CUTS

A basic file folder has a tab made out of the same material as the folder. Most styles of folders are made with front flaps undercut to increase the tab heading area. Special-purpose folders may have tabs that double the thickness of the folder from the top of the tab to the top of the undercut (called "double tab" or "two-ply" file folders). These tabs are good for active files. Other tabs are made of stronger material such as plastic.

The tab cut describes the number of tabs across the top edge of the file folder. Table 9-13 describes the different cuts. Folders usually are packaged with an equal number of tabs so the labeled tabs in the file drawer are staggered evenly.

OTHER FOLDER TYPES

There are several other important types of file folder:

Plastic file folders: Made of durable and flexible polyethylene or polypropylene, these are good for heavily used folders because they resist spills and stains and are rarely damaged by handling. Many have a nonslip surface to prevent sliding when stacked. They come in a variety of colors and are good for a color-coded system.

Hanging file folders: Most file drawers are equipped for a hanging file system or can be converted by using a metal frame. Files hang at a uniform level from rod-like projections or hooks at the top, allowing tabs to remain visible and preventing folders from sliding down into the drawer. Many have removable plastic tabs into which paper labeling tabs can be inserted—and removed and changed, and tabs can be used in a variety of positions. They are available in a range of colors and thus can be used in a color-coded system.

Interior manila folders: Shorter than regular manila folders, these are specifically designed to be used inside hanging file folders to make it easy to remove material from the

Table 9-13 Tab Cuts

Cut	Description	Use
Straight	Tab length is the full width of folder.	Multiple labels; extra long headings.
Half	Tab length is one-half the width of folder; tabs are staggered in sets of two.	Long headings.
Third	Tab length is one-third the width of folder; tabs are staggered in sets of three.	Most common; most folder labels are designed for this folder and do not fit other cuts.
Fifth	Tab length is one-fifth the width of folder; tabs are staggered in sets of five.	Less room for writing; most popular for numerical filing systems.
Two-fifths	Tab length is two-fifths the width of folder; tabs are either right of center or far right.	Long headings.
Shelf or end cut	Tab is on the end of the folder instead of the top; scored expansion bottoms accommodate more material.	Open shelf filing systems where records are stored in horizontal rows rather than in file drawers.

hanging folder without taking the folder out of the drawer. The height and tabs are designed so as not to block or interfere with hanging folder tabs.

Bellows (expansion) folders: These are available with pockets and may be labeled alphabetically or numerically.

Box bottom hanging folders: These folders have flat, reinforced bottoms for filing heavy, bulky material; closed sides keep smaller items from slipping out.

File folders with fasteners: Folders are available with fasteners attached in various positions to secure papers inside them; self-adhesive varieties are available as well as the standard version with plastic or metal prong fasteners that thread through the folder.

LABELS FOR FILE FOLDERS

File folder labels are available in self-adhesive, dry back, and removable types. They come in either sheets or rolls. They may be white or white with a color border. A wide range of border colors is available, including coral, lavender, and black as well as the traditional colors of yellow, blue, and red. File folder labels can also be one color, ranging from lightly tinted pastel shades to neon colors. Self-adhesive label protectors, which are clear Mylar laminate, can be used to protect top or end tabs on folders.

Self-adhesive labels for hanging file folders can be applied to plastic folder tabs or to their paper inserts. If the labels are put on the outside of the plastic tab, the tab inserts are unnecessary. These labels will not snag or peel off and are available in a variety of colored borders.

Preprinted inserts are also available for tabs; they eliminate typing of labels. The inserts are usually alphabetical, numerical, daily, monthly, or by states. Legal exhibit labels are also available preprinted.

File folder labels for dot-matrix printers are available on continuous forms to use with tractor feed printers. Color borders are also available.

GUIDES

File guides are used for dividing file drawers into categorized sections, thus preventing misfiling and wasting time. File guides can be 18-point manila, for inactive to semiactive files, or 25-point pressboard for semiactive to active files. Manila guides cost less than pressboard but are less durable. Guides are available with plain tabs, and monthly, daily, or alphabetic preprinted tabs. File guides are available for hanging file folders. Tabs are either made of the same paper as the guide or made of plastic or steel.

Out guides indicate that an entire folder has been removed from the files. Out guides range from 11- to 17-point paper with either end or tab cuts. Usually they are a bright color such as red or orange. The guide may include a printed form on which to write the date and by whom the file was removed or it may have a small pocket for a charge-out card.

COLORS

Color folders allow the classifying and coding of files by color. Color coding can be done with colored labels, file folders, hanging file folders, or labels. Color coding has several advantages, including the following:

- It guides the eye to correct files and reduces filing and retrieval time.
- It increases filing accuracy because misfiled items stand out.
- It provides additional subdivisions of filed material beyond label headings.

STORAGE BOXES

Corrugated cardboard filing boxes can be used for long-term storage of checks, documents; cards, forms, printouts, and tapes. The boxes usually need to be assembled. They have built-in handles and can be ordered with a color-coded system, which can save as much as 50 percent in filing and retrieval time. Some boxes are constructed to stand up under more than half a ton of stacking pressure, which maximizes storage floor space.

WRITING INSTRUMENTS AND CORRECTION SUPPLIES

New colors, improvements in style, a variety of types, and a wide range of prices provide many options. Because each writing instrument has advantages for its recommended use, it is likely that you use several different kinds. Many formerly low-end products have been developed with high-tech, aesthetically pleasing designs. Despite increased use of computers and electronic typewriters, office professionals still write some things in pen, marker, and pencil.

PENS

Pens are available in the following types:

Ballpoint: Most popular office pen, ballpoints may either be disposable or have a changeable refill. The ink dries quickly and does not smear, it writes through carbon copies, and it may be erasable. They range in price from expensive to very inexpensive.

Fountain: Enjoying a resurgence in popularity, fountain pens have a prestigious look. They can use a variety of brightly colored inks. Some are disposable, while others are refillable or have disposable ink cartridges.

Rollerball: These are becoming very popular for office use. They are available in several colors. The tips have a metal ball encased in a plastic or metal stem. Because they write darker and smoother than ballpoint pens, they are good for drawing, ruling, and detail work as well as writing. They can write through carbon copies; they are usually nonrefillable. Some rollerball pens are available with permanent waterproof ink, which is popular in banks and financial and legal offices.

Porous point or *felt tip:* These flow easily and have the crisp, precise lines of a ballpoint; however, their points are made of plastic, which may soften with age. The ink is often brighter in color than that of a ballpoint, and they are usually disposable. Although they will not write through carbon, they are good for detail work, ruling, sketching, and labeling floppy disks.

MARKERS

Markers are available for highlighting information, writing on surfaces, and writing on white boards and transparencies. Below are descriptions of various markers:

Highlighters: These are often used to call attention to information in reading material with bright see-through colors such as yellow, pink, and orange. They can make very fine or very bold lines, depending on the tip. Some can highlight on thin paper without bleeding through; some are nonsmearing and thus can be used to highlight over ink; some will not show up on copies. A highlighter that will not smear or remove ink is available for use with fax machine paper (and any other thermal process paper).

Permanent markers: These are good for writing on nonporous surfaces such as cellophane, glass, metal, and transparent tape. They are suitable for mailing labels since the ink does not run when wet. They are not recommended for ordinary writing because the ink bleeds through paper. The ink dries quickly and will not smear. They are available in a wide variety of colors, but some have a distinctive irritating odor. Chisel (or wedge) tips can make fine, medium, or bold strokes; bullet tip (pointed) makes a heavier mark.

Easel pad markers: Designed to write on easel pads, these are available in a variety of colors. Look for chisel tip and waterbased ink that will not bleed through paper.

Dry erase markers: These are designed for use on whiteboards only; they cannot be used on paper because they dry out quickly. They are available in many colors and have little odor, and they erase with a dry cloth or eraser. Some may also be used on glass, unpainted metal, and glazed ceramics. Whiteboards and dry erase markers are popular because they eliminate chalk dust around computers.

Visual aid markers: Available in both permanent and erasable (if waterbased) forms, these are used for writing on acetates, such as transparencies. Available in a wide range of colors, they are designed to remain brilliant and clear under heat and light.

PENCILS

Traditional woodcase lead pencils are still found in many offices, although mechanical pencils have become very popular because they have different lead thicknesses and low prices.

The older turn-type mechanical pencils held only one lead at a time and needed frequent reloading. The newest and best mechanical pencils advance the lead automatically and insert new leads as old ones are used up. Lead is available in widths of 0.5, 0.7, and 0.9 millimeters. The 0.5-mm lead is the most popular and is used for general writing and detail work; heavier lines can be drawn with 0.7- and 0.9-mm lead. Mechanical pencils are good for drafting, accounting, and general office work.

ERASERS AND CORRECTION SUPPLIES

Erasers are available for pencils, carbons, ink, and typewriters and for erasing graphite from drafting film. Electric erasers make erasing large areas of ink and pencil easy. There are special erasers to remove India ink from film and to remove film lead from drawing film and paper.

There are various types of correction supplies. They are detailed in Table 9-14.

COMPUTER, FAX MACHINE, AND COPIER SUPPLIES

Changes in technology have resulted in a greater variety of equipment in the office, and so there is a wide range of supplies for equipment such as computers, fax machines, and copiers.

COMPUTER DISKS

Computer disks come in various sizes, depending on the computer used. The two most popular sizes of disks are $5\frac{1}{4}$-inch and $3\frac{1}{2}$-inch. The $5\frac{1}{4}$-inch disk is also called a floppy disk and is susceptible to dust, dirt, fingerprints, and liquids. The $3\frac{1}{2}$-inch disk has a superior construction of rigid plastic that protects the magnetic medium from potential hazards. The $3\frac{1}{2}$-inch disk is smaller, easier to carry, and can store more information than the larger disk. However, the $5\frac{1}{4}$-inch disk is less expensive than the $3\frac{1}{2}$-inch disk.

Disks can be ordered preformatted for PCs, although there is an additional charge for this service. Disks are available in colors that allow for color coding data. Some disk manufacturers offer a service to restore lost data at no charge, and other disks are certified to be 100 percent error-free and have lifetime guarantees of free replacement. Although many disks look similar, there are differences in the way data is stored, depending on the computer system used. The following are typical abbreviations for disks:

Table 9-14 Correction Supplies

Type	*Description*	*Use*
Correction fluid	Available in white and a variety of colors to match paper; dries quickly; custom orders match company stationery.	Designed for specific types of ink, such as computer printouts, fax paper, handwriting, photo-copies, carbons, typed originals.
Correction film	A thin opaque film placed over original information; error is retyped, film is removed, new information is typed in; covers most inks and leads.	Typewriters.
Self-adhesive correction tape	Backing peels off, exposing adhesive, in a variety of widths; tape is placed over the area to be changed and new information can be typed in; eliminates smearing.	Typewriters. Designed so erasing is not necessary.
Removable cover-up tape	Strips in a variety of widths ($\frac{1}{6}$ inch is specially designed to block out one line of type or copy) that are removable and repositionable.	Good for covering confidential material or notes on originals to be photocopied.

SS   = single side (data stored on one side)
DS   = double side (data stored on two sides)
SD   = single density
DD   = double density
QUAD = quad density (also called high density)

The density indicates how closely the computer spaces the magnetic spots when it records a file. Most disks are double density (DD) and may also be used on single-density machines.

Hint: Do not buy disks of higher density than required by the computer system.

DISK STORAGE

There are boxes with roll tops or hinged lids in oak, polystyrene, transparent acrylic, or plastic to store both $5\frac{1}{4}$- and $3\frac{1}{2}$-inch disks. Some boxes have locks for security, movable dividers, built-in handles, the ability to pop up for an easel display, or can be attached to the side of the monitor. Rigid dividers are important for $5\frac{1}{4}$-inch disk storage boxes to prevent warping.

Table 9-15 Power Problems and Causes

Problem	Effect	Possible Causes
Surge	Increase in voltage	Switching of other equipment on or off.
Spike	Sudden increase in voltage	Lightning, utility company load-switching, power coming on after outage.
Outage	No voltage	Weather, power-line breaks, power system failures.
Sags/brownout	Decrease in voltage	Power company reduction during high demand periods, overloads.
Noise	Interference	High-frequency voltages from local electrical devices, including fluorescent lights.

Table 9-16 Power Protection Devices Available

Device	Surge	Spike	Sag	Outage	Noise
Surge protector	Yes	Yes	No	No	Some
UPS (uninterruptible power systems)	Yes	Yes	Yes	Yes	Some
SPS (standby power system)	No	No	No	Yes	No
Power conditioner	Yes	Yes	Yes	No	Yes

Plastic three-hole punched disk holders fit in $8\frac{1}{2}$-by-11-inch notebooks. There are also three-ring holders designed to keep documentation together with disks. For convenient storage in file folders or binders, there are self-adhesive pockets with pressure-sensitive backs that stick to most surfaces.

Traveling diskette holders come in a range of sizes, including a 20-disk carrying case with X-ray protection and a wallet-sized nylon holder for antistatic protection.

DISK MAILERS

Disk mailers are designed with a sturdy construction to offer protection from bending, static, and moisture. The mailers provide a preprinted address area with first-class postal identification and a warning such as: "Caution: Do not bend or fold. Avoid exposure to all magnetic fields."

SURGE PROTECTORS

Computers are sensitive to problems with the power supply. Such problems include surges, spikes, drops, noise, brownouts, and blackouts. Surges generally last longer than spikes, but both usually occur so fast that they are not noticed. Noise interference can be transmitted to the power line by things such as nearby radio and TV stations, loose electrical connections, and fluorescent lights. (See Table 9-15.)

A loss of power or a sudden surge of power can cause serious damage to the circuitry of a computer, disk drive, printer, and communications equipment as well as erase valuable data. A surge protector is a cost-effective method of insuring that computers, printers, and fax machines are protected from unpredictable weather or current changes. Surge protectors divert any excess electricity out the ground line and away from electrical equipment. Surge protectors prevent hardware damage and data transmission errors.

Some surge protectors have desktop remote controls and alarms to warn when the voltage drops below safe levels. Other surge protectors protect against spikes coming over the phone lines and are ideal for fax machines, modems, and answering machines.

DATA SWITCH BOXES

Data switch boxes allow several PCs to share the same peripherals without expensive networking hardware and software. Switch boxes are particularly helpful to laser printer users. The boxes can queue print jobs either manually or automatically.

FAX/PHONE LINE SHARING

Instead of adding another phone line, equipment is available to add a fax machine to an existing telephone line without interfering with the phone or answering machine already there. There are models designed for single-line, two-line, and multiple-line phone systems. They are compatible with tone and rotary (pulse) dialing, which allows continued phone operation during power failures.

LASER PRINTER AND COPY MACHINE TONER CARTRIDGES

Toner cartridges are used by laser printers and some copy machines. Toner is a dry, powdered substance that is attracted to electrically charged areas on the machine's photo-sensitive revolving drum. Toner cartridges can be ordered in color for some copy machines.

Toner should not be exposed to direct sunlight or room light for more than a few minutes because it uses a developing process similar to that of film in a camera. Light can cause the developing roller inside the cartridge to be damaged.

Some service bureaus can recharge toners, either locally or through the mail. If the recharging is done by mail, the empty toner cartridge is shipped in its original box, where it is recharged and returned. Note, however, that some laser printer manufacturers recommend against refilling cartridges because it may cause damage to the printer.

RIBBONS

Ribbons for the same machine may look alike or look totally different due to packaging, colors, and design features. Different part numbers in the user's manual represent differences in design, ink color, length of ribbon, and material, so it is possible for one type of ribbon to have more than one part number. If a ribbon was manufactured by the original

Table 9-17 Ribbon Types

Type	*Description*	*Use*
Correctable	A one-time use ribbon; ink does not penetrate the paper, so the typed image may be lifted off using a specially formulated lift-off tape (sold separately from ribbons). Because of the ease of correction, this ribbon should not be used for negotiable instruments (check writing) or offset/multilith application. Newer electronic typewriters have a magnetic memory correction process and do not require a correctable ribbon.	Typewriters not originally designed for correctable ribbon use.
Multistrike	Solvent coated reusable film; the ink coating allows multiple strikeovers in a single area on the film before advancing; offers higher character yield than correctable ribbons; more expensive than single-strike ribbons but will print more than five times the number of characters; print is permanent, so correction fluid or cover-up tape is necessary for corrections.	Electronic typewriters, daisywheel printers; recommended for correspondence.
Poly or single-strike	A one-time use film ribbon; produces a single strike on the ribbon and then advances; print is permanent, so correction fluid or cover-up tape is necessary for corrections.	Electronic typewriters; recommended for executive correspondence, erasable bond, and other hard-to-image papers.
Nylon or fabric	Continuous fabric loop is economical; print is permanent, so correction fluid or cover-up tape is necessary for corrections; may cost more than a multistrike ribbon but lasts longer.	Electronic typewriters; dot matrix printers; recommended for everyday and draft-quality printing.

equipment manufacturer and made in strict compliance with the device, it carries the abbreviation "OEM."

One way to avoid duplicating orders of ribbons is to establish an in-house list of machines and their ribbons. The list would include statements such as "Margaret's typewriter in Personnel takes X ribbon."

Table 9-17 lists the different types of ribbon.Ribbons for printing calculators and cash registers are nylon and are available in black, purple, or a combination of black and red.

Typewriters use correctable ribbons with lift-off tape or tabs, and nylon or poly ribbons, depending on the model type and manufacturer's recommendations.

> **Hint:** Light or partial characters and jammed or broken ribbons may be caused by worn or damaged printwheels, improper installation of the printwheel and ribbon, or incorrect pitch selection and impression control settings.

Printers use nylon ribbons. The width, length, caliper, and thread count vary with each specific ribbon. For the highest performance of printer ribbons, check the owner's manual for complete instructions on installation. Most ribbons have safety clips installed on the ribbon for protection during shipping and storage. It is important to remove all clips before installation or the ribbon might not advance, causing light printing, jamming, or breakage of the ribbon.

Nylon ribbons can be reinked, which involves adding ink to the ribbon so it can be used again. Reinking can be done in the office with a reinking kit or by sending ribbons to a service bureau. Reinking ribbons is a good way to save money on computer ribbons, which are used up rapidly when one does a great deal of printing.

CHAPTER 10

THE OFFICE WORKSTATION

A basic element of every office is the workstation. The workstation is a place where the worker can think and perform an assigned set of tasks. For the administrative assistant, the workstation is the action center for organizing and processing information, telephone calls, electronic messages, and files; for greeting visitors, maintaining reference materials, and performing other executive-support activities.

TYPES OF OFFICE WORKSTATIONS

The development of open-space planning has changed the look of offices significantly. Open offices use panels to create a maze of workstations consisting of systems furniture. Systems furniture includes partitions, desks or work surfaces, storage units, and accessories. Although offices with fixed walls and conventional furniture are still prevalent, the open office concept provides the greatest amount of flexibility for meeting changing business and financial trends.

A workstation is designed according to the needs of each individual office professional. There are workstations for receptionists, secretaries, administrative managers, supervisors, middle managers, and executives. Each workstation is designed to provide the necessary privacy, work surface, and storage for the task(s) being performed.

The workstation must physically support a variety of daily tasks. One's physical and psychological well-being are upset by bad design or poorly adjusted office components, such as the desk, chair, and computer. "Syntonic" is a term that means receptive to and in harmony with the environment. Syntonic design integrates or "harmonizes" all aspects of planning to create an office support system that maximizes productivity while meeting human needs. The integration of people, tools, and the workplace is necessary for efficient offices.

COMPONENTS OF A WORKSTATION

The workstation is composed of office seating, work surfaces, storage containers or files, and privacy panels.

SEATING

The most important component is the office chair. It has to support office professionals in the performance of most office tasks. Lower back pain, the number-one office health problem, is often caused by improper seating. Some researchers believe that there is no one correct seating position. The user, therefore, should be able to adjust the chair to his or her specific anatomical or physical characteristics and favorite seating positions.

Desirable features to consider when selecting an office chair include the following:

Height adjustment: Most office chairs can be raised or lowered to make sure one's feet touch the floor properly. Height adjustment is also important to ensure that one's arms maintain a correct angle for keyboard use. Very short people can use a slanted footrest to support their feet.

Lumbar support: A slight concavity in the lower back of the chair is important to minimize lower back pain. It helps to support the normal alignment and the natural curve of the lower spine, in a manner similar to the standing position.

Hint: A thin pillow will provide support if the back of the chair is flat.

Side arms: A chair with side arms helps to take pressure off the wrist when keyboarding and also can support leaning positions.

Waterfall seat: Prolonged sitting cuts off blood circulation to the legs. A sloping, rounded front edge on the seat takes strain off the thighs. Such a seat, called a waterfall seat, improves circulation.

Forward tilt: This feature locks the seat in a forward tilting position. This is very helpful when keyboarding for long periods of time.

Back tilt: This feature helps one recline, which is at times comfortable and necessary. Several manufacturers' chairs allow the user to lock two or three angles.

Base and casters: A five-star base prevents tipping. Dual-wheel or single-wheel casters allow easy movement over both hard and soft surfaces.

WORK SURFACES

Much office work is done on the most important work surface, the desktop. Other work surfaces may hold equipment, paper-flow sorting trays, telephones, and writing and reference materials.

Because there are various sizes and shapes of paper and office equipment, the surface must have adequate depth. A surface must be a minimum of 24 inches deep, for example, to hold binders with printouts, and 30 inches deep to accommodate a personal computer. Sometimes it is possible to adjust the height of the work surface to better accommodate an individual's needs.

CHAIR EVALUATION CHECKLIST

	YES	NO
A. HEIGHT		
1. Is the range of height adjustment adequate?	——	——
2. Can the chair height be easily adjusted?	——	——
3. Can the adjustment be made from the seated position?	——	——
4. Are adequate footrests available?	——	——
B. BACKREST		
5. Does the chair have a high backrest?	——	——
6. Does the backrest interfere with arm movements?	——	——
7. Is the lumbar support adequate?	——	——
8. Is the tension of the backrest adjustable?	——	——
9. Does the backrest tilt back?	——	——
10. Does the backrest lock in position?	——	——
11. Can the backrest be adjusted up and down?	——	——
12. Can the backrest be adjusted forward?	——	——
C. ARMRESTS		
13. Does the chair have armrests?	——	——
14. Are the armrests appropriate for the job?	——	——
15. Are armrests optional?	——	——
16. Do armrests interfere with movement?	——	——
D. SEATPAN		
17. Does the seatpan have a rounded front edge?	——	——
18. Does the seatpan tilt?	——	——
19. Is seatpan tension adjustable?	——	——
20. Does seatpan lock in position?	——	——
E. SAFETY		
21. Is the chair stable?	——	——
22. Does the chair have a 5-leg base?	——	——
23. Are casters matched to the floor?	——	——
24. Can casters be changed?	——	——
25. Are all adjustments safe against self or unintentional release?	——	——
26. Does chair meet all applicable fire codes?	——	——
F. COMFORT		
27. Is the chair adequately padded?	——	——
28. Are materials appropriate?	——	——
29. Is the chair comfortable?	——	——
G. OTHER		
30. Can the chair be easily maintained?	——	——
31. Can maintenance be performed in the field?	——	——

Figure 10-1 Chair evaluation checklist.

STORAGE

Adequate storage space improves the organization of an office's workspace. Recorded information is stored on many media, such as paper, magnetic floppy disks, microfilm, microfiche, CD-ROM, and optical disks. Each medium requires its own unique type of storage container. Fixed or mobile pedestals, binder bins, overhead flipper door cabinets, and lateral or vertical file cabinets help in organizing and storing information media, reference manuals, and supplies. (See the sections on Managing Paper-Based Records and Computer Software in Chapter 12 for more information.)

PRIVACY PANELS

Privacy panels are movable walls that can be as short as 40 inches high or as tall as the ceiling. Open-plan offices use movable panels that are lower than ceiling height to provide privacy. Since all desks, partitions, and other equipment can be moved easily, the workstations can be rearranged in a matter of hours, instead of days.

WORKSTATION ADJUSTMENT

Ergonomics is the study of the relationship between the worker and the work environment. (The term comes from the Greek words *ergon* meaning "work" and *nomos* meaning "law.") It takes into account the individual characteristics of the worker. Ideally, every office workstation should meet the physical, psychological, and work requirements of the individual.

Ergonomic principles are partly based on the study of anthropometrics. This involves the measurement of size and proportions of the human body. The height of a table and the width of a seat pan, for example, should fit the bodily dimensions of workers.

Ergonomic principles are also based on biomechanics, the study of the human body's structure and functions. Activities such as sitting for long periods, bending, lifting, and reaching can strain various body parts. Working positions should try to minimize fatigue and wear and tear on the body caused by such activities.

To conform to these principles, five focal points of adjustment are essential in any workstation: seating, work surface, video display terminal, lighting, and storage.

SEATING

Because office professionals spend most of their time in a chair, it is a crucial factor in comfort and efficiency. The proper chair must fit the individual and the job. A starting point for determining correct chair height is to equal the distance from the floor to the crease behind the knee. The height of the chair should be set to distribute body weight as evenly as possible, 14 to 17.5 inches for women and 15.5 to 19.2 inches for men.

Other important features include the following:

GUIDELINES FOR WORK SURFACES

WORKSPACE	YES	NO	NOT APPLICABLE
1. Is there adequate space to perform all tasks?			
2. Is there adequate space for all equipment?			
3. Can any workspace be shared?			
4. Can the workspace be adapted for either right or left hand use?			
5. Are all items of equipment and job aids which must frequently be used within the normal arm reach of the worker?			
6. Does the arrangement of the work area allow access to all equipment and job aids without excessive twisting?			
7. Are equipment, documents, writing surfaces, telephones, etc., arranged in the most efficient way?			
8. Is adequate space provided for storage of copies, handbooks, documents, and personal belongings?			
9. Are different heights necessary for different tasks?			
10. Are the heights of all working surfaces correct?			
11. Are working surfaces adjustable in height?			
12. Are surfaces user-adjustable?			
13. Can working surfaces be tilted?			
14. Is the surface thin enough to allow adequate leg space and a correct working height?			
15. Is there adequate legroom so the worker can adopt different postures?			
16. Is the area under the work surface free of obstructions that might interfere with movements between different tasks?			

Figure 10-2 Guidelines for work surfaces.

- Swivel-tilt, which allows freedom of movement so users can respond easily to changes in task requirements
- Easy-to-reach, adjustable controls, including a height adjustment handle on chairs with a pneumatic lift and a tension-control knob
- Adjustable armrests to minimize strain on the forearms and wrists
- Adjustable back support for the upper back

WORK SURFACES

Most work surfaces are 26 to 29 inches high. Since people vary in height, this is not always satisfactory. Most office professionals prefer a work surface located slightly above elbow height. This allows the arms to rest on the surface without leaning forward too far.

VIDEO DISPLAY TERMINALS

Administrative assistants often spend many hours a day looking at video display terminals (VDTs). Prolonged work at the terminal can lead to neck and back problems if both the keyboard and the display are not in the correct position. Most workers prefer the centerline of the screen to be slightly below eye level.

Here are guidelines for working at a VDT:

❑ The VDT should rest on the work surface and preferably not on top of the CPU (i.e., the disk drive).

❑ Source documents should rest flat on the work surface to the right or left of the keyboard or on a document holder parallel to the screen. Viewing distances should range from 24 to 36 inches.

❑ The keyboard should be placed on an adjustable shelf to minimize fatigue. The main table should allow the monitor to be positioned at an angle for easy viewing.

❑ Either lowering the work surface or using attachable keyboard supports will help to lessen strain on the forearms and wrists during keyboarding.

Hint: To increase the functionality of a workstation, an adjustable and rotating monitor mounting arm removes the monitor from the table to free the surface for other uses. It raises the monitor 3 to 5 inches to reduce the viewing angle problem.

Hint: Adjustable VDT tables with two surfaces ensure good posture by allowing the keyboard and screen to be adjusted independently to the appropriate levels.

LIGHTING

Glare and brightness in a work environment, especially where VDTs are used, can cause eye fatigue and hamper employee productivity. Appropriate lighting can reduce if not eliminate most problems. Workers need to have as much control as possible over their individual workstation (lighting) to assure visual and physical comfort. Ways to adjust the lighting within a workstation include (1) the ability to dim overhead lighting and (2) the addition of a desk lamp for lighting for specific tasks.

Indirect, ceiling-mounted or ambient light in combination with adjustable, task-specific lighting works best to help eliminate computer lighting problems. Light levels should serve for all tasks within the office.

Hint: The National Lighting Bureau is a good source of information on lighting issues and working with lighting consultants. This bureau has published a number of guides related to VDTs and lighting systems. The NLB is located at 2101 L Street NW, Suite 300, Washington, DC 20037.

CHECKLIST FOR OFFICE LIGHTING

	YES	NO	NOT APPLICABLE
1. Is the level of illumination proper for hard copy tasks?	____	____	____
2. Is the level of illumination proper for VDT use?	____	____	____
3. Are task lights provided as necessary?	____	____	____
4. Are lights flicker-free?	____	____	____
5. Are lights clean and well maintained?	____	____	____
6. Is the worker's field of view free of sources of glare?	____	____	____
7. Is the worker's field of view free of reflections from display screens, keyboards, desk, papers, etc.?	____	____	____
8. Are windows covered with blinds, drapes, or other means of controlling light?	____	____	____
9. Are lights covered with glare shields?	____	____	____
10. Are panels used to block glare and reflections?	____	____	____
11. Are workstations positioned to avoid glare and reflections?	____	____	____
12. Are VDTs fitted with filters to reduce reflections?	____	____	____
13. Are VDTs equipped with brightness and contrast controls?	____	____	____
14. Can VDTs or tables be tilted to reduce reflections?	____	____	____
15. Are contrasts within the visual field within recommended limits?	____	____	____
16. Are reflectances of walls, floors, and ceilings within recommended limits?	____	____	____

Figure 10-3 Checklist for office lighting.

ORGANIZING THE WORKSTATION ENVIRONMENT

An office space plan shows the organization and placement of workstation components, including work surfaces, filing and storage cabinets, and chairs. Office space plans should meet the psychological and physiological needs of workers. As the users of workstations, office professionals should have some say in such planning.

One's state of mind can directly influence one's efficiency. For example, when a worker perceives his or her office space to be unsatisfactory, poor morale is the result. Personal preferences regarding placement of the telephone, personal computer, and other office tools are also essential.

Hint: Most people do not like to sit with their backs to the hallway nor to have more than one entrance into a workstation.

Environmental disturbances from lighting, noise, and climate (including heat levels and air quality) can cause physiological stress.

PLANNING OFFICE SPACE

Space planning for administrative staff workstations in large companies is usually done by interior designers or facility managers. However, administrative staffs should have some input into the design of their workstations, to help arrange the work space properly to match the tasks. In small offices, administrative assistants may set up their own workstations.

To organize a workstation for maximum task support, begin with a task analysis. This is a process that profiles what people do and maps this onto a physical setting to see how people do it. Demands associated with different activities will fall into common categories. This information aids the planner in determining proper lighting, acoustics, and workspace requirements.

The next step in the design of a workstation space plan is to divide the workstation into work focus zones. These are the locations in the workstation where a specific type of work is done. Office tasks can be put in six basic categories: data entry; information acquisition; information transaction; analysis and problem solving; creative and imaginative thinking; and meeting and conferring. An office space plan should allow space for each type of work that will be done there.

The third step is to plan the arrangement of work resources, equipment, and materials within each zone. Resources should be positioned for ease of equipment operation, with materials easily reached and visual displays comfortably placed for ease of viewing.

MANAGING CABLES

As advances in information technology continue, the changes in today's office equipment continue at a pace faster than most offices can handle. This sometimes requires the rearrangement of office interiors, including reorganization of wiring. Managing the cables is usually left up to the electricians and facilities design managers.

LAN MANAGEMENT

Vital to a successful office is the ability to tie all company information together. In order to achieve that goal, a local area network (LAN) usually needs to be established. A LAN allows people in a department to share information with each other electronically as well as to share common resources such as printers and large hard disks.

LANs are comprised of cables—twisted-pair, coaxial, and fiber optics—connected to controller cards installed at each computer. More recently, wireless LANs have been developed that use radio frequencies or infrared light instead of cables.

WORKSTATION ACCESSORIES

There are many accessories that add to the efficiency of a workstation and that can personalize it. These range from paper management accessories to computer support accessories.

ERGONOMIC QUICKCHECK

TABLE HEIGHT	
• Non-VDT tasks (fixed height)	29"
• Non-VDT tasks (adjustable height)	26–30"
• VDT screen and keyboard same surface (fixed height)	26–27"
• VDT screen and keyboard same surface (adjustable height)	23–30"
UNDERSIDE OF TABLE	
• Minimum height	24"
• Minimum depth:	
• Knee level	16"
• Foot level	26"
• Minimum width	27"
TABLE THICKNESS	1.0–1.5"
TABLE SIZE	
(VDT screen and keyboard on same surface)	36" min (w) x 30" (d)
KEYBOARD SUPPORT SURFACE HEIGHT	
• Fixed height	27" (max)
• Adjustable height	23–30"
KEYBOARD SUPPORT SURFACE ANGLE	
• Fixed slope	0 degrees
• Adjustable slope	0–10 degrees
SCREEN VIEWING ANGLE (line of sight)	
• 0° (to top of screen) and	
• 40° (bottom of screen)	
SCREEN VIEWING DISTANCE	13–28"
REACH DISTANCES	
• Near reach	11.3" radius
	33.5" width*
• Far reach	22.4" radius
	57.2" width*

*Fingertips of left hand to fingertips of right hand when hands in near or far reach position.
   • near reach: distance fingertips can reach when upper arm is relaxed.
   • far reach: distance fingertips can reach when arm is fully extended.

Figure 10-4 Ergonomic quickcheck.

Paper Management Accessories

By aiding the storage and retrieval of paperwork, paper management accessories help to control paper usage within the workstation. Paper management accessories include desk racks with paper holders, as well as vertical and horizontal paper trays and organizers that mount onto wall panels or inside a cabinet. Forms, computer printouts, and reference material can easily be stored in these accessories. Some accessories can be transported to the next workstation. Other accessories include paper holders for computer printer paper and paper catchers for continuous form paper as it moves through the printer.

Computer Accessories

Computer accessories are intended to help users save space, protect data, and increase comfort. Accessories include antiglare filters or screens, monitor arms and swivel bases for adjusting monitors to user comfort, articulating drawers for keyboards, and workstation furniture designed specifically for computers.

Hint: Glare can be reduced and contrast improved with a light background and dark text or graphics.

Additional accessories include copy holders, disk files, switching systems, static mats, computer tool kits, footrests, surge protectors, and security and antitheft devices.

Personal Accessories

The way a workstation is decorated and maintained reflects its user's efficiency, professionalism, taste, and status. Policy on personal accessories varies from company to company and department to department.

Here are guidelines to follow when personalizing the workstation:

❑ Minimize clutter. A work surface that is bare except for the project being worked on and a few stylish accessories conveys an image of control and taste.

❑ Only those items being used should be on the primary work surface. Calculators, business card files, paper clip containers, extra pens and pencils should be put away when not in use.

❑ The "in" box should be well managed. An overflowing "in" box represents its owner's lack of efficiency besides taking up valuable work space. A wall-mounted "in" box is more efficient but it, too, needs to be properly managed.

❑ Keep projects organized. Projects should be neatly labeled and filed out of the way, not kept in a heap on the corner of a work surface.

❑ When selecting art for the workstation, restraint and respect for the corporate culture are paramount.

❑ Fabric panel walls should be kept clear. Mounting things to the fabric panels will keep it from absorbing sound.

❑ Use fabric art on solid walls to improve acoustics.

❏ Accessories that are permanently on the work surface should be chosen for utility and style. An accessory should pass the following test: Does it give its owner pleasure to use it and look at it? Is it in good taste?

Hint: Diplomas and certificates on the wall usually advertise insecurity and lack of taste, except for doctors and lawyers.

PART III

SPECIALIZED OFFICE PROCEDURES

CHAPTER 11

OFFICE MANUALS AND PUBLICATIONS

Successful managers keep their employees informed and involve them in decisions that affect employee welfare. Publications, such as policy and procedures manuals, job description manuals, and company newsletters, can have a positive impact on the employer-employee communication process. Since office professionals have good organizational and formatting skills, they often assume major responsibilities for preparing these documents.

POLICY MANUALS

A **policy manual** incorporates general guidelines governing how a company will operate to accomplish its purposes. These guidelines form the basis for management decision making. Policies may be covered in one manual, and procedures that describe how to do certain activities or tasks may be covered in a separate manual; or they may be combined in one manual. If they are combined, policy statements and procedures must be clearly separated and identified.

Although the board of directors makes the final decisions regarding company policies, top-level managers are responsible for seeing that the policies are written. They may write the policy statements themselves, hire technical writers, or assign the writing to someone else within the company. To lessen the possibility of an employee initiating an unfair treatment action against the company, and to be sure the policies comply with state and federal laws, an attorney may write or review policy statements. Middle management, supervisory, union, and employee input is always necessary and is especially important in the initial and evaluative stages of the process.

PURPOSE

Policy manuals are given to employees to explain the guidelines under which they must function. Employees can check the manual to determine what courses of action are appropriate rather than having to refer all their questions to their supervisors.

Since policy manuals are written documents, all employees will receive the same information. If managers apply the policies uniformly, employees should receive fair and equal consideration. Although new employees undergo an orientation when they begin working, the amount of information they are expected to grasp is often felt to be overwhelming. Therefore, new employees especially appreciate copies of policy manuals.

CONTENT

The amount of information in a policy manual varies with the type and size of the company and with the level of its employees. Exceptions to policies will sometimes occur, so do not try to incorporate every case in one general statement. The following are policy manual topics, divided into two categories, company information and general personnel policies:

Company Information
- Historical summary
- Company goals
- Philosophy and basic beliefs
- Board of director's policies—authority, organization, meeting notification, and conduct
- Conflict of interest—board members, management, employees
- Stockholders—voting rights, responsibilities to them
- Organizational chart
- Departmental responsibilities
- Company organization/subsidiaries/branch offices—location, function
- Commitment to customer service
- Public relations—handling confidential information, information clearance
- Product lines and services
- Building usage/building names—authorization for outside use by groups, selection of building names
- Budget and finance—responsibility, financial reports, distribution of reports
- Company closings/takeovers/mergers
- Political activity
- Ethics
- Commitment to environmental concerns
- Support of community affairs and development

General Personnel Policies
- Affirmative action and equal opportunity position
- Recruitment standards/applications/reference checks
- Personnel files—content, maintenance, access

- Benefits, such as insurance, pension, and savings
- Retirement/vesting
- Vacation allowances
- Company services, such as company store, merchandise reductions, education, childcare, and elder care
- Performance appraisals/promotions/incentives
- Grievance procedures/probation/termination
- Leaves, such as emergency, illness, personal, jury duty, bereavement, maternity and family, and military
- Hours of operation/overtime provisions/outside employment limitations
- Attendance and punctuality—expectations, disciplinary action
- Dress codes
- Holidays
- Payroll provisions, such as pay periods, and exempt or non-exempt status
- Part-time work/student employment/temporary help
- Work-related injuries/insurance/compensation limits
- Drugs/alcohol—prohibited use, testing, disciplinary actions
- Illness in the workplace/life-threatening diseases/confidentiality of medical records/AIDS issue
- Sexual harassment—definition, disciplinary actions
- Safety/building security
- Office furniture and decor
- Copyright protection
- Patents/inventions/trademark usage
- Purchasing—equipment requests, vendor selection, contracts
- Travel—approval, restrictions, ownership of frequent-flier miles
- Mail services/telecommunications/printing—availability, restrictions
- Records retention/destruction guidelines
- Use of off-site equipment or facilities—restrictions, authorization
- Conference attendance/speaking engagements/honorariums
- Civic responsibilities/jury duty/membership in local professional organizations
- Charity/office contributions/office celebrations

If a policy is new or controversial, such as testing for drugs or banning smoking on the premises, a short factual statement justifying the policy is helpful. (An example appears in Figure 11-1.) In such cases, send a cover memorandum to all employees explaining the rationale for the new or changed policy.

All policy changes must have appropriate approval. Do not write or distribute a memorandum concerning a change in policy to employees before that policy change has been cleared by all the necessary parties. Always include an effective date on new or revised policy statements.

The tone of a policy reflects management's attitudes toward employees. Avoid using phrases that sound autocratic or condescending. Use a positive approach when writing policies.

XYZ COMPANY

3000 SERIES   PERSONNEL AND AFFIRMATIVE ACTION

A. Personnel

    3920   Drug-Free Workplace

Congress signed the Drug-Free Workplace Act of 1988 into law on November 18, 1988. XYZ Company receives federal money and is, therefore, subject to the provisions of the Act. In an effort to comply with the Act and to continue to provide employees with a safe, drug-free environment at XYZ Company, the Board of Directors has adopted Board Policy 3920, Drug-Free Workplace.

Employees are prohibited from engaging in the unlawful manufacture, distribution, possession, or use of a controlled substance in any building or on any property under the control and use of XYZ Company. (See Health and Safety Code 11007 for a definition of the term "controlled substance.")

Any violation of this policy by an employee of XYZ Company may result in (1) requiring the employee to participate satisfactorily in an approved drug abuse assistance or drug rehabilitation program; or, (2) carrying out disciplinary action up to and including termination.

Reference: Health and Safety Code 11007
            Drug-Free Workplace Act of 1988

Adopted: July 31, 19--

Figure 11-1 Policy in report form.

Use: All full-time employees are entitled to ten days of sick leave per year.

Do not use: No more than ten days apply toward sick leave per year.

Software that helps create employee manuals is available. The software includes numerous policy topics from which a company selects those that pertain to its operation. The writer then responds to preprogrammed questions about these topic selections. The software includes explanations, pros and cons, and legal requirements for each policy. Based on the answers given and the software's stored information, a policy for a specific company can be written.

FORMAT

The first policy manual produced by a company takes considerable time to develop and compile. Once begun, new policies may be added without rekeying the entire manual. (For a comprehensive discussion on formatting and designing reports, see Chapter 18.) Specific guidelines for organizing the final copy of the policy manual follow:

Check policy manuals from other companies for format possibilities.

Store policy manuals in three-ring binder notebooks. New or revised policies may be inserted or old ones removed as needed.

Begin each policy statement on a separate sheet of paper. A new policy statement should always begin on a right-hand page. Continuation pages may be printed on both sides or on one side only. Since pages in a policy manual may change because of insertions of new policies or increases or decreases in the number of pages in a revised policy, do not number policy manual pages consecutively. Instead, indicate the number of pages devoted to each policy:

3005   Equal Employment (page 2 of 2)

State the name of each policy in a title line. If using a memorandum to inform employees of a new or revised policy, show the exact title of the policy and its number in the subject line of the memo.

3680   Memberships in Local Civic Organizations

SUBJECT: Board Policy 3680—Memberships in Local Civic Organizations

Organize the manual so policies that include similar topics are near each other. Cross-reference those items that pertain to more than one policy:

Leaves: Sickness
Leaves: Emergency
Leaves: Personal
Leaves: Jury (See also Civic Responsibilities)

Use dividers to set apart major categories of policies within the same manual, such as Board of Directors, Management, and Personnel.

Develop a numbering system that uses numbers and letters and allows for expansion.

1000 Series	BOARD OF DIRECTORS
	A. Organization of the Board
	1000 Authority
	1005 Officers
	1010 Meeting dates
	1015 Agendas
	1020 Meetings
	B. Conflict of Interest
	C. Compensation
2000 Series	MANAGEMENT
3000 Series	EMPLOYEES

Use subheadings when policy statements consist of more than one page.

Indicate whether the policy statement is new or whether it is a replacement for a previous policy. Indicate the date the policy becomes effective. At the bottom of each page, use a stamp that lets the reader know how to handle policy statements.

Replacement for Policy <u>3020,</u> dated <u>8/27/87</u>

or

New Policy _____

Effective Date _____ 6/30/92 _____

Include codes, references, or regulation numbers that apply to the policy at the bottom of the last page of the statement. Omit lengthy references to the law within a policy statement.

Reference: Section 703, Title VII of the Civil Rights Act.

Hint: Keep a master list of major policies. Include the names and numbers of the procedures that pertain to each policy. When the policy is changed, check the master list and make the appropriate changes in the procedures.

Prepare a detailed index of the policy manual. Keep it current as new policies or changes are made. Distribute the updated index material with each new policy or policy change.

Use notebooks with attractive cover designs that can be used for more than one year.

EVALUATION

A company may involve personnel other than top management in the process of evaluating policy statements. Office professionals may be asked to review the policies on an individual basis, or they may be asked to review them as members of a committee. The following questions will assist the office professional in providing input into the evaluation process:

❑ Were suggestions and ideas solicited from employees? The more involved the employees are in the process, the more support they will provide when the time comes to implement the policies.

Hint: To simplify this process, provide employees with the names of the policy review committee members and with forms that have the following headings:

Name (Optional):_____

Department (Optional):_____

Policy Number:_____

Policy Title:_____

Suggested Change (Note: Please use a separate form for each suggested change.)

❑ Is the manual attractive? The way material is packaged makes a statement about the importance of the policies as perceived by top management.

❑ Are the policies clearly stated? Is the language direct and simple?

❏ Is the reason for a new or controversial policy explained?

❏ Is it easy to locate the policy by topic? Is the organization of the manual logical?

❏ Are there any omissions in the policy statements? Are there statements that could be misinterpreted?

❏ Is the manual concise? Excessive reading material can be intimidating and employees may therefore ignore it.

❏ Has the manual been checked for proper grammar, punctuation, word usage, capitalization, and word division?

❏ Are the policies up to date? Is there a plan for a periodic revision and review of the policies?

Hint: When employees make suggestions about policy statements, file them in an appropriate subject folder and use them for the next revision or review. Maintain a file for each subject covered in the policy manual.

❏ Is a policy manual distribution list available? For example, some companies may distribute an all-inclusive policy manual to its managers or supervisors only.

Hint: If your department is in charge of distributing manuals or policy statements, assign that responsibility to one person or do it yourself. Prepare a list of employees to whom the manuals must be distributed and have these employees sign their names as they receive their copies. Be sure someone in your office inserts new policies or revisions in the existing manuals.

PROCEDURES MANUALS

Written procedures are necessary for policies to be carried out effectively. A **procedures manual** provides employees with instructions for performing specific activities or tasks. An **employee handbook** is another term to describe this type of manual. Supervisors or the people usually doing the tasks write the procedures.

PURPOSE

Well-written procedures manuals are simple and easy to understand. Even employees who have never performed the tasks or activities before should be able to follow the detailed instructions without difficulty. Since all employees receive the procedures manual, everyone has the same instructions, and therefore tasks should be performed similarly in all departments.

The manuals serve as guides for all employees. Specific written procedures save time since new employees need not ask coworkers or supervisors for assistance if they can refer to their procedures manual. Experienced employees use procedures manuals to remind them how to do tasks or activities that they perform infrequently.

CONTENT

The content depends on the policies established by the board and the type of procedures manual being written. One type of procedures manual may deal only with a specialized topic area, such as a company correspondence manual. Another may involve procedures for one department area, such as the accounting department or the mailroom. Yet another may include general information and procedures that apply to everyone in the organization. Some sample topics for the latter type of manual include the following:

Introductory Information
- Organization chart
- Responsibilities of departments/divisions
- Floor plans/office numbering systems/maps
- Names and telephone numbers or extensions of top management and department heads
- Telephone numbers of division secretaries
- Hours of operation
- Glossary of frequently used words, trademarks, and accepted abbreviations

Personnel Information
- Time cards/paychecks/payroll tax information/payroll data changes
- Vacation requests/holidays
- Leaves—procedures, forms, notification
- Jury duty
- Resignations—timelines, forms, notification
- Tardiness/absenteeism—notification
- Insurance—coverage, forms, claims
- Company library use/recreational facilities
- Education—tuition reimbursement, on-site training
- Physical examinations/substance abuse testing
- Childcare/elder care—applications, costs
- Performance evaluations—probation, procedures, timelines, forms
- Grievances—appeals, procedures, timelines, forms
- Retirement—benefits, pension fund disbursements, forms
- Breaks/lunch—cafeteria privileges, hours, infractions
- Parking/keys/security/passwords/company visitors
- Injuries—reporting procedures, forms
- Relocation—benefits, family provisions

Task-Related Information
- Supplies purchase and control—authorization, forms
- Equipment selection, purchase, repair
- Fax/electronic mail—restrictions, directions
- Software—backup, selection, copyrights

- Computer assistance—on and off premises
- Reprographics—forms, services, approval, copyrighted materials
- Travel—approval, reports, reimbursement, forms
- Records disposal/transfer
- Mail services
- Telephone—coverage, services, protocol
- Meetings—notice, room reservations, catering requests, forms
- File identification or filing systems
- Company vehicles—responsibility, reservations, forms

WRITING PROCEDURES

When the procedures apply to the entire organization, managers and supervisors write the procedures for their particular areas of responsibility. When the procedures are task related, office managers, supervisors, or their designees write the procedures. When the procedures concern office tasks, the designees are often office professionals. They perform the tasks and have the most knowledge about the steps involved.

Writing clear procedures requires logical thinking and attention to detail. The following suggestions will assist in writing procedures.

Clarify the reasons a procedure is necessary by answering these questions before beginning to write:

- Who will perform the task? For example, procedures for new employees require more detail than those written for the experienced workers.
- What is the purpose of this procedure? Why is it done *this* way?
- What equipment and supplies are required?
- With what work area or areas is this task associated? Who is involved in the activity?
- What is the first step? The next?

Examine the current company procedures manual. Prepare a list of changes or recommendations made since the last revision. If preparing a manual for the first time, review other company manuals to determine how these organizations write or format procedures.

Request assistance from coworkers. For example, if you are writing a procedure for handling petty cash, ask the person who performs the task to list the steps in consecutive order.

Hint: Before describing how to do a task, watch it being done. Use a tape recorder to record notes while the person is working.

Include only the information needed to complete the tasks. Excessive explanatory material slows a worker's progress in completing a task. Note, however, that although a subtask may seem obvious to someone who does it regularly, a new worker will not necessarily know that each step is necessary.

Divide the task into its logical parts. For example, a procedure might be necessary to clarify changes in reprographic services. In this case, a logical breakdown is to write instructions for using the convenience copier, the centralized printing center, or off-premise commercial services. Use subheadings and list the procedures by service area.

Select a numbering system and use it consistently throughout the procedures manual. One example of a numbering system for a section of a procedures manual follows:

36. Travel
    F. . . .
    G. Company Automobiles
       1. Approvals and authorizations for use
       2. Timelines
       3. Reservation procedures
       4. Accident reporting
       5. Automobile care and maintenance
       6. Forms (attached)
    H. . . .

This example identifies "Travel" as a section heading. Within that section, one subheading is "Company Automobiles." Under that subheading are suggested paragraph headings involving procedures for requesting the use of a company automobile.

Identify who is to do the task. Divide the procedure into two parts: *Who Performs the Activity* and *Action.* Another format identifies who is to perform the task and then lists responsibilities below.

Use short imperative sentences rather than lengthy narrative ones.

Use: Obtain Form No. 942, Educational Benefits Approval, from the secretary to the assistant personnel director in the Human Resources office.

Do not use: Educational leave is available to employees and may be applied for by obtaining Form No. 942, Educational Benefits Approval, from the secretary to the assistant personnel director in the Human Resources office.

Use a job title, as in the above example, rather than the name of the individual, since an individual may change his or her position. Be consistent when using titles. For example, do not refer to the division secretary in one step and to the same person as an assistant to the division manager in a later step.

Consider the background of the employees who will be using the procedures. Define all the technical terms used in a procedure.

Indicate the meaning of an abbreviation the first time it is used, such as Purchase Requisition (PR). Place the abbreviation in parentheses. The abbreviated form is then acceptable in the remaining steps of the procedure.

Present only one step at a time. Number each step in chronological order as it should occur.

Do not begin an instruction on one page and continue it on the next page. Complete the entire instruction on one page.

Use graphs, flow charts, and equipment diagrams when applicable. Use caution with photographs. In the reproduction process, photographs may become fuzzy, causing a loss of detail that may make the photographs less useful.

Provide samples of the forms required to do a task. Use code letters or numbers to designate the information that is placed on each line. Here is an example of a portion of a reprographic work order that illustrates the use of code letters to refer to instructions.

No. of Copies:____G__

Account to be Charged:____H__

The letters G and H refer to codes listed on a separate sheet. For example:

(G) Indicate a number 1–20. (The maximum number of copies allowed is 20.)

(H) Use the three-digit account number assigned to the project. (Your supervisor has the number.)

Identify *very* clearly any warnings for dangerous jobs or precautions about possible problems. Write the warnings in all necessary languages. Place the warnings at the beginning of the instructions and repeat them if they are part of one of the procedural steps. In order to draw attention to the warning, highlight it, place it in bold type, or capitalize it.

Hint: If language appears to be a barrier to understanding any activity, write the *entire procedure* in the languages needed.

Have an employee who is unfamiliar with the procedure try to do it by reading the manual. Rewrite and clarify if necessary.

Summarize the steps at the end of each procedure. Since experienced workers may forget how to do a step, a summary can be helpful so as to avoid starting at the beginning and reading each step to locate the problem.

Indicate the status of the procedure—new or revised. (See information on format under Policy Manuals section above.)

Refer the user to additional manuals, such as special forms manuals or correspondence manuals, to complete a task.

Identify the policy or government regulation that pertains to the procedure. When the policy or law changes, procedures are likely to change also. More than one procedure may be affected. The policy or regulation identification on *all* the affected procedures makes it less likely that a procedure will be missed in the revision process. Here is an example of a reference line with a code number and also a policy number:

Reference: California Education Code 72292
                   Governing Board Policy 3110

Proofread procedures for punctuation, capitalization, grammatical accuracy, and spelling.
Include cross references when needed to clarify the procedures.
Avoid sexist language. Use "his or her" or the plural form "their."

Select a title for the procedure carefully. The most effective titles are brief yet clear. For example, "Educational Benefits Process" is not a clear title; a more definitive title is "Educational Tuition Reimbursement—Applications."

FORMAT

The memo and the report are the two most common formats used to announce a revision in a procedure or a new procedure. A memo is more appropriate for short procedures. The memo should include a statement explaining the purpose of the procedure and why it must be followed; then the instructions follow. (A sample appears in Figure 11-2.) Employees should also be asked to add the document to their procedures manuals.

A report is usually divided into two sections—the heading (which includes background information) and the instructions. The report form is used when the procedure is lengthy. A sample of a portion of a procedure written in report form appears in Figure 11-3. A cover sheet is attached to a procedure written in report form. An accompanying memo usually reminds employees to remove the old procedure and add the new one in its place or to insert the new procedure.

The following suggestions apply to both formats unless noted otherwise. (For a comprehensive discussion on formatting and designing reports, see Chapter 18.)

Use a looseleaf binder for procedures. Use $8\frac{1}{2}$-by-11-inch paper. Looseleaf binders offer the greatest flexibility since new pages can be inserted easily. These binders are easy to use, since they open flat and are easy to store upright on a desk.

If procedures change frequently, try to get them placed on-line so employees can access them via the computer.

If the procedures are used regularly in areas where dust and dirt accumulate, consider laminating the materials or placing them in plastic sheet holders.

Use a type font that is large enough to be read easily; for example, 10 point or larger. In some areas where machines are used, the procedures may be posted at a distance and therefore require large type. (See Chapter 19 for more information.)

Position the visual aids so they are close to the related text. Label the visual aids consistently throughout the document; for example, "Figure 7: Completed Expense Report." A visual aid is effective only if it adds to the written material and if each part is clearly labeled. If the part is not referred to in the text, do not label it in the diagram. If a diagram is reduced in the duplication process, be sure its label remains readable.

Use a list format. Indent the steps from any narrative that precedes them. The visual effect emphasizes organization and helps the reader follow instructions easily.

Identify the summary steps by indenting the abbreviated steps or by placing a box around the summary.

Prepare a detailed table of contents and index when organizing the procedures.

Identify pages as follows: "Page 2 of 4 pages."

Display any forms as originals or in a reduced format and place the instructions for completing the forms on separate pages. Place the forms on the left and the instructions on the right to facilitate their use.

TO: Telephone Users
FROM: Sandra Orlando
SUBJECT: Telephone-Long-Distance Access
DATE: May 21, 19--

The following procedures are necessary to access your Extended Class of Service (ECOS) for long-distance telephone calls. Using this procedure will make long-distance access more expedient for you and will provide prompt service to our customers.

1. Obtain your Extended Class of Service (ECOS) account code from your immediate supervisor. Retain the code in a location that will not be readily available to other employees.

2. Pick up the telephone headset and dial the desired outside number.

   a. If the number dialed is within your Basic Class of Service (BCOS), your call will go through.

   b. If the number dialed is outside your BCOS, you will hear a feature set tone (the tone you hear when you use the #7 call forward).

3. Enter your 6-digit account code to gain access to your ECOS area at the sound of the feature set tone. If your call is within your ECOS, your call will be processed.

4. Maintain a record of long-distance calls on the form attached. Your call will be logged based on your ECOS account code, not on the extension number of the telephone used.

5. Contact your supervisor if you have questions on the use of this service.

The effective date for these procedures is May 28, 1992.

jmm
Attachment

Figure 11-2 Procedure in memo format.

JOB DESCRIPTION MANUALS

A **job description manual** is a compilation of specific jobs within a company that describes the jobs and lists their duties and requirements. The Human Resources Department is usually responsible for preparing and maintaining the manual; however, input is necessary from those who perform the jobs and from their supervisors.

XYZ COMPANY

Reference:	Board Policy 3920
	Drug-Free Workplace
Effective Date:	April 20, 19--
Previous Revision:	NA
Procedure:	Drug Abuse Violations
Distribution:	Department Managers

DRUG ABUSE VIOLATIONS (page 1 of 2 pages)

PURPOSE

XYZ Company is committed to providing a drug-free workplace for its
employees. To ensure this commitment, department managers need to be
aware of employees exhibiting behaviors that may be drug-related and
follow these procedures.

DEPARTMENT MANAGERS

1. Contact the Director of Human Resources immediately if an
    employee is suspected of drug dependency. Document your
    concerns and outline a plan of action.

2. Confront the employee displaying behaviors of being under the
    influence of drugs. (See Attachment A for a list of behavioral clues.)
    Determine whether the employee is at risk to self or other
    employees.

3. Release an employee who is at risk or who is unable to complete the
    remainder of his or her assigned activities for the remainder of the
    day or shift. Arrange for transportation to the employee's home.
    a. Ask the employee to contact a friend or family member to drive
        him or her home.
    b. Drive the employee home yourself.
    c. Request taxi service to take the employee home. Complete a taxi
        voucher form and submit it to Accounting. (Attachment A.)

4. Complete the following steps if the employee denies being under the
    influence of drugs.
    a. Request that the employee voluntarily agree to a drug screen.
        Obtain a signed Employee Voluntary Consent Form.
        (Attachment B.)
    b. Contact the Company physician to order the required test.
    c. Place employee on administrative leave until the review is
        complete.

Figure 11-3 Procedure in report format.

PURPOSE

Job descriptions provide management with information that is helpful in hiring, placing, and promoting personnel or useful in restructuring or eliminating positions. Supervisors use job descriptions when they evaluate employees' work. Ideally, they should compare actual work performance to the specifications listed in the job description. In large companies, Human Resource personnel do the initial screening and rely heavily on job descriptions. Screening applicants is easier if the job descriptions are clear and identify specific requirements for specific areas. Companies are very aware of discrimination charges and other legal conse-quences that can result from hiring or termination decisions. Well-written job descriptions communicated to employees can assist in the defense of these decisions.

Employees use job descriptions to inform them of their responsibilities and to plan for promotions or determine career paths. They also find them helpful when requesting salary increases or job reclassifications.

CONTENT

Job descriptions from other companies may be good models for determining format and content for your manual. Other information sources include interviews with workers and supervisors, observations by Human Resource personnel, or formal job analyses by outside consultants. The best information sources are the people who do the jobs.

Two ways to facilitate the collection of information from employees are (1) question-naires and (2) task diaries completed during a specified period of time. The advantage of the questionnaire is the inclusion of the same questions for all employees, which makes data categorization and interpretation easier. As office professionals perform new tasks or assume responsibilities for additional activities, they should include these on their job descriptions. This information is useful for performance appraisals as well as for writing or revising job descriptions.

Job descriptions should include the following information:

General information, such as name, department, job title, classification, work area location, and supervisor's title. Job titles are important since they lend prestige to positions and are used to compare jobs with similar titles. Assign a title that is definitive; for example, "payroll benefits clerk" rather than "accounting clerk."

Hint: The *Dictionary of Occupational Titles* is one source of job titles. The publica-tion and periodic supplements are available at most libraries or from the U.S. Depart-ment of Labor, Employment and Training Administration, 200 Constitution Avenue NW, Washington, DC 20001. The *Career Information Center* (CIC) publications include definitions of jobs, and also cover work characteristics, education and training requirements, and earnings and benefits. The CIC is available from Glencoe Publish-ing Company, 15319 Chatsworth Street, Mission Hills, CA 91345.

Salary structure information, such as salary range, regular and overtime hours, full- or part-time status, and exemption status. An *exempt* status means that some positions are not subject to certain provisions of the Fair Labor Standards Act (FLSA); for example, overtime and minimum wage. Managerial and professional positions often fall into this category. Employees paid by the hour are not exempt from the overtime payment and minimum wage requirements of the FLSA.

Job overview. The overview is a brief summary of the job. Using one description for "similar" jobs can be misleading; therefore, some companies prepare a job description for each position in the company. For example, an overview of an entry level sales division clerk position might be "provides data entry support for the Software Sales Division. Communicates with customers and sales personnel."

Duties. Duties are those which the job now entails. Do not list duties that have been changed or eliminated. Identify duties by the frequency with which they are done—daily or monthly—and in order of their importance.

> **Hint:** When describing duties, use action verbs such as those listed in the section *Work Experience* in Chapter 2. Describe duties rather than specific tasks; for example, "organizes monthly conference meetings" rather than "prepares monthly agendas" or "sends out notices of meetings."

Supervisory responsibilities, such as number of employees supervised and the type of supervision provided.

Intercompany contacts; for example, daily contact with a specific department or with customers.

Working environment; for example, size of office; single workstation or multiple workstations; job safety; travel requirements; physical requirements; type or level of pressure, such as the requirements of high production quotas.

Education required for the position; for example, high school, four-year degree, special licenses, and certification, such as CPS.

Experience and skills required for the position. Job standards require careful analysis and identification and must comply with the Equal Opportunity Act. Do not include standards that are unrelated to job duties.

Date of job description.

> **Hint:** Job descriptions require reviews. Rather than updating a job description when it is needed for a job announcement, establish a timeline for periodic evaluations of all job descriptions, such as once a year.

One side of the job description sheet includes the general information, summary, and duties; the reverse side outlines the job qualifications and specifications. Follow a similar format for all job descriptions. (A sample job description appears in Figure 11-4.)

Position title: Administrative secretary
Division: Sales and Marketing
Department: Marketing Research
Reports to: Department manager
Salary status: Exempt

JOB SUMMARY:
The executive secretary, under the general supervision of the
department manager, performs routine secretarial duties as well
as a variety of tasks that require planning and organization to
meet deadlines and quality standards. The position requires
interpersonal skills necessary to coordinate the work flow among
the six to eight office support staff members in the department.

DUTIES AND RESPONSIBILITIES:
• Composes routine correspondence
• Opens, routes, sorts, and prioritizes the department manager's
  mail
• Maintains the department manager's calendar
• Responds to mail and telephone inquiries or to surveys from
  other agencies
• Gathers information and prepares sales reports
• Maintains confidential files
• Prioritizes departmental work
• Delegates tasks to office staff
• Exercises supervision over department office support staff
• Edits product releases and brochures to maintain consistency
  in format and content
• Schedules conference and exhibit assignments on the computer
  calendar for department staff members
• Makes all travel arrangements for staff
• Prepares materials for department meetings and maintains
  file for agenda items
• Prepares press releases
• Recommends staff procedure changes
• Collects, compiles, and delivers office payroll time sheets to
  Personnel

Figure 11-4 Job description.

Job Description
Administrative secretary
Page 2 of 2 pages

QUALIFICATIONS:
A.A. degree
Five years' support staff experience
Advanced English usage, spelling, punctuation, and business
    vocabulary skills
Decision-making and management skills
Operating skill on the computer
Operational skills on basic office equipment
Written and oral communication skills
Interpersonal and problem-solving skills
Report-writing skills
Knowledge of advanced public relations procedures
Keyboarding skill of 70 words a minute
Ability to organize, schedule, and follow instructions
Ability to maintain confidential or sensitive information

PHYSICAL DEMANDS AND WORKING CONDITIONS:
Positions are primarily sedentary.
Worker may be required to attend off-premises meetings or
    conferences.

LICENSE REQUIRED:
Possession of a valid and appropriate driver's license

CAREER LADDER:
Executive assistant
Confidential administrative assistant

Approved: Richard Bennett
Date of Approval: August 21, 19--
D.O.T. Reference: NA

Figure 11-4 *(cont'd)*

WORKSTATION MANUALS

A **workstation manual** or **desk manual** provides a source of information unique to a specific position. The employee at the workstation prepares the information. The manual does not circulate throughout the company and is not an official company publication.

PURPOSE

The workstation manual serves as a guide for a temporary worker substituting for an absent employee or as an introduction for a new employee. Referring to the manual when questions arise will save time and create less tension in the office. In addition, the manual provides the supervisor with an overview of the many tasks that are performed at a particular workstation.

CONTENT

Some information in a workstation manual may also be included in a company-procedures or special-topics manual. It is, however, necessary to make a precise cross reference to the original source. The following items are recommended when compiling a workstation manual.

Overview of the position.
Organization chart.
Products/subsidiaries.
Location of personnel/telephone numbers:
- Immediate supervisor
- Supervisor's superior
- Supervisors for whom work is performed
- VIPs within the department or organization
- VIPs outside the organization, such as customers, clients, suppliers, and lawyers
- Key personnel responsible for specific areas
- Office personnel to contact for assistance
- Frequently called numbers
- Distribution lists including names of people who receive copies of the typical documents produced in your office

Tasks to be completed daily with recommended timelines. To identify typical daily tasks, refer to your time management logs. (See Chapter 3.) Indicate whether the tasks are typically completed in the morning or in the afternoon.

Tasks completed periodically; for example, the weekly submission of time sheet hours or the monthly replenishment of petty cash.

Current committees/projects in progress:
- Chairpersons
- Meeting dates

- Responsibilities/special procedures
- Timelines

Telephone etiquette:
- Standard office greeting/number of rings allowed before answering
- Long-distance call procedures and charges
- VIP calls—those which the supervisor always takes
- Transfer procedures
- Outside call procedures
- Message taking and distribution procedures
- Screening preferences
- Paging and forwarding procedures
- Personal use of office telephone
- Responses to frequently asked questions

Hint: A quick reference outline is helpful in explaining how the telephone system works, for example, how to transfer or forward a call. Keep it simple so information can be quickly obtained.

Mail handling:
- Times of delivery and collection
- Incoming mail/mail register
- Distribution responsibilities/items to route
- Outgoing mail including cablegrams, Telex, and Mailgram procedures
- Overnight/courier services
- Network protocol/fax/electronic mail

Filing:
- System explanation
- Coding procedures
- File label preparation
- Charge-out procedures
- Tickler file maintenance
- Shredding or disposal procedures
- Confidential information

Hint: If files are in a locked drawer or cabinet, identify the people who have access to specific files. Keep the list of people up to date.

Correspondence:
- Formats
- Special terminology, trademarks, and abbreviations
- Signatures required
- Stationery and envelopes
- Copies—number and distribution
- Form letters

Hint: Sample formats of letters, memos, reports, and envelopes are helpful. Identify margin settings and other special notations, such as attention, subject, distribution, and attachment lines.

Forms:
- Purpose
- Samples
- Location
- Required copies/distribution
- Approval/required signatures

Hint: A completed form is more helpful than a blank form. Identify the source of information for completing each form. If calculations are necessary, give instructions to show how to obtain the figures.

Supplies:
- Location
- Requisition procedures

Travel:
- Travel requests
- Travel preferences of supervisor
- Travel agents
- Itineraries
- Ticket pickup
- Mileage reimbursement
- Expense reports

Equipment repair:
- Reporting procedures/forms
- Telephone numbers

Computers:
- Operating procedures
- Assistance/hotline numbers
- Security
- Log-on instructions

Software:
- Types
- Access codes
- File naming procedures
- File location
- Precautions/security

Reprographics:
- In-company services/location
- Copy limitations/chargebacks

- Request forms/rush requests
- Repair service
- Overhead transparencies/special requests
- Publication and copyright guidelines

Visitors:
- Frequent visitors—names and positions
- VIP visitors (those whom the supervisor will always see)
- Security procedures

Meetings:
- Minutes/agendas
- Scheduling procedures
- Room/food requests

Bank deposits/reconciliations.
Timecards.
Petty cash.
Special reference materials.
Breaks/lunch.
Parking/office keys/security.
Dress/office appearance.
General precautions.
Efficiency hints.
Employer information:
- Professional memberships—meeting dates and dues
- Anniversaries/birthdays
- Family—names and telephone numbers
- Social security, passport, and credit card numbers

WRITING PROCEDURES

A workstation manual requires attention to detail and constant review. The following procedures will assist in organizing the manual.

Make a list of all the tasks performed and responsibilities involved with the position before beginning to write. Include information on material locations as well as hints or precautions. Individual index cards work well. Sort the cards and place them in categories; for example, place all telephone-related tasks together.

Obtain input from your supervisor. Prepare a copy of the manual for his or her desk.

Use cross references. For example, a specific task may require the shredding of all draft copies. Rather than describing the shredding procedure each time it is needed, direct the user to the one section where it is described in detail.

Compile the materials into a three-ring looseleaf notebook. Arrange the material by subjects. Use dividers to separate the sections. Number pages consecutively.

Store the instructions on a separate disk or create a training directory on the hard disk. A new employee will then have access to up-to-date instructions.

Hint: A temporary agency may help its employees by preparing disks of workstation instructions for those companies who are its major clients. Temporary workers could then become familiar with procedures *before* beginning a job.

Prepare a detailed table of contents.

Obtain input from the people who use the manual. Include a "comments" sheet at the front of the manual for this purpose. Consider these comments when making revisions.

Review the tasks periodically, and note any changes in the margins of the manual. This eliminates preparing new sheets each time a change occurs, yet it keeps the manual up to date. Prepare new inserts as needed.

INSTRUCTION MANUALS

A new piece of equipment or a software package usually comes with an **instruction manual** or an **owner's guide.** A **quick reference guide,** which is a shorter version of the instruction manual, may also be available.

Department supervisors should keep at least one copy of all instruction manuals in a centralized location. Each user should have access to the instruction manuals.

PURPOSE

Instruction manuals explain how to use specific products. They can also answer repair questions. Checking the manual before calling the repair center can save time and expense. When you call a hotline number for assistance, the person who responds to your question may refer you to a section in the instruction manual for future reference. Instruction manuals are also useful in training sessions and often serve as the textbooks.

CONTENT

Instruction manuals vary in format, size, and style, but they all include similar topics, such as the following:

- Disclaimer notices
- Warranty and liability statements
- Copyright protection
- Table of contents
- Unpacking/setup procedures
- Installation procedures
- Equipment diagram and list of parts
- Care and handling of equipment
- Getting started
- Standard operating procedures
- Precautions
- Advanced operations
- Glossary

- Appendices
- Troubleshooting pointers
- Warranty registration
- Site-license agreement

EVALUATION

Well-written instruction manuals can be helpful in learning how to operate new equipment or software, whereas poorly written manuals cause frustration and wasted time. The following questions can help to determine the potential effectiveness of an instruction manual:

❏ Is the language simple and clear?

Hint: Before a salesperson leaves the demonstration, ask to see a copy of the manual. Work through the steps of the first several procedures. Omissions or difficulties in following the first few procedures are signs of a faulty manual.

❏ Are terms explained?
❏ Is the material written logically? Is it arranged from the simplest to the most complex tasks? Is it direct or is there excess information that causes confusion?
❏ Is it readable? Are the steps in a procedure numbered? If not, are there lead-in statements such as "To make a copy of a volume, choose option B"? Are there sufficient headings and subheadings to divide topics? Are the paragraphs short?
❏ Do diagrams accompany instructions? Showing what happens *after* an instruction has been followed is helpful.
❏ Is there an index and is it easy to use?

Hint: To test its thoroughness, select several items and see if the pages provide the necessary information.

❏ Is there a hotline number that can be called for information?
❏ Does it permit a beginner to get started with the main task and learn others as needed?
❏ Is a quick reference guide available? Is each procedure summarized for easy reference or review?
❏ Is the manual well bound so that it will not fall apart with use? Is it a convenient size?
❏ Does it have a section listing error codes? Are cautions already identified? Are there procedures for making corrections?
❏ Are care and handling instructions clear?
❏ Are peripheral devices and limitations identified?
❏ Are there appendices for extra information that is not found in the instructions?

REFERENCE MANUALS

A **reference manual** is a source for checking specific information. Examples of reference manuals include dictionaries, atlases, office manuals, directories, and thesauruses. Since office professionals refer to these reference manuals frequently, they should be kept within easy reach. Computerized versions of such reference sources as dictionaries and thesauruses may also be accessible as separate software packages or as integral parts of word processing programs. Databases with directory information are also available.

DICTIONARIES

Standard unabridged dictionaries and abridged dictionaries are indispensable for spelling, definitions, word division, and pronunciation. In addition, some dictionaries include foreign words and phrases, grammar rules, abbreviations, forms of address, directories of colleges and universities, weights and measures, metrics, signs and symbols, and common English names. Unabridged dictionaries can include twice as many words as the standard abridged dictionary. Specialized dictionaries are available for such areas as law, medicine, accounting, insurance, electronics, and education.

THESAURUSES

A thesaurus can be helpful in writing or editing documents. It provides alternatives for words that are used frequently. Instead of repeating the same word in a sentence, a synonym can be selected from the thesaurus.

> **Hint:** Dictionaries and thesauruses should be up to date. Check for new editions in *Books in Print*, which is available at most libraries. Recommend new editions when these references become five to seven years old.

ATLASES

An atlas provides geographical information in the form of maps (often in color), with names of large cities and capitals. It also presents information on climate, air routes, the solar system, and the economy, in addition to census data and other statistical and demographic information. An atlas is useful in making travel arrangements, setting up geographic files, checking world locations, verifying spellings, and determining mileage.

DIRECTORIES

Directories contain names, addresses, and special data about people or businesses. Types of directories include telephone directories, toll-free number directories, ZIP Code directories, and city directories, as well as various types of professional membership directories.

Telephone directories of large cities are on file in libraries or central telephone offices. Companies can also rent telephone directories that include addresses from telephone companies.

The *National Five Digit ZIP Code and Post Office Directory* is a valuable reference source for checking the accuracy of ZIP Codes on outgoing mail. The directory is arranged by geographic location. A copy may be purchased at the counter in your main post office, or you may contact the U.S. Postal Service.

City directories list names, addresses, and occupations of the residents in a city or area. They may also contain a list of businesses and their officials or owners. Private companies collect the information and publish the directories.

Polk's Directory lists entries by specific city. Entries may be accessed by the entrant's name, address, telephone number, and place of work. You may obtain copies by writing to Polk's, 7168 Envoy Court, Dallas, TX 75241. Haines and Company publishes *Haines Criss-Cross Directory*, which covers an area rather than a specific city. Copies can be ordered from Haines at 8050 Freedom Avenue NW, North Canton, OH 44720. Check with your local public library for additional information.

To locate a particular directory in print, check the local library for the *Guide to American Directories*, which describes the many trade and professional directories published in the United States, or the *Directory of Directories*, which identifies business directories by country, state, and region, as well as by the type of business or the products available.

Computerized reference services are valuable sources of information. Your public library is an excellent place for locating such sources. *The Directory of On-Line Databases* from Cuadra Associates in Los Angeles or *Computer Readable Databases* from Gale Research in Detroit give the names of thousands of accessible databases available on-line throughout the world.

OFFICE REFERENCE MANUALS

An **office reference manual** is an indispensable source of information for office workers. This type of manual offers suggestions and information on a variety of office topics. The use of one office reference manual throughout the organization is more efficient than having separate manuals for each department. In a recent Professional Secretaries International® (PSI®) research study on reference materials, 52 percent of those surveyed indicated they made the recommendations about which office reference manual to purchase.

An appropriate selection of a reference manual requires research and input from the prospective users. Once input has been obtained, recommend that a committee of office professionals use this information to make the final selection.

If all office professionals use the same office reference manual, they should have the opportunity to attend training sessions regarding the contents and the effective use of these manuals. Recommend that a group of office professionals be responsible for presenting information on the reference manuals at all orientation sessions for new employees.

OTHER REFERENCE MATERIALS

Other useful references include books of quotations, etiquette guides, and parliamentary procedure manuals. For matters of editing and printing style, consult *The Chicago Manual of Style* (University of Chicago Press, 1982) and the U.S. Government Printing Office's *Style Manual* (1986).

SPECIALIZED LIBRARIES

Some companies establish their own specialized libraries. These libraries are usually private and available to company employees. Although some specialized libraries may be limited to a few major subject areas, their specific holdings are comprehensive and current. Access to a specialized library that does not contain classified or confidential information may be possible for people who are not company employees or members of an association. An explanation that outlines the need for the specialized information (preferably in writing) should be prepared before requesting access to any special collection.

Several reference indexes are available to assist in locating special library information. *The Directory of Special Libraries and Information Centers* provides addresses, telephone numbers, and the titles of those in charge of special libraries, archives, research libraries, and information centers. Another directory, *New Special Libraries,* provides regular updates to this directory.

COMPANY NEWSLETTERS

Company newsletters provide businesses with opportunities to communicate with employees (referred to as internal newsletters), or with vendors and current or potential customers (referred to as external newsletters). Management determines the purposes of the newsletters and approves their final publication. The emphasis in this chapter is on internal newsletters.

Because of their organizational skills and their knowledge of word processing or desktop publishing, office professionals assume a major role in producing internal newsletters. They may have responsibility for collecting the information, editing the material, writing an article, or printing and distributing the final copy.

A newsletter may be designed specifically for office professionals. Include such items as practical suggestions and timesavers, product information, course suggestions, grammar tips, and sources for information. This type of newsletter also provides an excellent means for promoting membership in professional organizations.

CONTENT

Determining newsletter content requires a clear understanding of management's goals in publishing the newsletter and the number of issues to be published. For example, is the immediate goal to introduce new ideas? to boost morale? to communicate management's activities? to make announcements? to provide information? to feature individuals in personal or work activities? Is one general issue published monthly or is this a weekly bulletin? Knowledge of these goals not only clarifies the content but also determines the order of the articles in the newsletter.

Examples of content ideas and possible headlines for newsletters include:

Messages from management.
Example: "A Message from the President" or "Straight from the Top."

Company sales/production quotas.
Example: "XYZ Company Reports Increased Sales for 4th Quarter."

Forecast reports.
Example: "A New Year: What Does It Hold for XYZ Company?"

New products/services.
Example: "XYZ Company Receives Recognition by Chamber of Commerce."

Research.

Company financial information.

Policy changes and explanations.

Current legislation or news items that impact the company.
Example: "Water Conservation—Our Responsibility."

General company information.
Example: "Your Financial Future/New Savings Plan for XYZ Employees."

Department/division features.
Example: "How Do I Talk to My Supervisor?"

New technology.

Local companies.
Example: "Have You Met the Next-Door Company?"

Personnel moves.
Example: "Roberts Named Sales Operations Manager" or "Donaldson Promoted."

Hint: Rather than simply featuring an employee who has moved along a career ladder, go a step beyond and include advice from the individual. For example, "Roberts, XYZ's New Sales Manager, Gives 12 Tips for Getting Customers."

New personnel.
Example: "How New Employees Learn the Job."

Education/training.
Example: "Check Out These New Courses."
___✔___WordPerfect, Intermediate
___✔___Report Writing

Employees' work-related achievements/team accomplishments.
Example: "We Do It Best as a Team" or "The Suggestion That Worked."

Presentations made by employees.
Example: "Peters Addresses Professional Secretaries International®."

Health information.
Example: "Dealing with Alcohol Abuse."

Safety reminders.
Example: "Take Time to Check for Safety."

Cautions.
Example: "A Note of Caution/Machines Need Routine Care."

Cost-saving reminders.
Example: "When Are Courier Services Really Necessary?"

Task-related information.
Example: "Advice from an Office Temp."

Ethics issues.

Feature articles on employees.
Example: "Inside XYZ Company" or "Profile/A Closer Look."

Hint: It is often difficult to become acquainted with coworkers. Distribute a form for employees to complete (voluntary) and include one or more "features" in each issue.

Calendar of events/activities within the company.

Surveys/suggestions.
Example: "What Employees Need at XYZ Company."

Hint: Once a survey has been taken, always report the results. Follow-up articles are also interesting; for example, the above survey can be followed with an article on how XYZ Company is meeting these needs.

Employees' personal achievements/awards.
Example: "On Our Own Time."

Attendance/longevity records.

Tours, community events, volunteers.

Announcements—births/deaths/retirements.

Recreational activities/scores.

Request for newsletter items.

Hint: The content must represent the company's needs. Get ideas from as many employees at all levels as possible. Include a form each time the newsletter is published that makes it easy for employees to respond.

EDITING/WRITING NEWSLETTERS

The editing task is less demanding if writers are carefully selected or if one person does the writing. Rewriting poor copy is often more difficult than writing the original copy. Rewriting can also cause friction with the author and may change the original intent of the article. Several suggestions for writing and/or editing articles follow.

Answer the basic reporting questions—who, where, when, what, why, and how—in the first paragraph. Articles must be informative and creative and yet practical for the readers. Write a headline that highlights the action in the first paragraph; for example, "Dayton

Corporation Sponsors $3000 Scholarship." Use secondary headlines in smaller type.

Rank information in a story. After the lead sentence, which is the attention getter, continue to write the material as you have ranked it. If space runs out, you still have the most important parts of the story included.

Establish a timeline and monitor it regularly. Include articles that are timely. Past events should not be written about as if they are still occurring. The calendar of events must be up to date and should not include dates of events that have already passed.

> **Hint:** New programs may create interest and appear timely. But do not include them unless their progress can be described. An announcement of a program in the planning stages can be premature and can confuse readers.

Eliminate statements that are not relevant to the major point of the article. Information in the articles should not be repeated.

Use the language of the audience for whom the newsletter is written.

Write short paragraphs to maintain interest. Use one new idea in each paragraph. Subheadings and captions are effective. Keep the sentences short.

Distinguish opinions from facts. If it is an opinion, state this in the article. Avoid superlatives or judgmental statements.

Avoid using customer or vendor names unless you have authorization to do so. Some companies may interpret the use of their names as product endorsements.

Place regularly occurring material in the same location each time the newsletter is printed. Use the same heading for the column. For example, the "Calendar of Events" may be boxed on the lower left corner of the last page of each issue.

Indicate the approximate number of words an article should have when you ask others to write. Request that the articles be double-spaced, have headlines, subheadings, and captions, and include photographs or illustrations if applicable.

Request vertical black and white glossy photographs. They are easier to use in columns where space is limited. If using two photographs on the same page, vary the sizes.

> **Hint:** A company may obtain permission to use photographs of its employees at the time employees are hired. Check with the Human Resources Department to be sure proper procedures for photo releases are followed.

Consult with the author of an article before making extensive editorial changes. If writing the article, check the accuracy of all facts. Get written permission before writing about a person and a sign-off acceptance signature after it is written or after it has been changed extensively.

Proofread carefully. Use a reference manual and dictionary. If interviewing, check spellings and details before leaving the interview. It is especially important to check the spellings of names and products.

Put the date, volume, and number on the front of each issue of the newsletter.

Include the name, address, and telephone and fax numbers of the company as well as the name of the editor. Include the dates of publication. Box the information on the first or last page.

Example:

Published biweekly for present and retired XYZ Company employees.
For additional information, contact the editor, (Name).

AMC
1220 Becker Road
Eau Galle, FL 32611
Telephone (407) 296-5433
Fax (407) 756-6586

CHAPTER 12

RECORDS MANAGEMENT

Predictions were made in the early 1980s that increased use of computers would mean less paper in offices. What has actually occurred, however, is the exact opposite: paper use has grown. Each day American businesses produce an estimated 1 billion pieces of paper. Office professionals are constantly dealing with mounting piles of paper and a diminishing amount of storage space.

Records management includes management of paper records, micrographics, magnetically stored documents, and optical information systems. Records management starts with the creation or receipt of information and ends with the destruction or storage of the information. Office professionals must be aware of available systems and options in order to manage records with the most efficient and productive methods.

TYPES OF RECORDS

Records can be either active or inactive. Active office files should contain only useful, current information. Records consulted frequently, several times a month or more, are considered active. They must be immediately accessible and should be in the main file area. Semiactive records are ones referred to approximately once a month. They may be stored in less accessible drawers or cabinets either in active storage or elsewhere on the same floor. Records used infrequently, less than once a month, are considered inactive. Inactive files need not be in the immediate work area. Inactive records can be moved to a basement, a storage unit or warehouse off-site, or natural underground caves specifically used for long-term storage. Off-site storage uses low-cost equipment, maximizes space, and costs less per square foot than office floor space. Because the records are inactive, a delay in retrieving them is acceptable.

RETAINING RECORDS

You should develop a records retention schedule to avoid keeping information longer than needed. A retention schedule tells how long to keep records in the office, when to destroy them, and when to transfer them to inactive storage facilities. In determining how long to retain records, consider the following:

❑ How useful and how active the record is. Move inactive records to another storage area.
❑ Legal retention requirements for federal, state, and local government agencies. Research these requirements carefully and consult with an attorney.
❑ Long-term value to the organization for research or to the community for scholarly purposes.

> **Hint:** Charitable and religious organizations usually retain a recorded history of their development.

VITAL RECORDS

Approximately 1 to 3 percent of business records are vital. Vital documents are those necessary for continuous operation of the business in the wake of fire, flood, earthquake, or other disaster. These records can be used to reconstruct a company's legal or financial status and to preserve the rights of the organization, its employees, customers, and stock-holders.

Vital records include:

- Insurance policies
- Documents of incorporation or partnership, certifications, licenses, leases, deeds, and titles
- Tax returns and supporting materials
- Warranties for office equipment, computers, and machinery
- Copyrights
- Personnel records
- Financial records such as accounts receivable balances
- Banking and payroll records
- Pension and profit-sharing documents
- Word- and data-processing backup tapes or disks
- Company policy manuals and departmental procedures manuals

Not all vital records are stored forever; only the most recent update of some information, such as accounts receivable, is considered vital.

Copies of vital records should be made for protection. Vital records can be protected using one of the following methods:

Dispersal: Copies may be stored at different locations during routine distribution of materials. This method is often used when companies have several locations. Dispersal may also be to banks, insurance companies, government agencies, or accounting firms.

Duplication: Copies of vital records can be made as part of regularly scheduled duplication; they may be in any medium, whether disk, microfilm, or paper.

On-site storage: Vital records can be stored in fireproof cabinets, vaults, or rooms; this is normally acceptable only for temporary storage. There must be proper environmental controls and sufficient security.

Off-site storage: Off-site storage facilities could be company-owned, commercial, or shared with others. They must have environmental controls for temperature, humidity, air circulation, and control of insects and rodents. Access should be restricted to ensure security.

TYPES OF FILING SYSTEMS

Most offices use several different filing systems. There are five major ways to store records, whether those records are on paper or on micrographics or magnetic media. Some offices may use a combination of one or more of the following systems:

Alphabetic: Files are kept under the names of individuals, businesses, and government organizations and filed by the sequence of letters in the alphabet. This is the system used in most offices. It is better for small companies and for individual files. Use standard filing rules for consistency in filing and retrieval.

Numeric: In this system, a code number is assigned to individuals, businesses, or subjects. Once the code number is assigned, no decisions have to be made as to how to file records. They are simply filed in numeric order. However, this method requires an index to find material. A numeric filing system works well for records that can be filed by policy numbers, product numbers, patient billing numbers, or customer account numbers. It is also easily learned by those not familiar with English.

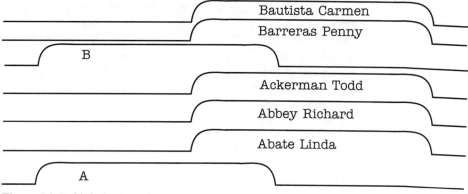

Figure 12-1 Alphabetic style.

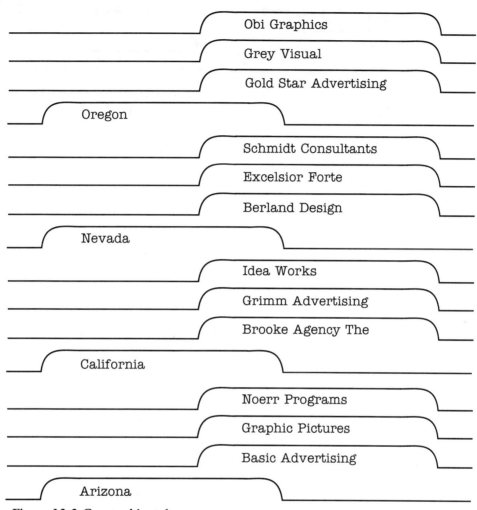

Figure 12-2 Geographic style.

Subject: Records are filed alphabetically by topic or category rather than by individual name or business name. This method is best for companies that store records by inventory or merchandise names. It is often combined with an alphabetic system. Such a system can be one to the most difficult to design and maintain. Major filing categories often are:

Accounting   Equipment
Advertising   Expense account
Associations   Finance
Budget   Insurance
Conferences and conventions   Inventory
Credit department   Legal

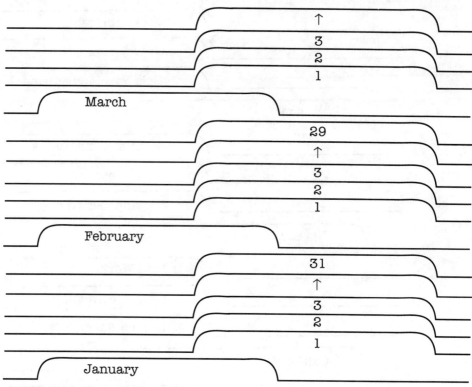

Figure 12-3 Chronological style.

Office systems	Safety
Personnel	Sales
Property	Travel
Records management	Vacations

Geographic: Records are arranged alphabetically according to names of geographic locations. This system works best for sales data broken down by geographic territories. Each geographic territory can be separated by file guides, as in this example:

Chronological: Records are arranged by date (usually year/month/day). This system is used especially for temporary filing and tickler or reminder files.

If material may be filed under one or more names or subjects, a cross reference should be made. File the material under one name or subject and file a cross reference to that name or subject under the other. Insert a permanent guide in the proper alphabetical position among the regular file folders for cross reference information.

Hint: Use the back of an old file folder.

For example, Dan Imler has a painting service called Dan & Son Painting. All materials are filed in the folder labeled Imler Dan. A cross reference is placed in the files under Dan & Son Painting. The cross reference reads as follows:

Dan & Son Painting
see
Imler Dan

FILING RULES AND STANDARDS

ARMA, the Association of Records Managers and Administrators, is a professional organization for the records management field that develops and promotes standards for records management.

ARMA Simplified Filing Standard Rules*

1. **Alphabetize by arranging files in unit-by-unit order and letter-by-letter within each unit.**

As written		As filed	
	Unit 1	Unit 2	Unit 3
Professional Artists Inc	Professional	Artists	Inc
Professional Secretaries International	Professional	Secretaries	International
Rapid Messenger Service	Rapid	Messenger	Service

2. **Each filing unit in a filing segment is to be considered. This includes prepositions, conjunctions, and articles. The only exception is when the word "the" is the first filing unit in a filing segment. In this case, "the" is the last filing unit. Spell out all symbols; e.g., as &, $, #, and file alphabetically.**

As written		As filed		
	Unit 1	Unit 2	Unit 3	Unit 4
Brinker & Pisenti	Brinker	and	Pisenti	
The Buffy Antiques	Buffy	Antiques	The	
Campbell & Associates	Campbell	and	Associates	
Creative Journeys of Napa	Creative	Journeys	of	Napa
$ and Cents	Dollars	and	Cents	
Flights of Fancy	Flights	of	Fancy	

3. **File "nothing before something." File single unit filing segments before multiple unit filing segments.**

*Based on ARMA International "Alphabetical Filing Rules." Copyright © 1972, 1985, 1986. All rights reserved. Published with permission of and by arrangement with the Association of Records Managers and Administrators, Inc.

As written	Unit 1	Unit 2	Unit 3	Unit 4
			As filed	
A Grand Innovation	A	Grand	Innovation	
A to Z Bookkeeping	A	to	Z	Bookkeeping
Able Auto Painting	Able	Auto	Painting	
C & W Ford	C	and	W	Ford
C G Products	C	G	Products	
Cooperfield Books	Cooperfield	Books		

4. Ignore all punctuation when alphabetizing. This includes periods, commas, dashes, hyphens, and apostrophes, etc. Hyphenated words are considered one unit.

As written	Unit 1	Unit 2	Unit 3
		As filed	
Brides 'n Maids	Brides	n	Maids
Cody's Books	Codys	Books	
Cluckler All-Steel Building	Cluckler	AllSteel	Building
Parker-West Advertising	ParkerWest	Advertising	
Sonoma Package Co.	Sonoma	Package	Co

5. Arabic and roman numbers are filed sequentially before alphabetic characters. All Arabic numerals precede all roman numerals.

As written	Unit 1	Unit 2	Unit 3	Unit 4
			As filed	
1 Hour Photo	1	Hour	Photo	
4 Star Foods	4	Star	Foods	
49er Pet Warehouse	49er	Pet	Warehouse	
355 Park Hotel	355	Park	Hotel	
V Star Foods	V	Star	Foods	
A-1 Equipment Rental	A1	Equipment	Rental	
Four Star Foods	Four	Star	Foods	
One Hour Photo	One	Hour	Photo	

6. Acronyms, abbreviations, and radio and television station call letters are filed as one unit.

As written	Unit 1	Unit 2	Unit 3	Unit 4
			As filed	
Am. Patent Services	Am	Patent	Services	
GE Consumer Service	GE	Consumer	Service	
KOLB TV	KOLB	TV		
WSRO 1350 AM	WSRO	1350	AM	

7. **File under the most commonly used name or title. Cross-reference under other names or titles which might be used in an information request.**

As written	As filed			
	Unit 1	Unit 2	Unit 3	Unit 4
Dan & Son Painting	Dan (See Imler Dan)	and	Son	Painting
Cellular Car Service	Cellular (See Sonoma Communications Inc)	Car	Service	
The Violin Shop	Violin (See Loveland Mike)	Shop	The	

EXAMPLES FOR APPLYING THE SIMPLIFIED FILING RULES

PERSONAL NAMES

1. *Simple Personal Names:* **Use the last (surname) as the first filing unit. The first name or initial is the second filing unit. Subsequent names or initials are filed as successive units.**

As written	As filed			
	Unit 1	Unit 2	Unit 3	Unit 4
A. Miriam Harms	Harms	A	Miriam	
Deanna Pebbles	Pebbles	Deanna		
Paul B. White	White	Paul	B	

2. *Personal Names with Prefixes:* **Surnames which include a prefix are filed as one unit whether the prefix is followed by a space or not. Examples of prefixes are: D', Da, De, Del, De la, Della, Den, Des, Di, Du, El, Fitz, L', La, Las, Le, Les, Lo, Los, M', Mac, Mc, O', Saint, St., Ste., Te, Ten, Ter, Van, Van de, Van der, Von, Von der.**

As written	As filed			
	Unit 1	Unit 2	Unit 3	Unit 4
Gary D'Alois	DAlois	Gary		
Jesse Del Moral	DelMoral	Jesse		
Andrea C. LaDow	LaDow	Andrea	C	

Peter J. McCabe	McCabe	Peter	J
Terry V. O'Connor	OConnor	Terry	V
Linda St. Andrew	StAndrew	Linda	
Jane C. Van Der Slice	VanDerSlice	Jane	C
Albert Vander Werf	VanderWerf	Albert	

3. *Personal Names with Personal and Professional Titles and Suffixes:* **Suffixes are not used as filing units except when needed to distinguish between two or more identical names. When needed, a suffix is the last filing unit and is filed as written, ignoring punctuation.**

As written	As filed			
	Unit 1	Unit 2	Unit 3	Unit 4
John P. Lynch, C.P.A.	Lynch	John	P	CPA
John P. Lynch, Jr.	Lynch	John	P	Jr
John P. Lynch, M.D.	Lynch	John	P	MD
Mr. John P. Lynch	Lynch	John	P	Mr
John P. Lynch, Ph.D.	Lynch	John	P	PhD
Senator John P. Lynch	Lynch	John	P	Senator

4. *Personal Names Which Are Hyphenated:* **Ignore the hyphen and file the two words as one unit.**

As written	As filed			
	Unit 1	Unit 2	Unit 3	Unit 4
Peggy Davis-Farrell	DavisFarrell	Peggy		
Danielle Griffin-Amcor	GriffinAmcor	Danielle		
Carol Lytle	Lytle	Carol		

5. *Pseudonymous and royal and religious titles:* **Pseudonyms are filed as written. Personal names which start with a royal or religious title and are followed by only a given name(s) are filed as written.**

As written	As filed			
	Unit 1	Unit 2	Unit 3	Unit 4
Dr. Seuss	Dr	Seuss		
Prince Charles	Prince	Charles		
Sister Mary	Sister	Mary		

6. *Foreign Personal Names:* **If the surname is identifiable, file the name as any other personal name is filed. If there is a question about the surname, use the last name as the first filing unit and make a cross-reference from the first name.**

As written	As filed			
	Unit 1	Unit 2	Unit 3	Unit 4
Liang Li	Li	Liang		
	Liang	Li		
	(See Li			
	Liang)			
Yang Mo	Mo	Yang		
	Yang	Mo		
	(see Mo			
	Yang)			
Yew Cong Wong	Wong	Yew	Cong	
	Yew Cong			
	Wong			
	(See Wong			
	Yew Cong)			

7. *Nicknames:* **When a person commonly uses a nickname as a first name, file using the nickname. Cross-reference from the given name only if necessary.**

As written	As filed			
	Unit 1	Unit 2	Unit 3	Unit 4
Susie Sziber	Sziber	Susie		
Bob Tagnoli	Tagnoli	Bob		
Buck Wood	Wood	Buck		
	(See Wood			
	John C)			

BUSINESS AND ORGANIZATION NAMES

1. **Business and organization names are filed as written according to the Simplified Standard Rules and using the business letterhead or trademark as a guide. Names with prefixes follow the example for personal names with prefixes above.**

As written	As filed			
	Unit 1	Unit 2	Unit 3	Unit 4
A & T Automotive	A	and	T	Automotive
Aardvark Transmissions	Aardvark	Trans-missions		
Dee-Jay's Sash & Glass	DeeJays	Sash	and	Glass
Kelly Kline				
Photo Studios	Kelly	Kline	Photo	Studios
U-Save Auto Rental	USave	Auto	Rental	
Van Koonse Glass Co.	VanKoonse	Glass	Co	

2. <u>Subsidiaries of businesses will be filed under their own name with a cross-reference to the parent company if needed.</u>

As written	As filed			
	Unit 1	Unit 2	Unit 3	Unit 4
Comstock Michigan Fruit	Comstock (See also Curtice Burns Foods Inc.)	Michigan	Fruit	
Curtice Burns Foods, Inc.	Curtice (for Divisions see: Comstock Michigan Fruit Iowa Fresh Foods Nebraska Produce, Inc.)	Burns	Foods	Inc

3. <u>Place names in business names will follow the Simplified Filing Standard Rule that each word/filing unit is treated as a separate filing unit.</u>

As written	As filed			
	Unit 1	Unit 2	Unit 3	Unit 4
California Parenting Institute	California	Parenting	Institute	
Oakland Coliseum	Oakland	Coliseum		
Sonoma County Transportation	Sonoma	County	Trans-portation	

4. <u>Compass Terms in Business Names. Each word/unit in a filing segment containing compass terms is considered a separate filing unit. If the term, includes more than one compass point, treat it as it is written. Establish cross references as needed.</u>

As written	As filed			
	Unit 1	Unit 2	Unit 3	Unit 4
North Bay Regional Center	North	Bay	Regional	Center

North Coast Drywall	North	Coast	Drywall
North West Design	North	West	Design
Northwest Community Center	Northwest	Community	Center

GOVERNMENT/POLITICAL DESIGNATIONS

When filing governmental/political material, the name of the major entity is filed first, followed by the distinctive name of the department, bureau, etc.

    This rule covers all governmental and political divisions, agencies, departments, and committees, etc., from the federal to the county/parish, city, district, and ward level.

Federal: **Prefix with the name of the government and eliminate the department; i.e., Department of the Interior, Department of the Treasury, etc. File titles of the office, service, or bureau, etc., by their distinctive names.**

United States Government
Army

United States Government
Federal Bureau of Investigation

United States Government
Interior

United States Government
Treasury

United States Government
Veterans Administration

State and local: State, county, parish, city, town, township and village governments/political divisions are filed by their distinctive names. The words "county of," "city of," "department of," etc., if needed and as appropriate, are added for clarity and are considered filing units.

Note: If "of" is not part of the official name as written, it is not added.

As written		As filed		
	Unit 1	Unit 2	Unit 3	Unit 4
Iowa Highway Patrol	Iowa	Highway	Patrol	
Marin County Library	Marin	County	Library	
City of Healdsburg	Healdsburg	City	of	

Foreign governments: **The distinctive English name is the first filing unit. If needed, the balance of the formal name of the government forms the next filing unit(s). Divisions,**

departments, and branches follow in sequential order, reversing the written order where necessary to give the distinctive name precedence in the filing arrangement.

States, colonies, provinces, cities, and other divisions of foreign governments are filed by their distinctive or official names as spelled in English. Cross-reference written name to official native name where necessary.

As written			As filed	
	Unit 1	Unit 2	Unit 3	Unit 4
Brazil	Brazil			
Paris, France	Paris	France		

MANAGING PAPER-BASED RECORDS

Paper accounts for 95 percent of the filing in the United States. It is estimated that on average a company doubles its total number of records every ten years.

The advantages of paper records are that they are affordable for an office of any size; they are an acceptable form of record for legal purposes; and people are comfortable working with paper. On the other hand, paper records can take up a great deal of space; they are vulnerable to water and fire damage and to loss; file security can be a problem; and only one person at a time can use a paper document.

Paper filing systems should meet the following guidelines:

❏ Records necessary for daily operations are easily retrieved. Active files are the ones closest to the user.

❏ Records accessed infrequently are stored in a separate, less accessible location.

❏ Access to confidential information is restricted.

❏ A retention schedule is developed; records are destroyed when they are no longer of value to the company. (See the sections on Retaining Records and on Transfer and Disposal in this chapter.)

REORGANIZING AN EXISTING PAPER-BASED FILING SYSTEM

If information cannot be accessed quickly and stored easily, it can be organized following these steps:

1. Prepare a written list of existing files.

2. Categorize files as active or inactive. Remove inactive files from the list.

3. Decide whether any materials (speeches, public relations material, client files) need to be separated from the main filing system.

Hint: A special file should contain enough material to fill up half a file drawer.

4. Organize the inventory list by broad categories. Usually one heading and two subheadings per category are sufficient. Get suggestions from others who are using the files.

Hint: Use a word processing outline feature, which makes updating easy and can generate a printed list.

5. Make any cross references needed. (See the section on Types of Filing Systems earlier in this chapter.)

6. Prepare a summary list, which is a map of the contents of the drawers with broad categories of material contained in each.

7. Prepare labels to put on the actual files. (See the heading *Preparation of File Folders* below for additional information.)

8. Train those who will use the filing system. Distribute the summary list.

EQUIPMENT

With the ever-increasing amount of paper in the office, storage has become a major problem for many companies. Filing equipment is available in a wide range of designs and sizes. No more space should be allocated for records than is necessary.

The following are some of the major types of filing equipment and their uses.

Desk-size filing units and two-drawer file cabinets: These are used for files that are accessed daily; they do not, however, utilize space efficiently.

Four- or five-drawer vertical file cabinet: These are the most popular format for active files; the five-drawer version has 25 percent more storage space than the four-drawer version. The letter-size version is the most popular style. A disadvantage is that it can be used by only one person at a time.

Lateral file cabinets: These are lengthwise units whose drawers or shelves are opened broadside; they are available with two to six drawers or shelves. When open, all records are visible. They may be used as barriers between working areas, and they require 40 percent less floor space than a four-drawer vertical file cabinet.

Open-shelf file units: These lateral units have open shelves like a bookshelf. They are good for high-volume filing and have the advantage of being accessible to more than one person at the same time. All records are visible. Filing and retrieval can be done approximately 20 to 40 percent more quickly than with file cabinets, and they require 50 percent less floor space than a four-drawer vertical file cabinet. Security, however, is a problem.

High-density mobile filing units: These vertical units make a large number of active documents readily accessible. Floor space is saved by not having aisles between the file units; since the units are on tracks or rails, and they are mobile, only one aisle is ever created at a time. Units can be moved either manually (the user pushes the units back and forth) or mechanically. They can increase file space by as much as 200 percent.

Rotary files: Rotation brings records close to the user with little user movement; some versions are automated. Records may be filed vertically or flat. Only one request can be processed at a time, however.

Heavy cardboard boxes: These boxes (12 by 10 by 15 inches) are used for inactive files; they are sealed and labeled and usually stored away from the main work area. Two letter-size file drawers are equivalent to three boxes. The same size is capable of storing both legal- and letter-size documents, as well as odd-size documents and cards. They are structurally secure over a long period of time and provide some degree of waterproofing.

SELECTION OF EQUIPMENT

The selection of filing equipment for paper-based records depends upon determining the following information:

1. The amount of floor space available. Vertical file cabinets take up the most space, followed by lateral and open-shelf cabinets. High-density mobile filing units take the least amount of space. Make sure there is adequate aisle space between cabinets. In addition, determine whether moving inactive files to storage will increase the floor space.

2. Number of people accessing the files at one time. Note that vertical cabinets may be used by only one person at a time. As density increases (seven or eight shelves high), accessibility decreases.

3. The method of filing. Determine the most appropriate method: alphabetical, numeric, subject, or geographic. Decide whether to use top or side tabs or bar codes.

4. Number of files pulled each day.

5. Number of refiles each day.

6. Type and size of records.

7. Security concerns. Open shelving is appropriate in a filing area that is accessible only to authorized personnel. In other areas, use cabinets with doors that lock to restrict access.

8. Weight capacity of existing floor. Consult with a structural engineer for load capacity before purchasing new equipment.

9. Corporate growth plans. Are there plans to merge or consolidate operations? Are there plans to move?

10. Corporate budget for filing and storage.

11. Environmental requirements.

To determine the cost of a system, follow these steps:

1. Compute the current filing inches of space.

> 175 pieces of paper = 1 file inch
> Vertical file cabinet = 25 filing inches per drawer
> Lateral file cabinet = 50 filing inches per shelf

2. Convert filing inches to square feet needed for equipment.

Equipment	Aisle space (inches)	Total square feet of office space needed
Letter-size vertical file	28	7.5
Legal-size vertical file	28	9.0
30-inch lateral cabinet	6	6.5
36-inch lateral cabinet	6	7.0
42-inch lateral cabinet	6	7.5

3. Multiply square feet times the cost of office space per square foot.

For example, Company A requires 2,000 inches of filing space. If approximately 20 four-drawer vertical file cabinets are used, 150 square feet of floor space is needed. If floor space averages $30 a square foot, the total annual floor space costs are $4,500.

But if high-density mobile files are used, 2,000 inches of filing space would fit in 42 square feet of floor space. If floor space averages $30 a square foot, total annual floor space costs are $1,260.

FILING SUPPLIES

The type of folders you should select depends on the following:

- Size of records
- Length of time the file is active
- Need for special features such as fasteners, pockets, or closed sides
- Anticipated volume

Here are descriptions of typical types of file folders:

Top-tab: The identifying tab is at the top. Made of either manila or pressboard material, these are used in vertical cabinets or lateral cabinets with drawers.

End-tab: The identifying tab is at the end of the folder. Made of either manila or pressboard material, these are used with flat shelving, lateral cabinets with flat shelves and flipper doors, and lateral units with buckets that slide on rails.

Hanging folders: These are designed to replace the manila or pressboard folder. The label holder can be placed in any position across the top of the folder. They are popular because they make records easily accessible and hold more information than regular file folders. However, they occupy 33 percent more drawer space, thus increasing equipment cost and floor space needs by 33 percent.

Folders with fasteners: These have metal fasteners at the top of the folder. They are used for very active records if records are transferred to several workers or if the internal order of documents is important.

Pocket folders: These are partially enclosed folders that expand from $\frac{3}{4}$ inch to $3\frac{1}{2}$ inches or more. They are used for odd-sized and loose materials.

PREPARATION OF FILE FOLDERS

Follow these steps in preparing file folders:

1. Select folder type (see the previous heading *Filing Supplies*).

2. Choose third, fifth, two-fifths, shelf, half, or straight cut folder tabs. (See the section on Filing and Records Management Supplies in Chapter 9 for tab descriptions.)

3. Decide on folder weight. (See the section on Filing and Records Management Supplies in Chapter 9 for more information on folder weights and uses.)

4. Determine the organization of the tabs. There are three main types of organization:

❏ *Type one:* Use a set tab position for each category of information to allow for quick retrieval. For example, for an alphabetical list of customers, reserve the first tab position for

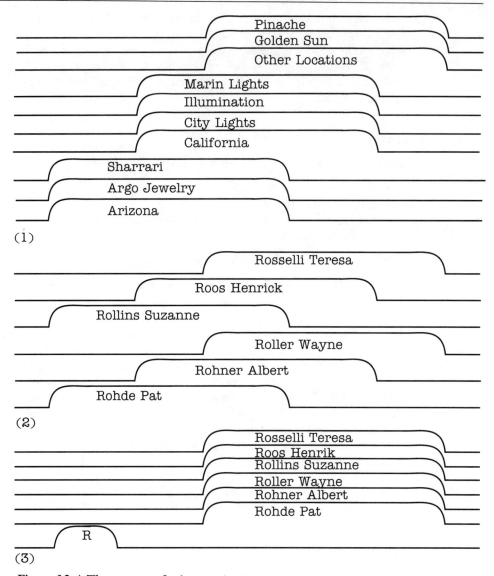

Figure 12-4 Three types of tab organization.

customers in Arizona, the second position for those in California, and the third position for everyone else.

❑ *Type two:* Use the first position tab, then the second position tab, and then the third position tab. This is good for a file system that does not change. If it does change, new file folders are added and items are no longer in order. Finding folders then becomes more time-consuming.

❑ *Type three:* Place all title information on the same position on each file folder. Filing new folders in this system is easy.

5. Use a computer to prepare labels.

Hint: Helvetica bold type font style works well. Use 24-point for headings, 18-point for major subheadings. Capitalize the first letter of each word; headings in all capital letters are difficult to read.

6. Prepare file labels uniformly.

Hint: Always start label names in the same location close to the top of the label, with a one- or two-space left margin.

7. Use simple words, such as "Advertising," "Legal," "Personnel."

Hint: Omit punctuation.

8. Use file guides. File guides serve as dividers, precede the file folders, and identify the major or subject headings. Guides are made out of heavy pressboard, fiber, or manila stock. (For additional information, see Chapter 9.)

Hint: Precede every five to ten folders with a guide.

9. Include a general or miscellaneous folder for each letter of the alphabet to file any material that has no folder. Place it behind the last name folder under that particular letter, and file material in it alphabetically. Review four times a year in order to purge or refile documents if possible. Start a new folder when a subject has five to ten pages of related documents.

10. Label file drawers.

COLOR CODING

Color coding may be used with any type of filing system. Colored file folders and labels allow quick identification and location of folders.

Use labels with a color bar at top by assigning a specific color bar to specific file groups. For example, personnel files could be red, customer files might be green, and creditor files could be yellow.

Use letters or numbers preprinted on a colored and/or patterned background to identify a partial name or subject. For example, the first three letters of a customer's name could be color coded. All customers with names beginning with these first three letters are easily identified as a group. This color-coding system adds an extra step in file preparation.

Solid color labels are recommended only when confidentiality is needed; use pastel colors for easy reading. For example, all personnel files could have yellow labels.

The following should be kept in mind when using color:

- Keep the system as simple as possible; e.g., make all the A's one color, all the B's one color, etc.
- In a numeric filing system use ten colors, since the most common system is based on ten digits.
- Use color folders to indicate certain types of files; e.g., blue could be for correspondence.

• Use different color labels for folders with the same name; e.g., "Steven White, Jr." could have a yellow label; "Steven White, Sr.," a green label.

FILING DOCUMENTS

Not everything must be filed. Information that will not be used in the future should be thrown away or recycled. Company newsletters, bulletins, newspapers, and vendor catalogs are best placed in a notebook on a bookshelf.

The following tips are helpful when filing:

❏ Underline or write file headings on documents. Then if an item is removed from the files, it will be refiled in the same folder.

❏ File documents daily to avoid accumulated filing.

❏ Remove rubber bands and paper clips; discard envelopes, routing slips, cover memos, and duplicates; staple multipage records together; mend tears with tape.

Hint: Keep one copy of each draft until the final document is inactive, then discard all previous drafts.

❏ Rough-sort documents into major categories; for example, a rough-sort for alphabetic documents is A–L and M–Z.

Hint: Both alphabetic and numeric sorting organizers are available from office supply sources.

❏ File the most recent papers in the front of the folder; place the document facing up, with the top of the page at the left edge of the folder.

❏ Crease the score marks at the bottom of manila folders when papers are a quarter of an inch thick (about 25 sheets of paper). Manila folders hold approximately 100 pieces of paper. If the folders are not scored for every quarter inch of paper, the file label cannot be seen and the folder will slide into the file drawer or shelf and damage the contents.

❏ Replace worn folders with new ones.

❏ Allow 3 to 4 inches of working space in vertical files.

RETRIEVAL AND CHARGE-OUT

A file can be quickly located if employees charge out files before using them. The following charge-out methods can be used:

Charge-out request: Write down the name of the file (either on a 3-by-5-inch slip of paper or a printed charge-out request); place the charge-out request in an out guide, which is a folder with a pocket for filing documents when the file is missing; remove the charge-out paper when the folder is returned. If the folder is to be used at the filing cabinet, a charge-out request is not necessary.

Out guide: Write on the out guide the name of the folder, when it was removed, and who removed it; place the out guide where the file was located; remove the out guide when the folder is returned. Out guides would be used in the following circumstances in small offices: (1) the file is loaned to someone outside the office; (2) the file is taken outside the office by an employee; or (3) an employee expects to use the file for a week or more. The advantages to using charge-out procedures are as follows:

❏ Identifies employees using the files.

Hint: If employees are in a hurry and do not feel they can take the time to complete the charge-out information, assign a special color out guide to be placed in the files in case of emergencies.

❏ Allows monitoring of the time a file was taken.

Hint: Use a color charge-out guide for each week of the month to help identify files missing for longer than necessary. For example, week 1 could be yellow; week 2, red; week 3, green, etc.

❏ Determines activity levels for use of the files.

SAFETY

The following safety precautions should be observed:

❏ Close all drawers or reference shelves after using them.
❏ Open only one drawer of a vertical cabinet at a time to keep the cabinet from tipping over.

Hint: Newer cabinets are equipped with counterbalances to avoid this problem.

❏ Weigh down the bottom shelf of lateral equipment before loading the top shelf. Once the cabinet is loaded past the middle shelf, it will not tip over.

Hint: Store paper or folders on the bottom shelf while loading the cabinet for the first time.

COMPUTER SOFTWARE

Document management software (also called records management software) makes it easier and faster to store, retrieve, and index information. This software is most advantageous when a paper-based filing system becomes overwhelming to maintain because of the volume of records.

Although requiring a high initial investment cost, records management software has numerous advantages, including the following:

- It provides a method to track files that are not in the filing cabinet.
- It reduces the possibility of misplaced or lost files.
- It generates reports showing who has taken out files and when they are due.
- It helps in making decisions about which records are to be moved to long-term storage.

There are three basic types of records managements software that manage paper-based records.

The first type is software that is developed in-house. Such software is highly specialized in its applications. It can take considerable time to create, however, and development costs are usually high.

The second type is database software, such as Lotus or dBase. Such software is available at a reasonable cost, and users can tailor it to meet their specific needs.

The third type is document management software, which is inexpensive, requires no development, and can be implemented quickly. It is usually compatible with IBM PCs; some may run on minicomputers. It typically uses a bar-code system, so that tracking is done by scanning labels.

Another method of controlling records is to store all records on computer. Such an electronic record storage system eliminates the need for paper records. Magnetic computer tape is the most commonly used medium for long-term storage of electronic records.

The major advantages of electronic records are that they require less storage space than paper records, can be retrieved quickly, and are easily transportable. The disadvantages include security problems that stem from unauthorized access, the fact that they are easier to destroy than paper records, and the initial cost of the hardware and software. Electronic record storage systems require the following components:

- A computer
- A way to enter documents into the system, such as with scanners or by copying from floppy disks
- A high-capacity storage system, such as an optical disk (optical disks are discussed later in this chapter)
- A screen that can display the image of the stored document
- A laser printer or similar high-speed output device
- Networking capabilities with other users
- Records management software

Most computers can store a tremendous amount of data. It is important that electronic files be managed properly. Some of the important steps in managing these files are the following:

❏ Use consistent standards for logging and naming documents when storing them. Most standards use letters, numbers, or a combination of both.

❏ Periodically clean up electronic files—either eliminate them or store them on disk. A crowded hard disk slows the access speed of finding information because the hard disk head must move farther across the disk in order to find files.

❏ Back up important documents. The backup method you should use is determined by the amount of data that you need to store. Floppy disk backup works well for up to 10MB (megabytes) of data. Tape cartridge backup is used for backing up 10 to 80 MB hard disks and for backing up information from local area networks. Tape cartridges are a separate unit and can back up a hard disk drive in less than 10 minutes. (See Chapter 8 on *Backing up Software* for additional information.)

❏ Store disks and tapes properly, using diskette trays or lateral filing. (See the section in Chapter 9, *Disk Storage*, for additional information.)

MICROGRAPHICS

About 4 percent of business information is stored on microforms. Microforms are photographic reductions of larger documents.

Microforms have several advantages. They are an excellent method for storing both active and inactive records, since they take up only a third of the space needed for paper documents. Once recorded, information cannot later be misfiled, since a microform is either a roll or a sheet of film. In addition, microforms are more durable than paper as well as being easily and economically duplicated and economically mailed.

Microforms also have their disadvantages. The initial cost of equipment is high. Readers are necessary (note that readers for microfilm and microfiche are different). Also, microforms must be stored in a controlled environment, and they cannot be updated without refilming.

A microfilm is a roll of film with miniature pictures of pages. A microfiche is a sheet of film with miniature pictures of pages. Both microfilm and microfiche are referred to as microforms.

Microfiche is better for smaller databases; one sheet can store hundreds of images. It is read by placing the fiche on a platen and scanning for the proper index.

Microfilm, although more expensive than microfiche, is one of the most cost-effective methods of storing documents. It is usually used to store large databases of information (typically several thousand images can be stored on one roll of film).

Another way of creating microforms is a method called computer output microfilm/microfiche (COM). Information from the computer is transferred directly to the microfilm/microfiche—it is not printed on paper first. The major advantage of using COM is its speed and the amount of work that can be handled. A COM recorder can film at the rate of 585,000 lines per minute.

Computer-assisted-retrieval systems (CAR) can help operators find specific microform images accurately and quickly using a computer. CAR systems consist of (1) a microfilm reader, (2) microfilm cartridges storing the images, and (3) a computer storing the image database. The computer operator enters the document ID number, the database tells the operator which microfilm cartridge to load, and the computer searches for the image.

OPTICAL DISKS

Only about 1 percent of the filing in the United States is done on optical disk. Optical disks are similar to CDs in the way they look and operate. Optical disk technology is used with computer systems that communicate with and display images from the optical disk. The disks also work with database software, which organizes and searches the optical disk for the requested images. Optical disks are primarily used by companies with large storage demands, a need to distribute large amounts of information, and high-security requirements.

Optical disks have several advantages. They are not affected by magnetic fields or other problems that might affect a hard disk. They take up less space than paper storage. Information cannot be misfiled because the computer does the filing and searching. Data can be accessed by a number of authorized operators at the same time.

As with other electronic systems, one disadvantage is the initial cost of equipment. In addition, optical disks may not be acceptable in courts of law in some states as a storage medium. And they are not acceptable to tax authorities as a storage medium.

Optical disks can either be CD-ROM, WORM, or erasable. Each technology is designed for a different purpose.

CD-ROM: This is the oldest optical disk technology; CD-ROM stands for "compact disk, read-only memory." Although about the size of a floppy disk, they can store approximately 250,000 pages of text or 40,000 pages of images; these images can be retrieved instantly to a screen or by a laser printer. Once made, however, they cannot be updated.

WORM: These are used for advanced data storage. WORM stands for "write once, read many." This is a more flexible medium than CD-ROM, because data can be added to the WORM disk; however, once added, data cannot be changed (although it also cannot accidentally be destroyed). WORM disks can store handwritten memos, signatures, and drawings and can also be used as backup storage for personal computers.

Erasable storage disks: This newest development in the area of optical storage allows writing, erasing, and reading of data, just as with a computer hard drive. Storage capacity ranges from 500MB to 1GB (gigabyte). The erasable disk is in a cartridge that can be removed from the computer. It can be used for backing up a fixed hard drive and network servers for local area networks.

TRANSFER AND DISPOSAL

When records are transferred from the active filing area to less expensive inactive filing areas, two transfer methods are most commonly used.

The *perpetual* method is used for records that are no longer active because the files have been closed by an event or a date (e.g., legal cases). This method is not suitable for files of a continuous nature. The *periodic* method is used for records that are regularly transferred after a given time period (e.g., semiannually or annually). Ultimately, vital records are transferred to permanent storage and all other records are destroyed.

A signed authorization is needed to destroy records that have legal retention requirements. This authorization itself becomes a vital record and is proof that destruction was part of normal business operations. If destroyed records are subsequently subpoenaed by a court, the authorization is proof that the records are no longer available.

Three methods of disposal are available. Nonconfidential records can be discarded as waste paper or recycled. Confidential records can first be shredded, then discarded or recycled. If the volume of records to be disposed of is large, a records management service firm can be hired to eliminate them.

FORMS MANAGEMENT

Forms are either on preprinted paper or on a computer screen. They contain permanent information with blank spaces for variable information. From 85 to 90 percent of the costs of filling out forms are for the personnel who complete, process, and use them. The goal of forms management is to minimize the cost of forms and at the same time increase work efficiency and effectiveness. These goals can be accomplished by following these steps:

❑ Consolidate or eliminate unnecessary forms. Determine if the form is needed. Analyze other forms to find relationships or duplications. Decide whether the forms or items on the form can be combined, eliminated, or simplified.

❑ Automate forms applications and systems. Maintain a computer listing of all approved forms. It might also be worthwhile to investigate forms management software packages or software packages with desktop publishing features.

❑ Maintain a forms file that includes specification sheets, design copies, order histories, and copies of all forms.

❑ Centralize purchasing and printing for cost savings.

❑ Review all forms annually or when equipment or procedures change.

DESIGNING FORMS

The following are components of effective business form design:

❑ Use spacing appropriate for equipment it will be used with. For example, check the vertical spacing on the form using the computer printer, an optical scanner, or a wand.

❑ Include requests for all important information (e.g., area code, ZIP Code). Make certain the instructions are adequate. Avoid unnecessary information and illegal questions.

❑ Group items so the user can concentrate on one small area at a time. It is best to put the most frequently used items at the top of the form.

❑ Use checklists and boxes for information. Place instructions above the lines or the boxes.

❑ Avoid having too many words and lines on a page, and use a combination of dark and light lines to guide the reader's eyes through the form.

————————Use light single lines as guides

━━━━━━━━Use heavy lines for major breaks

════════Use double lines to break up the form into distinct sections or for totals

❑ Use several type sizes and styles, including bold and italic, to draw attention to important items.

❑ Avoid wide margins unless needed for binding, because wide margins waste paper.

❑ Make sure lines and boxes are of adequate size to enter data.

❑ Include a form number and revision date in a standard location, such as a lower corner; identify forms with the organization's name and address. Include the company logo if the form is used outside the organization.

❑ Use color only if it serves a purpose.

❏ Use standard form designs and paper size if possible. Avoid sizes that are difficult to file or microfilm. Make certain the form fits in a business envelope. Use paper of appropriate weight and quality.

❏ Include an adequate number of parts so that as many carbon copies as needed are made when the form is filled out. Multipart forms are often the least costly way to duplicate information.

❏ Number all pages of multipage forms.

Identify each copy on its face if appropriate; for example,

    Copy 1—Office
    Copy 2—Customer
    Copy 3—Accounting

SECURITY OF RECORDS

Maintaining the security of records is an important part of protecting the assets of an organization. The following tips help secure written, oral, and computerized data:

1. Lock files when they are not in use; secure the office and file keys.
2. Audit who uses the files and for what reasons.
3. Shred confidential documents and printouts that are no longer needed.
4. Avoid leaving confidential information on desks accessible to the public, on the computer screens, in the fax output tray, or in the copy machine.
5. Protect computer passwords and system dial-in phone numbers; change passwords often; do not post passwords in the work area.
6. Log off the computer system when leaving the terminal.
7. Use tamper-proof interoffice envelopes.
8. Avoid mentioning confidential information over a cellular phone.
9. Keep magnets, paper clips, telephones, staples, and ballpoint pens away from diskettes.

CHAPTER 13

ACCOUNTING AND BOOKKEEPING

Business records provide management with information to make sound decisions. They also provide a measurement of an organization's stability and its potential for growth.

Office professionals often have the responsibility to collect and present the data required for accurate records. In smaller companies, these responsibilities may include handling cash, checking accounts, bank reconciliations, payroll, and billing as well as journalizing and posting transactions and preparing financial statements. In larger companies these financial responsibilities are more time-consuming and complex; they require a greater level of specialization.

Regardless of the size of the company, office professionals must understand basic bookkeeping principles. This understanding is especially vital as companies computerize their record-keeping functions. Realizing *why* a process is done a specific way will help a worker avoid or locate errors that may occur and make the work more meaningful and challenging.

Financial and managerial accounting are the two major accounting classifications. The goal of **financial accounting** is to prepare financial statements and present them to interested individuals outside the company. **Bookkeeping** involves procedures for recording financial data and is part of the financial accounting process.

Managerial accounting requires much of the same information accumulated in the financial accounting process, but management uses the information to plan, schedule, and control the company's internal activities. Cost accounting, financial forecasting (budgeting), auditing, and income tax accounting involve additional specialized accounting functions. Our emphasis is on financial accounting procedures.

Companies operate on either an accrual basis or a cash basis. Operating on an **accrual basis** means that all revenue and expenses are recorded at the time they are incurred regardless of when cash is actually received or expended. Companies operating on a **cash basis** record revenue only when cash is received, and they record expenses only when cash is disbursed.

RECORDING FINANCIAL INFORMATION

To be consistent and provide an orderly recording of financial information, a company must identify the accounts it expects to use and give a number to each account. This **chart of accounts** is used to identify the accounts that must be charged when making entries in journals and ledgers. (See Figure 13-1.)

JOURNALS

A **journal** is a diary in which daily business transactions are recorded from source documents such as checks, invoices, and cash register tapes. Journal formats vary. Some companies use a general journal and record *all* transactions in it. (See Figure 13-2.) Other companies subdivide tasks and use special journals to record transactions in areas such as sales, purchases, cash receipts, and cash disbursements. Others use a combined journal form. (See Figure 13-3.)

LEDGERS

Once a transaction is entered in the journal, or journalized, the next step is recording or posting these transactions in a **general ledger.** The ledger may be in card, single-sheet, or bound-book format. Each account in the chart of accounts has a space in the ledger. (See Figure 13-4.) In addition to a general ledger, companies may use accounts receivable ledgers (records of customers who owe money) (see Figure 13-5) and accounts payable ledgers (records of creditors to whom money is owed).

In the **double-entry** system of accounting, both a debit entry and a credit entry are required in the journal and the ledger for any transaction that involves an exchange of money or property or that adjusts or corrects existing information. A debit is entered on the *left side* of a ledger account; a credit is entered on the *right side*. When recording transactions, the total debits must equal the total credits.

Most businesses use the double-entry system of accounting, whether they record their entries manually or electronically with a computer. However, some small businesses use the simpler **single-entry** system, in which each transaction is entered only once as a sum due to or owed by the company.

There are several standard classifications of accounts. **Assets** are items that are owned by a company. **Current assets** include cash, inventory, and other assets that have a high probability of being turned into cash readily, usually within a year. **Plant assets** are long-term assets, such as equipment and land, with benefits that carry over into future accounting periods. Asset accounts increase on the debit side and decrease on the credit side of a ledger.

Liabilities are amounts owed or services yet to be rendered by a company. They also are broken down into current and long-term accounts. Accounts payable and salaries payable are examples of **current liabilities**. A mortgage is an example of a **long-term liability**. Liability accounts decrease on the debit side and increase on the credit side of a ledger.

Corner Bookkeeping Service
Chart of Accounts

100–199
110   Cash
111   Petty Cash
120   Accounts Receivable
130   Prepaid Insurance
140   Prepaid Rent
150   Office Supplies
160   Office Equipment
161   Accumulated Depreciation on Office Equipment
170   Office Furniture
171   Accumulated Depreciation on Office Furniture

200–299
210   Accounts Payable

300–399
310   D. R. Johnson, Capital
320   D. R. Johnson, Drawing
399   Income Summary

400–499
410   Service Fees

500–599
510   Salaries Expense
520   Supplies Expense
530   Insurance Expense
540   Rent Expense
550   Utilities Expense
551   Telephone Expense
560   Depreciation Expense/Office Equipment

Figure 13-1 Chart of accounts for a service company.

Owner's equity, which is also called capital, or net worth, represents the owner's claim against the firm's assets after subtracting the liabilities. In corporations, owner's equity is called stockholders' equity or shareholders' investment. Owner's equity accounts decrease on the debit side and increase on the credit side of a ledger.

Revenue results from the sale of goods, the rendering of services, or the use of money

Date		Entry Description	Ref	Debit		Credit	
1992							
Sept.	4	Equipment		1995	00		
		Accounts Payable,					
		Donnelly Corp.				1995	00

General Journal — Page 201

Figure 13-2 General journal.

Combination Journal for Month of _____ 19___   Page ___

Cash		Ck #	Date	Explanation of Entry	Ref	General		Accounts Receivable		Accounts Payable		Service Income	Salaries Expense	Utilities Expense
Dr	Cr					Dr	Cr	Dr	Cr	Dr	Cr	Cr	Dr	Dr
	1800.00	4	June 3	Rent Expense		1800.00								
980.00			June 4	Sales				2000.00				2980.00		

Figure 13-3 Combined journal.

or property. Revenue accounts decrease on the debit side and increase on the credit side of a ledger account. **Expenses** are the costs involved in an effort to produce revenue. Expense accounts increase on the debit side and decrease on the credit side of a ledger account.

FINANCIAL STATEMENTS

Financial statements are reports on the operations or financial position of a business during a given fiscal (or financial) period or on a given date. An **income statement** shows whether a firm operated at a profit or at a loss during a fiscal period, which may be a year, a quarter, or a month. If revenue is greater than expenses, there is a net income; if expenses are greater than revenue, there is a net loss. A **balance sheet** shows the financial picture of a business

	Accounts Payable					Account No. 210	
Date	Explanation	Ref	Debit	Credit		Debit Balance	Credit Balance
1992							
Sept. 4	Inv. 9920A	GJ 201		1995	00		1995 00

Figure 13-4 Accounts payable account in the general ledger.

Wm. Weiler Associates			Credit Referrals:					
2092 North Oak Street								
Des Moines, IA 50301								
Telephone: 515-633-9201			Checking Account Reference:					
Fax: 515-633-9222								
Comments:								
Date		Entry Description	Ref	Debit		Credit		Balance
October	1	Balance	✓					83,000 89
	18	Sales Invoice AJ965	SJ90	396	40			83,397 29
	29	CK 9065	CR550			83,000	89	396 40

Figure 13-5 Customer's record in accounts receivable ledger.

on a specific date rather than during a fiscal period. It includes three major classifications of accounts—assets, liabilities, and owner's equity.

A **statement of owner's equity** shows any changes in the owner's claim as a result of additional investments, net income, or net loss; it also shows any draws against the company by the owner. A **statement of retained earnings** shows the changes in income that have occurred but that have not been paid out as dividends to stockholders.

Headings are very important on financial statements. Each heading must include the company name, the name of the statement, and the date or time period of the statement. Dollar signs should be next to the first figure in a column and next to all totals. Double rules indicate that a process is complete.

Hint: Some accounts may be of more interest than others to your supervisor. Highlight these accounts on any financial statements or reports directed to your department.

SPORTING GOODS, INC.
Income Statement
For the Month Ended October 31, 1992

Operating Revenue

Sales		$327,000.00
Less Sales Returns and Allowances	$800.00	
Sales Discounts	500.00	1,300.00
Net Sales		$325,700.00

Cost of Goods Sold

Merchandise Inventory, October 1, 1992			$80,000.00
Merchandise Purchases		$150,000.00	
Less Purchases Returns and Allowances	$3,000.00		
Purchases Discount	6,900.00	9,900.00	
Net Purchases			140,100.00
Merchandise Available for Sale			220,100.00
Less Merchandise Inventory, October 31, 1992			85,000.00
Cost of Goods Sold			135,100.00
Gross Profit on Sales			$190,600.00

Operating Expenses

Selling Expenses

Sales Salaries Expense	$85,000.00	
Supplies Expense	6,000.00	
Delivery Expense	1,500.00	
Advertising Expense	12,000.00	
Total Selling Expense		$104,500.00

Administrative Expenses

Office Salaries Expense	$22,000.00	
Rent Expense	15,000.00	
Utilities Expense	3,000.00	
Insurance Expense	3,000.00	
Office Operations Expense	550.00	
Telephone Expense	1,200.00	
Depreciation Expense/Equipment	500.00	
Total Administrative Expenses		45,250.00
Total Operating Expenses		149,750.00
Net Income		$40,850.00

Figure 13-6 Income statement.

SPINNETI LAWN AND GARDEN SUPPLIES
Balance Sheet
December 31, 1991

ASSETS

Current Assets
Cash		$25,000.00	
Petty Cash Fund		100.00	
Notes Receivable		3,000.00	
Accounts Receivable	$30,000.00		
Less Allowance for Uncollectible Accounts	600.00	29,400.00	
Merchandise Inventory		83,000.00	
Supplies		200.00	
Prepaid Insurance		2,500.00	
Total Current Assets			$143,200.00

Plant and Equipment
Equipment	$15,000.00		
Less Accumulated Depreciation/Equipment	4,000.00		11,000.00
Total Assets			$154,200.00

LIABILITIES

Notes Payable	$18,000.00	
Accounts Payable	39,000.00	
Salaries Payable	9,500.00	
Sales Tax Payable	5,900.00	
Total Liabilities		$72,400.00

OWNER'S EQUITY

Tony Spinneti, Capital	$81,800.00
TOTAL LIABILITIES AND OWNER'S EQUITY	$154,200.00

Figure 13-7 Balance sheet.

USING THE COMPUTER FOR ACCOUNTING AND BOOKKEEPING

Computerized accounting programs range from programs that produce checks and reconcile bank statements to multiuser, fully integrated systems on a network. Computer application modules can include such programs for check writing, bank reconciliations, accounts receivable, accounts payable, inventory control, payroll, job costing, billing, order entry, and general ledger.

The program may have a single application, or several integrated applications. For example, an accounts receivable module may automatically update inventory, billing, job costing, and general ledger records. Integrated programs allow additional functions to be added as these functions become necessary. Multiuser software depends on a network that allows many users to be on-line at one time and prevents an item taken from inventory by one clerk from being sold at the same time by another.

Numerous accounting packages are available, so it is important to investigate them thoroughly before purchasing. With a background in accounting principles, you can help your supervisor(s) determine whether the software is acceptable to your particular requirements. Here are some questions to ask when choosing accounting software:

❏ What are the hardware or system requirements? Is there enough storage capacity (memory) to run the program *and* handle the number of transactions the business requires? Are reliable data backups and protection procedures included?

❏ Are the menus arranged so the submenus are not lost when the user goes from one module to another? Are windows available so that two or more items of information can be viewed at the same time?

❏ Do modules operate individually or do they rely on a general ledger package?

❏ Is the chart of accounts flexible? Are options available for financial reports or check statement forms? For example, are forms predefined; are they capable of modification; or are they free form, making it possible to create an original format? Do the financial reports provide information for comparative balances, such as budget to actual or current year to previous year? Do they provide year-to-date balances and indicate percentages of increase or decrease in the various accounts?

❏ Are transactions automatically posted to the general ledger immediately after they have been entered? Is there an effective audit trail procedure?

❏ Does the software manufacturer have an 800 number to call for assistance? Are there on-line tutorials? Is the documentation easy to understand and indexed for quick reference?

❏ Is there an opportunity to work through a sample company's transactions and reports? Is it possible to set up an imitation company before entering the company's actual information?

❏ Is it possible to transfer data to spreadsheets and word processing programs? If so, which ones? Does the program allow data to be exported or imported from other spreadsheet programs?

❏ Is there a module that allows the information to be displayed in graphic form?

❏ Is the program capable of printing mailing labels? Will it allow printing on standard business forms?

> **Hint:** Other companies may use the same software you are investigating. Ask for their input before you make a final decision.

(Additional help for choosing software can be found in the section on Selecting Software in Chapter 8.)

HANDLING CASH RECEIPTS

When a business uses a cash register to record its sales, a tape inside the register shows each sale and the total sales for the day. When a business issues receipts for the cash it receives, the receipts should be prenumbered for security purposes. Cash register tapes and copies of the receipts are the source documents for recording sales and cash receipts. Cash and checks should be deposited daily.

If you obtain funds for others, place the money in a sealed envelope and separate it from other cash. Handle checks made payable to cash with extreme care. Indicate the amount on the outside of the envelope and on a sheet of paper that goes inside the envelope with the money. Insist that the money be re-counted by the person accepting it.

CHECKS

The party who signs the check is known as the **maker** or **drawer**. The financial institution upon which the check is drawn is the **drawee**, and the party who will receive payment is the **payee**.

When checks are received in payment for goods and services, check for signatures, correct dates, and correct amounts. The figure on the check must match the written amount. If it does not, return the check to the maker or obtain written verification of the correct amount.

If the payee's name is written incorrectly on the face of the check, the payee should endorse it as written and then endorse it again correctly before depositing. If a check is received and funds are not available to cover it, call the maker of the check immediately to determine how payment is to be covered. Retain the dishonored check in your files.

> **Hint:** A company may call the bank to verify that sufficient funds are available to cover the check at that specific time. The company cannot ask how much money is in the account.

ENDORSEMENT

All checks require immediate endorsement, that is, a signature. An **endorsement** transfers ownership of a check or other negotiable instrument. All checks, as well as traveler's checks, money orders, and bank drafts, require a blank, full, or restrictive endorsement. The place for an endorsement is at the left end of the back of a check.

A **blank endorsement** means only the signature of the payee appears. This type of endorsement is not recommended for general business use. A check with such an endorsement should never be sent through the mail. (See Figure 13-8.)

Occasionally, a business will use a **full endorsement**. The purpose of a full endorsement is to transfer ownership of a check to someone other than the payee. The payee endorses the check and in addition writes "Pay to the order of" and the name of the party to whom the check is being transferred. (See Figure 13-9.)

A **restrictive endorsement** is the most common type of endorsement used by businesses,

Figure 13-8 Blank endorsement.

since it limits the way a check can be used. A typical restrictive endorsement says "For Deposit Only," followed by the bank's name, depositor's name, and account number. When banking by mail, this type of endorsement provides the safest method of transferring a check. (See Figure 13-10.) Most companies use a stamp or machine to endorse checks quickly and safely. For security purposes, keep the stamp for endorsing checks in a locked drawer.

BANK DEPOSITS

A **deposit ticket** preprinted with the identification number of the bank and the account number of the customer provides a record of the deposit for the bank and for the depositor. A signed **signature card** on file at the bank gives an employee the authorization to make deposits as well as to sign checks. It is necessary to have a signature card on file at the bank for each employee who has this authorization.

The following procedures for handling bank deposits should help you to speed up banking transactions.

Figure 13-9 Full endorsement (also, qualified endorsement).

❏ Use coin wrappers, provided by banks, for large amounts of coins. Write the amount, name, and number of the account on the outside of the wrapper before filling it with coins. Inexpensive counters are available that automatically sort coins.

❏ Place bills of the same denomination face up in the bill wrappers supplied by the bank. If the bills are not all the same denomination, arrange them so the largest denominations are on top and the smaller denominations are on the bottom. Secure these bills with a rubber band. Record the amount of money included in each wrapper.

❏ Prepare deposit slips in duplicate. Keep one copy until the bank reconciliation process is complete and all deposits are acknowledged.

❏ List the coins, currency, and amounts for each check on the deposit slip. If checks are drawn on the same bank, list them together. To identify checks, use the name of the bank on which the check is drawn or use the numbers on the top half of the American Bankers Association (ABA) number. ABA numbers indicate the state or city of the bank and the bank number. The numbers in the bottom half of the ABA number indicate a Federal Reserve number and are not necessary on the deposit slip. Arrange the checks so they are in the same order as they are listed on the deposit slip.

❏ Total the currency, coin, and check amounts and place the total in the appropriate

```
FOR DEPOSIT ONLY
RAPIDS NATIONAL BANK
NOLAN & SONS
8643-08
```

Figure 13-10 Restrictive endorsement.

location on the deposit slip and also in the checkbook or check register. A check register not only has check forms but also space to record detailed information about a check.

❏ Deposit the money by taking it directly to the bank, using the night depository or mailing it. Never mail coins or currency, only checks. Banks provide special bags to customers for making night deposits.

HANDLING CASH PAYMENTS

Companies pay for most purchases by check. Check forms and stubs vary. Some companies prefer to use their own printed check forms; others use the checks supplied by their banks. **Voucher** check forms are detachable but have a permanent in-book slip on which to record detailed information concerning the check. A separate **check register** may be used to record information about checks that are issued. Always complete the stubs, voucher forms, and entries in a check register before writing the check. If several invoices are paid with one check, list each invoice number and amount on the stub or voucher form.

Hint: Always follow the company's internal control procedures. Never assume sole responsibility for receiving cash, making deposits, writing checks, recording cash entries, and reconciling checking accounts. Before issuing a check, always be sure the payment has been reviewed and approved by a company official.

Check stubs, copies of voucher forms, or check register entries are the major source documents for making journal entries for cash payments. Information for any of these forms must include the amount of the check, the date, the payee's name, the reason for the check (invoice number, reference notation, brief explanation), the balance before the check was written, and the new balance after the check is written.

If it is necessary to stop payment on a check, call the bank immediately to inform them of the date and number of the check, the payee's name, the drawer's name, the amount, and the reason for the stop payment. Keep a supply of stop-payment forms in the office; these forms satisfy the bank's request for written verification of the transaction. Banks usually charge for stop-payment service. Once the payment is stopped, don't forget to add the amount to the checkbook balance and make the correcting journal entries.

PROCEDURES FOR PREPARING CHECKS

Many checks are computer generated or are produced with check protector equipment. A **check protector** prohibits someone from making changes in check amounts. The device imprints the amount in figures and words (often in color) on the check. There may still be a need, however, to prepare some checks with a typewriter or a pen. Never use a pencil to write any part of a check.

The following suggestions are helpful in writing checks:

❏ Use the current date on checks; do not postdate or predate them.

❏ Enter the payee's full name as far to the left as possible. Draw a line or type dashes to fill in any remaining blank space to prevent the insertion of other names on the check. Titles such as *Ms., Mr.,* or *Dr.* are not necessary. Verify the spelling of a payee's name.

❏ If a check is made payable to an individual who is acting in an official capacity for an organization, such as a county treasurer, write the name of the payee followed by a specific title on the check. This makes it clear that the money is going to the organization and not the payee's own account.

❏ Place the check amount in figures as close as possible to the dollar sign to prevent the insertion of any additional numbers.

❏ Express the amount of the check in words beginning at the far left of the space provided on the check. Only the first letter of the first word needs to be capitalized. The figures 21 (twenty-one) through 99 (ninety-nine) are the only ones that require hyphens. The word *and* is used only between the dollars and cents amount. If the check is for an even dollar amount, fill in zeros for the cents:

Five hundred twenty-nine and 00/100 —————————————————— DOLLARS

❏ Express amounts using as few words as possible. For example, the amount $1645.29 takes up less space if written "Sixteen hundred forty-five and 29/100" rather than "One thousand six hundred forty-five and 29/100."

❏ Circle any amount following a dollar sign that is less than $1. In addition, write "only" before the amount written in words and place a line through the word Dollars.

$\boxed{.75}$

Only seventy-five cents ————————————————————— ~~DOLLARS~~

❏ Do not erase, cross out, or make changes on a check. Write "VOID" on any check that has an error. Make a notation on the stub or voucher form or in the check register when a check has been voided. File the voided checks.

PROCEDURES FOR HANDLING PETTY CASH

Sometimes a payment is too small to justify writing a check; a petty cash fund is a practical way to handle these small expenditures. Usually management designates one person to be in charge of petty cash. The procedures for handling petty cash are as follows:

❏ Have management establish the petty cash fund amount. Once established, the designated amount in the petty cash fund does not vary unless management decides to increase or decrease it.

❏ Always keep the petty cash in a locked box or drawer. If large amounts are not necessary, recommend that the fund be kept small.

❏ Complete a voucher form for every request for petty cash. (See Figure 13-11.)

❏ Do not allow general access to the petty cash fund. Establish procedures for allowing access and obtain approval of management for the procedures. For example, management should specify the amount to be maintained in the fund, specific employees who can use the fund, type of record on which to record amounts paid out, reconcilement steps, signatures required, and steps to reimburse or replenish the fund.

❏ Maintain control by prenumbering the voucher forms. If a mistake is made, write "VOID" on the voucher and in the petty cash record.

PETTY CASH VOUCHER   No._____86_____
Date _____ Amount _____
Paid to _____
Purpose _____
Account/s Charged _____
Issued by _____
Amount of Purchase _____   Received Payment
Cash Returned _____
Cash Owed _____   Signature

Figure 13-11 Petty cash voucher.

Petty Cash Record for Month of _____1991   Page _____

Date		Explanation of entry	Vou #	Petty Cash				Payment Distribution						
				Received		Paid		Supplies		Advertising Expense	Delivery Expense	Other Accounts		
												Account Name	Amount	
1992														
May	1	Established	—	200	00									
		Fund check												
		# 8196												
	1	Labels/	1			8	00	8	00					
		PWP Project												
	2	Floral Rental/	2			30	00					Misc. Expense	30	00
		Open House												

Figure 13-12 Petty cash record.

❏ Record every disbursement in a petty cash record. (See Figure 13-12.) Check the chart of accounts to identify the appropriate general ledger accounts to charge. All petty cash disbursements increase or decrease the amounts in the general ledger.

❏ Verify that the cash remaining in the petty cash fund and the total of the vouchers equal the amount for which the fund was established. Complete this verification once a week.

❏ Replenish the petty cash fund at the end of a specified time period by preparing a check request (or the check) for the amount that will bring the fund to its original amount. If authorized to prepare the check, make it payable to Petty Cash. Cash the check; add the amount to the petty cash box and record the receipt on the petty cash record. Use the cash short and over account when the cash on hand in the fund and the voucher totals are not equal. The cash short and over account accommodates overages or shortages that result from errors made in paying or receiving cash.

❏ Prepare a summary petty cash report for management. The petty cash report lists the amounts charged to *each* general ledger account and the total petty cash expended for the time period. Attach the paid vouchers and receipts.

❏ Prepare a journal entry debiting the accounts charged for the disbursements and crediting cash.

Hint: Replenishing the petty cash fund does not change the original size of the fund. Do not debit or credit the petty cash account at the time you replenish the fund.

SPECIAL PAYMENT FORMS

When an ordinary company check is not appropriate or acceptable, one of the following forms of payment may be appropriate:

Certified check: A bank employee stamps "Certified" on the face of an ordinary company-prepared check. This stamp indicates that the amount is available for payment and the bank has earmarked the funds. There is a fee for the service, and a depositor cannot issue a stop-payment order on a certified check. Certified checks need to be included when reconciling the bank statement.

Cashier's check: A bank employee prepares a cashier's check written on the bank's own account rather than on the depositor's account. The depositor reimburses the bank with a payment equal to the cashier's check plus a fee paid to the bank for issuing the check. The depositor may be the payee on a cashier's check and in turn may endorse it to the appropriate creditor, or the cashier's check may be made payable directly to the creditor to whom the payment is due.

Bank draft: A bank draft is helpful when large amounts of money are being transferred from one location to another, when a payment is due in another location, or when payment is due in foreign currency. A bank employee issues a bank draft on funds in another bank rather than on its own funds. The depositor reimburses the bank that issued the draft for the amount and pays the bank a fee.

Money order. Money orders are negotiable instruments and are used most frequently by people who do not have checking accounts. Banks place restrictions on the amount for which individual money orders may be written; however, more than one money order may be purchased for a fee and made payable to a creditor. Money orders are also available for a fee at post offices and at various retail stores.

Traveler's checks: Traveler's checks are useful when it is inconvenient to carry large amounts of cash. Only the person who purchases traveler's checks can use them. At the time of purchase, the user signs the check in the presence of a representative of a financial institution. Each time a traveler's check is cashed, the user signs the check again in view of the person who accepts it as payment. The checks come in $10, $50, $100, and $500 denominations and are also available in many foreign currencies. The numbers on a set of traveler's checks provide a record in case the checks are lost or stolen. Make a list of these numbers for the traveler as well as for the office files.

Direct deposit service: Direct deposit service may be used for payroll. The company is authorized by the employee to deposit the employee's net pay to a designated financial institution. This eliminates the need for a payroll check. The employee receives only a record of the payment listing such items as regular and overtime hours, gross and net wages, individual tax deductions, and voluntary deductions. Signed authorizations are necessary for employees who wish to participate in direct deposit of their payroll checks.

Automatic withdrawal: A company may authorize the bank to deduct certain designated payments from its checking account and transfer them to the parties to whom the payments are due.

RECONCILING THE BANK STATEMENT

Each month a depositor receives a statement from a bank showing the beginning and ending account balances and any additions or subtractions from the account. Included with the statement are the **canceled checks** (those checks presented and cleared for payment), deposit slips, and credit and debit memos. Credit memos are reminders to add amounts to the ledger accounts and checkbook; debit memos require subtractions.

Some banks retain the canceled checks and simply list the check numbers and amounts on the statements—a process referred to as **check truncation.** The depositor has a checkbook in which either carbons or entries are made each time a check is written so a record

GRAEBER NURSERY
912463-09
RECONCILIATION OF BANK STATEMENT
June 15, 1992

Bank Statement Balance		$29,642.00
Add Deposits		
June 14		8,320.00
		37,962.00
Less Checks Outstanding, June 15		
No. 2078	$5,815.00	
No. 2082	1,655.00	
No. 2083	62.00	7,532.00
Adjusted Bank Balance		$30,430.00
Check Register Balance		$31,581.00
Less: Bank Service Charge Expense	81.00	
NSF	1220.00	1,301.00
		30,280.00
Add: Interest Received		150.00
Adjusted Check Register Balance		$30,430.00

Figure 13-13 Bank reconciliation company format.

of the check is available. If a copy of the original check is needed, the depositor may obtain one for a fee from the bank.

PROCEDURES FOR RECONCILING THE BANK STATEMENT

Reconciling the bank statement is the process of identifying the differences between the book or checkbook balance and the bank balance and bringing these two balances into agreement. Companies often use software programs to reconcile their statements. Reconciliation takes place monthly, as soon as possible after the statement arrives. The bank reconciliation process is not a task to treat lightly or to postpone until time permits. The paperwork, or lack of it, provides auditors with important clues about a firm's financial arrangements. Do not delegate this responsibility to a new or inexperienced employee without training the person and supervising the work.

Banks provide reconciliation forms on the back of the statements mailed to their depositors. Some companies prefer to use their own reconciliation formats. (See Figure 13-13.)

The following procedures are helpful in reconciling bank statements.

Use an appropriate heading that gives the date, account number, and account name, whether you use the bank's form or the company's.

Enter the balance found on the bank statement.

Verify that all deposits in transit from last month's reconciliation as well as all deposits made since the last reconciliation are listed on the statement. **Deposits in transit** are deposits that are already recorded in the depositor's books but that did not reach the bank in time to be included in the statement. List any deposits still in transit and add the total to the bank statement balance.

Compare the canceled check amounts with the bank statement amounts. If they agree, place a checkmark next to the statement amount.

Place the canceled checks in numerical order. Compare the canceled checks with the check stub or check register entries. Also, compare the canceled checks with any outstanding checks listed on last month's reconciliation form. Use a checkmark, preferably in color, on the stub or register to indicate the check has cleared the bank for payment. Checks without checkmarks are **outstanding checks** and have not been deducted by the bank at the time the statement was prepared.

List the amount of each outstanding check along with its number. Obtain a total amount and subtract it from the bank statement balance. This figure represents the **adjusted bank balance.**

Enter the current balance from the checkbook. Be sure the balances in the checkbook and in the cash account in the general ledger agree before doing the reconciliation.

Look for any credit memos listed on the bank statement. Credit memos include such items as collections made for the depositor by the bank or deposit slip errors in the depositor's favor. Compare the list with the entries on the stubs or in the check register. Add those items not yet recorded to the checkbook balance. Give a brief explanation of each credit memo.

Add any interest that has been earned on the checking account to the checkbook balance.

Look for any debit memos listed on the statement. Debit memos include such items as payments the depositor has authorized the bank to deduct automatically, such as mortgage or insurance payments, deposit slip errors that decrease the depositor's cash, or nonsufficient funds notifications. These notices let the depositor know that a check that was accepted in good faith was not payable by the drawer's bank due to lack of funds. Compare the list with entries on the stubs or in the check register. Subtract those items not yet recorded from the checkbook balance. Include a brief explanation for each debit memo.

Subtract fees for overdrafts and for credit card discount fees. The latter are charges made by the bank for handling bank charge card slips.

Once these additions and subtractions are completed, the result indicates the **adjusted checkbook balance.** Compare the adjusted bank balance and adjusted checkbook balance. If the balances do not agree at this point, try these steps to find the errors.

❑ Compute the amount of the difference between the adjusted bank balance and the adjusted checkbook balance. The amount may be an outstanding check that was omitted from the list or a deposit that was not added.

❑ An amount may have been added to a balance when it should have been subtracted or vice versa. Divide the difference by two and the answer may provide a clue. Look for any checks, credits, or debits that equal the answer.

❑ A decimal slide may occur, such as writing $15 for $150. Divide the difference between the two balances by nine. If the answer is a whole number with no remainders, decimal slide may have occurred. For example, suppose the adjusted checkbook balance is $925 and the adjusted bank balance is $790. The difference of $135 divided by nine is $15, a whole number. This figure may be the one causing the discrepancy.

❏ If these methods are not successful, begin at the point of the last reconciliation and add and subtract all entries in the checkbook again.

❏ Finally, if all else fails, contact the bank.

Place the notation "reconciled," the date of the reconciliation, and any corrections, including reasons, on the next available stub in the checkbook or on the next available line in the check register. Write "Correction made (date) from ($x) to ($y)" on the check stub on which the error was made.

Journalize and post any adjustments pertaining to the checkbook side of the reconciliation. All debit memos result in a decrease to cash.

File the bank statements in chronological order by date with the most recent form on top.

File the checks in numerical order in a separate file designed for check retention. Legal requirements for retaining financial records are not the same in all states due to different statutes of limitations.

Hint: As canceled checks are filed each month, color code them to identify the retention periods. For example, code all checks that must be kept permanently with a red sticker. A column indicating the retention period for records is also helpful in a check register.

Hint: Review each month's outstanding checks to investigate checks that have not cleared. Write or telephone the payee to find out if the check was received. If a deposit is not listed on the bank statement and is not in transit, contact the bank as soon as possible to locate the deposit.

USING TECHNOLOGY FOR CHECK WRITING AND RECONCILIATIONS

Single proprietorships or small partnerships and corporations often find that personal finance software for single-entry or double-entry accounting is adequate for monitoring cash flow and reconciling bank statements. Large companies may use a single, comprehensive software package. Before purchasing a software program, however, a company must identify its current and future needs.

Answers to the following questions will be helpful in assessing personal finance software:

❏ Is the program designed for single-entry or double-entry bookkeeping? How much accounting theory is required to operate the program?

❏ Is there automated check writing? Once the amount in figures is entered, does the amount in words automatically appear? Are the amounts entered automatically in a check register? Is there an option to indicate reminder dates for mailing the checks?

❏ Is a preliminary cash report possible? Is it possible to change or delete transactions and *then* prepare payments? Can items be selected and placed on hold for later payments?

❏ Can the program handle handwritten and voided checks? Are checks printed in voucher number or due date order? Is it possible to make partial payments on invoices? If multiple invoices are paid with one check, are all invoice numbers listed?

❑ If a check is sent out monthly (for example, the rent payment), is there a shortcut or a code so the entire check does not have to be reentered?

❑ Are transactions categorized into deductible and nondeductible tax items?

❑ Are accounts listed by categories (for example, assets, liabilities, etc.)? Does the program produce statements (balance sheet, income statement, cash flow reports)? Do the statements provide year-to-date analyses as well as current fiscal period information?

❑ Can the program still be used if the business expands?

❑ Do vendors' accounts indicate such items as name, address, phone number, terms offered, and payment deadlines? Is it possible to print a report of all vendors? Is it possible to print out a report of selected vendors?

❑ Can the vendor's mailing information be printed on the check to take advantage of mailing in window envelopes?

HANDLING PAYROLL

Every company needs a record of the time its employees work, the amount of wages or salaries paid, and information necessary for completing budgets and tax reports. Office professionals assume various levels of responsibility for payroll tasks, ranging from completing their own timecards to completing federal tax documents. Many companies use computers to do payroll, have contracts with commercial payroll service organizations, or use their bank's payroll services. Many small companies still do their payroll manually. Those who understand the concepts of payroll accounting have a level of expertise that is helpful when interacting with CPAs, accountants, and managers and when supervising other employees.

PAYROLL RECORDS

Most companies find that several types of records will provide them with the information they need to meet the requirements of federal and state regulations affecting payroll. Whether the payroll is done manually or on the computer, the same information is needed.

A **master employee list** of all employee names, numbers, addresses, Social Security numbers, phone numbers, departments, hourly rates, overtime rates when applicable, and the number of exemptions provides the basic source of information for the payroll and personnel departments.

A **timecard** or **report** shows the hours worked by each employee. This manual procedure requires careful review and a supervisor's signature. Formats for time reporting vary widely for employees paid hourly wages, for those paid weekly or monthly salaries, and for those hired on a commission, piece-rate, or job-costing basis.

The **payroll register** or journal summarizes information for a specific payroll period and includes time and earnings information on every employee on the payroll. If space permits, a separate column in the payroll register for each deduction is best. Otherwise, a supplemen-

Payroll Register

Week Ending <u>November 9, 1992</u>   Department: <u>Sales</u>

Emp. no.	Employee Name	Marital Status	W.H. Allowance	Earnings			Taxable Earnings				Deductions							Net Paid	Ck. No.	Accounts to be Charged	
				Reg.	O.T.	Total	FICA	Medi-care	FUTA	SUTA	FIT	FICA	Medi-care	SIT	Union dues	Other*	Total			Sales Salaries	Office & Adm. Sal.
	Totals																				

*M = Medical Insurance, T = Tax Shelter Annuity, C = Charitable Contributions

Figure 13-14 Payroll register.

Employee Earnings Record

Employee: _____   Employee No. _____

Address: _____   Date Employed _____

_____   Withholding Allow. _____

_____   Marital Status: _____

Telephone: _____   Regular Rate $ _____

Department: _____   Overtime Rate $ _____

Social Security No. _____   Date Terminated _____

Hours		Earnings				Deductions							Net Pay	Ck. No.
Reg.	O.T.	Reg.	O.T.	Total	Accumulated Earnings	FIT	FICA	Medi-care	SIT	Union dues	Other*	Total		

*M = Medical Insurance, T= Tax Shelter Annuity, C = Charitable Contributions

Figure 13-15 Employee's earnings record.

tary record is necessary for each deduction. The totals on the payroll register provide the data needed for journal entries. (A sample register appears in Figure 13-14.) Office supply stores stock similar forms.

An **employee earnings record** is maintained by most companies. This record provides a place to accumulate payroll data from one period to the next so that at the end of a fiscal year Wage and Tax Statements, or W-2 forms, may be sent to each employee. When recording the payroll manually, the earnings record helps to determine the point when an employee reaches the basic amounts for such taxes as FICA, state unemployment, or federal unemployment. Once these amounts are reached, taxes no longer have to be deducted from the employee's earnings, and employer contributions and tax expenses are no longer required.

Procedures and forms for reporting **sick leave** vary from company to company and often from department to department within a company. Information can be entered on a database program so that periodic reports can be generated for distribution.

PAYROLL TAXES AND OTHER DEDUCTIONS

Payroll deductions, such as income taxes and FICA taxes, are mandatory. Other deductions may be optional, such as union dues, charitable contributions, insurance premiums, and savings plan contributions.

FEDERAL INCOME TAX (FIT)

The employee's number of exemptions (earnings not subject to income taxes), marital status, payroll time period, and gross wages determine the amount of that employee's FIT deduction. Form W-4 provides the authorization for deducting an appropriate amount of federal income tax from an employee's gross wages. The federal government furnishes tax-withholding tables in the booklet *Circular E: The Employer's Tax Guide.* Income taxes withheld by the employer are recorded as liabilities of the company.

STATE, COUNTY, OR CITY INCOME TAX

The same procedures for determining federal income tax deductions also apply for calculating state, county, or city income taxes. The forms to fill out vary in each state and locality. Special tax-withholding tables are available from the appropriate government agencies.

FICA TAX

The FICA tax (Federal Insurance Contribution Act) covers Social Security, old-age, disability, and survivor benefits as well as Medicare for persons over 65 years of age. The federal government sets the percentage of gross wages to be taxed and the maximum base on which the tax must be paid. The base and/or the percentage usually increase from year to year. But both usually do not change in the same year.

The employer is responsible for paying FICA taxes to the government equal to the total amount contributed by all employees in each payroll period. To determine the amount, multiply the total in the FICA taxable earnings column of the payroll register by the current FICA percentage rate. The contributions withheld for employees are liabilities of the business, and the employer's matching contribution is a payroll tax expense.

UNEMPLOYMENT TAXES (SUTA/FUTA)

State unemployment taxes (SUTA) temporarily assist employees who become unemployed as a result of changes they cannot control, such as mergers, layoffs, and cutbacks. SUTA rates and tax bases vary from state to state.

Federal unemployment taxes (FUTA) help defray the costs incurred by the states in administering unemployment programs. Employers receive a credit (the maximum percentage is designated by law) against their federal unemployment tax for monies they pay to the state.

To determine the SUTA and FUTA amounts, multiply the totals in the FUTA and

SUTA taxable earnings columns of the payroll register by the appropriate tax rates. For information on bases and rates, contact the state unemployment commission. Unemployment taxes are expenses of the business.

OTHER PAYROLL DEDUCTIONS

Deductions other than those mandated by law include such items as contributions to retirement accounts or plans, insurance premiums, and union dues. Retirement plan vesting rights and payroll termination dates must be carefully documented so payouts are accurate. The employer records pension payments as an expense of the business and records employees' contributions as a liability.

In the case of insurance premiums, the employer records any amounts withheld from the employees as a liability. Employees often pay their union dues through payroll deductions. The employer records this deduction as a liability and at the appropriate time transfers the dues to the union treasurer.

PAYROLL FORMS AND REPORTS

The employer records and transfers to the appropriate agencies the amounts deducted from employees' earnings or contributed by the company. The following forms and reports are necessary to document employees' authorizations for deductions and the prompt transfer of contributions.

Form SS-4: If an employer does not have an employer identification number, which is used on all payroll forms and reports, Form SS-4 must be completed. It is available at any IRS or Social Security office.

Form SS-5: If an employee does not have a Social Security number, he or she must complete Form SS-5. The Social Security Administration provides the forms.

Form OOAN-7003: Employees must complete this form if they change their names.

Form W-4: All new employees must complete a Form W-4 (Employee's Withholding Allowance Certificate), on which they indicate the number of withholding allowances they wish to claim. The employer files these forms and uses the number of allowances the employee indicates to compute federal and state income tax deductions. Each exemption represents an amount of income that is not taxable. Employees are responsible for requesting any changes in the number of withholding allowances.

Form W-2: Each year on or before January 31, the company must provide its employees with W-2 forms (Wage and Tax Statements) for the preceding year. Employees need these multipart forms to prepare their personal federal and state income tax returns. The employer distributes copies to the Social Security Administration; state, city, or local tax agencies; and employees, who receive several copies to file with tax returns and to retain in their files. The employer retains a copy in the office files. When an employee cannot be located, the employer does not send a copy of Form W-2 to the Social Security Administration but keeps it in the company files for at least four years. If an employee loses a W-2 form, the company reissues another form with the word "reissued" on the new statement. A reissued Form W-2 should not be sent to the Social Security Administration.

Form W-3: An employer must send a Form W-3, the Transmittal of Income and Tax Statements, along with copies of all the W-2 forms to the Social Security Administration. The due date for the W-2 forms and the W-3 transmittal form is the last day of February. Optical scanners are used for reading the W-3 forms, so the information must be typed, and none of these forms may be stapled or folded. Dollar signs may not be used, but a decimal point should be included with the monetary amounts on the forms.

Form 8109: Each time employers deposit income tax and FICA deductions and contributions, they complete Form 8109 (Federal Tax Deposit Form). Once a company obtains an employer identification number, federal tax deposit coupon books are mailed to the company automatically. Form 8109 must include the amount deposited, the tax period, and the type of tax being deposited.

Form 941: Every three months, employers report the amount of income taxes and FICA taxes deducted or contributed on a Form 941 (Employer's Quarterly Federal Tax Return). Form 941 is due at the regional IRS office one month after the quarter ends. For example, the first quarter ends March 31, and the report is due April 30. Any undeposited tax amounts for the quarter are also due at this time.

Form 940. The employer reports FUTA taxes already submitted during the year on Form 940 (Employer's Annual Federal Unemployment Tax Return). The form is due on January 31 of the next year. Any undeposited tax amounts are also due at that time.

SPECIAL CONCERNS ABOUT HANDLING PAYROLL

The employer must deposit federal income taxes withheld and the FICA taxes (employees' and employer's contributions) in a timely manner with a bank authorized to accept such payments. If the deposit is not made according to the rules, the employer faces a fine. In case an emergency keeps you out of the office, be sure someone else is aware of the need for the prompt deposit of these taxes.

USING TECHNOLOGY TO HANDLE PAYROLL

Payroll is often one of the first areas that companies computerize. The payroll module can operate as a separate system or be integrated with the general ledger system. The following questions will be helpful in selecting the best software:

❑ Is there a limit on the number of employees the program can handle? Is there a limit on the number of deductions that can be handled? Are reports generated for each type of deduction per pay period?

❑ Can different compensation modes be accommodated, such as salary, commission, hourly wage, tips, piece rate, pay advances, vacation pay, bonus, per diem, and contract?

❑ Are sufficient tax tables available? Which taxes are included? Does the software company offer tax updates each year? What is the cost? Are both manual and automatic calculation modes available? Can the user set any of the tax rates?

❏ Can payroll expenses be distributed by department? For example, an employee may be assigned to more than one department with different pay rates. Can departmental timecard reports be generated?

❏ Does the program maintain quarterly, monthly, weekly, and year-to-date earnings and deduction accumulations? Are W-2 forms automatically prepared at the end of the year? Can they be prepared automatically at other times as well? Does the program automatically update each employee's earnings and deductions?

❏ Can the payroll be processed without immediate check printing? Is there a report that can be reviewed for incorrect data entries? Is a check register prepared for each payroll period?

HANDLING CUSTOMER BILLING

A company's favorable cash flow depends on prompt payments by its customers. The longer accounts are outstanding, the longer it takes to collect them; some will remain uncollectible. Internal controls are important when working with credit customers. The tasks of recording the journal entries, preparing invoices and statements, receiving customer payments, and mailing the bills require some check-and-balance procedures.

PROCEDURES FOR HANDLING BILLING

The billing task is one of the final steps in a sequence that begins with selling merchandise to a credit customer. With an orderly set of procedures in place, the sales invoice can be completed in a timely manner and mailed the same day as the shipment. The **sales invoice** includes all the details of the sale. It is the source document necessary for making journal and ledger entries.

The following are useful procedural guidelines for handling the various stages of billing:

❏ Review each item of merchandise on the customer's purchase order to be certain descriptions match stock numbers and prices.

❏ Check the pricing options and the credit terms for approval.

❏ Verify the extensions and recalculate the totals on the customer's purchase order. Indicate that this has been completed by placing checkmarks next to the verified figures.

❏ Initial the purchase order after completing a task. A purchase order that has a verification stamp with each task listed in sequence is helpful in tracking the sequence of responsibility.

❏ Prepare multiple copies of the sales invoice and distribute the copies as follows: sales representative/sales, inventory control, shipping and transportation, accounts receivable/accounting, and two copies for the reminder file. To eliminate errors in filing and distribution, use different colors for each copy.

❏ Post the information on the sales invoice to the accounts receivable subsidiary ledger, which is a record of a customer's new sales as well as payments on previously purchased merchandise.

Customer Name	Inv	Inv Date	Terms	0–30	31–60	61–90	91–120	Over 120
			HICKSON DISTRIBUTORS					
			AGED ACCOUNTS RECEIVABLE					
			AUGUST 31, 1992					
Arnold. C. L.	89651	June 15	n/30		359.00			
Bixby Metal	90311	July 15	n/30	865.20				

Figure 13-16 Aged accounts receivable report.

❑ Maintain a chronological file to have control of the dates when payments are due.

❑ Send bills at certain designated times each month. Some companies prefer cycle billing and send bills to certain preestablished groups throughout the month. Arranging groups by sections of the alphabet, by account numbers, or by geographic locations works equally well for cycle billing. An example of a billing schedule follows:

Customers Whose Last Names Begin with	Mailing Date
A–D	1st
E–H	6th
I–L	11th
M–P	16th
Q–T	21st
U–Z	26th

❑ Send one of the reminder invoices as notification that a payment is due five days after the due date. Include a short note, such as: "This is the amount you owe us on (date). We are sending a copy of the original sales invoice so you can review the details of the purchase you made with us."

❑ Send the second of the reminder invoices (if payment is still ignored) 20 days after the first reminder. If necessary, follow this notification with a series of reminder letters. Each letter becomes more insistent, and the time between letters becomes shorter.

❑ Send a collection letter that is both courteous and specific. Gimmick letters, such as the "string attached" theme, may work once, but only if a specific course of action is outlined and a direct request for payment is made. Never overwhelm the message with the gimmick.

❑ Prepare reports to assist management in identifying credit problems and slow-paying customers. An aged accounts receivable report shows those accounts that are overdue by 30, 60, 90, or more than 90 days. (See Figure 13-16.) An aged accounts receivable report arranged by salesperson flags problems unique in specific areas or with specific personnel. A report that arranges outstanding balances from the highest to the lowest identifies those to be collected first.

USING TECHNOLOGY TO HANDLE CUSTOMER BILLING

Companies use accounts receivable software frequently; many assume it will be the answer to prompt collections and therefore increased cash flow. This may be true, but only if such issues as credit approval and price structuring have been addressed. With the increase in the number of service-oriented businesses, time-on-task billing is becoming critical for their success. In these instances, time spent on each process needs to be monitored to see how much it costs to produce the revenue being generated. Although the monitoring may be documented manually, it is more effectively controlled by using a computer program.

Accounts receivable and billing functions may be two separate software modules or they may be combined. The following questions will assist office professionals as they research this software:

❏ Is there a limit to the number of accounts receivable the program can handle? Is the numbering system flexible?

❏ Does the program automatically update such records as inventory, job costing, and the general ledger? Is invoicing done within the accounts receivable module or is a separate module for billing necessary?

❏ Does the program provide the option of handling customer accounts using either the balance-forward method or the open-item method (each invoice is a separate record)? Does it allow the user to identify codes for terms and credit lines so that select customers may receive payment terms different from other customers? Does it automatically calculate finance charges and discounts?

❏ Does the program print product as well as service invoices? When are invoices printed— at the time they are entered, at the end of the fiscal period, or periodically according to the billing cycle?

❏ Are aged reports printed? If so, for how many periods (30–60 days, 61–90 days, etc.)? Does the program print reports showing collections, sales invoices, individual customer ledgers, and a general ledger control report?

❏ Does the program include a procedure that stops credit after a certain point (for example, a certain number of days without payment or a certain number of times payment is not made on time)?

❏ Is it possible to keep track of the number and amount of sales made by each salesperson? Can data be sorted by such items as ZIP Code, customer type, or volume of sales?

CHAPTER 14

TRAVEL PLANNING

Although electronic technology provides organizations with many effective communication options, companies often have more productive results from person-to-person contacts than from telephone calls or letters. Company representatives who travel must have economical, informative, and accurate travel plans. Office professionals have an active role in travel planning; they make the travel arrangements, obtain and organize the information, and handle the follow-up tasks after the traveler returns.

OBTAINING TRAVEL INFORMATION

You may get assistance in making travel arrangements from sources such as a commercial travel agency, an in-house travel or transportation department acting as a travel agency, electronic travel services, or a company employee designated to handle travel requests. In addition, you can contact airlines, hotels or motels, and car rental agencies directly for up-to-date schedule and rate information. Numerous publications also provide excellent reference sources.

COMMERCIAL TRAVEL AGENCIES

Commercial travel agencies can arrange business or personal trips efficiently. In most cases, routine reservation services are free to customers. A company usually selects a travel agency and then establishes an open credit account with that agency. Especially if you work for a small company, you may play a major role in selecting a travel agency and agent. To make a wise selection, you should answer the following questions:

❏ What agency or agencies are other local firms using? Are they satisfied with the service they receive?

❏ Have any complaints about poor service been filed against the company? The local Better Business Bureau can supply this information.

❏ Is the agency a member of a travel trade association such as the American Society of Travel Agents (ASTA) or the Association of Retail Travel Agents (ARTA)? Membership in ASTA, for example, indicates that criteria governing an agent or agency's financial status and ethical practices have been met and the agency has been in business with the same owner for at least three years. ASTA also maintains a Consumer Affairs Department that reviews customer complaints and tries to resolve conflicts through arbitration and mediation.

> **Hint:** If a problem occurs, immediately send copies of all correspondence, dates of telephone calls, names of people contacted, agencies involved, and any documentation involving the action to the ASTA Consumer Affairs Department, ASTA World Headquarters, 1101 King Street, Alexandria, VA 22314.

❏ Are the agents certified? The Institute of Certified Travel Agents offers two types of proficiency designations: the Certified Travel Counselor (CTC) and the Destination Specialist (DS). To obtain a CTC rating, agents must complete an advanced program in travel management and have at least five years' experience in the travel industry. To receive the DS rating, agents must have expertise in one or more specific areas of the world and have a year of travel experience.

> **Hint:** To obtain a list of CTCs in a local area, send a stamped, self-addressed envelope to the Institute of Certified Travel Agents, 148 Linden Street, PO Box 82-56, Wellesley, MA 02181.

❏ Have the travel agents traveled extensively themselves? Do they appear willing to investigate alternative arrangements, give you the best schedules and prices, and take the time to answer questions?

❏ Is the agency independent, part of a national franchise, or a member of a consortium? A **consortium** is a number of smaller agencies who have formed a group to obtain benefits that the larger agencies receive. For example, as a member of a consortium the volume of business will be larger, and this increases the discounts available to customers.

❏ Does the agency specialize in business travel? Does it book hotel accommodations for large groups? Can it compare costs of meeting rooms and make conference arrangements?

❏ What type of computer reservation system (CRS) does the agency use? Is it possible for the agency to send tickets to companies electronically; for example, through satellite ticket printing? Are the printed itineraries and tickets readable? Are the boarding passes attached or enclosed with the ticket?

❏ Is the appearance of the travel agency professional? Are the brochures current and attractively arranged?

❏ Are the billing procedures acceptable? Are summary statements prepared that list each trip, date, and cost of trip by employee? Is it possible for the agency to track mileage to be applied to frequent-flyer benefits?

IN-HOUSE TRAVEL DEPARTMENTS

Because travel costs are a significant budget item, companies require detailed records of money spent. Some companies operate their own in-house travel agencies with designated employees who monitor travel requests and expense reports. This allows companies to get the lowest fares possible and to control the classes of service (first, business, or coach) booked by employees. Some companies have policies concerning frequent-flyer benefits that result from business travel, either for the company or for the employee. In-house controls provide an effective way to track these benefits.

Computerized systems similar to those used in travel agencies can also be leased to companies. A company's travel policies, such as preferred airline, first-class privileges, number and level of company representatives per flight, and any per diem limits may be programmed into the system. The computer will then selectively display only those flights that meet the travel guidelines. It is possible to book the reservations through the computer and receive tickets through the company travel office, pick them up at the airport, or have them mailed.

By using a microcomputer, modem, and communications software, companies can access a computer network with a travel service. To use a network service, companies pay a monthly fee plus telephone charges or a charge based on time used. The travel service is free. The following is just a sample of the types of travel information available through a network:

- Up-to-date flight information; flight restrictions
- Lowest airfare information; on-time statistics; train travel
- Credit card arrangements
- Airline meal selections; seating preferences
- On-line reservation capabilities with tickets held at the airline or delivered
- Flight changes; layover times; stops en route
- Hotel and restaurant information for the United States and overseas; banquet and meeting room facilities; local events; city guides
- Weather information and Department of State travel advisories
- Suggestions and tips on travel

PUBLISHED TRAVEL REFERENCES

State travel and tourism departments provide information on outstanding features of the state. The Chamber of Commerce is a good source for local information. Public libraries and bookstores often have copies of consumer travel publications as well as tourist guides. Auto clubs supply information on lodging, restaurants, and places of interest to its members.

Hint: Most airlines, car rental agencies, and hotel chains have toll-free 800 numbers to call for reservations. If you do not have a directory of 800 numbers, telephone 1-800-555-1212 to obtain the 800 number you need. Weather information (current and three-day forecasts) is available for U.S. and foreign cities by dialing 1-900-Weather.

Reference publications provide detailed information about transportation and accommodations. To use these references effectively, it is necessary to keep them up to date. Even though travel agencies maintain this information, you can use these published references for preplanning. Their use can save on-line computer time or telephone contact time with a travel agent. The references, however, are expensive and the price may be too high for a small firm. Following are several published travel references:

Official Airline Guide ® (OAG ®): This guide contains detailed airline schedules. Cities are arranged alphabetically and listed by destination and origin with the airlines that service them. Information for each flight is arranged chronologically by the time of departure. Times are stated in local times. Additional information includes flight numbers, days the flights operate, number of stops and in which cities, food service, types of airplanes, baggage allowances, and the airline's 800 number for reservations. Ground information includes distances to the city from the airport, types of airport transportation available, car rental agencies and their toll-free numbers, and helicopter service. Two editions exist: the North American version, which is updated twice a month, and the Worldwide version, which is updated once a month. The *OAGEE,* an electronic edition, is also available.

OAG ® Pocket Flight Guides: These pocket guides are quick references for checking scheduled direct flights. They also include airline reservation telephone numbers of all carriers in each listed city, departure and arrival times, names of airlines and flight numbers, class of service, type of aircraft, and stops en route. The guides, which are updated monthly, are available in four editions: North America, Latin America/Caribbean, Europe/Middle East/Africa, and Pacific/Asia.

OAG ® Travel Planner Hotel and Motel Redbook: Published four times a year, this reference contains detailed hotel listings (some with ratings), airline and ground information, car rental and rail directories, airport diagrams, country and city maps, and currency conversion rates. A section for each country features a calendar of events, banking and business hours, consulate office information, and travel document requirements. There are two editions of this reference, the Pacific/Asia and the European. A North American edition, *OAG ® Business Travel Planner,* is also available.

Official Hotel and Resort Guide: Several volumes contain descriptive information about hotels, motels, and city attractions. Maps, room rates and ratings, number of rooms, fax and Telex information, and telephone numbers are useful when trying to determine the best accommodations. The guides come in a looseleaf format with updated pages mailed regularly to subscribers.

Hotel and Travel Index: The listings in this reference are alphabetically arranged by country, state, and city. Publication of this large, comprehensive index is on a quarterly basis. It is available in single issues or by subscription and includes telephone numbers, Telex and fax information, addresses, number of units, and credit cards accepted.

Official Railway Guide: Rail timetables and fares for Amtrak as well as for trains in Canada and Mexico are available in this guide, which is published eight times a year. Information on large city commuter rail transit services is useful to business travelers.

Thomas Cook Timetables: Schedules for Europe are available in the *Thomas Cook Continental Timetable.* The *Thomas Cook Overseas Timetable* lists schedules for all other worldwide railway systems. Both guides show maps of the area traveled, visa requirements, and time zones.

The Official National Motorcoach Guide/The Official Canadian Guide. These guides include fares and schedules for bus lines in the United States, Canada, and Mexico. Copies are available monthly. Single issues may be purchased.

UNDERSTANDING TRAVEL TERMS

Regardless of your source for professional travel assistance, you should understand the terms and acronyms you will encounter. Most important are terms used in airline travel, accommodations, and car rental.

AIRLINE TRAVEL TERMS

Business travelers have three classes of airline service from which to choose:

❑ *First class* offers wider seats and more space than other classes of service. It also offers quality food service, free drinks, and attentive, personalized service. Because of these extras, first class is quite expensive.

❑ *Business class* is less expensive than first class, but the passenger also receives special benefits, such as more space for carry-on items, free drinks, above-average meals, and a quiet working atmosphere. Special streamlined check-in procedures may be available for both first-class and business-class passengers.

❑ *Coach-class* seats are not as wide, and there is limited leg room. With more passengers moving around the cabin, coach class is less quiet and less appealing as a working area. It is the least expensive class of service.

If the flight is listed as **direct,** the plane makes stops in one or more cities, but passengers do not change planes. A **nonstop** flight has no stops between the departure and arrival cities. A **connecting** flight requires a plane change.

Fare structures are determined by destination and also by such factors as the amount of advance purchase time required, class of seating, the refundable status of the ticket, and the day of the week and time of travel.

> **Hint:** Nonrefundable tickets have penalties attached if plans change and the trip is not made. The entire cost of the ticket or a percentage of the cost may be lost. If the cancellation is due to a family medical emergency, a physician's letter will void the penalty. When making reservations, be sure to request information about the penalties for canceled trips.

For a traveler on **standby status,** there is a possibility that a seat will become available at the time of the flight. If one is available, the person travels as a regular customer. A traveler on a **waitlist** is one who wants to fly at a time when the flight is already filled. The traveler's name is placed on a numbered list. If a seat becomes available as the result of a cancellation (within 24 hours of flight time), travelers are accepted from the waitlist in the order of the assigned number and type of booking.

A **stopover** involves spending more than 12 hours in a location that is an interruption in the trip. An **open-jaw** trip is one in which the passenger returns to a city other than the one in which the trip originated. An **open ticket** is valid between two cities but indicates no specific reservation. For example, it may be used if a return trip cannot be finalized at the time the reservations were made.

Most airlines offer **frequent-flyer** incentives to encourage customers to use their services. Members may take free upgrades in class of service or save the miles and take a discounted fare trip or a free trip later.

Airline club services are available for an annual fee. Members may use these airport facilities for making telephone calls (local calls may be free), photocopying, storing luggage, using the fax machine, or working or relaxing in a quiet area. Meeting rooms may also be booked, and refreshments are available.

Accommodation Terms

Hotel rates and service depend on the type of plan offered. **Budget hotels** have low prices and cater to the traveler on a limited budget. **Executive** rooms are deluxe accommodations and expensive. Rooms are often advertised with ratings; a four-star rating is very high. Some businesspeople prefer **all-suite** hotels, with living room, bedroom, bath, and often kitchen facilities. This type of arrangement is useful when meetings are to be held in hotel rooms. A **concierge** is a hotel employee who assists guests with such tasks as making theater reservations or suggesting restaurants. A concierge may be assigned to a specific floor or floors in a hotel.

The **American plan (AP)** is a rate that includes, in addition to the room, all meals daily. The **modified plan (MP)** offers breakfast and dinner. The **breakfast plan (BP)** includes full breakfasts each day. The **continental plan (CP)** includes a continental breakfast (often muffins or sweet rolls, juice, and beverage) each day. The **European plan (EP)** offers no meals. A **rack rate** is the official posted rate of a hotel room. **Corporate rates,** which must be requested, are available to business travelers and are less than the quoted normal daily hotel or motel rates. The **frequent-stay benefit** allows regular customers to receive discounted rates or extra services such as upgrades in rooms, late check-outs, car rental discounts, and special attention to reservations. Some frequent-stay programs have incentive ties to frequent-flyer membership programs.

Car Rental Terms

Car rental agencies use different classifications when describing their cars. Most agencies use the term **deluxe** to describe their largest, most expensive model. A **standard** model is a full-size car. A **compact** is regular size, and a **subcompact** is a small car.

A **drop-off charge** is the amount a car rental agency charges when a car is rented at one location but returned to another. If a car is rented under a contract that specifies **unlimited mileage**, the driver pays a set amount for a designated time period; the payment is not based on the number of miles traveled, as is the case for a **limited mileage** plan.

A **collision damage waiver** or **liability damage waiver** increases the cost of a rental considerably. Most travelers will not need these waivers since they are covered by their own personal automobile insurance policies and by some credit card plans.

MAKING RESERVATIONS

When making reservations of any type—airline, hotel, or car—company policy as well as the preferences of the person traveling are important considerations. If other company employees are traveling also, you must work with others to coordinate travel arrangements. To insure a trip free from annoying distractions, reservations must be accurate and complete. You should handle these tasks prior to making reservations:

Research the travel policies of the company. Well-written policies specify such items as whose signatures are required for travel approval, per diem allowances, travel restrictions, procedures for using company credit cards, and the documentation necessary for expense reports.

Identify travel agencies, airlines, car rental agencies, and hotels and motels that the company prefers to use.

Maintain a permanent file of the traveler's preferences that includes these items:

- Days of the week for travel
- Departure times (early morning, mid-day)
- Airline and seating arrangements

Hint: If the traveler has coach-class seating, he or she may not want a center seat on a plane where the seats are three across. When reserving seats, a window or aisle seat can be requested.

- Restrictions on costs

Hint: Membership in associations such as the American Management Association or the American Association of Retired People allows special hotel and car rental rates. Some companies also have accounts with specific hotels and car rental agencies that allow them special rates for their employees. Always give the name of the organization and member number for which a special rate is available when making the reservation.

- Location of hotel; type of accommodations; services needed at hotels or motels; type of room and location of room; rooms allowing or prohibiting smoking
- Type and size of car; ground transportation
- Times and locations for meetings upon arrival

Verify the trip details, such as destination, dates, and meeting times and places with the traveler.

Prepare a planning guide to use when making reservations. (See Figure 14-1.) Before making the final reservations, be certain the traveler approves the arrangements.

Hint: Box in or highlight the information that must be given to the travel agent or reservation assistant so you do not forget information when making reservations. Record every detail about the reservation made.

Hint: To make the planning guide easily recognizable, use colored paper. Keep a copy of the guide in the files. It is an excellent source for preparing the itinerary.

TRAVEL PLANNING GUIDE

Name _____ Department _____

Credit Card: Type _____ Number _____ Expiration date _____

Frequent Flyer Information:

Airline _____ Number _____

Preferences of Traveler: Place a checkmark in the column labeled "Information Given" each time a reservation is made through a travel center. Many travel agencies also keep this information on file for their clients.

Information
Given

Airline Preferences

_____ Carrier Preference _____

_____ Seating Preference _____

_____ Days of Week _____

_____ Departure Times _____

_____ Special Needs _____

_____ Other Preferences _____

Accommodation Preferences

_____ Hotel/Motel Chain/Other _____

_____ Hotel/Motel Location _____

_____ Floor/Room Location _____

_____ Type of Accommodations _____

_____ Services _____

Car Rental Preferences

_____ Model, Type, Size _____

_____ Services _____

Name _____ Department _____

Telephone: Work _____ Ext. _____ Home _____

Airline: _____

Number of People Traveling: _____   Travel Dates: _____

Destination City/Cities: _____

Routing:

Option 1:

Departure

| Date | Departure | | Arrival | | Airline and Flight No. | Airport |
	City	Time	City	Time		

Restrictions: _____

Return Trip

| Date | Departure | | Arrival | | Airline and Flight No. | Airport |
	City	Time	City	Time		

Restrictions: _____

Figure 14-1 Travel planning guide.

Option 2:

Departure

	Departure		Arrival			
Date	City	Time	City	Time	Airline and Flight No.	Airport

Restrictions: _____

Return Trip

	Departure		Arrival			
Date	City	Time	City	Time	Airline and Flight No.	Airport

Restrictions: _____

Class of Service: _____ Seat: _____ Type of Plane: _____

Special Meals: _____ Verified: _____

Booking Date: _____ Option: ____ Name of Agent: _____

Confirmation Date: _____ Name of Agent: _____

Airline Telephone Number: _____

Cost: _____ Method of Payment: _____ Ticket Pickup: _____

Flights Preceding Option Selected: _____

Flights Following Option Selected: _____

Transportation to Destination: _____

Distance to Destination: _____

Comments: _____

Traveler's Approval: _____

Hotel/Motel Accommodations

Hotel/Motel Name: _____

Address: _____ Phone No.: _____

Booking Date: _____ Confirmation Number: _____

Date of Arrival: _____ Date of Departure: _____

Type of Room: _____ Number of People: _____

Check-in Time: _____ Check-out Time: _____

Meeting Facilities/Size: _____ Banquet Facilities/Size: _____

Directions to Hotel: _____

Courtesy Transportation: _____

Cost: _____ Guaranteed Arrival: _____ Method of Payment: _____

Special Services: _____

Cancel by: _____

Reservations Agent: _____

Traveler's Approval: _____

Car Rental

Company Name: _____

Name of Driver or Drivers: _____

Model, Type, Size of Car: _____

Special Services: _____

Dates Car is Needed: _____

Incoming Airline and Flight Number: _____

Pickup Location: _____ Drop-off Location: _____

Cost: _____ Method of Payment: _____

Date of Reservation: _____ Agent: _____

Figure 14-1 *(con't)*

Begin a trip folder for each person who is traveling. Collect all materials that pertain to the trip and file them in the folder. File the trip folder behind the planning guide. Place all written confirmations, appointments, addresses, and telephone numbers in an $8\frac{1}{2}$-by-11-inch envelope within the folder. Include hotel brochures, restaurant suggestions, maps of the city, and transportation options that will be helpful when the traveler arrives at a destination. This trip folder will be the basis for organizing the materials that will accompany the traveler on the trip.

Remind the traveler to write or call the people with whom meetings are being scheduled. Document travel arrangements and dates of visit as well as addresses and telephone numbers that might be used while at this location. Request directions to the meeting locations as well as directions within the building, such as floor and room numbers. Confirm all meeting dates and times two days before the traveler leaves.

AIRLINE RESERVATIONS

The airline reservation is the first reservation made after the trip has been approved and tentative appointments have been scheduled. The reservation agent or travel agent needs the following information before booking the flights:

❏ Departure city, date, and time

Hint: When booking a flight, request information on flights scheduled before and after the one that is actually being booked. Include this information as a note on the itinerary so alternative arrangements can be made in case a flight is delayed or there is a seat on an earlier flight.

Hint: To assist the agent and to obtain the best selection of fares, indicate general departure times, such as mid-morning or before 10 a.m., rather than exact hours.

❏ Arrival date, time, and destination

Hint: Distances from cities to airports vary. Allow sufficient time between scheduled meetings and airline departure and arrival times. Be especially careful with scheduling during rush-hour traffic periods.

Hint: Nonstop flights to the destination city are most desirable. If a flight requires a connection in cities where the weather may be bad or where a terminal change is necessary, allow sufficient time between flights.

❏ Restrictions on costs; special rates for conference groups

Hint: Companies may request that employees stay over a Saturday night to save on airline fares. Be sure to consider the extra hotel charges when comparing rates.

❏ Number of people traveling
❏ Names, addresses, and telephone numbers of passengers
❏ Frequent-flyer mileage information

Hint: When using frequent-flyer credits, make reservations directly with the airline. Maintain a list of frequent-flyer mileage numbers so that they are available when reserving the flight. Make sure the agent has the frequent-flyer numbers so that credit can be given for each trip.

❑ Class of service; type of flight; seating preference; smoking or nonsmoking; handicap accommodations if applicable

❑ Special meals, such as vegetarian, low fat, low sodium, kosher, Hindu, and Moslem

Hint: Verification of special-request meals should be made approximately 48 hours before flight time to assure availability of the meals. Order the special meals at the time the reservation is made.

❑ Airline and flight numbers

❑ Name of destination airport or airports

❑ Type of ground transportation and where to get it; mileage to city center

❑ Shuttle service

Hint: Shuttle reservations are not necessary. Passengers purchase tickets through a machine or en route. Check for luggage restrictions since some shuttle flights allow only carry-on bags.

❑ Arrangements to pick up tickets; method of ticket payment

❑ Airline telephone service

❑ Airline club availability

❑ Airline service centers

Hint: The centers offer services similar to those of airline clubs; however, travelers do not have to be members. Travelers pay only for the services they use. Since charges vary from center to center, check costs carefully.

❑ Name of agent making the reservation

❑ Date of booking

❑ Date of confirmation

Hint: Many airlines and some countries require that you confirm a return flight 24 to 48 hours before departure.

❑ On-schedule information

Hint: FlightCall, a service offered through the *Official Airline Guide* ® (*OAG* ®), provides information indicating whether a flight is on time. Using FlightCall is often quicker, though more expensive, than calling the airline. The number is (900) 786-8686.

HOTEL OR MOTEL RESERVATIONS

Travel agents can reserve hotel or motel accommodations. You can also call the hotel or motel directly or use "800" reservation numbers provided by the larger hotel and motel chains. Include this information on the planning guide to assist you in making hotel or motel reservations:

❏ Name of person and company
❏ Arrival date and time; departure date and time; guaranteed late arrival

Hint: If the reservation is guaranteed late arrival, the hotel charges the customer whether the room is used that evening or not. If changes in accommodations are made while en route, the person traveling must inform the hotel or motel to avoid charges. In addition, remind the person traveling to contact the hotel or motel if arrival time has been delayed beyond 6 p.m. to avoid cancellation of the room. When making the reservation, find out the cancellation policy of the hotel or motel.

❏ Cost restrictions

Hint: Promotional rates may be available. Ask for them when making the reservation.

❏ Number of persons per room; bed size; smoking or nonsmoking room; room location (e.g., away from vending machines); top, first, or concierge service floor
❏ Method of payment (credit card number)

Hint: Since credit cards are used so frequently, keep a list of personal and corporate credit card numbers in a special file. Mark it "confidential" and keep it in a locked drawer.

❏ Specific location of hotel or motel

Hint: Careful booking is required since there may be several hotels in the area that are part of the same chain. Request specific location information—city, address, telephone numbers, and proximity to meeting location.

❏ Type of plan, such as European, continental, or modified
❏ Courtesy airport pick-up and return; hours of operation; pick-up location; procedures to obtain the service
❏ Check-in and check-out times
❏ Laundry/cleaning services; hairdressers (appointments necessary?); pool; exercise facilities; evening drinks/refreshments; room-service hours; telephone service/extra charges
❏ Secretarial services; private office suite availability; equipment availability; modem capabilities

Hint: Specific information may not be available by calling an 800 number when making reservations. To be certain of equipment facilities call the concierge at the hotel.

Hint: Some hotels reserve a floor for business travelers. There is usually an area where guests can relax, obtain concierge assistance, and mingle with other businesspeople. Others are developing business centers, which are equipped with up-to-date equipment and software.

Hint: The Association for Computer Training and Support publishes *Traveling with a Laptop Computer.* A free copy is available by sending a stamped, self-addressed envelope to ACTS, 27 Sagamore Road, Raquette Lake, NY 13436.

❑ Business advisors for briefings on protocol in foreign countries; access to on-line news services

❑ Suites or conference rooms; banquet and meeting facilities

Hint: Hotels are very helpful in arranging group meetings or conferences. Contact the hotel sales manager or convention sales coordinator for information.

❑ Confirmation number

Hint: Hotels may overbook or lose a reservation. Always request written confirmation of a hotel reservation. Obtain the name of the reservation clerk and the confirmation number.

CAR RENTAL RESERVATIONS

Car rental agencies have rental locations at airports or short distances from airports, at some hotels, and at downtown or suburban locations. When making car rental reservations, the following items of information will be helpful:

❑ Dates for which the car is needed; pick-up and drop-off times; pick-up and drop-off locations

Hint: Pick-up and drop-off locations may be off the airport premises.

❑ Name of person renting and names of drivers
❑ Flight number of arriving flights if applicable
❑ Cost restrictions; discounted rates; insurance charges; out-of-state or out-of-country restrictions; age limitations of drivers
❑ Limited or unlimited mileage
❑ Model, type, and size of car
❑ Drop-off charge; charges for late drop-off
❑ Frequent-flyer coupon restrictions and information
❑ Cellular telephone availability and cost

COMPANY CARS, PLANES, AND CHARTER FLIGHTS

A company may provide a car for an employee to use for business travel. Someone in the company is responsible for reserving the cars and keeping maintenance records on them. Since other employees also use company cars, it is important to reserve the car as early as possible in the trip-planning process so one is available when needed.

State or city tourist bureaus issue road maps and city maps as well as general information about the area. It takes time to obtain these materials, so such information needs to be requested early in the planning process.

Hint: If a person travels to certain locales frequently, maintain a file of maps, lists of good restaurants, limousine services, and other information for those areas. Arrange the materials by city or state and keep the files up to date.

Hint: To make expense reporting and record keeping easier, prepare a mileage chart showing the number of miles between cities to which the person often travels.

If a company has its own planes, consult the person who keeps the records for reserving a seat. This person is usually responsible for contacting the pilots, verifying departure dates and times, and following the guidelines for determining which employees (and family members, if applicable) are eligible to use the service.

When a number of people travel to the same meeting, chartering a small plane may be economical and time-efficient. To identify companies that operate charter flights, check the Yellow Pages of the local telephone directory under "Aircraft Charters and Rentals." To obtain information about the cost of a charter flight, you must indicate the length of the trip, the number of stops, size of plane, overnight stays for crew members, in-flight catering, jet or nonjet, and the number of passengers.

ARRANGING INTERNATIONAL TRAVEL

International business activity has increased greatly, and thus more company employees are traveling to foreign countries. Travel agents provide the best assistance for planning these business trips; however, you will also need information about travel documents, foreign customs, security, and foreign currency as you organize the details involved in foreign travel.

TRAVEL DOCUMENTS

The documents necessary for travel vary from country to country. Sources of information about a country's entry requirements or travel restrictions include the following:

❏ Airline offices serving the countries being visited
❏ Travel agents
❏ Foreign government tourist bureaus with offices in the United States
❏ *Foreign Entry Requirements* (U.S. Government Publication M-164), which includes such information as required travel documents, immunizations, embassy or consulate addresses and telephone numbers, time required for processing travel documents, and currency regulations

> **Hint:** For a free copy, check at a U.S. passport agency or write to the U.S. Department of State, Bureau of Consular Affairs, Washington, DC 20520. Another more general publication, *Your Trip Abroad*, is available from the Superintendent of Documents, U.S. Government Printing Office, Washington, DC 20402-9371.

❏ Nearest embassies or consulates of the countries to be visited

> **Hint:** For locations of these embassies or consulates, check *The Congressional Directory*; a copy is available at most public libraries. Consulates and embassies are helpful in emergencies or when trying to contact a person traveling in a foreign country.

❏ Citizens Emergency Center for Travel Advisory Information, Department of State, Washington, DC 20520, which issues warnings about areas of political unrest, terrorism, currency restrictions, and hotel shortages in specific regions or countries

PASSPORT

A **passport**, issued by the U.S. Department of State, is required for every U.S. citizen who plans to travel in a foreign country. It is valid for ten years and gives a citizen the right to leave the United States, receive protection, if necessary, within the country being visited, and reenter the United States after traveling. A passport is not necessary for a citizen traveling to Mexico, Canada, the West Indies, the Caribbean, and some South and Central American countries. It is wise to apply for a passport well in advance since it may take three to six weeks to obtain.

First-time passport applicants need to appear in person at a State Department passport agency, at an appropriately designated courthouse (federal, state, or county), or at a U.S. post office. The applicant needs to bring the following:

❏ Proof of identity—driver's license or government identification card
❏ Proof of citizenship—birth certificate, certificate of naturalization, certificate of citizenship, or report of birth abroad of a citizen of the United States. If these are not available, secondary proof, such as a baptismal certificate, voter registration verification, elementary school records, or insurance papers, is also acceptable.
❏ Photographs—two identical 2-by-2-inch color or black-and-white photographs taken during the past six months. The Yellow Pages in the local telephone directory will indicate those photography studios where passport pictures are taken and processed. The date of the photograph and the owner's signature should be written on the backs of the two photographs. Make several extra copies of the photographs. In case a passport is lost in a foreign country, extra photographs can expedite getting a replacement passport from the U.S. Consulate.
❏ Fee

If a person had a passport in the past and now wishes to renew it, a shorter form mailed to the nearest passport agency is acceptable. The necessary documents include an application form, the old passport, two photographs, and the fee.

Hint: Passport numbers and dates for renewal should be recorded in the "travel preference" folders maintained for all managers in order to remind the users of dates when passports must be renewed.

Hint: Order a 48-page passport with space for numerous visa stamps if the person travels a great deal to foreign countries.

VISA

A **visa** is a permit to enter a certain country for a specific purpose on a specified date. If a visa is required in a country, the consulate of that country issues one by stamping the passport. A travel agent can obtain a visa for a traveler by sending the passport, an application, and any necessary fees to the consulate. Many countries in Asia, the Middle East, the South Pacific, and Eastern Europe require visas. In a very limited number of cases, a visa may be issued upon arrival in a country. Some countries require letters of reference or proof from travelers that they have transportation in and out of the country; some restrict the length of stay.

TOURIST CARD

The tourist card grants entry to a country without a passport or visa. Tourist cards for a country such as Mexico are available from the country's embassy or consulate office, official tourist offices in the United States, some travel agencies, airlines serving that country, or at the port of entry.

INTERNATIONAL DRIVING PERMIT

The permit verifies that the data on a regular license is valid; the information is written in the language of the country in which it is needed. A fee, a completed application, and two passport photographs are required. Permits remain in effect for one year from the date of issue. They are available from the American Automobile Association (AAA) or the American Automobile Touring Alliance, 888 Worcester Street, Wellesley, MA 02181.

INTERNATIONAL CERTIFICATE OF VACCINATION

The United States does not require vaccinations before returning; however, some countries do request documentation of certain vaccinations for such diseases as cholera or yellow fever before entering. International certificate of vaccination forms are available through local or state public health offices or passport agencies. The form requires a physician's signature and the health department's stamp.

> **Hint:** For up-to-date international health information, order a copy of *Health Information for International Travel,* U.S. Government Printing Office, Washington, DC 20402. It lists required and recommended vaccinations by country and recommends ways to maintain health while traveling. Always use a current copy, since regulations concerning proof of vaccination change. There is a fee for the booklet. The International Travelers Hotline, (404) 332-4559, is another source for region-by-region information concerning required vaccinations. The Public Health Office may also have this information, but always ask the date of their sources.

> **Hint:** If vaccinations are needed, remind the traveler to allow time for the vaccinations to become effective, such as five days for cholera.

CERTIFICATE OF REGISTRATION

The certificate of registration allows a traveler to register any personal foreign-produced item, such as a watch or camera. This eliminates any customs delays when entering the country. Documents, such as a bill of sale, jeweler's appraisal, or receipt, are proof of prior possession.

COMPUTER DECLARATION

Some countries require entering travelers to declare computers and other electronic equipment at customs. Forms such as Application for a Valid License (BXA-622P) and Digital Computer Systems Parameters (ITA-6013P) provide information on make and model, equipment diagrams, and specific hardware descriptions. The Office of Export Licensing processes the forms and assigns a validated license number.

The validated license number is needed to complete the Shippers Export Declaration form, which is required for customs. The United States Department of Commerce has the forms in stock.

> **Hint:** Electrical power and outlets in a foreign country may be different from those in the U.S. An adapter and/or a transformer may be required for electrical appliances. Check this before embarking on a trip. When scheduling meetings in foreign countries, request information about the type of equipment available and its compatibility with the items the traveler will be bringing.

CUSTOMS DECLARATION

Articles purchased in certain foreign countries and brought back to the United States are subject to customs declaration; there are, however, exemptions. The Department of the Treasury, U.S. Customs Service, publishes *Know Before You Go* and *Customs Hints for Returning U.S. Residents,* which are designed to assist travelers who have made purchases in foreign countries.

FOREIGN CURRENCIES

Once travel plans are completed, there may be a need to obtain foreign currency. Traveler's checks in dollars or a foreign currency are a popular way for business travelers to handle money. Worldwide travel companies, such as American Express, banks with foreign exchange facilities, and some travel agents, through airline-sponsored reservation systems, sell traveler's checks in foreign currencies. The customer may receive foreign traveler's checks by registered mail or, for an additional fee, by overnight delivery, or they may be picked up in person.

Credit cards are accepted in most foreign countries. The conversion rate may be less than the charges involved with traveler's checks.

Large banks usually have certain currencies available for those travelers who want cash before they arrive in a country. Current exchange rates are published in some local newspapers and in the *Wall Street Journal,* or they may be obtained by calling the bank or the reference librarian at the public library.

CULTURAL AWARENESS

Company employees who represent their firms in foreign countries will find it helpful to acquire general information about the countries as well as knowledge of the customs and values of the people with whom they will be working. Office professionals can assist in collecting and organizing this information so it can be used by anyone who travels internationally or associates with foreign visitors.

GENERAL INFORMATION

Find out as much as possible about topics such as economic climate, history, the political party in power, education, recreational facilities and events, business ethics, and negotiation strategies. A current atlas will provide general information about a country. People who have visited the country, businesspeople who have done business there, or college professors who teach language or area studies courses are also excellent resources for general information about specific countries.

LANGUAGE

Everyone appreciates a visitor's attempts to communicate in the native language of the host country. Small language translators are available, often with correct pronunciations. Practice the pronunciations for such appropriate courtesy phrases as "Thank you" and "It was a pleasure meeting you." If business is to be conducted in English, the English used must be understandable. Superlatives such as "fantastic" or "absolute disaster" are confusing. Two-word verbs, such as "break up" or "win back" should be avoided. Acronyms, slang, and jargon, such as "ballpark figures," are difficult for foreigners to interpret.

GREETINGS/ADDRESS

Greetings range from handshakes to bows to friendly slaps on the back. For example, handshakes are a common form of greeting and saying goodbye in the western European countries. Japanese businesspeople often bow and then shake hands.

Addressing someone with his or her title and last name is appropriate in most countries. Determine who will be visited, and write down the pronunciation of each name. Place this information in the appropriate meeting folder.

EYE CONTACT

To Americans, eye contact signifies honesty; but in some countries, such as those in Latin America, keeping the eyes lowered shows respect.

BUSINESS CARDS

Business cards are very appropriate in international situations. It is courteous to print one side of the card in English and the other side in the language of the country visited.

TIME

In some countries, meetings and appointments often begin late; however, this does not devalue the importance of the business to be conducted or provide a reason for others to be late. In other countries, however, promptness is imperative. Afternoon breaks of two hours or more are common in many European countries. In such cases, appointments are best made for the morning hours.

Central European businesses may close during July or August for vacation. Long weekends are also customary. Banks and some businesses in Muslim countries are open on Saturday and Sunday but closed on Friday.

Time differences between various parts of the world affect travel preferences as well as optimum meeting times.

Holidays vary from country to country. Some are regional or local only. To avoid scheduling appointments on holidays, check with the country's consulate or embassy in the United States.

Jet lag may make it necessary to allow some time for readjustment. Avoid scheduling meetings too close to arrival time at the destination city.

MEALS AND TIPPING PRACTICES

In some countries, such as Greece or Spain, the time for the evening meal is relatively late. Huge banquets are often given in China. Travelers to Asian countries may wish to learn to use chopsticks. Discussing business during a meal may be inappropriate.

Tipping practices vary. Prepare a list of tipping suggestions for each country the traveler plans to visit and include it with the materials to be taken on the trip. Current tourist manuals found in bookstores or public libraries are useful sources of information for tipping practices. In many countries, a percentage tip is included on the bill, so additional tipping is not necessary.

BODY LANGUAGE

Head shakes may have different meanings or even opposite meanings in different countries. A nod may simply mean that the message has been heard; it does not necessarily indicate agreement. Requesting feedback is appropriate and wise at various stages of a discussion.

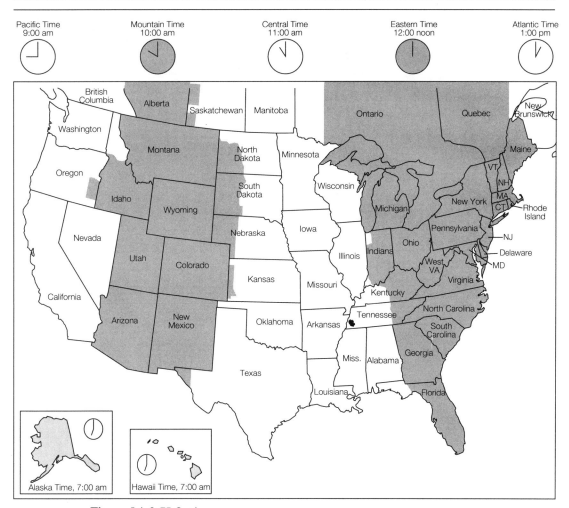

Figure 14-2 U.S. time zones.

In Japan, it is polite to use both hands when receiving or giving items, such as business cards. In India, it is inappropriate to use the left hand for such purposes.

GIFT GIVING

Appropriate gifts include products from the United States or an illustrated book. In some western European countries, a gift is not given at the first meeting. Giving a banquet for Chinese businesspeople is an appropriate gift, but receiving a clock as a gift is considered bad luck in China. No gifts of liquor should be given in the Middle Eastern countries, since alcohol is forbidden by the Muslim religion. Return dinner invitations or theater invitations are customary forms of gifts in most countries.

Table 14-1 Time Differences Around the World

| Country | Time Zone | | | |
	EST	CST	MST	PST
American Samoa	−6	−5	−4	−3
Argentina	+2	+3	+4	+5
Australia (Sydney)	+15	+16	+17	+18
Austria	+6	+7	+8	+9
Belgium	+6	+7	+8	+9
Bolivia	+1	+2	+3	+4
Brazil	+2	+3	+4	+5
Chile	+1	+2	+3	+4
Colombia	+0	+1	+2	+3
Costa Rica	−1	+0	+1	+2
Cyprus	+7	+8	+9	+10
Denmark	+6	+7	+8	+9
Equador	+0	+1	+2	+3
El Salvador	−1	+0	+1	+2
Fiji	+17	+18	+19	+20
Finland	+7	+8	+9	+10
France	+6	+7	+8	+9
Germany	+6	+7	+8	+9
Greece	+7	+8	+9	+10
Guam	+15	+16	+17	+18
Guatemala	−1	+0	+1	+2
Guyana	+2	+3	+4	+5
Haiti	+0	+1	+2	+3
Honduras	−1	+0	+1	+2
Hong Kong	+13	+14	+15	+16
Indonesia	+12	+13	+14	+15
Iran	$+8\frac{1}{2}$	$+9\frac{1}{2}$	$+10\frac{1}{2}$	$+11\frac{1}{2}$
Iraq	+8	+9	+10	+11
Ireland	+5	+6	+7	+8
Israel	+7	+8	+9	+10
Italy	+6	+7	+8	+9
Ivory Coast	+5	+6	+7	+8
Japan	+14	+15	+16	+17
Kenya	+8	+9	+10	+11
Korea	+14	+15	+16	+17
Kuwait	+8	+9	+10	+11

EST-Eastern Standard Time   MST-Mountain Standard Time
CST-Central Standard Time   PST-Pacific Standard Time

Table 14-1 *(con't)*

Country	Time Zone			
	EST	*CST*	*MST*	*PST*
Liberia	+5	+6	+7	+8
Libya	+7	+8	+9	+10
Luxembourg	+6	+7	+8	+9
Malaysia	+13	+14	+15	+16
Monaco	+6	+7	+8	+9
Netherlands	+6	+7	+8	+9
New Zealand	+17	+18	+19	+20
Nicaragua	−1	+0	+1	+2
Nigeria	+6	+7	+8	+9
Norway	+6	+7	+8	+9
Panama	+0	+1	+2	+3
Paraguay	+1	+2	+3	+4
Peru	+0	+1	+2	+3
Philippines	+13	+14	+15	+16
Portugal	+5	+6	+7	+8
Romania	+7	+8	+9	+10
Saudi Arabia	+8	+9	+10	+11
Senegal	+5	+6	+7	+8
Singapore	+13	+14	+15	+16
South Africa	+7	+8	+9	+10
Spain	+6	+7	+8	+9
Sri Lanka	$+10\frac{1}{2}$	$+11\frac{1}{2}$	$+12\frac{1}{2}$	$+13\frac{1}{2}$
Sweden	+6	+7	+8	+9
Switzerland	+6	+7	+8	+9
Tahiti	−5	−4	−3	−2
Taiwan	+13	+14	+15	+16
Thailand	+12	+13	+14	+15
Tunisia	+6	+7	+8	+9
Turkey	+8	+9	+10	+11
U.S.S.R. (Moscow)	+8	+9	+10	+11
United Arab Emirates	+9	+10	+11	+10
United Kingdom	+5	+6	+7	+8
Vatican City	+6	+7	+8	+9
Venezuela	+1	+2	+3	+4
Yugoslavia	+6	+7	+8	+9

Colors are significant and should be considered when choosing gifts; for example, white and black are associated with mourning in Japan. The same is true of purple in Latin American countries. Red and gold are good colors in China.

AGE AND SEX

Age is highly honored in some countries. A younger person, therefore, may be less successful in business negotiations. In other countries women may find it difficult to conduct business transactions.

CORRESPONDENCE

Generally, business letters from foreign countries are formal and courteous. Some letters may begin with references to the weather or with personal comments.

The tone of your own business correspondence should not be overly familiar. The use of clear, precise English is helpful to a foreign reader. Short sentences limited to one idea and paragraphs of seven to eight lines will clarify major points. If several points are made, precede them with "first," "second," etc. To avoid confusion in dates, write them out; for example, use "October 8, 1990," rather than "10/8/90," which may be interpreted as August 10.

If measurements or money are mentioned in correspondence, use metric units and current monetary conversion rates. To avoid misunderstandings, indicate both the dollar amount and the amount in the appropriate foreign currency. (For metric equivalents and conversions, see Tables 14-2 and 14-3.)

DECISION MAKING

A company's trustworthiness is an important factor in conducting foreign business. To establish a favorable perception of trustworthiness, such items as the history of the company, its founders, and personal information about the people attending the meeting are helpful and may be sent to the foreign company before the visit.

In some countries the most important matters are left until the end of a meeting; in others, omitting details suggests evasiveness. Knowing such differences before a meeting and organizing the materials accordingly can aid in negotiations.

In some Asian countries decisions are often made by a group, not left to one person. The time needed to make decisions, therefore, may be lengthy, which can be a factor in scheduling meetings or business trips.

REFERENCES FOR FOREIGN TRAVEL

Numerous guides exist on customs, etiquette, and general information about foreign countries. Other resources include airline magazines, tourist books, and a foreign country's tourist office. Two excellent sources of information are the Business Council for International Understanding, The American University, Washington, DC 20016, and the David M. Kennedy Center for International Studies, Brigham Young University, Provo, UT 84604.

Table 14-2 Metric Equivalents

Linear Measure	
U.S. CUSTOMARY	METRIC
1 inch	25.4 millimeters (mm)
	2.54 centimeters (cm)
1 foot (12 in.)	304.8 millimeters (mm)
	30.48 centimeters (cm)
	0.3048 meter (m)
1 yard (36 in.; 3 ft.)	0.9144 meter (m)
1 rod (16.5 ft.; 5.5 yds.)	5.029 meters (m)
1 statute mile (5280 ft.; 1760 yds.)	1609.3 meters (m)
	1.6093 kilometers (km)
METRIC	U.S. CUSTOMARY
1 millimeter (mm)	0.03937 in.
1 centimeter (cm)	0.3937 in.
1 meter (m)	39.37 in.
	3.2808 ft.
	1.0936 yds.
1 kilometer (km)	3280.8 ft.
	1093.6 yds.
	0.62137 mi.

Liquid Measure	
U.S. CUSTOMARY	METRIC
1 fluid ounce (fl. oz.)	29.573 milliliters (ml)
1 pint (16 fl. oz.)	0.473 liter (l)
1 quart (2 pints; 32 fl. oz.)	9.4635 deciliters (dl)
	0.94635 liter (l)
1 gallon (4 quarts; 128 fl. oz.)	3.7854 liters (l)
METRIC	U.S. CUSTOMARY
1 milliliter (ml)	0.033814 fl. oz.
1 deciliter (dl)	3.3814 fl. oz.
1 liter (l)	33.814 fl. oz.
	1.0567 qts.
	0.26417 gal.

Table 14-2 *(con't)*

Area Measure

U.S. CUSTOMARY	METRIC
square inch (0.007 sq. ft.)	6.452 square centimeters (cm²)
	645.16 square millimeters (mm²)
square foot (144 sq. in.)	929.03 square centimeters (cm²)
	0.092903 square meter (m²)
square yard (9 sq. ft.)	0.83613 square meter (m²)
square rod (30.25 sq. yd.)	
square mile (640 acres)	2.59 square kilometers (km²)

METRIC	U.S. CUSTOMARY
1 square millimeter (mm²)	0.00155 square inch (sq. in.)
1 square centimeter (cm²)	0.155 square inch (sq. in.)
1 centiare	10.764 square feet (sq. ft.)
1 square kilometer (km²)	0.38608 square mile (sq. mi.)

Capacity

U.S. CUSTOMARY	METRIC
cubic inch (0.00058 cu. ft.)	16.387 cubic centimeters (cc; cm³)
	0.016387 liter (l)
cubic foot (1728 cu. in.)	0.028317 cubic meter (m³)
cubic yard (27 cu. ft.)	0.76455 cubic meter (m³)
cubic mile (cu. mi.)	4.16818 cubic kilometers (k³)

METRIC	U.S. CUSTOMARY
1 cubic centimeter (cc; cm³)	0.061023 cubic inch (cu. in.)
1 cubic meter (m³)	35.135 cubic feet (1.3079 cu. yds.)
1 cubic kilometer (km³)	0.23990 cubic mile (cu. mi.)

Avoirdupois Weights

U.S. CUSTOMARY	METRIC
1 grain	0.064799 gram (g)
1 ounce (437.5 grains)	28.350 grams (g)
1 pound (16 oz.)	0.45359 kilogram (kg)
1 short ton (2000 lb.)	907.18 kilograms (kg)
	0.90718 metric ton
1 long ton (2240 lb.)	1016 kilograms (kg)
	1.016 metric tons

Table 14-2 *(con't)*

	Metric Units		
EASY ESTIMATION GUIDE (rounded off for rule-of-thumb estimations)			
PREFIX	METRIC UNIT	U.S. EQUIVALENTS	
milli- = $\frac{1}{1000}$	1 millimeter = 0.039 inch		
centi- = $\frac{1}{100}$	1 centimeter = 0.39 inch		
deci- = $\frac{1}{10}$	1 decimeter = 3.937 inches	= 0.32 foot	
	1 meter = 39.37 inches	= 3.2 feet	= 1.1 yards
deka- = 10	1 dekameter = 393.7 inches	= 32 feet	= 10 yards
hecto- = 100	1 hectometer = 3937 inches	= 328 feet	= 109 yards
kilo- = 1000	1 kilometer = 39300 inches	= 3280 feet	= 1090 yards

ARRANGING TRAVEL FUNDS

Company guidelines for obtaining travel funds are usually very specific and require strict adherence to established schedules and procedures. Company credit cards, cash advances, and personal payments to be reimbursed later are ways to fund travel.

COMPANY CREDIT CARDS

A company often issues company credit cards to individual employees. These cards remain the property of the company. A list of all employees who are issued individual credit cards for travel purposes must be kept up to date so that when an employee leaves the company the expenses charged to that credit card are cleared before another employee receives the card privileges.

CASH ADVANCES

A cash advance allows a traveler to receive funds before leaving on a business trip. Since all costs are not known in advance, it is necessary to estimate such expenses as food and business entertainment. A typical cash advance form requires the following information before the accounting office issues cash or a check:

- Date of request
- Purpose of trip
- Travel location
- Dates of trip
- Amount requested—may or may not require a breakdown of individual expenses
- Signature of person traveling
- Approval of supervisor

Table 14-3 Metric Conversions

METRIC TO U.S.	U.S. TO METRIC
LENGTH	
millimeters × 0.04 = inches	inches × 25.4 = millimeters
centimeters × 0.39 = inches	inches × 2.54 = centimeters
meters × 3.28 = feet	feet × 3.04 = meters
meters × 1.09 = yards	yards × 0.91 = meters
kilometers × 0.6 = miles	miles × 1.6 = kilometers
VOLUME	
milliliters × 0.03 = fluid ounces	teaspoons × 5 = milliliters
milliliters × 0.06 = cubic inches	tablespoons × 15 = milliliters
liters × 2.1 = pints	cubic inches × 16 = milliliters
liters × 1.06 = quarts	fluid ounces × 30 = milliliters
liters × 0.26 = gallons	cups × 0.24 = liters
cubic meters × 35.3 = cubic feet	pints × 0.47 = liters
cubic meters × 1.3 = cubic yards	quarts × 0.95 = liters
	gallons × 3.8 = liters
	cubic feet × 0.03 = cubic meters
	cubic yards × 0.76 = cubic meters
MASS	
grams × 0.035 = ounces	ounces × 28 = grams
kilograms × 2.2 = pounds	pounds × 0.45 = kilograms
short tons × 0.9 = metric tons	metric tons × 1.1 = short tons

AREA

METRIC TO U.S.

square centimeters × 0.16 = square inches
square meters × 1.2 = square yards
square kilometers × 0.4 = square miles
hectares (ha) × 2.5 = acres

U.S. TO METRIC

square inches × 6.5 = square centimeters
square feet × 0.09 = square meters
square yards × 0.8 = square meters
square miles × 2.6 = square kilometers
acres × 0.4 = hectares
(the hectare is not an official Sl unit, but is permitted)

TEMPERATURE

degrees Fahrenheit   − 32 × 5/9 = degrees Celsius
degrees Celsius   × 9/5 + 32 = degrees Fahrenheit

To be sure the amount received matches the amount requested, count the money received from the accounting office, and do not sign a receipt form until this has been verified. Place the cash or check in an envelope for the manager, include a copy of the signed request form, and obtain a signature from the person who accepts the money. File that signed copy in the preliminary trip folder; it will be helpful in preparing the expense claim.

PERSONAL PAYMENTS

When payments for travel expenses are handled personally by the traveler, receipts for all expenditures are necessary for reimbursement. Since many of the payments may have been on the traveler's personal credit card, it is advisable to make copies of all receipts. The originals accompany the expense claim.

LETTERS OF CREDIT

Handling travel funds with a letter of credit allows a traveler to obtain funds up to a designated amount from banks. Such a letter states that the person is a customer in good standing at the bank issuing the letter. The letter acts as an introduction in financial institutions and allows the bearer to make withdrawals up to the amount of the specified credit line.

PREPARING THE ITINERARY

The **itinerary** is a chronological outline of travel plans prepared for each person who is traveling. Even though the airline prepares a flight itinerary, it is helpful for the traveler to have more detailed information presented on a day-by-day basis.

The planning guide provides an excellent source of information for the itinerary. Itinerary formats may vary, but the information is similar on all. (See Figure 14-3.) This information includes:

❑ Dates and times of departure and arrival.

Hint: Include the day of the week as well as date. Note all time zones. If the international date line is crossed, be sure the dates are accurate.

❑ Departure and arrival cities.

Hint: A city may have more than one airport. For example, Chicago has both Midway and O'Hare. Choose the airport closest to the meeting location. Clearly identify the destination airport on the itinerary.

Hint: If the flight crosses time zones, use the local arrival time. Indicate the number of hours of flying time between destinations. If applicable, include the amount of layover time.

ITINERARY
SANDRA MCNEELEY
May 6-8
National Pharmaceutical Sales Conference

WEDNESDAY, MAY 6

1:30 p.m.	Leave Chicago/O'Hare Field
	American Airlines Flight No. 836
	Nonstop; lunch
5:10 p.m.	Arrive Boston/Logan Int.
	Hotel Transportation Provided
	Phone: 267-9314
	Hotel: Revere Square Hotel, 9135 Revere Square
	Dates: May 6 and 7
	Confirmation No. 156J92CD
	Guaranteed Arrival

NOTE: Upon arrival, contact Tom Kennedy regarding conference presentation.

THURSDAY, MAY 7

7:30 a.m.	Breakfast meeting with Donald Hallahan and
	Courtney Watson, Revere Square Coffee Shop
	Advertising Review Promotion Campaign

NOTE: Contact conference headquarters for conference handouts.

10:00 a.m.	Presentation to National Pharmaceutical Sales Conference,
	Decker Hall, Revere Square Hotel
11:45 a.m.	Luncheon with Jon Blake, new account,
	Pullman Room, Regency House
4:00 p.m.	Meeting with all regional sales managers,
	Hall B, Revere Square Hotel
7:30 p.m.	Conference Banquet,
	Boston Room, Revere Square Hotel

FRIDAY, MAY 8

7:30 a.m	Breakfast meeting with Tom Kennedy, Hotel Coffee Shop
10:00 a.m.	Exhibits Review with Sandra Milo,
	Grand Ballroom, Revere Square Hotel
12:00 noon	Conference Luncheon,
	Boston Room, Revere Square Hotel
3:10 p.m.	Leave Boston/Logan Int.
	American Airlines Flight No. 462
	Nonstop; snack
5:30 p.m.	Arrive Chicago/O'Hare Field

Figure 14-3 Sample itinerary.

❏ Airline; flight numbers; seat assignment; meals provided.

❏ Airport transportation; cost; times of operation; telephone numbers of limousine services.

❏ Car rental agency; type of car; charge card used.

❏ Lodging accommodations; confirmation numbers; written confirmations; telephone, fax, or Telex numbers; guaranteed arrival time; date reservation was made; name of person who made the reservation; credit card used; services available, such as exercise facilities or secretarial.

❏ Appointments for each day; date; address; room and building; time of meeting; names of people involved; reason for meeting; contact persons and their office and home telephone numbers.

> **Hint:** If social engagements are scheduled, indicate the type of dress required.

❏ Reminders for each appointment, such as where to find materials needed for each meeting or personal information about the people at the meeting.

> **Hint:** If an appointment is some distance away from the airport, indicate its distance so the meeting can end in time. Highlight times when a connection time is short or extra materials are needed. Leave a reminder if a task must be completed, such as making a reservation if a return time or date was left open.

When the itinerary is up to date, prepare two copies for the traveler (one to carry and one for the luggage), one copy for the office files, and one copy for the manager in charge. The traveler may also wish additional copies for family and/or friends.

ORGANIZING TRAVEL DETAILS

Even though materials may be collected as soon as the initial plans for a business trip are in place, it is not always possible to complete everything before the trip begins. Some last-minute tasks include the following:

Check the tickets against the information in the trip planning folder. Check the itinerary to be sure times, dates, and locations match the tickets.

Organize materials and supplies that will be needed for the trip. A checklist for each traveler is helpful. The following are examples of items to include on the list:

❏ Copy of itinerary
❏ Tickets
❏ Motel or hotel information
❏ Money, letters of credit, or traveler's checks

> **Hint:** If traveler's checks are used, give the traveler a list of the check numbers, to be kept separate from the checks. Keep a second list in the office. In case of loss, the check numbers will be available for a refund. (See the section *Special Payment Forms* in Chapter 13 for a discussion of traveler's checks.)

❏ Speeches and reports

Hint: In case the original copy of a speech gets misplaced, mail or fax a copy to a specified individual at the location of the meeting. Send handouts ahead of time so they will not have to be carried on the plane. Allow sufficient time for the items to reach their designated locations and verify that they were received. If the materials are sent to a hotel, indicate the name, date of arrival, and specific meeting for which they will be used. If they are sent to a business, address the package to a specific person in that organization.

❏ Business cards; company letterhead and envelopes, preaddressed mailing envelopes; company forms, Post-it notes, manila envelopes, legal pads, folders; paper clips, stamps, notepads, tape, rubber bands, calendar
❏ Notes on the area, on special customs, and on etiquette (for foreign countries)
❏ Items that must be delivered; wrapped gifts
❏ Airline timetables; maps
❏ Expense account forms; office checks

Hint: The traveler may need a reminder to keep track of expenditures, so include a blank expense claim form and an envelope for receipts. If the expense claim is filled out while traveling, the details are more easily remembered than if the traveler waits until returning to the office.

❏ Passport; visa
❏ Vaccination certificates; international driver's license or permit
❏ Medical prescriptions

Hint: Since medical or eyeglass prescriptions are important and difficult to replace, be sure they are in the materials to be carried by hand. Include a personal health information card with blood type and allergies.

❏ Credit cards

Hint: A list of card numbers and toll-free numbers of the credit card companies is helpful in case the cards are lost. Prepare a list for the office and one for the traveler.

❏ Frequent-flyer numbers
❏ Telephone credit card; emergency telephone numbers
❏ Portable slide projector or overhead projector
❏ Slides or transparencies

Hint: Audiovisual presentations are less frustrating if the materials are sequenced and numbered before the trip begins.

❏ Laptop computer; batteries; recharger; extra disks, software; summary of keystrokes to activate the modem, fax, printer, and programs
❏ Portable fax; dictation equipment; portable printer with paper; spare ink cartridges; portable photocopier; cables
❏ Adapters for three-prong plugs (some locations may have only two-prong outlets); car battery adapters for electronic equipment; adapters for use in foreign countries
❏ Surge suppressor; battery packs

Hint: Make copies of this list for use in organizing travel materials. Ask the traveler to check the items that need to be packed. Include one completed copy in his or her files and keep one in the office.

Contact the airline, travel agency, hotel or motel, or car rental agency if any changes in travel plans are made. Confirm the airline reservation a day before departure.

Place materials for each appointment in a separate folder and place them in envelopes with clasps. Prepare a label with the company name and date of appointment for each folder as well as for the envelope. Number each envelope in consecutive order according to the information on the itinerary. In case the envelopes are mixed up, the numbers will make it easy to rearrange. Include helpful information such as recent correspondence, an annual report of financial information, names of people contacted previously, officers' names, and product or service updates for each company.

Place airline tickets and confirmations in a special envelope labeled "Tickets." Do not pack the tickets, passports, visas, or traveler's checks in the luggage that is to be checked. If a ticket is lost or stolen, the traveler must buy a new one. The airline will reimburse the traveler for the cost of this purchase, but it may take as long as four months to receive the refund.

Contact the airline to determine the number, weight, and size restrictions for luggage that may be carried on the plane. Sort materials in two groups—one for hand-carried luggage and one for checked luggage.

Make photocopies of airline tickets, passport identification page, driver's license, and credit cards. Keep one set at the office and give the other set to the traveler.

COMPLETING FOLLOW-UP TASKS

Well-planned business travel includes monitoring the office tasks that must be completed during and after a manager's absence. While the manager is away, the office professional assumes responsibility for the daily office tasks necessary to operate efficiently. When the manager returns, the office professional often prepares the expense report and follows up on the tasks resulting from the trip.

HANDLING TASKS DURING A MANAGER'S ABSENCE

You should decide which tasks the manager must handle upon returning to the office and which you can handle without immediate supervision. The following suggestions will assist you in organizing work so time is used efficiently.

Maintain a day-by-day activities list. Highlight the priority action items to alert the manager who calls the office regularly. Compile questions that need to be asked when he or she calls. Identify the best time to contact the manager. Obtain fax numbers for the places where the manager has scheduled meetings. Clarify how paychecks or money transfers should be handled *before* the trip begins.

Understand the parameters of authority while the manager is away from the office. Discuss emergency procedures and delegation of tasks *before* he or she leaves. Know who has been authorized to handle emergencies and to make major company decisions.

Sort the mail and distribute it to the appropriate individuals. When another manager has been designated to be in charge, be sure all pertinent items are sent to that person.

Maintain folders for mail received and actions taken. Label the folders as follows:

❏ Immediate attention
❏ Actions completed

> **Hint:** Maintain a log of each task or action taken. For easy reference, attach this log to the inside of the "Actions completed" folder. Include a copy of the paperwork connected with each action.

❏ General reading
❏ General correspondence
❏ Signature required
❏ Phone calls; visitors; appointments made; activities in the office

Compose routine correspondence as needed. Sign the letters as follows:

Sincerely yours,

Barbara Williams
Executive Assistant to J. T. Todd

Forward mail or fax items to predesignated locations. Maintain a record of these items along with dates they were forwarded. Keep copies in a folder labeled "Items sent to (name)." If mailing items, number each item and inform the manager of the number of items enclosed. Indicate the number and type of items being forwarded and keep a list for the office files.

Maintain a list of all telephone calls and all appointments made each day. Prioritize the calls and keep a list that will be helpful to a manager. Always update the appointment calendars. Place in parentheses to identify they were made in the manager's absence. As directed, cancel and reschedule appointments and committee meetings during the manager's absence.

COMPLETING EXPENSE REPORTS

Completing expense reports is another task that requires attention after a trip is over. Some businesses require receipts for all company money spent; others have per diem allowances, which require only receipts for expenses above the limits. Follow explicitly the company guidelines for categorizing travel expenses. If you have questions about travel expenses, discuss them with the person submitting the expenses. Study company policy and ask for clarification when needed.

When filling out expense reports, you should:

Complete the expense claim paperwork as quickly as possible. If a receipt is missing or a gap in activities is evident, it will be easier for the manager to remember the event now rather than later.

Review the receipts and notes made by the manager while traveling. If any part of the trip was canceled, check the monthly credit card statements carefully for excess charges.

Categorize the receipts by transportation, registration, food, lodging, business entertainment, and miscellaneous (tips, tolls, parking, telephone and fax charges, secretarial services, postage charges).

Attach all required receipts to the expense claim forms. Make copies of each receipt for the files. Keep these receipts for five years. Legitimate business expenses include the following:

❑ Transportation (airline, shuttle, railroad, bus, taxi, limousine, or rapid transit); car rentals; automobile costs at the current IRS rates or established company rates per mile; parking fees; flight insurance
❑ Lodging; meals; tips
❑ Laundry and cleaning costs; telephone, fax, mail, and shipping charges; business supplies
❑ Exhibit charges; conference registration fees
❑ Conference room charges
❑ Business entertainment expenses

Indicate the type of entertainment, names of clients (titles and companies represented), dates, location (city, state, and street location), duration, and the purpose of the meeting when itemizing the business entertainment expenses on the claim form. The IRS reviews these amounts very carefully and specifies that they must relate to the business being conducted. The expenses may be incurred directly before or after a business activity takes place as well as during the activity.

> **Hint:** *Travel, Entertainment, and Gift Expenses,* a booklet published by the IRS, lists rules for handling deductible travel expenses. You can obtain a copy from the IRS or, in many cities, from the public library.

Compare the total expenses incurred with the cash advance made. If money is owed to the company, get a check for the difference from the traveler and attach it to the expense report.

Review the completed expense claim carefully. Check all calculations at least twice. Obtain the necessary signatures and submit the claim for payment. It is important to have the necessary documentation and to be sure the claim is accurate the first time it is submitted so reimbursements will not be delayed.

HANDLING POST-TRAVEL TASKS

When the traveler returns to the office, numerous tasks will need completion. Some suggestions for handling these follow-up activities include:

❑ Avoid scheduling lengthy, important meetings the first day or two after the trip.
❑ Explain what activities have taken place during the travelers's absence. Schedule time on your appointment calendar to discuss the items in the "Immediate attention" and "Actions completed" folders.

❑ Compose thank-you letters for courtesies that were extended to the traveler during the trip. Write the appropriate follow-up letters.

❑ Replace all materials that were removed from the files for use during the business trip. The checklists of materials that were packed for the trip provide a reminder of those items that were taken out of the office. If necessary, prepare labels and folders for new contacts or subjects that were the result of the trip.

❑ Change computer files and, if necessary, reprint and distribute updated versions to the appropriate parties. Send copies of all items promised by the manager to the appropriate contacts.

❑ Record comments about travel and hotel preferences in the travel preference folder.

MEETING PLANNING AND MANAGEMENT

Successful meetings are the result of careful planning and management. There are two types of meetings. A **formal meeting** is a structured, planned meeting with a prepared agenda, such as an annual sales meeting, yearly conference, or convention. An **informal meeting** is generally held on company premises and can be held regularly or called at the last minute.

PLANNING A MEETING

Whether the meeting is formal or informal, the process of planning for a meeting is the same. Certain questions must be answered by the person calling the meeting so that the meeting planner can act:

- What is the purpose of the meeting?
- How long will the meeting run?
- Who should attend?
- What equipment and aids will be needed?
- Where should the meeting be held?
- When is the best time to hold the meeting?

To determine the time and place of the meeting, you need to notify participants of the meeting and determine their availability. Reserve at least three available dates and times. Ask them to hold these times open until they are called back later in the day to confirm the meeting's date and time. After contacting all participants, review the schedule to see what date and time are acceptable to all. You may have to undertake this process several times to arrive at an acceptable date and time.

Depending on the complexity of the meeting, scheduling, budget, and other forms may be necessary. Such meeting forms may be available through the company or, if not, an office supply store may carry standard forms. The American Management Association produces a manual, *Conference and Workshop Planner's Manual,* that contains sample planning schedule, budget, equipment and supply checklist, registration form, and speaker-appraisal forms.

MEETING FUNCTIONS

The functions involved in planning and running a meeting depend on how the organization operates, the type of meeting, and whether the planning and execution of the meeting rests with one person or with committees. All or some of the following functions must be addressed in planning a meeting:

- Budget
- Agenda
- Attendees
- Meeting notices and agendas
- Guests, speakers, or program participants
- Site and facilities
- Equipment and audiovisuals
- Exhibits and demonstrations
- Refreshments and meals
- Minutes and proceedings

NOTIFICATION OF MEETING PARTICIPANTS

Notification of participants can be made by telephone, by mail, or by computer through the electronic mail system or network communication system, if available. The meeting planner should make a list of those to be notified, make sure all have been informed, and check responses so that a final list of attendees can be prepared. Participants should be informed of the day, time, and place of the meeting, the topic to be discussed, and the identity of other participants. An agenda and supplementary material should also be distributed; for example, directions to the meeting location are often provided.

In addition, supplementary material should be gathered for the meeting. The meeting room should have enough chairs, pads, pencils, and paper. All charts and graphic material should be displayed, and any audiovisual equipment and/or computer technology should be checked and set up for use.

AGENDA

An agenda is a list of all matters to be brought up at the meeting. Agendas vary with the type of meeting. Informal meeting agendas simply list the items to be discussed during the meeting. Formal meeting agendas detail times, events, speakers, and locations of events.

Hint: All papers and documents pertaining to matters that will be discussed at the next meeting should be kept in a meeting folder. The folder should contain copies of the meeting notice, a list of those to whom notices were sent, drafts of resolutions to be taken up at the meeting, and an outline of the minutes of the last meeting. An agenda can be prepared from material accumulated in the current meeting folder.

In formal meetings, the bylaws of an organization usually state the order of business of the meeting, and an agenda can be prepared from this model. A typical agenda for a director's meeting might include:

- Reading of the minutes of the last directors' meeting
- Presentation of reports of officers and committees
- Adoption of a resolution approving the minutes of executive committee meetings
- Current business

The agenda should list each item to be acted upon. A copy of the agenda with copies of all minutes, reports, and resolutions attached should be furnished to each participant. (See Figure 15-1.)

MEETING ROOM FACILITIES AND SUPPLIES

As soon as a date for the meeting has been determined, a meeting room must be selected. Most companies have conference rooms available for small meetings of company personnel. For large meetings, an off-site area may have to be selected. This may entail reserving a ballroom in a hotel or teleconference rooms in a number of cities. In selecting a meeting site several factors must be considered:

- Size of group and purpose of meeting
- Budget
- Ambience, acoustics, privacy
- Ventilation
- Support services (e.g., catering, audiovisual equipment)
- Dependability of service

Once a meeting room has been selected, you must determine how the room is to be set up. There are numerous arrangements to select from, depending on the number of people participating and the size of the room itself. Common room setups include:

Theater style: Suitable for large audiences; designed for lecture presentation and/or audiovisuals; speaker is visible, on raised platform

Classroom style: Suitable for taking notes; works well with long, narrow room; attention directed to speaker

Boardroom style: Good for small groups; communication facilitated; formal setting

U-shape style: Allows speaker access to each participant; good for medium-size group; promotes interaction

T-shape style: Good for panel discussion; accommodates small groups

Roundtable style: Informal; prompts discussion; good for small group work

Meeting room facilities should be checked for lighting, heating, and ventilation. Microphones, slide projectors, overhead projectors, video machines, screens, and the like need

(a)

MEETING OF THE HIGHER EDUCATION ADVISORY COMMITTEE
May 17, 19--

AGENDA
1. Discuss latest product proposal.
2. Review new product literature.
3. Update list of potential clients.
4. Report on previous sales calls to top six universities.

(b)

SALES MEETING CONFERENCE

Monday, March 16

8–9 a.m.	Breakfast	Tiffany Room
9–10:30 a.m.	Opening Session	Ballroom A
	James Hughes, Senior VP	
10:30–11 a.m.	Break	
11 a.m.–Noon	Selling to Higher Education	Ballroom A
	Peter Mann, Consultant	
Noon–1 p.m.	Lunch	Terrace Room

Tuesday, March 17

8–9 a.m.	Breakfast	Terrace Room
9–10 a.m.	Marketing Communications	Ballroom A
	Tina Sanford, Mgr.	
10–Noon	Individual seminars	
	(Consult packet for seminar	
	information and locations)	
Noon–1 p.m.	Lunch	Evergreen Room

Figure 15-1 Sample agendas for (a) informal meeting, (b) formal meeting.

to be properly set up and working. During the meeting, be sure to provide enough memo pads, pencils, water and glasses, and ashtrays (if smoking is permitted). If coffee or tea is to be served, check your supplies and equipment (if the meeting is held at the company's facilities) or arrange for them to be served by someone else.

Hint: Several publications are available as references for meeting facilities. They include *Successful Meetings,* published by Bill Communications, Inc., 633 Third Avenue,

New York, NY 10017, and *Official Meeting Facilities Guide,* published by Reed Travel Group, 500 Plaza Drive, Secaucus, NJ 07096. Professional organizations for meeting planners can also provide information and insight into meeting planning and facility selection.

TELECONFERENCES

Teleconferences are meetings that take place between groups of people in different places through the use of electronic communications, such as audio conferences and video conferences. (Teleconferences are discussed in detail in Chapter 22, Electronic Communications.)

TAKING MINUTES

Minutes are an accurate recording in outline form of the actions that occurred in a meeting. For informal meetings, the minutes should be brief and simple. Formal meetings require more complex minutes.

You may be asked to take minutes during the meeting. Skillful minute taking is an art that takes practice to develop. Here are some guidelines to follow:

❑ Get a copy of the agenda beforehand if you were not the person who prepared it. If technical or unfamiliar jargon is used, find a way to familiarize yourself with common terms. Minutes of past meetings, handouts for the meetings, and glossaries of relevant subjects are appropriate sources.

❑ Take thorough notes.

> **Hint:** Consider using a small tape recorder. You will have to get permission to do so from every participant. If even one objects, do not use it.

❑ Record verbatim all resolutions, amendments, decisions, and conclusions.

> **Hint:** A resolution is a formal statement of the group, approved by a vote of the group. After a resolution is drafted and approved, it must be signed, distributed, and incorporated into the minutes. Resolutions may be for achievements, sympathy, promotion of special events, etc. Each paragraph in a resolution begins with the words WHEREAS or RESOLVED, either in capital letters or underlined.

❑ Record all important statements verbatim.

❑ Use eye-catching symbols to mark any item that may need action.

❑ Write a rough but complete draft as soon as possible and submit it for review to the supervisor in charge of the meeting.

❑ Transcribe the minutes as soon as possible after the meeting. Do not add your own opinions. Be sure you have the chairperson approve and sign the minutes before they are distributed.

❑ Send handouts to anyone who was absent from the meeting.

❑ Include any follow-up meeting information at the bottom of the minutes, such as the date, time, and location.

❑ Correct the minutes at the next meeting, if necessary. For formal meetings, corrections are made on the official copy with red ink (if possible) and initialed in the margin. Minutes should never be erased or rewritten. If corrections are extensive, they should be written on a separate page and attached to the original minutes. A marginal note should be included at the side of the item in the original minutes indicating a correction is attached.

When putting formal minutes into their final form, use the following outline:

1. Name of group, place, date, and time of meeting.

2. Listing of those present, identifying officers and other officials.

3. Call to order; reading of minutes of previous meeting and approval, corrections or amendments.

4. Reports of officers and committees.

5. Unfinished business; discussion, motions.

6. New business and action taken.

7. Motions, including names of those involved in total motion, if amended, and names of seconders.

8. Date and location of next meeting.

9. Adjournment and time of adjournment.

10. Signature of secretary and, if required, the chairperson.

Corporate minutes should be typed on plain white paper (watermarked for official corporate stockholders' and directors' meetings). If the minutes are brief, double-space the body and triple-space between paragraphs. If the minutes are long, they should be single-spaced for the text and double-spaced between headings. When side subheadings are used, it is not necessary to indent the paragraphs. Allow a one-and-one-half-inch left margin and a one-inch right margin. The title should be capitalized and centered. (See Figure 15-2.)

When filing the minutes, be sure to include all handouts and the agenda for future reference. By law, corporations are required to keep minutes of stockholders' and directors' meetings. Such minutes are considered legal records and should be guarded against tampering.

FOLLOW-UP ACTIVITIES

After the meeting, you must follow up on a number of details, including distribution of the minutes to proper individuals, collection of any extra materials, review of charges and receipts, and writing of "thank you" letters to speakers, participants and hotel staff (if appropriate). It is also important to maintain an accurate meeting folder for reference.

The checklist in Figure 15-3 is a helpful reminder to keep in front of you throughout the process of planning for a meeting.

MEETING OF PLANNING COMMITTEE
September 7, 19--

ATTENDANCE

The monthly meeting of the planning committee was held in the conference room of Manville Hospital at 10 a.m. on September 7, 19--. Dale Stetzer, Vice President of Marketing, presided. Present were Mary Farr, George Rowen, Sue Gates, Ted Smith, and Larry Taylor.

REPORTS/MOTIONS/NEW BUSINESS

1. Sue Gates presented a report on the proposed east wing renovation. Further information is to be given at the October 9 meeting.
2. George Rowen reported on the progress of the sewer project. Completion is expected by early spring, 19--.
3. A new service contract was approved for the computer equipment.

MEETING DETAILS

The next meeting of the planning committee will be held on October 9 at 10 a.m., Conference Room A, Manville Hospital.

ADJOURNMENT

The meeting was adjourned at 12 noon.

Peter Ren, Recorder

Figure 15-2 Sample minutes.

1. Three months prior to meeting:
   _____ a. Book a meeting location.
   _____ b. Identify and contract with support services.
   _____ c. Notify attendees regarding details of meeting.
   _____ d. Prepare travel arrangements for attendees.
   _____ e. Identify local events and get information.
   _____ f. Plan a program of formal and recreational events.
   _____ g. Plan a topical program and identify speakers.
   _____ h. Invite speakers and VIP's.

2. Three weeks before meeting:
   _____ a. Confirm menus, room setups, and supplies with the hotel, in writing.
   _____ b. Reconfirm speakers, formal and recreational events.
   _____ c. Mail agendas and other pertinent information.
   _____ d. Reconfirm attendees.

3. One week before your meeting:
   _____ a. Ship material to hotel for delivery at least 24 hours ahead of your arrival.
   _____ b. Confirm arrival of materials prior to your departure to the meeting.
   _____ c. Make arrangements to collect from the hotel, pack and ship back to your office any unused materials.
   _____ d. Bring a master set of handout materials with you and make arrangements for duplicating additional materials if necessary.
   _____ e. Confirm food and beverage requirements at least 48 hours prior to the meeting.
   _____ f. Bring your own supplies of tape, shipping labels, paper clips, pens, pencils, note pads, badges, scissors, masking tape, magic markers, etc.

4. Upon arrival at the meeting location:
   _____ a. Meet with the convention coordinator and confirm all details and walk through the meeting site.
   _____ b. Confirm with the audiovisual coordinator that needed equipment will be available.
   _____ c. Meet with the bell captain and the maitre d'.
   _____ d. Confirm the attendees list with the front desk and the room assignments if possible.
   _____ e. Arrange for any gifts that are to be delivered to the attendees' rooms, e.g., fruit basket.
   _____ f. Double check that meeting room locations are posted in the hotel lobby.

Figure 15-3 Meeting planner's checklist.

5. Meeting days:
   _____ a. Walk through meeting room spaces at least one hour before start of program.
   _____ b. Confirm that speakers have checked into the hotel. Leave notes in their mailboxes to contact you.
   _____ c. Check with the audiovisual coordinator regarding equipment and supplies for each meeting room.
   _____ d. Be available at all times should an emergency develop.

6. Final meeting day:
   _____ a. Meet with the hotel meeting coordinator to review invoices, receipts, and arrangements for returning unused materials.
   _____ b. Disburse appropriate gratuities.

CHAPTER 16

MAILING DOCUMENTS

Once documents have been created, they must be distributed efficiently and economically. Whether the documents are coming into the company or leaving the company and whether they are distributed by the U.S. Postal Service or transmitted electronically, office professionals must know the guidelines for each method of delivery.

U.S. POSTAL SERVICE

The U.S. Postal Service (USPS) offers a variety of domestic and international mail delivery services. **Domestic** mail service covers all classes of mail handled in the United States, its territories and possessions, the areas comprising the former Canal Zone, and Army/Air Force (APO) and Navy (FPO) post offices. It also includes mail for delivery to the United Nations in New York City. **International** mail service covers mail received from or mailed to foreign countries.

For detailed information about USPS services, the *Domestic Mail Manual* and the *International Mail Manual* are useful references. These manuals are the sources for the descriptive information—classes of mail and services provided by the USPS—summarized in this chapter and are available from the Superintendent of Documents, U.S. Government Printing Office, Washington, DC 20402-9371, on a yearly subscription basis. They are also available at local post offices. The USPS also issues a free newsletter, "Memo to Mailers," which includes updates on mailing services. To be placed on a mailing list, write to the Editor, Memo to Mailers, U.S. Postal Service, Washington, DC 20260-3122.

FIRST-CLASS MAIL

First-class mail consists of such items as letters; postal cards (sold by the post office); postcards (sold commercially); bills; typewritten, handwritten, or photocopied messages; price lists; statements of account; checks; printed forms; and computer-generated matter with the characteristics of business or personal messages.

Sealed first-class mail items are not subject to postal inspections. First-class mail may be sent special delivery, certified, COD, or registered. The sender may also obtain a certificate of mailing. (See below, *Special Services for Domestic Mail* and *Special Services for International Mail.*)

To qualify as first-class mail, items must weigh 11 ounces or less and be at least 0.007 inch thick. (See below, *Priority Mail,* for information on items weighing more than 11 ounces.) Items that are $\frac{1}{4}$ inch thick or less must be at least $3\frac{1}{2}$ inches high, at least 5 inches long, and rectangular in shape. If these standards are not met, the Postal Service will return the items to the sender.

First-class items of 1 ounce or less are considered nonstandard if they exceed a height of $6\frac{1}{8}$ inches, a length of $11\frac{1}{2}$ inches, and a thickness of $\frac{1}{4}$ inch. Nonstandard mail requires special processing, since automated sorting equipment cannot handle it. A surcharge is added to the regular postage for nonstandard mail.

First-class postal rates are based on weight, with the charge for the first ounce higher than the charges for the second and succeeding ounces. Rates for postcards and postal cards are less than for regular first-class items.

First-class mail is transported by the most efficient means available. Airmail is no longer a domestic classification, since air service is the usual method for moving all first-class mail. International mail still uses the airmail classification. The USPS forwards all first-class mail without charge for one year if it is informed of the new address.

> **Hint:** Less confusion results when companies inform their clients of address changes and complete change-of-address forms furnished by the USPS before they move. Remind employees within the department to complete change-of-address forms if they leave the company. Fewer pieces of mail will then have to be forwarded.

FIRST-CLASS BULK RATE OPTIONS

The options of presorted first-class, presorted carrier route, ZIP + 4 (presorted or nonpresorted), or bar-coded mail (presorted or nonpresorted) allow mailers to receive reduced rates on bulk first-class mailings. (Bulk mailings are mailings of many pieces.) To qualify for the reduced rates, mailers must do some of the work usually done by the USPS. They must also follow specific USPS procedures and meet certain eligibility requirements. Local post office personnel can assist mailers in selecting the appropriate option and in providing information to prepare the mailings accurately. Several of the requirements for first-class bulk rates are:

❏ A minimum number of items must be in a single mailing; for example, for presorted first-class, 3 or 5 digits, there must be 500 items or more.

❑ The mailer pays an annual fee, which allows the mailer to obtain rate discounts for presorted first-class, presorted carrier route, ZIP + 4, or bar-coded mail. The annual presort mailing fee is not the same as the one-time fee for a **permit imprint.** The permit imprint allows users to mail items without placing postage on them if payment is made from a previously established deposit account at the post office. The permit imprint may be stamped, copied, or printed on the envelope but not handwritten or typewritten.

❑ The ZIP Code must appear correctly in the address line.

❑ Each piece must be appropriately marked; for example, "ZIP + 4 Presort."

❑ Mailers must complete forms that indicate the total number of items in the mailing.

❑ Letters in the address should be a uniform size, and the line spacing must be consistent. Black ink on a white background is preferred. No reverse printing or bright colors are accepted.

❑ A **bar code** consists of a field of 52 bars that represent the nine numbers in the ZIP + 4 Code. The bar code must be on the addressed side of the envelope or package within the bar code read area. (See Figure 16-1.)

❑ Mailers must follow bundling requirements for each of the options. Bundled items must be placed in trays that are accurately labeled for immediate handling.

> **Hint:** The Postal Service provides trays, labels, and rubber bands without charge for bundling. Do not make the bundles more than 4 inches thick. If bundles are 1 inch or less, use one rubber band per bundle. If the bundles are 1 to 4 inches, use two rubber bands. Place the rubber band around the bundle lengthwise first; then place the second one around its girth (thickest part).

❑ The mail must be delivered to a postal facility by the mailer.

PRIORITY MAIL

Priority mail is first-class mail that weighs more than 11 ounces but no more than 70 pounds. It is useful for heavier mail that requires faster delivery than parcel post.

The combined length and girth (thickness) of a piece of priority mail cannot be more than 108 inches. The two measurements added together represent the size of the package.

Rates depend on the weight of the item and the zone to which it is being mailed. Priority mail offers a flat rate for all material that can fit into a special priority mail envelope. The envelopes are available at local post offices. Flat rates are also available for 3-, 4-, and 5-pound items.

Customers may request pickup service and pay one fee per call, not per item. Priority mail packages may be insured or sent COD. Mailers can obtain certificates of mailing. For extra fees, return receipts, restricted delivery, special delivery, certified, and registered services are also possible.

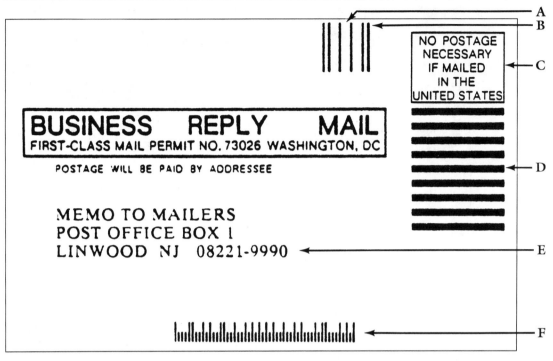

A   Top of Facing Identification Mark (FIM bar) must be within $\frac{1}{8}$" of edge and may touch edge. $\frac{5}{8}$" maximum length and $1\frac{3}{4}$" minimum to 3" maximum from right edge.

B   Rightmost edge of FIM bar must be a minimum of $1\frac{7}{8}$" to maximum of $2\frac{1}{8}$" from right side of envelope.

C   Minimum 1" wide, all caps and wording as shown.

D   Horizontal bars must be minimum 1" long and $\frac{1}{16}$" to $\frac{3}{16}$" thick and evenly spaced. Bars must not extend below delivery address line.

E   At least $\frac{1}{2}$" clearance between end of ZIP Code and horizontal bars.

F   Placement of bar code: Maximum of 4" to a $3\frac{1}{4}$" minimum from right side of envelope and $\frac{1}{4}$" from bottom edge.

Figure 16-1 Bar code placement (not drawn to scale).

EXPRESS MAIL

Express mail is the fastest service the USPS provides. It is a reliable service for mailing documents, letters, or packages up to 70 pounds. Express mail is not acceptable for mailings of more than 108 inches in length and girth combined.

Rates differ depending on weight and type of service. The cost includes insurance against loss or damage. If the item does not reach its destination within the time established, refunds are due the mailer. Express mail also offers a flat rate for all material that can fit into a special envelope. This flat-rate service saves time, since the envelope does not have to be

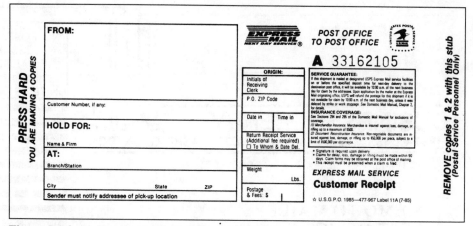

Figure 16-2 (a) Express mail customer receipt—post office to post office.

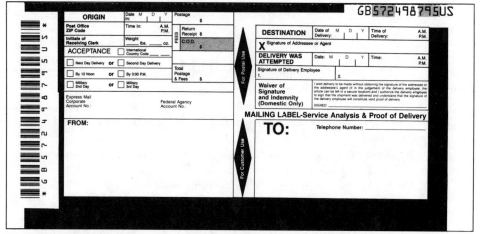

Figure 16-2 (b) Express mail customer receipt—post office to addressee.

weighed at the post office but may be placed with the company's outgoing mail or in a USPS collection box.

An express mail corporate account allows a company to deposit an estimated amount of express mail postage charges or $100, whichever is higher, in an express mail post office. When sending an express mail item, write the corporate account number on the appropriate express mail label. Express mail postage stamps for the exact amount of a basic express mail package are also available.

Express mail may be sent COD. By paying an extra fee, mailers may also request a return receipt, which offers proof of delivery. Restricted delivery service is not available for express mail.

USPS provides mailers with express mail envelopes, boxes, and tubes at no extra cost.

Mailers may request on-call express mail pickup service, or they may specify the scheduled times for pickup in their express mail custom designed service agreements, paying one fee per call.

Several options for service are available:

Express mail same day airport service (Label C): This service is available only between major U.S. airports. The mailer brings an item to an airport mail facility, and it is then sent to its destination on the next available flight. The addressee claims the item at the time designated by the originating airport mail facility.

Express mail custom designed service: The customer signs an agreement with the Postal Service that outlines pickup times and days, delivery dates and times, service levels, and so forth. The customer receives a guarantee for timely and consistent service according to the individual agreement specifications.

Express mail next day service: Two types of service are available: post office to post office (Label A) and post office to addressee (Label B). (See Figures 16-2 (a) and (b).) Mail deposited by a time designated by the local postmaster (often 5 p.m.) is delivered to the addressee by 12 noon or 3 p.m. the following day, or it may be picked up at the post office by 10 a.m. the next day, if the post office is open for regular service. Express mail next day service is not available in every city. Check with the local post office before preparing an item for express mail. Every post office has a copy of the *Express Mail Next Day Service Network Directory.* In this directory mailers can locate those post offices with express mail next day service. The directory also includes locations for express mail next day service mail and information on where the nearest express mail collection box is.

Express mail second day service: The types of service available with and the requirements for express mail next day service also apply to second day service. The major difference is that the mail is delivered the second day after it is mailed.

Express mail international service: See the heading *International Mail* below for information.

SECOND-CLASS MAIL

Publishers and news agents use this service to mail newspapers and periodicals in bulk. To be eligible for second-class mail privileges, the following requirements must be met:

❏ The item must be published at least four times a year. The publisher must file a frequency-of-publishing statement to indicate the number of issues to be distributed and an application for second-class mailing privileges at the local post office.

❏ Publications should be informational and not designed primarily as advertising or as promotional pieces.

❏ Circulation records must be available for periodic examination by post office personnel. Printing orders, invoices from printers, newsstand and vending machine sales and returns, and on-premise sales receipts are examples of records that publishers must keep to document their circulation activity.

❏ Subscription orders and receipts are the only enclosures allowed in second-class publications. Other types of enclosures require additional postage.

Hint: To mail single issues of newspapers or magazines, use third- or fourth-class service.

THIRD-CLASS MAIL

Third-class mail includes such items as circulars, catalogs, booklets, printed matter, photographs, keys, and general merchandise. Third-class rates are available to businesses and certain nonprofit organizations. The rates for qualified nonprofit groups are lower than the rates for business mailers. Third-class mail must weigh less than 16 ounces; if it is heavier, priority mail or fourth-class rates apply. Third-class mail must meet the same size requirements as first-class mail, with the exception of keys or other identification pieces. Postal Service personnel may inspect third-class mail, whether it is sealed or unsealed.

Third-class *bulk* rates apply to material with the same general message sent to different addresses. At least 200 pieces or 50 pounds will qualify for bulk mail rates. A company or organization must pay an annual bulk mailing fee; this fee is not the same as the one-time fee paid to mail under a permit imprint.

To send bulk shipments, mailers must use the bulk mail acceptance station at the post office from which they obtained the bulk mail permit. Postage depends on the weight of the item and level of presorting completed by the mailer. Payment is due before postal employees can accept and verify the accuracy of bulk mailings. Mailers must complete a mailing statement with each mailing.

Hint: Since all mailing statements are verified by postal employees, check all calculations carefully and answer each question. Submit a duplicate copy of the mailing statement to your accounting office. Organize a set of notes that outline bulk mail procedures; attach a copy of a completed statement for reference.

Third-class bulk mail must be properly sorted, bundled, labeled, and put in sacks. Mailers have six sorting options—basic, basic ZIP + 4, presort 3 or 5 digits, 5 digit ZIP + 4, ZIP + 4 bar-coded, and carrier route. Check with the local post office for assistance with bulk mail options and procedures. Several general guidelines for preparing third-class bulk mail include:

❏ Sort mail by ZIP Codes. For example, when ten or more pieces have the same five-digit ZIP Code, band them together and place a red pressure-sensitive label "D" on the top item in the bundle. Only the top item in a bundle requires a pressure-sensitive label. Attach this label at the bottom left of the envelope below the address line.
❏ Sort and label bundles with the same three-digit ZIP Code (green 3 label); bundles going to the same state (orange S label); bundles going to mixed states (tan MS label); and bundles sorted by firm (blue F label), city (yellow C label), sectional center facility (green 3 label), and state distribution center (facing slip labeled "All for SDC"). A **facing slip** is a label placed on a bundle of mail that indicates its contents and destination.
❏ Place rubber bands around the bundles to keep the items in place. If the package is 1 inch thick, use one rubber band around the width. If the package is larger, use two rubber bands—one around its length and one around its girth.

❑ Place the sorted mail into sacks according to the post office's distribution lists. Sacking is necessary when the number of items in a single mailing reaches 125 pieces or when 15 pounds accumulate, whichever comes first. Limit the amount of mail to 70 pounds maximum per sack; 40 pounds is preferable.

❑ Label each sack with specific information; use three lines. For example, this might be the information on a sack label:

> Chicago IL　　　　54432
> 3C LTRS
> Salinas CA

❑ Line 1 is for the destination and indicates the mail is for delivery to Chicago only. Line 2 is for the contents and indicates that the sack contains letters mailed third-class. Line 3 is for the original mailing office and indicates that the mailing originated in Salinas, California.

Hint: The Postal Service prefers machine-prepared labels rather than handwritten ones. Type the label so that the top line will not be covered by the label holder. Use accepted postal abbreviations for identifying a sack's contents, such as LTRS for letters and FLTS for flats.

FOURTH-CLASS MAIL

Fourth-class mail consists of mailable matter that weighs 16 ounces or more, with the exception of special or library classifications. The service is effective for large items that do not need priority or express mail attention. Packages must weigh 70 pounds or less and cannot measure more than 108 inches in combined length and girth. Parcels exceeding size or weight limits are not mailable using USPS services.

A company may include such written materials as instructions, a packing slip, or an invoice inside the parcel at no extra cost. When a letter is to be sent with a fourth-class parcel, attach it to the outside of the parcel and pay for the letter at the first-class rate and for the parcel at the fourth-class rate. Another way to include a letter is to place it inside the package, mark "Letter Enclosed" on the outside of the parcel, and pay the appropriate postal rates for the parcel and letter.

Fourth-class mail does not include a guaranteed arrival time. Two or more packages approximately the same size and shape may be mailed as a single package. They must not exceed fourth-class weight or size limits and must be wrapped together. Fourth-class mail may be subject to Postal Service examination whether it is sealed or unsealed.

The categories of fourth-class mail are:

Parcel post: Any fourth-class mail may be sent using parcel post rates. Rates for parcel post depend on weight, distance mailed, and whether an item is mailed and delivered within bulk mail or area service centers. There are eight postal zones in the U.S. Zone charts are available from local post offices. To qualify for bulk parcel post rates, 300 pieces or 2,000 pounds of fourth-class mail must be in the mailing. The pieces must be identical in weight but not necessarily in size or content.

Bound printed matter: This category includes promotional, advertising, and educational items. Material cannot be sent as loose sheets in a binder but must be permanently fastened with staples, binding, or stitching. At least 90 percent of the sheets must be imprinted with letters, figures, or characters. Bound printed matter must weigh at least 1 pound and no more than 10 pounds. Bulk rates are available for mailings of 300 or more pieces of material qualifying as bound printed matter.

Special fourth-class rate mail: Items that qualify for special fourth-class rates include books of at least eight printed pages; films (16 mm or narrower widths); printed music; printed objective educational test materials; sound and video recordings and/or scripts; playscripts or manuscripts for books, periodicals, and music; and medical information for those in the profession. Special fourth-class rate mail can qualify for presort rates. Mailers presort by ZIP Codes and follow specific marking, sacking, and labeling instructions.

Library rate: Library rate mail covers books, theses, printed music, periodicals, sound recordings, unpublished manuscripts, and museum materials. Items are eligible for library rates if exchanged or loaned between educational institutions, museums, public libraries, or specified nonprofit organizations and associations. An institution or organization name and address must appear in either the destination address or in the return address of each package. Items mailed by publishers also receive the special library rate when items are sent to educational institutions, public libraries, museums, or nonprofit organizations and associations.

OFFICIAL MAIL

Official mail does not require the prepayment of postage. Official mail can be franked mail or penalty mail. Only a few U.S. government officials, such as members of Congress, may use *franked mail* privileges. This mail is easily identified as it carries a real or facsimile signature in place of the stamp. The words "Public Document" and "Official Business" appear on the address side. *Penalty mail* carries the warning "Penalty for Private Use to Avoid Payment of Postage." It is used by government agencies for official government correspondence. The words "Official Business" also appear on the address side of the envelope.

SPECIAL SERVICES FOR DOMESTIC MAIL

As an office professional, you should understand the special services provided by the USPS. Since these services often involve fees, you should purchase only those that are necessary.

BUSINESS REPLY MAIL

Business reply mail consists of postage-paid envelopes or postal cards that are enclosed with other mailings to encourage recipients to respond. Mailers pay postage only on replies that are returned. Mailers pay the regular first-class postage plus a handling charge.

Business reply mail users require a permit, which is available for an annual fee. The words "First-Class Mail Permit No. xxx" and the name of the post office issuing the permit (city

---

| U.S. POSTAL SERVICE | **CERTIFICATE OF MAILING** | Affix fee here in stamps or meter postage and post mark. Inquire of Postmaster for current fee. |

MAY BE USED FOR DOMESTIC AND INTERNATIONAL MAIL, DOES NOT PROVIDE FOR INSURANCE—POSTMASTER

Received From:

_____

_____

One piece of ordinary mail addressed to:

_____

_____

_____

PS Form 3817, Mar. 1989 ★ U.S. GPO:1989-242-531/05281

Figure 16-3 Certificate of mailing.

and state) must appear on the address side. The Postal Service specifies certain design and format requirements for preparing business reply mail.

CERTIFICATE OF MAILING

The certificate shows that the Postal Service accepted the item and provides proof that an item was mailed. (See Figure 16-3.) It does not indicate that the item arrived at its destination. The certificate is available for all classes of mail, and it applies to domestic and international mail. The certificate fee does not include insurance on the mailed material. The person sending the item completes the certificate of mailing and pays the fee.

> **Hint:** Notations on the certificate that identify the items mailed are helpful for future reference; for example, an invoice number may be used. Make a note on the copy of the correspondence to indicate when the item was mailed. File the certificate in a separate folder for mail receipts.

CERTIFIED MAIL

Certified mail is a domestic mail service that provides the mailer with a receipt for an item sent by first-class or priority mail. The destination post office maintains a record of delivery for two years; the post office at which the mail originated does not keep a record.

For an additional fee, a return receipt or a restricted delivery receipt is available as evidence that the delivery occurred. The endorsement "Certified Mail" appears on the envelope. It travels with other first-class mail and does not receive special attention until it

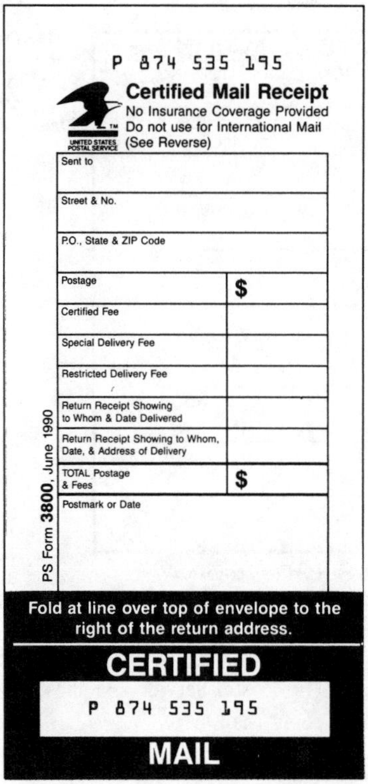

P 874 535 195

Certified Mail Receipt
No Insurance Coverage Provided
Do not use for International Mail
(See Reverse)

UNITED STATES POSTAL SERVICE

Sent to	
Street & No.	
P.O., State & ZIP Code	
Postage	$
Certified Fee	
Special Delivery Fee	
Restricted Delivery Fee	
Return Receipt Showing to Whom & Date Delivered	
Return Receipt Showing to Whom, Date, & Address of Delivery	
TOTAL Postage & Fees	$
Postmark or Date	

PS Form **3800**, June 1990

Fold at line over top of envelope to the right of the return address.

CERTIFIED

P 874 535 195

MAIL

Figure 16-4 Certified mail receipt.

arrives at the destination post office. At that time the postal carrier delivers it to the address and obtains the appropriate signature. Mailers of certified mail may request special delivery service for an extra fee.

Hint: The Postal Service provides blank certified mail coupons, Form 3800, Certified Mail Receipt. Enter the addressee's name and address. Check the boxes indicating the appropriate receipts needed. Enter the certified number on the return receipt card, self-address it, and attach it to the item being certified. Mark the date, attach the correct postage, and mail at any post office or deposit in any USPS mailbox. (See Figure 16-4.)

RETURN RECEIPT

A return receipt signifies to the mailer that delivery of an item took place. The return receipt may indicate to whom and the date delivered or it may indicate to whom, date delivered, and delivery address. Return receipts are available for certified, registered, COD, and express mail and for mail insured for over $50. They apply to domestic and international mailings. Fees for return receipts do not cover damages or losses to the items sent. (See Figures 16-5 and 16-6.)

Is your RETURN ADDRESS completed on the reverse side?

SENDER:
- Complete items 1 and/or 2 for additional services.
- Complete items 3, and 4a & b.
- Print your name and address on the reverse of this form so that we can return this card to you.
- Attach this form to the front of the mailpiece, or on the back if space does not permit.
- Write "Return Receipt Requested" on the mailpiece below the article number.
- The Return Receipt Fee will provide you the signature of the person delivered to and the date of delivery.

I also wish to receive the following services (for an extra fee):
1. ☐ Addressee's Address
2. ☐ Restricted Delivery

Consult postmaster for fee.

3. Article Addressed to:

4a. Article Number

4b. Service Type
☐ Registered ☐ Insured
☐ Certified ☐ COD
☐ Express Mail ☐ Return Receipt for Merchandise

7. Date of Delivery

5. Signature (Addressee)

8. Addressee's Address (Only if requested and fee is paid)

6. Signature (Agent)

PS Form **3811**, November 1990 ☆U.S. GPO: 1991—287-066 **DOMESTIC RETURN RECEIPT**

Thank you for using Return Receipt Service.

Figure 16-5 Return receipt—domestic.

POSTAL SERVICE OF THE UNITED STATES OF AMERICA
Administration des Postes des Etats-Unis d'Amérique

C5
Postmark of the office returning the receipt
Timbre du bureau renvoyant l'avis

PAR AVION

POSTAL SERVICE
Service des postes

RETURN RECEIPT
Avis de réception

To be returned by the quickest route (air or surface mail), á découvert and postage free.

To be filled out by the sender, who will indicate his address for the return of this receipt.
A remplir par l'expediteur, qui indiquera son adresse pour le renvoi du présent avis.

Name or firm — Nom ou raison sociale

A renoyer par la voie la plus rapide (aèrienne ou de surface), à découvert et en franchise de port.

Street and No. — Rue et no.

City, State and ZIP Code — Lieu et Pays

PS Form 2865
Mar. 1985

UNITED STATES OF AMERICA *Etats-Unis d'Amérique*

Figure 16-6 Return receipt—international.

RETURN RECEIPTS FOR MERCHANDISE

Return receipts are available only for priority mail and third- and fourth-class items. They allow the mailer to obtain a mailing receipt, a return receipt, and a record of delivery. They are not available for international mailings. Special delivery service can be obtained for a fee.

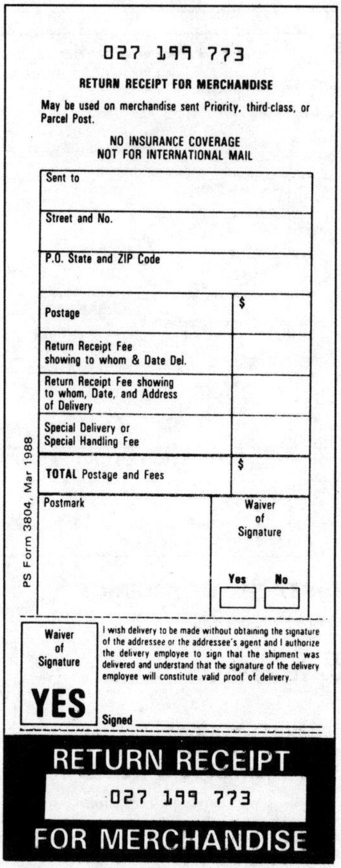

```
          027 199 773
    RETURN RECEIPT FOR MERCHANDISE
May be used on merchandise sent Priority, third-class, or
Parcel Post.

        NO INSURANCE COVERAGE
       NOT FOR INTERNATIONAL MAIL
```

Sent to	
Street and No.	
P.O. State and ZIP Code	
Postage	$
Return Receipt Fee showing to whom & Date Del.	
Return Receipt Fee showing to whom, Date, and Address of Delivery	
Special Delivery or Special Handling Fee	
TOTAL Postage and Fees	$

```
Postmark                    Waiver
                              of
                           Signature

                         Yes    No
                         [  ]   [  ]
```

PS Form 3804, Mar 1988

Waiver of Signature **YES**	I wish delivery to be made without obtaining the signature of the addressee or the addressee's agent and I authorize the delivery employee to sign that the shipment was delivered and understand that the signature of the delivery employee will constitute valid proof of delivery.
Signed _____	

RETURN RECEIPT
· 027 199 773 ·
FOR MERCHANDISE

Figure 16-7 Return receipt for merchandise.

Special handling can be obtained for a fee but only for third-class and parcel post. Articles with return receipts for merchandise must be mailed at a post office; they cannot be deposited in collection boxes. (See Figure 16-7.)

RESTRICTED DELIVERY

Restricted delivery allows a mailer to designate who can receive the item being mailed. Restricted delivery is available for COD, registered, and certified mail, and for mail insured for more than $50. It is not available for express mail service. The addressee or a designated representative must show proof of identity when the item is delivered.

★ U.S. GOVERNMENT PRINTING OFFICE: 1991–296-512

REGISTERED NO.		POSTMARK

To Be Completed By Post Office

Reg. Fee $	Special $ Delivery
Handling $ Charge	Return $ Receipt
Postage $	Restricted $ Delivery
Received by	

Domestic Insurance
Is Limited To
$25,000; International
Indemnity Is Limited
(See Reverse)

To Be Completed By Customer (Please Print) All Entries Must Be in Ball Point or Typed

Customer Must Declare Full Value $

☐ With Postal Insurance
☐ Without Postal Insurance

FROM

TO

PS Form **3806**, **RECEIPT FOR REGISTERED MAIL** *(Customer Copy)*
April 1991 *(See Information on Reverse)*

Figure 16-8 Registered mail receipt.

REGISTERED MAIL

Registered mail represents the most secure means of delivering valuable mail. A postal clerk records the arrival of a piece of registered mail at each point along its way. (See Figure 16-8.) These extra precautions result in a slower delivery.

To register a piece of mail, the sender brings it to a post office and declares the full value of the item. If the item is extremely valuable, only the main post office may be able to register it. If the item is fragile, inform the post office employee. The mailer receives a receipt once an item is registered.

First-class mail, priority mail, and COD parcels may be registered; business reply mail may not be registered. It is possible to obtain a return receipt or a restricted delivery receipt for additional fees. Additional insurance is also available.

Special attention is needed when preparing registered mail. Full names and addresses of the sender and the receiver are necessary. Seal packages with glue or plain paper or cloth tape only. Mark registered mail "Registered"; if return receipts are requested, mark "Registered, Return Receipt Requested" or "Registered, Deliver to Addressee Only."

RECEIPT FOR DOMESTIC INSURED PARCEL
(Not for International Mail)

ADDRESSED FOR DELIVERY AT *(P.O., State & ZIP Code)*

POSTAGE	¢	POSTMARK OF
INSURANCE FEE	¢	
SPECIAL DELIVERY	¢	
SPECIAL HANDLING	¢	
Total		
INSURANCE COVERAGE $		
		MAILING OFFICE

☐ Fragile   ☐ Liquid   ☐ Perishable

POSTMASTER *(By)*

SENDER—Enter name and address of addressee on the reverse and read information regarding insurance coverage and claims.

PS Form 3813, Feb. 1986

Figure 16-9 Insured mail receipt—domestic.

Hint: Valuable items such as stock certificates, merchandise, or jewelry should be registered. Send any item that cannot be replaced, valuable or not, by registered mail.

INSURED MAIL

Insurance is available to guard against loss or damage to items mailed at third- or fourth-class rates or to third- or fourth-class matter mailed at first-class rates. Insurance may be obtained for domestic as well as international mail. Return receipt and restricted delivery services are available for extra fees. Insured mail must be taken to the post office; it cannot be deposited in a collection box.

The post office at which the item is mailed does not keep a record of insured mail. The person receiving the mail signs a receipt that is filed at the destination post office.

The sender declares the value of the item to be mailed, usually for "less than $50" or "more than $50." An appropriate endorsement for insured mail is stamped on the parcel. The postal clerk issues a receipt to the sender. (See Figures 16-9 and 16-10.)

The receipt is necessary if a claim for loss or damage is ever made. Write the name and address of the addressee on the receipt and file it until you know that the parcel arrived safely.

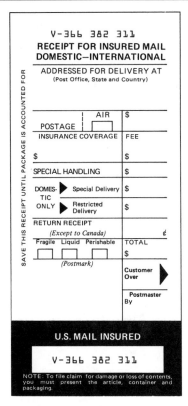

Figure 16-10 Insured mail receipt—international.

SPECIAL DELIVERY

Special delivery service is available for all classes of mail. It is available to all points within a 1-mile radius of a post office or within the city delivery limits of any post office. Special delivery may also be available for other urban and rural areas. Check with the local post office.

The fee for special delivery service, which must be paid in addition to regular postage, does not cover insurance against theft or loss. Fees depend on weight and the class of mail.

Postal Service messengers try to deliver special delivery mail to business locations before regular mail deliveries. Delivery hours are 7 a.m. to 11 p.m. On Sundays and holidays, deliveries are scheduled as necessary.

To make special delivery feasible, send the items so they will arrive during normal business hours rather than over a weekend. Avoid using a post office box as the address. Some post offices hold special delivery mail addressed to a post office box at a general delivery window. If the post office is not open, the item may not reach the addressee any faster using special delivery service than it would by regular mail.

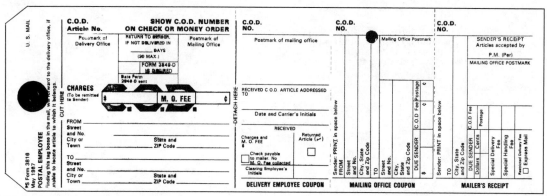

Figure 16-11 COD delivery.

SPECIAL HANDLING

Mail marked "Special handling" receives preferential handling treatment whenever possible. Special handling applies to third- and fourth-class mail and is available for COD and insured items. It does not include special delivery service or "special" care in handling fragile or breakable items. The weight determines the fee. The special handling fee is in addition to third- or fourth-class postage.

COLLECT ON DELIVERY (COD)

First-class, third-class, fourth-class, and express mail may be sent using COD service. Special handling, special delivery, return receipt, or restricted delivery services are all available. COD mail may also be sent as registered COD mail. The sender must prepay the postage and COD fee. The COD fee includes insurance against loss or damage and an amount to cover the potential failure of the addressee to pay for the merchandise. COD items cannot be placed in collection boxes but must be mailed at a post office. (See Figure 16-11.)

When the items are delivered, the receiver pays for the cost of the goods and the postage, up to a maximum amount of $500 per parcel. Payment may be in cash or by a check payable to the sender. When cash is involved, the sender receives a money order from the Postal Service for the amount collected.

INTERNATIONAL MAIL

The USPS offers land (surface) mail and airmail services to most foreign locations. Information on postal rates and fees is available in the Postal Service publication *International Postal Rates and Fees*. Companies with extensive international communications should have a copy of the *International Mail Manual*. This publication is available from the Superintendent of Documents by subscription; information updates are frequent.

International mail is classified into three categories.

LC mail (*lettres et cartes*): Items include letters and letter packages, postcards, and *aerogrammes*. The weight limit for LC mail is 4 pounds.

AO mail (*autres objets*): Items include printed matter, books, periodicals, and other items reproduced by processes other than handwriting or typing. *Small packets* are also in this classification. These may consist of small merchandise items, samples, or nonpersonal documents. If mailers send considerable quantities of mail to one address, an *M bag* is an alternative. An M bag can weigh no less than 15 pounds and no more than 66 pounds.

Parcel post (*colis postaux*): This classification is similar to domestic fourth-class mail. It includes items that do not require LC rates, and it is possible to insure the item. Maximum weights vary from 22 to 44 pounds.

Express mail international service (EMS): This is the fastest service available through the USPS to foreign countries. Weight limits and the allowed contents vary depending on individual country restrictions. The USPS provides no specific guarantee for this service since it depends on air connections between the U.S. and the destination. Most deliveries are made within three days.

International priority mail: International priority mail is primarily for businesses and is available for LC and AO mail classifications. It is faster than regular mail, but mailers must meet certain volume requirements and must sort the items according to USPS standards. The contents of the items do not have to be identical to qualify for the lower rates this service provides. The service is available to all foreign countries except Canada.

International surface air lift (ISA): This system for sending all types of printed matter is faster than surface mail. Mailers take their bulk items to designated airports (a list of these airports is available at local post offices) to be flown to the designated foreign countries. Once the items arrive, they are sent by surface mail delivery to the addressees. Costs are lower than airmail shipments. Rates vary from country to country.

SPECIAL SERVICES FOR INTERNATIONAL MAIL

These services are similar to special services for domestic mail. Registered mail is available for LC mail, small packets, and printed materials, but it is not available for parcel post items. Mail to most countries may be registered.

Special delivery is available in most countries, but each country has its own delivery regulations. The service is available for LC mail, small packets, and printed materials. Insurance covers parcel post items against loss or damage but is not available for LC mail, small packets, or printed materials. Maximum coverage varies according to the country.

Special handling is available only for parcel post, printed matter, and small packets. Usually preferential treatment is given only from the sender's office to the U.S. dispatch office. The fee does not cover preferential treatment after reaching the U.S. dispatch office and upon arriving in the foreign country.

Return receipt and restricted delivery services are similar to those available for domestic mail. COD delivery and certified mail are not available for international mail.

International reply coupons allow a sender to prepay a reply to correspondence sent to a foreign addressee. The sender buys reply coupons and sends them to an addressee; the addressee exchanges the coupon or coupons for surface or airmail letter stamps and returns a reply.

ALTERNATE DELIVERY SERVICES

Other delivery services are available besides the USPS. The costs, delivery times, and types of services offered vary. The Yellow Pages of a local telephone directory include companies that offer freight, delivery, and shipping services. Individual companies can provide information on rates, service charts, and limitations on items transported.

UNITED PARCEL SERVICE (UPS)

The United Parcel Service (UPS) delivers packages to individuals and businesses. In addition to ground service, air service—next day or second day—is available to destinations within the United States as well as to Puerto Rico, Japan, and numerous European countries.

UPS has an overnight letter and express service that promises delivery by 10:30 a.m. the next day. Mailers can request door-to-door service or they may drop off the item at a UPS facility or collection box. Fees differ depending on the service.

The sender must fill out a form that requests the sender's name and address, the recipient's name and address, and the contents of the parcel. The package must weigh 70 pounds or less. The size limitation for a package is 108 inches, length and girth combined. In addition to the protection against theft or damage already included in the basic UPS rate, the mailer may purchase additional insurance coverage.

AIR EXPRESS

Several companies, such as Federal Express, provide air express or courier express service for domestic and international deliveries. These companies will pick up a firm's or individual's letters, parcels, or heavy freight items and provide same day, next day, or second day delivery. The service is fast but expensive. Charges depend on the size and weight of the parcel.

Some companies have rates for items that are delivered by 10 a.m. and others for items delivered by 3 p.m. Volume discounts are often available. Pickup services vary among companies; some charge one pickup fee for any number of pieces; others charge a fee per piece. COD service may also be available.

> **Hint:** Courier services offer many delivery options. Experiment with several companies' services. Request the free services and information that courier service representatives offer companies.

Most courier companies are expanding their international markets. Some courier services operate their own planes; others rely on commercial flights. All major firms can track a lost item. Guaranteeing the arrival of the shipment or returning the fee for a lost item is part of the service offered by courier companies.

When calling to obtain rates, go over these details:

- Value of the parcel(s)
- Delivery date
- Number of packages
- Service; for example, overnight, international, or second day delivery
- Pickup service
- Weight of each parcel
- Destination
- Type of merchandise
- Day of the week for pickup as well as delivery

Hint: If your company does not have one person monitoring costs, it becomes everyone's responsibility to cut costs and improve service. Organize your work so it is not necessary to use expensive delivery services at the last minute. Use these services only for documents that must get delivered the next day.

LOCAL TRANSPORT SERVICES

Companies located in small cities may have to depend on local bus service for some deliveries. The cost is reasonable, and insurance is included in the basic charge. Depending on local schedules, same day service as well as Sunday and holiday service may be possible. In addition to rate information, the local bus company offices can indicate any limitations concerning the size and weight of a parcel.

ELECTRONIC MAIL DELIVERY SYSTEMS

An electronic mail or E-mail delivery system relies on telephone lines, computers, modems, teletypewriters, fax machines, computer networks (local area or public access), or satellites for the transmission of information. E-mail can be delivered instantaneously or, at the very latest, the same day.

E-mail service allows employees to send messages to other employees in the same building or to employees in branch offices at other locations. It enables employees in one firm to send information to other firms in the same city or across the country. It offers businesses opportunities to communicate with their clients in foreign countries.

Sending mail electronically offers additional options for handling information in a timely way. Changing technology demands that office professionals become knowledgeable about new equipment features and adopt operating procedures that justify costs.

ADVANTAGES OF E-MAIL

E-mail delivery systems have several advantages in addition to speed:

❏ Transmittals do not require paper.

❏ Differences in time zones do not cause difficulties for the sender or recipient, and "telephone tag" is no longer a problem. Messages are stored electronically to await retrieval.

❏ A message may be stored until the recipient decides to retrieve it. The sender may also store the message and send it when telephone rates are lower.

❏ The systems are operable 24 hours a day.

❏ The sender and the recipient of the message do not have to be in their offices at the same time in order to conduct business.

❏ Messages can easily be sent to multiple destinations at the same time.

❏ Messages may be transmitted directly to the intended recipient without going through another individual.

❏ Employees can communicate with each other from their desks.

❏ One message may be transmitted to numerous recipients. This eliminates the process of routing information, telephoning, or writing a memo.

❏ Messages do not have to meet interoffice mail or USPS pickup deadlines.

SPECIAL CONCERNS ABOUT E-MAIL

Business use of E-mail is expanding very quickly. With this rapid expansion, precautions are necessary. The following will help you use E-mail properly:

❏ Routine letters, memos, and reports usually do not require electronic transmittal. Determine the urgency of routine messages and use the appropriate delivery system.

❏ Some situations, especially those involving personnel problems, require face-to-face meetings. Using electronic mail to handle the problem often creates negative reactions.

❏ Keep electronic messages relatively short. Readers can handle viewing a screen of information but dislike paging up or down to check facts or connect ideas. Writers of messages have the same problem in proofreading from screen to screen.

> **Hint:** Proofread a document carefully. Take the time to correct each error. If the same E-mail message is sent to 100 clients and it is transmitted with an error, that results in 100 incorrect messages—not just one.

❏ In-house messages are usually less formal than other types of correspondence. However, the tendency to respond to a situation via electronic mail while angry or disappointed can result in serious problems. Sarcastic or judgmental remarks that reach other mailboxes by mistake cause embarrassment for the sender and others involved.

❏ Security remains a problem with electronic messages unless passwords and codes for classified communications are in effect and protected from internal as well as external misuse.

❏ Messages sent to specific individuals may not be picked up promptly, especially if the recipients are away from their offices for any length of time.

Hint: With some systems, employees who expect to be away from their desks or on vacation can leave an electronic message that will automatically be relayed to the sender.

❏ Messages are often printed twice; for example, a message may be printed on a fax machine using thermal paper and as a computer message appearing on the screen.
❏ Users may receive an excess of unwanted messages.

Hint: Screening devices can identify key words in a message and route the message to an answering machine or "folder" for later attention. Other alternatives are an unlisted number or an access code that must be entered by the sender before he or she can transmit a message.

❏ Accessing the various directories to locate E-mail addresses is time-consuming.

Hint: An international standard or set of rules called X.500 is being developed for E-mail directory services. Users will be able to access the directory to locate names and numbers of other users on other systems as well as their own. Each user will have one E-mail address rather than an address for each system to which the user is connected.

MAILGRAMS

A Mailgram is an electronic telecommunication service offered by Western Union and delivered by the USPS. A Mailgram lacks the professional appearance of a letter produced on quality paper or company letterhead.

The sender must contact Western Union and input a message via equipment such as a Telex, computer terminal, fax machine, or telephone. Western Union transmits the message electronically to the post office in the city where the recipient resides. The post office receiving station prints the message. Postal Service personnel place the message in a special window envelope and process it as first-class mail. If the post office receives the Mailgram by 7 p.m., a carrier delivers it with the next day's regular mail deliveries. The cost depends on the number of words.

TELEGRAMS

Senders transmit their messages to a Western Union office. Western Union sends the message by teleprinter to another Western Union office near the recipient. An employee in the receiving office calls the recipient or delivers the telegram, which appears on a special form that is easily identifiable. Messages should be brief and to the point, since the number of words determines the cost. The costs may be charged to a company's telephone number.

TELETYPEWRITERS

Teletypewriters are useful for companies that conduct a considerable amount of international business. They can receive and send messages day and night across different time zones. Operators key messages on machines that resemble typewriter keyboards. The keystrokes are transferred into codes that are sent over telephone lines. Companies may install their own teletypewriting equipment or use the Telex services provided by Western Union.

A store-and-forward feature allows a sending machine to hold messages and send them later if the receiving machine is busy. No one need be present to receive the message; a printed copy is made automatically. Newer models of teletypewriters also have screens, disks for storage, and limited word processing capabilities. Teletypewriter service is slower than other electronic mail services, and its cost is low. However, the costs are high for lengthy documents, so it is best used for short messages.

INTELPOST

INTELPOST (International Electronic Post) service is available for items that can be copied. Items are faxed from local post offices to Canada, Europe, South America, and the Near East and Far East. Faxed documents may be delivered by mail the following day or by same day special delivery, or they may be picked up by the addressee after an hour.

COMPUTER-BASED MESSAGE SYSTEMS

Using the computer to transmit messages from one terminal to others is another electronic mail delivery option. The sender uses the computer keyboard to input a message. Once the address or mailbox of the recipient is located, the message is transmitted to the addressee's computer by activating a transmit key. At the receiving workstation, the recipient checks the mail received, selects a message to view, and displays it on the monitor.

Computer-based message systems usually require the sender and receiver to have a personal computer, telephone, modem, and a communications software program. Other systems involve a keyboard and terminal, with transmittal through a mainframe computer or via a computer network. An internal electronic message system requires cables and wires to connect the computers. An external system uses telephone lines via modems to transmit signals to other locations.

FEATURES

Standard features of computer-based message systems allow users to send, receive, and edit documents and attach computer files to the transmitted materials. Several of these additional features may also be available:

Filter system software/call blockers: Users can prioritize electronic mail by programming the computer to place messages from their supervisors or customers in an "urgent" file.

Messages can also be forwarded to vacation or travel sites, other team members, or an answering machine. Some software can organize messages by the headings of messages or by key words within messages.

Distribution list/broadcasting: By typing a group name into the address location, all members in that group will receive the message. For example, sales representatives could make up one distribution list.

Blind-copy capability: Recipients do not see the names of other employees to whom the memo is addressed.

Message delivery status: This feature shows the sender what happened with the message. The choices usually include *receipt,* which simply indicates the message was received. *Read, unread,* and *response sent* indicate the recipient's action.

Message security and status: The sender has the option of declaring that the message is urgent or confidential.

Transmission speed: The transmission speed is measured in bits per second (bps) and ranges from 300 bps to 9600 bps.

Sorting: Recipients can sort incoming messages by sender, date sent, urgency level, or subject.

Calendar "to do" list function: Users can check others' schedules to determine when everyone is available for a meeting. They cannot, however, see what is scheduled on other employees' calendars and with whom these employees are meeting.

Access to other applications: Integrated software packages allow access to other spreadsheet or word processing applications while using the electronic mail feature.

Access to other systems/gateways: A *gateway* allows two products to communicate with each other. It allows the interconnection of separate electronic mail systems used internally or externally. Gateway support may be a part of the communications software package or it may be an optional package.

Free support and training: Select a communications software company with a toll-free telephone number and one that offers on-site training sessions. Warranty coverage varies. Compare the warranty carefully to be certain defective disks and program bugs are covered.

Hint: Waiting for technician help can be time-consuming. Ask if emergency calls are transferred immediately to an available operator. Check if an appointment time can be set for the technician to call back. This eliminates waiting on hold until someone is available.

PROCEDURES FOR HANDLING COMPUTER-BASED MESSAGES

With the use of electronic mail come new responsibilities. Follow these procedures for proper handling of computer-based messages:

Avoid sending a computer-based message if a personal telephone call or face-to-face meeting is just as convenient.

Write a brief message. Recipients of computer-based messages may read one screen of material, but when the message continues for several screens, they pay less attention to the information. Transmitting long messages may also be costly.

Hint: The same good writing techniques apply to computer-based messages as to any other written form of communication. Be concise; highlight key ideas by numbering them or indenting them from each margin. Outline your thoughts before sending a message so that your message is clear.

Allow the recipient time to respond. Even if the recipient has received a message, he or she may not find it convenient to take action immediately. Time differences, for example, may allow the sender to transmit a message when rates are lower, but the recipients may not be in the office to respond immediately.

Maintain an electronic index of all incoming and outgoing communications.

Organize your materials before logging on to a mainframe system or network. If the document is composed and edited during this log-on time, computer time is being misspent.

Follow the suggestions for proofreading and editing written correspondence. (See Chapter 20.) Even though the message is not intended for distribution, the recipient may reproduce it and send it to others.

Use a subject line and introduction that attracts the reader's attention. Some computer-based message systems allow a reader to preview a document. If the first few lines do not get to the point, the reader may ignore the rest of the message.

Use one of these message formats:

- Use interoffice memo headings. (See the section on Memo Styles in Chapter 17.)
- Enter the recipient's name followed by a colon as the greeting; for example, "Mrs. Johnson:" or "Bob:" It is not necessary to write "Dear." Enter the sender's name at the end without using a closing such as "Sincerely yours."
- Use interoffice memo headings but use the recipient's name for a more personal greeting; for example, "Mary, here are the up-to-date job cost figures which you requested this morning."

Send messages that have single subjects. They will be easier to locate later. If a portion of a message is to be distributed to another employee, it is easier to send a single short message to both rather than to delete irrelevant parts of a long message before transmitting to the other recipient.

Establish a schedule to check your mailbox for messages. The best times are midmorning and midafternoon. Schedule a time for sending messages so that you handle outgoing messages a few times a day without having constantly to interrupt other tasks. Urgent messages should of course be transmitted immediately.

Mark your calendar for meetings scheduled through electronic mail.

PUBLIC E-MAIL SYSTEMS

Electronic mail services are also offered by several companies. Services vary, but they offer similar operating procedures. Subscribers use a modem to dial an 800 number or a local telephone number to reach the public system. The sender signs on by name and identification number and creates a message using the system's software or using his or her own software.

Public E-mail systems may charge by the number of characters per message, with the first batch one price and each additional batch at a higher rate; by the number of messages sent; or by the amount of time on-line. Signup fees and setup times vary. Access to the system may be free, if it uses an 800 number, or there may be an access charge. Costs may be higher for prime time use.

INCOMING MAIL

Incoming mail includes USPS mail, special courier deliveries, intercompany correspondence, and electronic messages. Although incoming mail may arrive throughout the day, most USPS mail arrives at specified times. Office professionals often facilitate the handling of these documents by prioritizing, opening, and distributing them as soon as possible after delivery.

SORTING INCOMING MAIL

In companies with centralized mail departments, USPS mail is delivered by mailroom messengers or mobile delivery carts programmed to stop at designated locations. In other companies, postal carriers deliver the mail to each person's desk or to one person who then distributes it.

Once the mail is delivered, arrange it according to importance. Sort the mail on a desk with a clean space to avoid mixing current mail with other materials. Check the address of each item to be sure it has been delivered to the correct location. Return all mail that does not belong to the department to the mailroom or to the post office.

The following are useful categories for sorting mail by priority:

First priority: E-mail messages such as Telexes, telegrams, faxes, or Mailgrams; express mail; certified, registered, insured, or special delivery mail.

Hint: Because the Mailgram has become an advertising tool and a mass mailing device, it has lost much of the urgency it once had. Many do not belong in this first-priority category.

Second priority: personal or confidential mail. If a supervisor gives you permission to open personal, confidential, or private mail, attach a note to indicate that the envelope was marked as such. If you do not have permission to open this type of mail, place the unopened personal mail after the items listed above.

Third priority: first-class mail, interoffice mail, priority mail, airmail.

Fourth priority: packages.

Fifth priority: second-class mail—newspapers and magazines.

Hint: Magazines and newspapers may be important to a supervisor. Do not put second-class mail aside for later handling, but include it in each mail distribution.

Sixth priority: third-class mail—catalogs, advertising materials, pamphlets, and booklets.

Hint: Prioritize E-mail the same way as letters and memos.

SUPPLIES FOR OPENING THE MAIL

Several supplies are helpful in opening the mail.

❑ Letter openers. Small mail opener machines, either manual or electric, can save considerable time. Some models automatically feed the envelopes, even ones of various sizes. In addition, such equipment can open the envelopes on one end (or on one side and one end), stack the envelopes, and count them.

> **Hint:** When using a manual letter opener, place the envelope on a hard surface with the flap up. To cut the envelope, insert the letter opener halfway under the flap and quickly move it forward and outward. Avoid jagged edges or tearing the envelope by using a sharp opener and by holding it properly.

❑ Date and time stamp.

❑ Mail record, special services record, mail expected record, or a combination of these records. (See the heading on *Recording Incoming Mail* below.)

❑ Stapler, paper clips, adhesive message pad, pencils, and transparent tape.

❑ Mail stop directory. If mail needs to be routed to another location, include the mail stop location (if applicable) as well as the name.

❑ Routing slips.

PROCEDURES FOR OPENING THE MAIL

The following procedures are recommended for opening mail and removing the contents:

❑ Arrange the envelopes so the flaps face the same direction before opening them by hand or machine. Open all envelopes first; then remove and unfold the contents. To prevent discarding an enclosure, hold each envelope to the light to make sure the envelope is empty. Clip each envelope's contents together. Do not discard the envelopes until you have verified the addresses.

❑ Use a date stamp to record the receipt date of each item. Once the contents have been removed, stamp the document in the same location; for example, in the upper right on correspondence or on the back of catalogs. Include the time a document is received if it is important. The date and/or time may be handwritten, hand-stamped, or machine-stamped.

> **Hint:** If using a hand stamp, change the date immediately upon arrival at the office in the morning.

❑ Tap the lower edges of the envelope to allow the contents to fall to the bottom and avoid cutting them. If an item is cut, use transparent tape to repair the damage.

❑ If an envelope was opened when it should not have been, write "Opened by Mistake" on the envelope and initial it.

❑ Review each document for the sender's name and address, enclosures, and date. If the address on the envelope and document differ, clip the return address from the envelope and staple it to the letter. Make a note to verify the correct address with the sender. Once verified, change all mailing list notations and circle the correct address on the correspondence just received.

❏ Record an omission of a date or a major discrepancy between the date on the letter and the date of the postmark on a piece of adhesive notepaper. Attach the note to the correspondence for your supervisor's attention. Staple the envelope to the document. Any discrepancies may have consequences in legal matters.

❏ Verify the receipt of all enclosures. If an enclosure is missing, circle the enclosure line and indicate that the item is missing. If the amount in the message is different from the amount on an enclosed check, indicate the discrepancy next to the enclosure notation. Record the missing item(s) on the mail record and make a note to contact the sender as soon as possible.

> **Hint:** Unless your supervisor wishes to see each check, prepare a list of incoming checks and other reimbursements and submit the list to your supervisor daily. Include the date of the check, the maker, and the amount. A copy of the list is also helpful when the payments are submitted to the accounting department. If your supervisor is the payee, distribute those checks directly to her or him. Attach the check to the accompanying correspondence and place it in a folder. Make a photocopy of the check.

❏ Attach an enclosure to a document with a staple or a paper clip. Attach small enclosures to the front of documents and attach enclosures that are the same size or larger to the back of documents.

> **Hint:** A staple may damage an attachment, such as a photograph. Fold a small sheet of paper in half and place the attachment between the fold and document. Use a paper clip to attach them together.

❏ Draw a line through the last name that appears on an interoffice envelope and save for reuse. Check that all contents have been removed.

❏ Check parcels for first-class mail, such as an invoice or letter, that may be attached to the front of the package or enclosed inside.

❏ Verify that the contents of the package match the packing slip or invoice as well as the original requisition. Indicate the acceptance of the materials listed on the invoice with a signature or other designated approval before sending the invoice to accounting for payment. Note on the mail record that the ordered materials were received.

❏ Indicate that enclosures have been distributed to another location by writing a note on the original copy of the letter and on the mail record.

RECORDING INCOMING MAIL

In addition to recording the date and time that materials arrive, keep a record of the mail. The mail record is a daily list of mail received with follow-up actions and dates. A review of the record indicates how a document is being handled and to whom a document was routed. It helps in locating and tracing correspondence. Record those items that appear to need additional handling as well as certified, registered, express, priority, and first-class mail; interoffice mail; airmail; E-mail; and personal mail. File mail records in a three-ring $8\frac{1}{2}$-by-11-inch notebook.

A *special services record* lists only those documents requiring the sender to pay additional fees, such as certified, registered, and express mail. The *mail expected record* lists mail that is still expected, such as materials that have been ordered or items that are being sent under separate cover. If the mail expected is very limited, a note on your "to do" list is sufficient. Establish separate records for each special one-time event, such as a special publication or a conference that requires registration fees.

ANNOTATING MAIL

In addition to reviewing and recording mail, reminders or comments may be written in the margins of the correspondence, with underlining or highlighting of key facts. Refer only to the items that require your supervisor's attention; excessive annotation is ineffective. Before making notations on the correspondence, obtain your supervisor's consent. If the documents are distributed to other departments, the marginal notations or underscores may not be appropriate.

Nonreproducing pencils are useful when annotating correspondence since the notations do not reproduce when photocopied. Adhesive notepaper also works since it is easily removed before copies are made for distribution. Use a highlighter only with your supervisor's approval.

Many incoming documents require only brief acknowledgments or transmittal of material. Draft responses to such correspondence for your supervisor's signature or under your own name. Discuss your ability to handle certain types of correspondence with your supervisor.

DISTRIBUTING INCOMING MAIL

Once the mail is sorted by importance, it can then be divided into such categories as:

- Immediate action required
- For reply/routine mail
- For reply/other employees
- For reply/office assistant
- No reply needed—information only (e.g., thank-you notes, acknowledgment letters)
- Magazines, newspapers, publications
- For reading (e.g., announcements, reports not included in the first two categories, advertisements)

The earlier the mail reaches the right desk, the more time there is to respond to those items that require immediate action. Try to set aside the same times each day for handling the mail. Use these procedures for quick, effective distribution:

❏ Sort the first-class mail into such categories as invoices, client concerns, orders, or correspondence from suppliers.

❏ Use a consistent system for presenting the mail. Place it in folders or arrange it according to priority, with the most important documents on top.

> **Hint:** To identify priorities, use different colored folders. For example, place the documents for immediate action in a bright red folder.

❏ Place incoming mail in the same location on the supervisor's desk each time it is delivered. If folders are not appropriate, place a bulky item such as a book on top of the mail. Place the top sheet face-down so the materials are not visible to others.

❏ Assist your supervisor in handling the magazines and trade publications that he or she receives. Request a prioritized list of topics and publications. Prepare a list of articles in each magazine that correspond with these subjects. The supervisor can then select the magazines and articles to read. A second method involves preparing file cards for the articles that fall in an interest area. File these cards in the subject folders for each interest topic. A third method is to photocopy the table of contents of a magazine and highlight those articles in which the supervisor may be interested. Place this list in a folder marked "For Reading." Always keep reading files and subject lists up to date.

❏ Route materials to other departments or other employees by using routing slips. These slips may include names of employees who should review the material or take action. After the first person is finished with the material, he or she initials and dates the routing slip and passes the material on to the second person on the list. "Date received" and "date sent" may be included on the slip.

> **Hint:** The last person on a routing list should know what to do with the document once everyone has read it. Include on the routing slip the name of the person to whom the material should be returned or indicate if it can be discarded.

❏ If there are a number of people who must see the document, photocopying may be more expedient than routing the document. The size of the document and the time needed to copy it will determine the best procedure. Keep the original copy in the originating office.

❏ If actions are necessary, prepare a duplicate and attach it to the original kept in the office. This prevents the same document from being routed again. Making a note in the mail-expected record to indicate to whom the item was routed or the action expected is also helpful.

❏ Share materials from the files with other employees who are asked to take action on an assigned task. Attach these files when routing the materials. Make a notation in the mail record to indicate that the file materials are being routed.

❏ Ask for assistance in determining which advertisements and catalogs to save, if any. Store them in a separate location away from general files. Discard the older editions as soon as new ones are received.

❏ If an employee has left the company, forward personal correspondence to the employee's home. Cross out the company address on the envelope and write the forwarding address and the words "Please forward." If the document appears to be business related, forward it to that person's replacement, or to the immediate supervisor if a replacement has not been named.

OUTGOING MAIL

Efficient handling of outgoing mail speeds the communication process. Processing the mail so it is not delayed and following the USPS guidelines for addressing mail are responsibilities of office professionals.

PROCESSING OUTGOING MAIL

Before sending the mail to the mailroom or depositing it for delivery, several steps are needed to process it:

❑ Check that all letters have a signature. Be sure all attachments and enclosures are included.

❑ Type the envelope; do not address envelopes by hand.

❑ Combine mailings. If there are two letters to one company, place them both in the same envelope. Use both sides of the paper for lengthy reports; this practice saves paper and also postage costs.

❑ Check that all correspondence has been dated and that the address on the envelope matches the inside address. Verify the accuracy of the addresses by checking the current address list and making appropriate changes. When inserting the material in the envelopes, be sure the correct letter goes in the proper envelope.

❑ Verify the ZIP Code with the address on the original correspondence or locate it in the ZIP Code directory.

❑ Deposit all metered mail on the date stamped. Do not place metered stamps on the envelopes one day and wait until another day to do the mailing. If the mail does not make the last pickup, take it to another collection box or to the post office.

❑ Change the date on the postage meter each morning *before* other tasks are started. Metered mail is processed faster than stamped mail, since it does not have to be canceled at the post office.

❑ Avoid waiting until the end of the day to deposit mail. Take mail to the mailroom several times during the day. Mail deposited by 2 p.m. has a chance of being processed by 5 p.m. for next day delivery.

❑ Order postage for the postage meter when the remaining postage is enough for three days of mail. Reorder by telephone or take the meter in to the post office to be reset.

❑ Use a stamp dispenser that automatically moistens stamps as they are removed from the roll. Use the USPS order forms to order stamps or envelopes. USPS also has a service for ordering stamps by telephone. There is a charge for the service.

❑ Sort the mail into local and out-of-town bundles.

❑ Use window envelopes only if the address has four or fewer lines. More than four lines will not be fully visible in the window section.

❑ Inform mailroom personnel when a large mailing is planned.

❑ Insure mail for its proper value. Reimbursement is made on actual, not declared, value. Certified mail does not include insurance, but it does provide a receipt and is less expensive.

❑ Weigh all mail. Do not guess. Use a scale that measures to a fraction of an ounce. Check the scales periodically with the USPS scales to be certain they are accurate.

❑ Use postal cards to make routine announcements to clients and to send short messages to customers. Use business reply envelopes for return responses. They are less expensive than stamped, self-addressed envelopes.

❑ Place tape over a metal clasp on an envelope. This avoids damage to the envelope if it gets jammed in the sorting machine. Write "Please hand stamp" on the outside of the envelope if it contains bulky items.

> **Hint:** If materials must be clipped together or stapled, fold so that the paper clips or staples are in the inner fold of the document. Paper clips can get bent and cause a jam in a sorting machine.

❑ Obtain full value for the amount of postage used. If paying for one ounce, weigh the letter to determine if another announcement or promotion piece can be included. This eliminates two separate mailings.

❑ Use the smallest and strongest containers possible for wrapping packages. Do not use string and wrapping paper, since packages may also be processed by machines; use a filament tape. Do not use newspaper for protecting the contents; use lightweight stuffing.

❑ Include a letter with any disk that is being transmitted through the mail. Do not rely solely on a file named "Read.me" on the disk. Identify the contents of the disk and the sender in the transmittal letter and on the disk label. This procedure causes less confusion should the disk and letter be separated. Also, identify the software program and the hardware used.

❑ Prepare disks for mailing by placing them in cardboard or heavy plastic wrap before putting them in a box or padded envelope. On the outside of the box or envelope, indicate a disk is enclosed.

FOLDING AND INSERTING MAIL

Machines are available to fold, seal, and stamp mail. Correct folding and insertion give letters a professional look and make them easy for the reader to open and unfold. The steps involved in folding and inserting materials for the No. 10, No. $6\frac{3}{4}$, and window envelopes follow. Always use a flat surface for neater folds.

No. 10 Envelope

❑ With the document face-up on the desk, fold up the bottom third of the page first.

❑ Fold the top third of the letter down over the bottom third so the top edge is $\frac{1}{4}$ inch from the first fold.

❑ Insert the item so the open side of the document is at the back (side to be sealed) and to the top of the envelope.

No. 6¾ Envelope

❏ With the document face-up on the desk, fold the bottom half of the paper to $\frac{1}{4}$ inch from the top. Leaving the $\frac{1}{4}$ inch makes it easier for the reader to separate the pages.

❏ Fold the document in thirds. Start with the first one-third fold from the right side. Continue with the second one-third fold from the left side so the edge is $\frac{1}{4}$ inch from the right side.

❏ Insert so the last fold is toward the bottom of the envelope and the open edge faces the back of the envelope (the side to be sealed). Insert the document so the open edges are on the stamp side of the envelope.

Hint: If the folds are not parallel with the top and sides, the letter will look sloppy when unfolded. Fold the sections so they are exactly the same width. Avoid uneven edges and folds that are at angles.

Window Envelope

❏ With the document face-up on the desk, fold up the bottom third of the page first.

❏ Fold the top third of the document in the opposite direction so the edge touches the first fold.

❏ Insert the document so the last fold is at the bottom of the envelope and the address shows through the window.

❏ Postal guidelines call for a space of $\frac{1}{4}$ inch between the side and bottom edges of the window and an address.

Hint: Fold enclosures with the document or insert them so they are in the fold of the document.

ADDRESSING ENVELOPES

The USPS has provided guidelines for addressing envelopes so its mechanical and electronic equipment can read the addresses and speed the delivery of mail. (See Figure 16–12.)

State abbreviations: Use the standard two-letter abbreviations as given in Table 16-1.

ZIP Codes: Use nine-digit ZIP Codes, if known, or the five-digit ZIP Code. Letter-sorting machines sort envelopes by ZIP Codes. Optical character readers read the last two lines of an address. Bar code readers can process mail with imprinted bar codes at extraordinary speeds. Most countries have postal code systems. Canadian and British postal codes consist of numbers and letters arranged in two groups of three characters each; for example, F3N 4B2.

Address placement: Mail can be processed more quickly if the address is placed in a designated location on the envelope and arranged in a specific sequence. The USPS recommends the following for address placement:

❏ Locate the address lines within the OCR read area.

❏ Align the address so each line is straight.

❏ Allow an area $4\frac{1}{2}$ inches wide and $\frac{5}{8}$ inch from the bottom of an envelope for printing the bar code. Do not mark anything within the bar code boundaries.

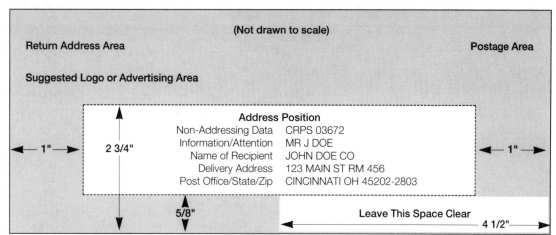

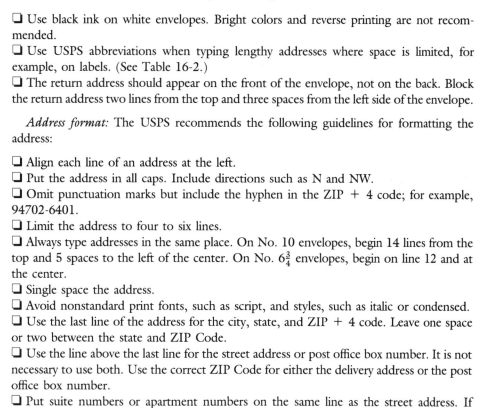

Any non-address information, such as logos, advertising, etc., should be placed above delivery address line.

Figure 16-12 Format for addressing an envelope.

❑ Use black ink on white envelopes. Bright colors and reverse printing are not recommended.

❑ Use USPS abbreviations when typing lengthy addresses where space is limited, for example, on labels. (See Table 16-2.)

❑ The return address should appear on the front of the envelope, not on the back. Block the return address two lines from the top and three spaces from the left side of the envelope.

Address format: The USPS recommends the following guidelines for formatting the address:

❑ Align each line of an address at the left.

❑ Put the address in all caps. Include directions such as N and NW.

❑ Omit punctuation marks but include the hyphen in the ZIP + 4 code; for example, 94702-6401.

❑ Limit the address to four to six lines.

❑ Always type addresses in the same place. On No. 10 envelopes, begin 14 lines from the top and 5 spaces to the left of the center. On No. $6\frac{3}{4}$ envelopes, begin on line 12 and at the center.

❑ Single space the address.

❑ Avoid nonstandard print fonts, such as script, and styles, such as italic or condensed.

❑ Use the last line of the address for the city, state, and ZIP + 4 code. Leave one space or two between the state and ZIP Code.

❑ Use the line above the last line for the street address or post office box number. It is not necessary to use both. Use the correct ZIP Code for either the delivery address or the post office box number.

❑ Put suite numbers or apartment numbers on the same line as the street address. If the address is too long, put the suite or apartment number on the line above the street address.

Table 16-1 Standard Address Abbreviations

United States and Possessions			
Alabama	AL	Missouri	MO
Alaska	AK	Montana	MT
Arizona	AZ	Nebraska	NE
Arkansas	AR	Nevada	NV
American Samoa	AS	New Hampshire	NH
California	CA	New Jersey	NJ
Colorado	CO	New Mexico	NM
Connecticut	CT	New York	NY
Delaware	DE	North Carolina	NC
District of Columbia	DC	North Dakota	ND
Federated States of		Northern Mariana Islands	MP
Micronesia	FM	Ohio	OH
Florida	FL	Oklahoma	OK
Georgia	GA	Oregon	OR
Guam	GU	Palau	PW
Hawaii	HI	Pennsylvania	PA
Idaho	ID	Puerto Rico	PR
Illinois	IL	Rhode Island	RI
Indiana	IN	South Carolina	SC
Iowa	IA	South Dakota	SD
Kansas	KS	Tennessee	TN
Kentucky	KY	Texas	TX
Louisiana	LA	Utah	UT
Maine	ME	Vermont	VT
Marshall Islands	MH	Virginia	VA
Maryland	MD	Virgin Islands	VI
Massachusetts	MA	Washington	WA
Michigan	MI	West Virginia	WV
Minnesota	MN	Wisconsin	WI
Mississippi	MS	Wyoming	WY

Table 16-1 *(con't)*

United States and Possessions			
Canada		*Directional Abbreviations*	
Alberta	AB	North	N
British Columbia	BC	East	E
Manitoba	MB	South	S
New Brunswick	NB	West	W
Newfoundland	NF	Northeast	NE
Northwest Territories	NT	Southeast	SE
Nova Scotia	NS	Southwest	SW
Ontario	ON	Northwest	NW
Prince Edward Island	PE		
Quebec	PQ		
Saskatchewan	SK		
Yukon Territory	YT		

❏ Identify the addressee on the top line of the address. The department name, if applicable, should appear on the second line and the company name on the third line.

❏ Use an "attention" line on the second line of an address if necessary.

❏ Put special service notations such as SPECIAL DELIVERY, CERTIFIED, or REGIS-TERED two lines below the stamp in all capital letters. Underscores are not necessary. The information must be above the OCR read area.

❏ Put handling instructions such as Confidential and Personal three lines below the return address and above the OCR read area. Capitalize the first letter of each word and under-score.

❏ When addressing mail to foreign countries put the name of the country on the last line in all capital letters.

Hint: Address formats differ in foreign countries. In European countries, the street name often appears first with the number following it. Write the address exactly as it appears on the letterhead.

INTEROFFICE MAIL

Interoffice mail may be delivered by mailroom personnel, intercompany transport, or E-mail. Most companies have distinctive envelopes for interoffice mail. Light brown envelopes with room for names and departments/locations of the recipients are the most common. They are $9\frac{1}{2}$ inches × 13 inches or 4 inches × $9\frac{1}{2}$ inches. The smaller size is appropriate for small notes. Avoid using the smaller envelopes for documents that must be folded to fit inside.

Table 16-2 Frequently Used Postal Abbreviations

Abbreviations for Street Designators (Street Suffixes)

Alley	ALY	Gardens	GDNS	Radial	RADL
Annex	ANX	Gateway	GTWY	Ranch	RNCH
Arcade	ARC	Glen	GLN	Rapids	RPDS
Avenue	AVE	Green	GRN	Rest	RST
Bayou	BYU	Grove	GRV	Ridge	RDG
Beach	BCH	Harbor	HBR	River	RIV
Bend	BND	Haven	HVN	Road	RD
Bluff	BLF	Heights	HTS	Row	ROW
Bottom	BTM	Highway	HWY	Run	RUN
Boulevard	BLVD	Hill	HL	Shoal	SHL
Branch	BR	Hills	HLS	Shoals	SHLS
Bridge	BRG	Hollow	HOLW	Shore	SHR
Brook	BRK	Inlet	INLT	Shores	SHRS
Burg	BG	Island	IS	Spring	SPG
Bypass	BYP	Islands	ISS	Springs	SPGS
Camp	CP	Isle	ISLE	Spur	SPUR
Canyon	CYN	Junction	JCT	Square	SQ
Cape	CPE	Key	KY	Station	STA
Causeway	CSWY	Knolls	KNLS	Stravenue	STRA
Center	CTR	Lake	LK	Stream	STRM
Circle	CIR	Lakes	LKS	Street	ST
Cliffs	CLFS	Landing	LNDG	Summit	SMT
Club	CLB	Lane	LN	Terrace	TER
Corner	COR	Light	LGT	Trace	TRCE
Corners	CORS	Loaf	LF	Track	TRAK
Course	CRSE	Locks	LCKS	Trail	TRL
Court	CT	Lodge	LDG	Trailer	TRLR
Courts	CTS	Loop	LOOP	Tunnel	TUNL
Cove	CV	Mall	MALL	Turnpike	TPKE
Creek	CRK	Manor	MNR	Union	UN
Crescent	CRES	Meadows	MDWS	Valley	VLY
Crossing	XING	Mill	ML	Viaduct	VIA
Dale	DL	Mills	MLS	View	VW
Dam	DM	Mission	MSN	Village	VLG
Divide	DV	Mount	MT	Ville	VL
Drive	DR	Mountain	MTN	Vista	VIS
Estates	EST	Neck	NCK	Walk	WALK
Expressway	EXPY	Orchard	ORCH	Way	WAY
Extension	EXT	Oval	OVAL	Wells	WLS
Fall	FALL	Park	PARK		
Falls	FLS	Parkway	PKY		
Ferry	FRY	Pass	PASS		
Field	FLD	Path	PATH		
Fields	FLDS	Pike	PIKE		
Flats	FLT	Pines	PNES		
Ford	FRD	Place	PL		
Forest	FRST	Plain	PLN		
Forge	FRG	Plains	PLNS		
Fork	FRK	Plaza	PLZ		
Forks	FRKS	Point	PT		
Fort	FT	Port	PRT		
Freeway	FWY	Prairie	PR		

Interoffice envelopes are reusable. The sender crosses out the previous name, inserts the material, and fastens, but does not seal, the envelope, usually with an attached string. Interoffice mail accumulates and is collected at scheduled intervals during the day.

Hint: If the material is confidential, use an ordinary envelope and seal it. Label it "INTEROFFICE MEMO" in the upper right corner so it will not get mixed in with the other classes of mail. Some companies have special envelopes for confidential interoffice mail that are labeled as such.

MAILING LISTS

Mailing lists are effective only when names, addresses, and job titles are accurate and up to date. Effective mailing lists are easy to reuse and manipulate.

Companies use mailing lists for such activities as sending out newsletters or informational bulletins to employees, maintaining vendor addresses, compiling customer lists, and marketing their products. The company prepares the lists in-house or rents, buys, or leases them from other companies.

Mailing lists can be compiled from numerous sources. These sources include:

- Company sales invoices
- Company payroll records
- Replies to advertisements
- Business license applications
- Professional organizations; for example, Kiwanis, Chamber of Commerce
- Utility companies
- Voting lists
- Auto registration lists
- Tax lists
- Warranty registrations
- City directories
- Telephone directories

Hint: *The Directory of Directories,* an annual publication from Gale Research Company, has listings for organization and business directories.

Many directories are neither up to date nor accurate. Using directories to build mailing lists can be time-consuming. Each address must be copied on an envelope or label or entered in a database and then printed on an envelope or label.

In-house preparation of mailing lists requires time and planning. Begin by identifying the appropriate fields to include in setting up a database. Then revise the fields as necessary once the database is established.

Several suggestions for specific fields include:

- Name/address/telephone number
- Social Security number (if known or applicable)

- Income level/sales volume
- Job title of the person making the inquiry or purchase
- Number of years the organization has been in the business
- Age category of individuals (when applicable)
- Geographic area
- Product areas
- Amount of order
- Date of first purchase; date of last purchase
- Frequency of orders
- Peak buying times
- Code for products in which an interest is shown
- Category of the company; for example, manufacturing, real estate, finance
- Level of inquiry; for example, branch office, department, project group

Mailing lists may be maintained on address labels, address plates, file cards, computer printouts, or as a database. Lists stored in computers are the most flexible. List processing or mail management software allows users to prepare and sort lists more efficiently; for example, mailing labels can be produced in ZIP Code order, which makes them easier to presort for bulk mailing. A mail management program may also permit the user to produce sacking labels. Word processing, database, or integrated software programs may also have mail management functions of varying sophistication. Addresses may be printed directly on envelopes or on gummed labels, or merged into accompanying letters or statements.

Hint: Printing directly on an envelope is more personal; a recipient will be more likely to open it rather than toss it away.

Hint: If numerous lists exist in different departments, bring address changes to the attention of other departments to avoid wasted postage costs and returned mail.

Hint: To eliminate duplicate names, sort by last name, Social Security number, or telephone number. Take the time to check the list for names that are obviously misspelled and for names that are listed more than once. If a prepared list and an in-house list are both used, an outside service bureau may save the company time by doing the purging and checking. Contact the local direct marketing association for names of service bureaus in the area.

If the in-house compilation of mailing lists becomes a formidable task, the lists may be rented, purchased, or leased from companies who prepare mailing lists or from those who loan lists. Lists come in different formats; for example, disk, labels, or printouts. When mailing lists are purchased, the maintenance of the list becomes the buyer's responsibility.

The lists may be rented for one-time use, or more than once if stated in the original agreement. Those who compile and own the lists can identify illegal use of their lists. Use the list only as specified in the rental agreement.

When ordering a mailing list, allow at least six weeks to order and receive the list, sort the names, and prepare the mailing. Time the mailing so it reaches potential clients by the beginning of the week or at seasonal slack times. After the holiday season and around tax deadlines or accounting closing periods, direct mail literature receives less attention.

The USPS can assist companies in updating mailing lists. If you write "Address Correction Requested" below the return address on the envelope, the post office will inform you of the correct address if known. The service is expensive and therefore most companies limit this service to current customer lists.

To remove your name or your company's name from commercial and/or nonprofit mailing lists, contact the Mail Preference Service of the Direct Marketing Association, 6 East 43rd Street, New York, NY 10017. Another way to decrease the influx of direct mail is to request companies with whom business is transacted to stop renting the company name to other organizations.

PART IV

OFFICE COMMUNICATIONS

CHAPTER 17

WRITTEN CORRESPONDENCE

Well-written correspondence is one of the most important factors in communicating a strong, positive corporate image. The office professional is expected to know how to correctly and attractively format correspondence for maximum impact using the most productive means available. In addition, many office professionals are expected to compose written communications for others.

For years the formats of memos and letters did not change. Computers, however, now allow the design of personalized form letters, printing of envelopes from prepared address lists, and discovery of errors by spelling, grammar, and style checkers. All of these advances in technology have brought about streamlined, uncluttered correspondence designed to improve operator productivity.

COMPONENTS OF LETTERS

Letters may include some or all of the following:

- Date
- Inside address
- Attention line
- Salutation
- Subject line
- Complimentary closing
- Writer information
- Initials of typist
- Notations

The inclusion of a component depends on the purpose of the correspondence and the letter style used.

DATE

All letters should include a date. Write the date as, for example, January 15, 19__. Spell out the month. Or use the military style of 15 January 19__ to avoid punctuation and save keying time. Place the date two or more lines beneath the letterhead; the shorter the letter, the more space is needed beneath the letterhead. Place the date either at the left margin or the center of the page, depending upon the letter style used (see the section on Letter Styles later in this chapter).

INSIDE ADDRESS

The inside address contains everything necessary for delivery of correspondence: the name, job title, company name, street address or post office box number, and the city, state, and ZIP Code.

Name
- Check on the correct spelling of the recipient's name.
- Use a courtesy title if it is known. Courtesy titles include *Dr., Mr., Mrs.,* and *Ms.* (See the heading *Salutation* below for determining whether to use *Ms., Mrs.,* or *Miss.*)

Hint: If you do not know whether you are addressing a man or a woman with first names like Lynn or Pat, omit the title of *Mr.* or *Ms.* It is best to use the simplified letter style. (See the section on Letter Styles in this chapter.)

- Omitting earned titles such as *Dr., M.D.,* or *the Reverend* may offend the reader, especially if that person has written your company using his or her title. Courtesy titles are not used if the earned title is included, and only one earned title is used: e.g., Louise F. Granger, M.D. (not Dr. Louise F. Granger, M.D.).
- *Esquire* (abbreviated as *Esq.*) can be used after the name of a lawyer, but no courtesy title should then be included: e.g., Shannon A. Duff, Esq. (not Ms. Shannon A. Duff, Esq.)
- Use a job title if the name of the person is not known.
- Use a period after most courtesy and earned titles (except *Miss*).
- Spell out *Professor* and *Reverend*.

Job Title
- Omit the job title if the exact title is not known.
- Place it either on the same line with the name, separated by a comma, or on the next line.

Company Name
- Check on the exact spelling and punctuation of the company name.
- Type the name exactly as it appears in the company's official letterhead, including *The, Inc.,* or *Co.*

Street Address or Post Office Box

- Spell out numerical names of streets and avenues if they are numbers less than 10: e.g., Seventh Street, Third Avenue, 15th Street.
- Use figures for all house numbers except One: e.g., One Commerce Boulevard, 2 Park Avenue, 102 Sunnyslope.
- Spell out *Avenue, Street, Boulevard,* etc.
- Place a PO Box number after the street address: e.g.,

3489 Westwood Road
PO Box 4388

- Omit periods after abbreviations: e.g., PO Box 34; 2 Elm Street, NW
  The trend toward dropping periods in the inside address is a result of USPS requests to eliminate punctuation on envelopes. Also, addresses on computer databases generally do not include punctuation.

City, State, and ZIP

- Include the full name of the city with no abbreviations. For example, San Francisco instead of SF.
- Use the two-letter state or province abbreviation recommended by the USPS. (See Table 16-1 in Chapter 16.)
- Place the ZIP or postal code one or two spaces after the state or province abbreviation.
- Use the ZIP + 4 code if known.
- A comma is not necessary between the city and the state, but one may be used.

The inside address should be single-spaced and placed at the left-hand margin. Locate it not less than two lines nor more than twelve lines below the date; placement depends on letter length. For longer letters, place closer to the date; for shorter letters, avoid extending the inside address beyond the middle of the page. Avoid going beyond the center of the page with the inside address. If necessary, carry over information to the next line, which should be indented five spaces. Avoid having more than six lines in an address; it may be necessary to combine lines.

Here are some examples of inside addresses:

Ms. Sarah Raintree
Sales Manager
Interim Personnel, Suite 203
4378 Southwest Boulevard
Chicago IL 60637

Dr. Gail Radtkey
Vice President
Lawrence Galleries
3892 Independence Avenue
Phoenix AZ 85773

Cameron Jacobson, M.D.
968 Lakeville Highway
Napa CA 94943

Mr. Roger Weiss, President
Creative Leisure
5948 Industrial Road
Trenton NJ 38943

Alexandra T. L. Freeman, Personnel
    Coordinator
4783 Redwood Highway
PO Box 5012
San Rafael CA 94530

ATTENTION LINE

An attention line is used when correspondence is addressed to a company but sent to the attention of an individual. If the recipient's name is known, put the name in the inside address, use a proper salutation (see the heading *Salutation* below), and eliminate the attention line. The USPS recommends placing the attention line first in an address. To be consistent, the attention line should be placed in the same position in the letter. Place the attention line at the left margin as the first line of the inside address. A colon is optional after the word *Attention*.

Attention Sharon Flanagan
Campbell Press
3902 Oakridge Drive
San Jose CA 49857

Dear Ms. Flanagan:

OR

Attention: Sharon Flanagan
Campbell Press
3902 Oakridge Drive
San Jose CA 49857

Dear Ms. Flanagan:

SALUTATION

A letter should always be addressed to an individual if the name is known. Below are suggested salutations.

ADDRESSED TO AN INDIVIDUAL

The most common salutation is *Dear*. Whether the first name or last name with title is used depends on the relationship between the writer and the recipient. Most people find it annoying to be addressed by their first name if they do not know the writer.

Use *Ms.* when addressing a woman, unless previous correspondence indicates she prefers the title *Mrs.* or *Miss*. Many women prefer the neutral term of *Ms.* over a term that denotes marital status.

If a person has an earned title such as M.D., Ph.D., or Ed.D., use *Dr.* in the salutation. Spell out the title *Professor*.

Avoid substituting a designation of business rank or position for a name; use "Dear Mr. Jones," not "Dear Personnel Director Jones." Similarly, write "Dear Ms. Reynolds," not "Dear Editor Reynolds."

The Honorable is used for individuals with high offices at the federal, state, or city levels. This title is still held after retirement. Table 17-1 provides sample salutations used for clergy, elected officials, military officers, and education officials.

WHEN RECIPIENT'S NAME IS NOT KNOWN

Traditional salutations of *Dear Sir* or *Gentlemen* are inappropriate if the recipient's name is not known. *Dear Sir or Madam* or *Dear Ladies and Gentlemen* are options. The following are other contemporary solutions to the gender problem: (1) Omit the salutation and closing and use the simplified letter format (see the section on Letter Styles later in this chapter). (2) Address the recipient by title: e.g., Dear Screening Committee, Dear Board Members, Dear Credit Manager.

A salutation can use either open or closed punctuation. Either is correct, but the style must be consistent in a letter. Open punctuation means there is no punctuation after the salutation or closing. Closed punctuation uses a comma after the salutation when the first name is used; a colon after the salutation when a title and last name are used; and a comma after the closing.

Abbreviate the titles *Mr., Mrs., Ms., Messrs.,* and *Dr.* Spell out all other titles. Type the salutation two lines below the inside address. If you will use a standard window envelope, start on line 12 from the top of the page.

SUBJECT

The subject line describes the purpose for writing a letter. The subject line is not necessary in business letters but is used when drawing the reader's attention to the contents of the letter. It is particularly helpful if recipients, such as government agencies, receive a volume of correspondence. No punctuation is needed.

Hint: Avoid *re,* an outdated Latin expression meaning the same as "subject."

Table 17-1 Sample Salutations

Person	Inside Address	Salutation
Elected Officials		
Chief Justice	The Chief Justice Supreme Court	Dear Mr. Chief Justice
Governor	The Honorable Richard Swan	Dear Governor Swan or Dear Governor
Judge	The Honorable Rosa Bezzari	Dear Judge Bezzari
Mayor	The Honorable Carolina Jung	Dear Mayor Jung
President	The President	Dear Mr. President Dear Madam President
Speaker of the House	The Honorable José Perez The Honorable Julia Payne	Dear Mr. Speaker Dear Madam Speaker
State Senator	The Honorable Lisa O'Leary	Dear Senator O'Leary
State Representative	The Honorable Mary Carter	Dear Representative Carter
U.S. Representative	The Honorable Betty Hamilton	Dear Representative Hamilton or Dear Ms. Hamilton
U.S. Senator	The Honorable Sam Nelson	Dear Senator Nelson or Dear Mr. Nelson
Vice President	The Vice President	Dear Mr. Vice President Dear Madam Vice President
Education Officials		
	Dr. J. Barbara Hall	Dear Dr. Hall
	Professor Quinlan Jones	Dear Professor Jones
Clergy		
Protestant clergy	The Reverend Sarah Gilligam	Dear Dr. Gilligam (with a doctorate degree) Dear Ms. Gilligam (without a doctorate degree)
Bishop of the Episcopal Church	The Right Reverend Randolph Jones	Dear Bishop Jones
Methodist Bishop	The Reverend George Rojas	Dear Reverend Rojas
Mormon Bishop	Mr. Gerald Hornaby	Dear Mr. Hornaby
The Pope	His Holiness, The Pope	Your Holiness
Cardinal	His Eminence, Paul Cardinal Bernardi	Your Eminence or Dear Cardinal Bernardi
Priest	The Reverend Father Peter Smoll	Dear Father Smoll
Nun	Sister Mary Margoilis or Mary Margoilis, R.S.C.J.	Dear Sister

Table 17-1 *(con't)*

Person	Inside Address	Salutation
Rabbi	Rabbi Benjamin Stein	Dear Rabbi Stein
Military		
First Lieutenant	First Lieutenant, Craig Garcia	Dear Lieutenant Garcia
Lieutenant Colonel	Lieutenant Colonel, Samuel Jacobson	Dear Colonel Jacobson
Noncommissioned officers in Army, Air Force, and Marine Corps	Master Sergeant Roger Webb	Dear Sergeant Webb
Enlisted person in Navy	SN Charles Brown	Dear Seaman Brown

COMPLIMENTARY CLOSING

The most popular and appropriate closing is *Sincerely*. *Sincerely yours* and *Cordially* are also well-accepted closings. *Respectfully yours* is used when writing to a high official, including the President of the United States or a high church official. If a closing has more than one word (such as *Sincerely yours*), capitalize only the first word.

Place the closing two lines below the last line of the letter. Use a comma after the closing if using closed punctuation; use no punctuation if using open punctuation. (See the heading *Salutation* earlier in this chapter for a definition of open and closed punctuation.)

WRITER'S NAME AND SIGNATURE

All letters should include the name and title of the writer. Enough space should be left between the complimentary closing and the typed name of the writer for a signature.

Name
- Place the writer's name four lines under the closing to allow space for the signature.
- Use the first name with or without the middle initial as preferred by the writer; place a period after a middle initial if used.
- Place earned titles after the name; place periods after earned titles if appropriate: e.g., Karen Fisher, CPS; Martin Pena, M.D.

Job Title
- Place the writer's job title on a line below the typed name:

Sincerely,

Ronald Rubik

Ronald Rubik
Sales Manager

Sincerely,

Debbie Paulsen

Debbie Paulsen
Administrative Assistant
    to Ronald Rubik

- If the letter is signed by someone other than the writer, sign the writer's name and use your initials.

Sincerely,

Sylvia J. Crinski gk

Sylvia J. Crinski
Vice President

- Professional, military, or academic titles appear after the writer's name:

Sincerely,

John Toten

John Toten, M.D.

Sincerely,

Leslie Duggins

Leslie Duggins, CPS

INITIALS OF TYPIST

The typist's initials are often included but may be omitted. Use lowercase initials at the left margin and place them two lines below the writer's title.

NOTATIONS

Notations include information such as the number and nature of enclosures and the number of copies and who received them.

❑ Place notations at the left margin two lines below the initials of typist.
❑ "Enclosure" is written out. More than one enclosure can be noted as follows:

Enclosures 2
Enclosure—Software
Enclosures
    Software
    Documentation Manual

❏ "cc" means carbon copy. Since carbons are obsolete in many offices, the notations "pc" for photocopy and "c" for copy are commonly used. The notation "bcc" or "bc" is used for "blind" copies, that is, for copies that the recipient of the document will not necessarily know about.

pc Richard Hernandez

c Adele Richards
  Marvin O'Leary

❏ No punctuation is needed.

LETTER STYLES

Most companies have designed letterhead and developed a letter style to identify, communicate, and project a corporate image. Letter styles are typically based on their perceived impact on others.

A letter style may have been developed before computers were common in an office; therefore the operator may need to do complex equipment adjustments to get that style on a computer. Modern letter styles take advantage of the capabilities of computers.

The most common letter styles are the block, simplified block, and modified block letter. The less centering and indenting in a letter, the easier it is to keyboard and revise, which increases productivity. Productivity can also be increased by having one standard letter format instead of having different styles for different writers.

The following general formatting rules apply to letters, no matter what style is used:

❏ Use a standard line length, which is typically 6 inches. Line length can be decreased for shorter letters. A line length longer than 6 inches is difficult to read. Start a new page if the letter runs long rather than increase the margins to more than 6 inches.

❏ Return four times after the date. The space may be increased or decreased depending on the length of the letter.

❏ Single-space the body; double-space between paragraphs.

❏ Use short sentences averaging no more than 20 words.

❏ Include at least two sentences in a paragraph.

❏ Keep paragraphs approximately the same length. Avoid more than 10 lines of type in a paragraph; divide a longer paragraph into two shorter ones.

❏ Use tabulated lists to make a letter look more interesting. Discreet use of underlining, italics, or bold print also adds interest.

❏ Begin lists at the left margin with a number followed by a period. Leave two spaces after the period and begin the text. If an item is longer than one line, succeeding lines should be indented to line up with the text.

BLOCK LETTER

In a block letter, all lines are flush with the left margin. (See Figure 17-1.)

Formatting Suggestions:
❑ Return two times after the inside address, salutation, the subject (if any), and before the closing.
❑ Return four times after the closing for the writer's information.
❑ Return two times after the writer's information for the initials of the typist and notations.

SIMPLIFIED BLOCK LETTER

This letter style reflects a trend toward eliminating the salutation and complimentary close. All lines are flush with the left margin. A subject line is used in place of the salutation. The simplified letter is the most efficient letter style to type.

There are two formats for simplified block letters. The major differences are in line spacing and capitalization. (See Figures 17-2 and 17-3.)

Style #1
❑ Type inside address with initial caps or in all capital letters as recommended by the USPS.
❑ Return three times after the inside address.
❑ Omit the salutation and use a subject line. The subject line may be initial capped or in all caps.
❑ Return three times after the subject line and begin the body.
❑ Omit the closing.
❑ Return four times after the body for the writer's information. The writer's name and title may be initial capped or in all caps.

Style #2
❑ Key the document only on even-numbered lines (line 12, 14, 16, or 18 depending the length of letter or use of window envelopes).
❑ Use only multiples of two for spacing. The inside address is a quadruple space from the date; the subject is a double-space from the inside address; the body is a double space from the subject line; the writer's identification is a quadruple space from the body to the writer's name.
❑ Type inside address with initial caps or in all capital letters as recommended by the USPS.
❑ Omit the salutation and use a subject line. The subject line may be initial capped or in all caps.
❑ Use the recipient's name in the beginning and near the end of the body.
❑ Omit the closing.
❑ The writer's name and title may be initial capped or in all caps.

June 5, 19--

Mr. Greg Lichau
Lark Creek Inn
Box 6329
Tahoe City CA 95730

Dear Greg:

Thanks to you and your staff again this year for the superior job
of handling our group so well! We like to come to Lark Creek Inn
because we know the meeting rooms are comfortable and pleasant and the food is excellent.

Next year we are planning our conference for August 12–16. If
by any chance our original dates become available, we would like
to be notified. We also would like to reserve our dates several
years in advance for the last week in July.

Thank you again for all you did to help make our conference a
success! We look forward to working with you again next year.

Sincerely,

Michelle Bryant
Conference Coordinator

ik

Figure 17-1 Block letter.

June 5, 19--

Mr. Michael Troy
Human Development Associates
203 S Willits
Visalia CA 93291

YOU DID AN OUTSTANDING JOB!

"Thanks" hardly seems like an expressive enough word for all
the time, effort, and planning that went into our conference,
Mike. You were so responsive to our needs and so willing to
make changes.

Just as last year, you did an excellent job and really gave the
balance we were looking for. I had a million little things to worry
about, and it was a relief to not worry about you or your presentation. I knew you would do a great job!

The enclosed evaluations are our best ever and reflect your ability to deliver the training we wanted. Thanks again, Mike, for
everything you did to make our conference a success.

Michelle Bryant
Conference Coordinator

ik

Figure 17-2 Simplified block letter #1.

June 5, 19--

Ms. Michelle Bryant
Conference Coordinator
The Learning and Guidance Center
6543 Lincoln Way
San Francisco CA 94367

The Conference Was a Success

Thank you, Michelle, for the evaluations of the conference, the
great pictures, and your lovely letter. This truly was an outstanding conference, deserving of the very high evaluations it
received.

Your organizational, management, and human relations skills
were very much in evidence. The standing ovation you received
reflected the recognition and appreciation for all your efforts.
Congratulations on an excellent job!

Being involved in the committee that planned, delivered, and
evaluated the conference was a wonderful experience. It is a joy
to work with such dedicated people as you, Michelle.

Robin Noll
Vice President

mj

Figure 17-3 Simplified block letter #2.

September 11, 19--

Ms. Michelle Bryant
Conference Coordinator
The Learning and Guidance Center
6543 Lincoln Way
San Francisco CA 94367

Dear Michelle:

Thank you so much for letting me observe your conference
at Lark Creek Inn on June 1. Your leaders did a marvelous
job of relating to the participants as well as educating them
in leadership, presentation styles, and problem-solving skills.

My experience will be relayed to the educators I work with.
We have a lot to strive for with your conference as a model.
Congratulations on a wonderful conference!

                              Sincerely,

                              Sandra Mandici
                              Project Consultant

lp

Figure 17-4 Modified block letter.

MODIFIED BLOCK LETTER

The modified block letter is somewhat more traditional. The date, closing, and writer's information start at the center. All other lines are flush with the left margin. This format looks balanced on the page. (See Figure 17-4.)

Formatting Suggestions

❑ Return two times after the inside address, salutation, and the subject (if any) and before the closing.
❑ Return four times after the closing for the writer's name and title.
❑ Return two times after the writer's name and title for the initials of the typist, if any.
❑ Return two times after the typist's initials for any notations.

MULTIPAGE LETTER

The first page of a multipage letter should be typed on letterhead. The rest of the pages should be typed on plain paper of the same size and quality as the letterhead. At least three lines of the letter should go on the last page with the closing (if used) and the writer's signature.

A heading should be placed at the top of the page that includes the name of the addressee, page number, and date in either of the following formats:

Dr. Christine Davis   2   April 19, 19__

Dr. Christine Davis
Page 2
April 19, 19__

Formatting Suggestions

❑ Leave a 1-inch top margin (start heading on line 7).
❑ Start the body three lines below the heading.
❑ Use the same margins as on the first page.

FORM LETTERS

A form letter is a letter sent to many people, usually about a repetitive or routine situation. Form letters save time in letter writing and keyboarding. A form letter is useful when people repeatedly ask for the same information. Form letters about products or the company can be prepared in response to customers who write with questions, requests, or complaints. They are also useful when the same information needs to be sent to more than one person, company, or group; for example, a letter sent to a list of customers.

Form letters should appear as if they were written for the recipient. This is easily done with the mail-merge function of many word processors. (See Chapter 8, Office Computer Software.) The following are suggestions for personalizing form letters:

- Use company letterhead and matching envelope.
- Include the recipient's name, title, and address in the inside address.
- Use a personalized salutation; for example, "Dear Ms. Garza."
- Customize by adding specific information if known; for example, "I enjoyed talking with you this morning."
- Personally sign each letter.

MEMO STYLES

A memorandum, or memo, is a short, informal message used in-house. The tone depends upon the relationship between the reader and writer. Because memos are to people in the same organization, jargon and technical terms may be used and the tone may be more informal than correspondence leaving the company.

Most memos contain the headings DATE, TO, FROM, and SUBJECT instead of an inside address, salutation, closing, and signature line. This information may be preprinted or typed on letterhead or plain paper.

DATE: The month is written out with a comma separating the day from the year: e.g., January 20, 19__. Military style of 20 January 19__ is acceptable to avoid punctuation and save keying time.

TO: This line includes the name and job title of the individual(s) who will receive the memo or copy of it.

FROM: This line includes the writer's name and title (if necessary). Writers sign their name or initials to show they have read and approved the contents.

SUBJECT: Use a concise phrase with action verbs if possible on this line.

The following general formatting rules apply to memos, no matter what style is used:

- Single-space the body; double-space between paragraphs.
- Align paragraphs at the left margin.
- Place the typist's initials two lines below the last line of the body.

PREPRINTED MEMO FORMS

Some companies use a standard, printed form with the company name printed at the top. The headings DATE, TO, FROM, and SUBJECT are typical on a preprinted form. Companies may include a variety of other headings to expedite communication. Align the typed text so that it begins two spaces after the longest preprinted word, which usually would be SUBJECT.

A preprinted form is more difficult to align on a computer printer than a form created by the typist. There are two popular formats: You can align the left margin with the printed heading, or you can align the left margin with the text you typed on the form. (See Figures 17-5 and 17-6.)

DATE   May 23, 19--

TO   Steve Posgate, Allan Brody, Tracy Brennan,
              Brett Rouzer, Antonio Ruiz, Janet Sandberg

FROM   Michelle Bryant, Conference Coordinator   *Michelle*

SUBJECT   Conference Details

The registrations are arriving and plans are under way for the
fifth Leadership Conference to be held June 1–4 at Lark Creek
Inn, Lake Tahoe.

Enclosed is the form confirming your attendance. Please fill this
out and return it to me by May 28 so I can proceed with the room
reservation list and make other necessary arrangements at Lark
Creek Inn.

Enclosure

Figure 17-5 Memo with preprinted headings #1.

You should use left and right margins of equal width and begin the body three lines from
the last preprinted heading.

INDIVIDUALIZED MEMO FORMS

Individualized memo forms can be developed for typed or word processed memos. They
can be stored as computer files or as macros. There are two styles of typed memo forms:
the traditional and the simplified. The traditional memorandum has typed headings such as
TO, FROM, and SUBJECT. This memorandum takes time to align properly. (See Figure
17-7.)

Formatting Suggestions for Traditional Memos
❏ Use a 6-inch line.
❏ Begin the date 1 inch from the top of the page (line 6) unless letterhead paper is used.
If letterhead is used, place the date at least two lines below the letterhead.

TO   Steve Posgate, Allan Brody, Tracy Brennan,
              Brett Rouzer, Antonio Ruiz, Janet Sandberg

FROM   Michelle Bryant, Conference Coordinator

DATE   May 23, 19--

SUBJECT   Conference Details

              The registrations are arriving and plans are under
              way for the fifth Leadership Conference to be held
              June 1–4 at Lark Creek Inn, Lake Tahoe.

              Enclosed is the form confirming your attendance.
              Please fill this out and return it to me by May 28 so I
              can proceed with the room reservation list and make
              other necessary arrangements at Lark Creek Inn.

              Enclosure

Figure 17-6 Memo with preprinted headings #2

❏ Return four times after the date. This space may be increased or decreased depending on the length of the memorandum.
❏ Type TO, FROM, and SUBJECT in all capitals. A colon after each heading is optional. Leave one blank line between lines of the heading.
❏ Leave two blank lines after the last line in the heading before the body.

The simplified memo omits the headings TO, FROM, DATE, and SUBJECT to save typing time. The parts of the memo are placed flush left on the same lines as they would appear in the simplified block letter.

Two different formats exist for simplified memos. The major differences are in line spacing. (See Figures 17-8 and 17-9.)

Formatting Suggestions for Simplified Memos
❏ Use a 6-inch line.
❏ Begin the date 1 inch (6 lines) or 10 lines from the top of the page unless letterhead

May 5, 19--

TO   Leadership Conference Participants

FROM   Michelle Bryant, Conference Coordinator

SUBJECT   Conference Details

Congratulations on your selection to the Learning and Conference Center Conference, June 1–4, at Lark Creek Inn, Lake
Tahoe! The overall objective of the conference is the development
of your leadership skills.

Enclosed are the following:
1. A map and directions to Lark Creek Inn.
2. A list of participants.
3. The program and activities for the conference.
4. Information about accommodations, cost, and dress.
5. Confirmation of Attendance form.

The only item which needs to be returned to me by May 15 is the
Confirmation of Attendance form. Please make all room arrangements through me and not Lark Creek Inn.

ik

Enclosures--5

Figure 17-7 Traditional memo.

July 10, 19--

Leadership Graduates

WHAT A GREAT GROUP OF LEADERS!

It was terrific having an opportunity to get to
know you this year at the Leadership Conference.
We hope you will proudly wear your leadership
pin and let others know about your experiences.

Enclosed is a group picture taken on the last day.
We are planning a newsletter specifically for you,
so look for it this fall. We will also plan to have a
special reunion at Lark Creek Inn in January.

Michelle Bryant
Conference Coordinator

ik
Enclosure--Picture

Figure 17-8 Simplified memo #1.

paper is used. If letterhead is used, place the date at least two lines below the letter-head.

❏ If you begin 1 inch from the top, triple-space between the date, name of recipient, subject line, and body.

❏ If you begin 10 lines from the top, double- or quadruple-space between parts of the heading.

❏ Place the subject line in all capitals.

❏ Return four times after the body for the writer's name and title.

ADDRESSING ENVELOPES

Mail addressed according to the USPS guidelines helps insure accurate delivery. (See Chapter 16, Mailing Documents.)

- Use paper with a minimum basis weight of 20 pounds.
- Include a return address in the upper left-hand corner.
- Line up addresses flush left.
- Allow at least 1-inch left and right margins.
- Place address horizontally.

July 10, 19--

Leadership Graduates

WHAT A GREAT GROUP OF LEADERS!

It was terrific having an opportunity to get to
know you this year at the Leadership Conference.
We hope you will proudly wear your leadership
pin and let others know about your experiences.

Enclosed is a group picture taken on the last day.
We are planning a newsletter specifically for you,
so look for it this fall. We will also plan to have a
special reunion at Lark Creek Inn in January.

Michelle Bryant
Conference Coordinator

ik
Enclosure--Picture

Figure 17-9 Simplified memo #2.

- Put address in all capital letters with no punctuation. Do not allow letters to overlap or touch.
- Typewrite or machine print. Use easy-to-read type styles, not italics or script. Securely fasten stickers and labels to prevent damage when going through automated equipment.

TIPS ON COMPOSING CORRESPONDENCE

1. Write only when circumstances are appropriate. In some instances, it may be better to place a phone call or handle in person.

Be aware that anything put in writing may be shown to others, even if it is not intended for them. Therefore, do not put anything in writing that you would not say publicly or you would not want published with your name. Never send correspondence in anger.

Hint: Wait 24 hours before sending a negative reply or something written in anger. You may decide not to send it after cooling off.

2. Know your audience. Determine what relationship exists or what relationship you wish to achieve. Demonstrate sensitivity to the needs and interests of the reader. Personalize correspondence if possible.

You may need to know the following items for audience analysis: occupation or position, gender, age range, education, income, and experience.

3. Have a specific objective. For example, ask for information or attempt to make a sale. Every piece of correspondence should have the subtle objective of building goodwill for your organization.

Hint: Always know the purpose before writing. It helps to answer this question: What do I want my reader to do (or know) when they finish reading what I've written?

4. Use the active voice. Voice shows whether the subject acts or is acted upon. In the active voice, the subject performs an action: *Our accountants completed the audit; We shipped your order on Friday, December 3*. In the passive voice, the subject is acted upon: *The audit was completed by our accountants; The order was shipped on Friday, December 3*. The active voice is more direct, even though both sentences state the same information.

The passive voice is often used to soften the impact of negative news: *Your order will be shipped when the enclosed order blank is returned*. This is less negative than the active voice: *We will ship your order when you return the enclosed order blank*.

Hint: Many computer grammar and style checkers can analyze sentences for active or passive construction.

5. Be concise. Use specific, concrete words. Eliminate unnecessary words. Avoid clichés and jargon.

Hint: The average sentence length should be fewer than 20 words.

Hint: Computer thesaurus programs can suggest synonyms and help you avoid repeating the same words. Computer grammar and style checkers can point out unnecessary words or statements.

Words and phrases to avoid:	Use
accompanied by	with
according to our records	(avoid)
acknowledge receipt of	(avoid)
as of this day	today
at the present time	now, presently
at your earliest convenience	(be specific)
attached please find	enclosed
be cognizant of	know that
consensus of opinion	consensus
deliberate upon	think about
disbursements	payments
due to the fact	because
enclosed please find	enclosed
forward	send
free of charge	free
herewith	(leave out)

increment	increase
in compliance with your request	as requested
in reference to	about
in the amount of	for
in the event of	if, in case
kindly	please
pursuant to our previous . . .	when we last
per your request	as requested
re	regarding
scrutinize	read, examine
subsequent to	after, since
take the liberty of	(avoid)
thanking you in advance	thank you
this is to acknowledge	(avoid)
up to this writing	until now
utilize	use
vitally essential	vital or essential

6. Be polite and courteous. Be positive by stressing what you can do instead of what you cannot do. Use the "you" attitude to convey warmth and friendliness. The "you" attitude is writing from the reader's point of view by emphasizing "you" and minimizing "we" and "I."

Hint: Some companies prefer the use of "we" rather than "I" in order to show that the writer is speaking for the company. Use "we" or "us" to show others share the message.

7. Get straight to the point unless the news is bad. Make the purpose of the correspondence obvious. Arrange material from general to specific. Start with a general statement and add facts that explain the statement.

Hint: The last paragraph is remembered the longest, so important information should be stated or restated there.

8. Reply promptly. If you cannot respond to a letter in a week, acknowledge it immediately and say when the requested information will be available: *Thank you for your letter. The information you requested will take several days to research. As soon as we have the information, . . .*

Hint: When saying "no" to a request or job applicant, delay the reply for a week so it does not appear that little thought was given to the response.

9. Use proper grammar, spelling, and punctuation. A computer grammar and style checker helps point out potential problems with sentence structure, punctuation, and writing style. A computer spelling checker locates misspellings and typographical errors.

10. Check for accuracy of dates and figures.

SAMPLE CORRESPONDENCE

ANNOUNCEMENT LETTER

An announcement letter is similar to a press release. It is a way to improve visibility and provide a reminder of a firm or products. An announcement may be made for the following reasons:

- Opening of a company or division
- New product or service
- Change of address
- New staff
- Promotion
- Anniversary
- Acquisition
- Merger

Suggested Features

- Communicates pride; some are very formal with only a few sentences
- Gives appropriate information such as names, dates, and addresses; has a clear purpose
- Addressed to the public or a company; envelopes addressed to individuals
- Uses company letterhead or a specially printed white or cream card with black ink

Sample announcement of new service

Milan, Inc., is pleased to offer 24-hour customer service for your convenience. Call toll-free 1-800-489-5984.

Sample announcement of new employee

Hirschfield and Nadler Law Office is pleased to announce that Patricia Issel has joined our staff as an associate in our probate department.

Sample announcement of a promotion

The President and Board of Directors of AMS Industries, Inc., are pleased to announce the promotion of Charles Leoni to Vice President. Mr. Leoni has been the Sales Manager for AMS in San Francisco for the past ten years and will join our corporate staff in Houston.

LETTER OF APOLOGY

Mistakes will occur, and it is important to apologize for them in a prompt letter of apology.

Suggested Features
- Blames the company, not a specific person or department
- States what is being done (or was done) to correct the error
- Explains how the error was made
- Apologizes for the error
- Reassures the customer that steps are being taken to reduce the chances of error in the future
- Closes positively

Sample letter of apology

Your book order was shipped air express on November 2. You should have the books by now.

In investigating the problem, we discovered your order code was entered incorrectly in the computer. Consequently, your order was shipped to another school. Since we pride ourselves on our data-entry procedure, mistakes like this are very infrequent. However, our computer programmer is adding an extra safeguard to our order program so we can avoid errors like this in the future.

I appreciate receiving notification of the problem in enough time to send the books before classes started. We believe you will be pleased with the revised edition of <u>Administrative Procedures.</u>

Best wishes for a successful school year.

CONFIRMATION OF APPOINTMENT

A confirmation of an appointment need not be sent for every appointment, but it can be used to verify a verbal conversation.

Suggested Features
- Is brief and limited to appointment information, including date, time, place, and names
- Is sent out immediately after the appointment is made

Sample letter of confirmation

This is to confirm our appointment on Monday, September 2, at 9:00 a.m. in Room 4026, 4th Floor, of the Economic Development Building, 722 Capitol Mall. A public parking garage is located directly across the street at 7th and Capitol.

I look forward to continuing our discussion on your proposal.

LETTER OF CONGRATULATIONS

Letters of congratulation build goodwill. They may be sent for the following occasions:

- Promotions and appointments to new positions
- Achievements
- Awards and honors
- Introduction of a new product
- Marriages, births, and anniversaries
- Retirements

Suggested Features
- Expresses interest sincerely and enthusiastically
- Avoids negatives
- Begins with the expression of congratulations
- Mentions the reason for the congratulations
- Ends with an expression of goodwill

Sample letter of congratulations for receiving an award

Congratulations for receiving the Distinguished Achievement Award from the National Media Association! I was so proud when they announced your name and the audience gave you a standing ovation.

No one is more deserving of this award than you. Congratulations on your consistent accomplishments. We are all celebrating for you.

Sample letter of congratulations for receiving an appointment

Congratulations on your appointment as Vice President of The Travel Center. You have worked hard, and I am thrilled your efforts have been rewarded. You will bring dynamic leadership to your position.

Our company offers any help you need as you move into your new position. We're behind you all the way!

EMPLOYMENT REJECTION

Examples of sample cover letters to use in a job search are in Chapter 2. Unsolicited letters of application should be answered briefly and immediately.

Suggested Features
- Conveys thanks for the interest in the firm
- Indicates positions are not available
- Expresses luck in job search

Sample letter of rejection

Thank you for your interest in North Bay News. Presently we do not have any positions available which match your background.

We will keep your resume on file and contact you if your experience meets our needs. We wish you success in your job search.

MEETING NOTIFICATION

Meeting notifications should be in writing. If the meeting will always be on the same day, same time, and same place, notification is sent when the meeting time and place are set, along with a listing of all the dates. If any dates are altered from the original schedule, notification should be in writing.

Suggested Features
- Is brief and limited to meeting information, including date, time, place, and names
- Is sent out immediately after the meeting date is set
- Includes any special items to be brought to the meeting; for example, budget figures, reports, or personnel manual
- Includes a tentative agenda and asks for input

Sample notification letter

Our regular staff meeting would fall on March 23 this month. Since many of us will be involved in planning for our national convention, the date has been changed to March 15 at 1:00 p.m. in the Board Room.

Attached is a tentative agenda. If you have any item you would like to add, please let me know by March 10. We will be discussing sick-leave policy, so bring a copy of the regulations distributed on January 20.

LETTER OF RESIGNATION

The letter of resignation is used to notify your boss that you are resigning from a position. Generally the letter should be positive, since these letters typically stay in a personnel file. If you resign because of a lack of promotional opportunities or because you did not receive a promotion, you may prefer to express those disappointments in the letter of resignation. Derogatory comments about the staff or company should be avoided.

Suggested Feature
- Includes the effective date, which is typically two weeks in advance of leaving.

Sample friendly letter of resignation

I am resigning effective June 1, 19__, after five years of stimulating and productive work at Ferraris, Inc. As you know, I will be moving to Seattle to take a position as administrative assistant to the president of Environmental Controls.

Moving back to Seattle fulfills a dream of being able to work in the environmental field in my hometown. I will miss all the good friends I've made at Ferraris, and I will particularly miss working with you. Thank you for making me part of the team.

Sample letter of resignation for lack of promotional opportunities

I am resigning as your administrative assistant effective June 1, 19__. Although I have learned a great deal working with you, I had hoped to have an opportunity to expand my responsibilities. I feel I need to find a position that will give me the chance to use more of my talents.

Thank you for all your help and support during these last three years.

REQUEST LETTER

A request letter should be clear and precise. Be brief and specific; cover only the information requested. If information is needed from two separate departments, write two letters.

Suggested Features
- Include all information necessary, such as item number, quality, price, color, and where to ship
- Use list form, which is easier to read than a letter

Sample simple request letter

Please send me 15 copies of your free brochure, "Telephone Techniques." We plan to use this brochure in training our support staff. Thank you.

Sample request letter

The Harrison House is recommended as a good meeting facility near the Kansas City Airport. Our Board of Directors is meeting October 5–8, 19__, and we need a meeting room and accommodations.

Date	October 5–8
	Arriving October 4. Staying the nights of October 4, 5, 6, 7; departing October 8.
Number	15. Need a room with a large enough table to comfortably seat 15; video projection and overhead availability. 15 single-occupancy rooms.
Food Service	One evening banquet; four luncheons. If possible, meals in a room separate from the meeting room.

Please send rates, meeting room sizes, recreational facilities, and catering menus. We will be making a decision on the meeting by March 1. I look forward to hearing from you.

SYMPATHY LETTER

Sympathy letters are written when a colleague (no matter what position in the company) has lost someone to death.

Suggested Features
- Expresses how you feel about the news
- Recalls something positive about the deceased
- Makes an offer to be of help or comfort
- Uses a sympathy card or is handwritten on personal stationery

Sample sympathy letter

I was shocked to hear about Jeff. He was so active and healthy.

Jeff was a wonderful, supportive man. He was always calm, even in times of crises. We all know how close you were and how much you will miss him.

I am thinking of you at this difficult time. Please let me know if there is anything I can do to help.

CHAPTER 18

REPORTS

Reports provide essential information for everyday operations and decision making. Businesses could not function without written reports. A fundamental component of many office professionals' jobs is to correctly format reports for their supervisors. In addition to formatting, some office professionals decide on content and write reports.

Reports range from informal interoffice memos describing seminar attendance to bound formal reports such as feasibility studies. Reports are categorized according to subject, intended audience, and length. Each type of report requires a different format and organizational style. Reports can be classified into two general categories by length. (See Table 18-1.)

SHORT REPORTS

Short reports are also called informal, semiformal, or semitechnical reports. They get right to the point, with objective reporting of facts in one to three pages. The subject of the report determines the number of subdivisions it has, if any. Short reports are typically routine and have a limited audience of coworkers or an immediate supervisor.

A short report will answer the questions who, why, where, when, what, and how. Some companies follow a specific procedure for organization of reports, while others leave the organization up to the author. A short report typically includes the following components:

- Purpose
- Findings
- Conclusion or Summary
- Recommendations

Hint: Some employers prefer to find the recommendations at the beginning of the report instead of the end to avoid having to read the entire report.

Table 18-1 Types of Reports

Type	Number of Pages	Examples
Short	Less than 4	Appraisal
		Audit
		Evaluation
		Incident report
		Inventory
		Investigation
		Laboratory report
		Procedure report
		Progress report
		Production report
		Recommendations
		Research report
		Status report
		Trip report
Long	4 or more	Annual report
		Feasibility study
		Grant proposal
		Investigation
		Evaluation
		Product analysis
		Project summary
		Task analysis

Detailed information such as drawings, charts, or cost analyses are usually placed at the end of the report in a section referred to as "Attachments" or "Appendices."

If a report is for in-house use, it is usually in memo format, while those reports going outside the company are typically written in the form of a letter. Memos are the least formal type of report format. Some companies may use standard, printed, letterhead forms. Memos use a heading with the following lines: TO, FROM, DATE, SUBJECT. There is no need for an inside address, salutation, complimentary close, or signature line. Be sure to include the name and job title of individual(s) who will receive the memo or a copy of it. (See Figure 18-1.)

Formatting Suggestions
❑ Printed heading: Set the left margin where the printed heading begins or two spaces after the longest guide word in the printed heading. Set the right margin equal to the left margin.
❑ Plain paper: Use a 6-inch line. Leave a 1-inch (6-line) top margin.
❑ Start the body of the report on the third line after the last line of the heading.
❑ Use single spacing with block paragraphs.

TO   Maria Gravelez, Supervisor

FROM   Judith Witmore, CPS, Administrative Assistant

DATE   August 3, 19--

SUBJECT   Evaluation of PSI Seminar in Salt Lake City

After attendance at the Professional Secretaries International
Convention in Salt Lake City, July 20–25, 19--, I recommend that
at least one support staff member have the opportunity to attend
each year. The information distributed at the convention is
extremely valuable and will be beneficial to all support staff at
Western Bank.

The sessions ranged from technical to practical to personal. Even
with the variety of the sessions, nearly all workshops focused on
the central theme of expanding and enhancing the contribution
of secretaries in the workplace.

The sessions I attended were as follows:
1. Office Automation in the 1990s
2. Anatomy of a Merger
3. How to Get Your Article Published in The Secretary
4. Secretarial Stress: The Hidden and Controlling Factor

Over 50 companies exhibited the latest in office technology,
demonstrating everything from fax machines to filing systems.

The convention was truly outstanding and is a highlight of my
professional career. I will be sharing what I learned with the
other office professionals at Western Bank at our monthly
meeting.

Figure 18-1 Short report in memo form.

December 7, 19--

Mr. Gary Thomas
Public Relations Director
Clemmons, Jones, and Grantz
3894 South Geary
San Francisco CA 94132

EVALUATION OF COMPANY NEWSLETTER

This is the third issue of your company newsletter that I have
coordinated and edited. I have the following recommendations,
which I think will enhance this communication.

Format
The format of two columns does not provide much flexibility in
layout and design. We are restricted in placement of pictures and
columnar headings. It is my recommendation that we move to a
three-column format.

Pages
The number of pages has ranged from four to ten. The first
newsletter had ten pages, and subsequent issues gradually
decreased to four. I recommend a standard number of pages,
preferably four, be set for the newsletter. If there is any
additional information that needs to be included in an issue, it
can be added as an insert.

Figure 18-2 Short report in letter form.

Gary Thomas
Page 2
December 7, 19--

Printing
We have used Mountain Printers because they gave the best
quote. As you know, we reprinted the last issue because of poor
print quality of pictures. I have previously worked with Zenith
Printers. The cost is approximately 10 percent higher, but the
quality is consistently excellent.

Use of Color
We have used color in every headline. This format seems to
make the newsletter look "busy." I recommend we use color only
on the masthead, dates, and flag sections. It will not only reduce
the cost but also enhance the image.

It has been a pleasure working with your professional staff. I am
anxious to hear your reactions to these recommendations. I will
be out of the office until December 15. Please call me anytime
after that date so we can talk.

Sarah Williams, CPS
Consultant

Figure 18-2 *(con't)*

(For more detailed information on memos, see the section on Memo Styles in Chapter 17.)

A letter has to appear more formal, especially if the report is directed to someone outside the company. It should be typed or printed on company letterhead. (See Figure 18-2.)

Formatting Suggestions

❏ Use a 6-inch line of 65 characters or fewer. Lines of more than 65 characters are tiring to the eye.

❏ Allow a top margin of 2 to $2\frac{1}{2}$ inches (between lines 12 and 15), depending upon the depth of the letterhead.

❏ Allow a bottom margin of 1 inch (6 lines).

❏ Use single spacing with block or indented paragraphs and one blank line between paragraphs.

❏ Begin the body on the second line after the salutation.

(For detailed information on letters, see the section on Letter Styles in Chapter 17.)

If the report is more than one page, type the continuation page on a blank sheet of paper. Leave a 1-inch top margin (start on line 7). Begin the body on the third line after the heading.

Hint: A header command on a word processing program can add the required information and the page number.

Formatting Suggestions

❏ Leave at least two lines of a paragraph at the bottom of a page. Carry over at least two lines to the next page.

❏ Do not divide the last word on a page.

❏ Always include at least two lines of copy after a heading before starting a new page.

LONG REPORTS

A long or formal report gives detailed information about a subject and usually requires extensive research. The audience may include stockholders or top-level managers. Such reports may influence long-range financial or organizational decisions. Often they are designed and printed out of house if they are important enough.

Long reports may include some or all of the following components:

Preliminary pages:

Cover, letter of transmittal, title page, table of contents, list of illustrations, abstract or executive summary

Body:

Introduction, background, problem, purpose, scope, main discussion (70 percent of the report), conclusions, recommendations

Table 18-2 Business Report Format

Left and right	6-inch line Bound: 1½-inch left margin; 1-inch right Unbound: 1-inch left margin; 1-inch right
Top of first page	2-inch margin Start title on line 13, body on line 15
Succeeding pages	1-inch margin Start page number on line 7, body on line 10
Bottom	1-inch margin Line 60 from the top

Page Numbers

Preliminary pages	Use sequential lowercase roman numerals beginning with i for the title page. Center at the bottom of the page. The title page has no number.
Body	Use sequential arabic numerals beginning with 1 for the first page. They may be in one of two styles: 1. One inch from the top of the page (line 7) at the right margin; body begins on line 10. 2. Centered at the bottom of the page on line 60; body begins on line 7.

Spacing

Body	Use 6-inch line. If you have no DTP capabilities, make it double-spaced with five-space paragraph indentions. If you have DTP capabilities, use flush left paragraphs and the default leading (see the heading *Leading* in Chapter 19).

Back matter:

Glossary, references/bibliography, appendix

Many businesses have a standard format, described in a style guide, to follow in writing a report. A standard format minimizes misunderstandings between the author and the person or persons keying and/or designing the report.

Table 18-2 gives details on a format typically used in business reports. Desktop publishing (DTP) capabilities will allow you some flexibility in typeface and size (see Chapter 19). For additional formatting suggestions, see the specific topics in this chapter.

Formatting Suggestions

❏ Leave at least two lines of a paragraph at the bottom of a page. Carry over at least two lines to the next page.

❏ Do not divide the last word on a page.

❏ Always include at least two lines of copy after a heading before starting a new page.

❏ Indent quoted material 5 spaces from both margins.

❏ Avoid dividing a quote or list of items unless at least two lines are at the bottom of a page and two lines are on the next page.

COVER

The cover should reflect the style of the rest of the report. An attractive cover helps persuade the reader to open the report and read it. A well-designed cover makes it easy to understand the subject of the report. For an important enough report, these elements should appear on the cover:

- Title of the report
- Name(s) of report writer(s)
- Name and address of the company

Formatting Suggestions:

❏ Illustrations should be used only if they are relevant and of high quality.

❏ Simple typography should be used, and it should be stronger than the type size and typeface chosen for the inside.

❏ The paper should be heavier than the paper used for the report itself.

❏ Standard covers can be preprinted that include the company name and address and a cut-out window. The title of the report appears on the title page and will show through the window.

❏ The same elements that appear on the title page can also be printed on the cover page. (See the section on Title Page below.)

❏ A cover page is not necessary for reports that are somewhat less formal. A title page can be used as the cover for such reports.

❏ The top margin should be 2 inches (12 lines) and the bottom margin should be 1 inch (6 lines).

LETTER OF TRANSMITTAL

A letter of transmittal may be used to convey a report from one organization to another, or from one person to another. It may be bound as part of the report or it may be attached to the front. A letter of transmittal summarizes the purpose, scope, and major recommendations of the report. (See Figure 18-3.)

A cover letter may be used instead. A cover letter includes a simple statement such as "Enclosed is a copy of. . . ." If reports are regularly distributed inside a company, a letter of transmittal is not necessary.

February 10, 19--

Mr. Louis Johnson
President
Pacific Telecommunications
4783 South Pima
Tucson AZ 85745

IMPROVING COMPUTER-USER COMFORT

Enclosed is the report, "Improving Computer-User Comfort,"
that you asked our company to prepare. The report summarizes
current research on the effects of computers on health and recommends changes for your computer users.

We interviewed over five hundred Pacific Telecommunications
employees in the last six months and consulted with health
experts in eye and wrist fatigue. We also reviewed all the current literature available for computer health hazards.

Our recommendations are as follows:
1. Antiradiation screens should be available for computer
    monitors.
2. Wrist supports should be used to help maintain proper wrist
    position during computer use and possibly reduce the risk of
    carpal tunnel syndrome.
3. Employees need adjustable chairs with a stronger back
    support.

You should find our report useful in reorganizing your computer
area for maximum comfort. If you have any questions or would
like to discuss our recommendations, please let us know.

Janet Wong
Consultant

Figure 18-3 Letter of transmittal.

TITLE PAGE

A title page is usually the first page of a document after the cover. (See Figure 18-4.) It usually contains the following elements:

- Title. The title should be brief yet informative.
- Name(s) of report writer(s). Include the title(s) of the writers and their contribution to the project or report (e.g., coordinator, editor, analyst).
- Name and address of the company or organization preparing the report.
- Date the report was written.
- Any agency or order numbers.
- Name of the firm for which the report was prepared (e.g., *Prepared for Professional Secretaries International*).

Formatting Suggestions
❑ All title page elements do not have to be included, nor must they be in the order given above.
❑ The layout should be consistent with the document, however. If the chapters start on the same line on the page, the title should start on that same line.
❑ A 6-inch line length is typical.
❑ The reader's eye will usually start a quarter of the way down the page.
❑ Avoid putting the longest line at the top of the page or below the visual center.
❑ Allow enough space for the left margin given the binding that will be used.
❑ The title page is actually counted as small roman numeral i, even though no number is typed on the page.
❑ A short title may be in bold print and capital letters. A long title in bold print and capital letters is difficult to read and takes up too much space.

TABLE OF CONTENTS

The table of contents lists the major sections of the report and the page numbers as well as all appendices. It allows the reader to see how the report is organized, what topics are covered, and where to find specific information. The table of contents may include a list of subdivisions and any subheadings that may be included under each subdivision. Include subheadings only if there are two or more, but do not include *any* subheadings if their inclusion would make the table of contents too long. (See Figure 18-5.)

Include a brief summary of the contents of each chapter if the subdivision titles are not sufficiently descriptive or if the contents need to convince the reader to look at the report.

If space is limited, the title page and table of contents may be combined on the same page.

Formatting Suggestions
❑ The left and right margins may be different from those of the report. The subdivisions and page numbers should be close enough together so the eye can link the two.

EFFECTIVE COMMUNICATION

The Art of Business Communication

Benjamin Strom

1992

Professional Secretaries International®

Kansas City, Missouri

Figure 18-4 Sample title page.

TABLE OF CONTENTS

ii

Figure 18-5 Sample table of contents.

❑ Rules (lines) can be used to separate subdivisions instead of leader lines (rows of dots).
❑ The top margin should be 2 inches (12 lines) from the top of the page and the bottom margin 1 inch (6 lines) from the bottom of the page.
❑ This page is counted as small roman numeral ii, centered on line 60 (the seventh line from the bottom of the page).

LIST OF ILLUSTRATIONS

This is a list of any illustrations and tables with their page numbers. (See Figure 18-6.) The single entry "Illustrations" and the page number is listed in the table of contents. If there are few illustrations, they can be listed in the table of contents.

Formatting Suggestions
❑ It is not necessary to use the same margins as the report, but you should use the same margins as the table of contents.
❑ If there is a list of illustrations, it is counted as small roman numeral iii, typed on line 60 (seventh line from the bottom of the page).
❑ The top margin should be 2 inches (12 lines) and the bottom margin 1 inch (6 lines).

ABSTRACT OR EXECUTIVE SUMMARY

The abstract or executive summary is a summary of what the report contains, including problems and conclusions. It may contain a listing of key points in sentences or miniparagraphs. Readers can see the contents of the report without having to read it. The abstract or executive summary immediately precedes the text, but it does not always have to appear on a separate page. Sometimes it is included in the cover letter preceding the document. If space is available, it may be on the title page or cover.

Formatting Suggestions
❑ The abstract may be less than a page; an executive summary is often two or three pages.
❑ If this page is used, it is counted as the next small roman numeral, typed on line 60 (seventh line from the bottom of the page).
❑ The top margin should be 2 inches (12 lines) and the bottom margin 1 inch (6 lines).

Here is a sample summary:

"Improving Computer User Comfort" summarizes the current research on the effects of computers on health and recommends changes for computer users. Employees were interviewed and health professionals were consulted. Current literature was reviewed.

It is recommended that the following accessories be made available for computer

ILLUSTRATIONS

iii

Figure 18-6 List of illustrations.

users: antiradiation screens for computer monitors, wrist supports to help maintain proper wrist position during computer use and possibly reduce the risk of carpal tunnel syndrome, and adjustable chairs with a stronger back support.

BODY OF THE REPORT

The body is the main text of the report and should be organized according to the nature of the report. Listed below are the sections included in most reports.

Introduction: An introduction tells the reader why the report was written and helps interpret what follows. It can be in a larger type size than or have different line spacing from the rest of the report.

Main discussion: The main discussion should be organized according to major topics and subtopics. Headings help readers identify major subjects and are included in the table of contents.

Conclusions: The conclusions tie everything together for the reader by presenting the findings of the report. Conclusions should be based on the information and documentation in the report and contain no new information.

Recommendations: Recommendations suggest what should be done based on the findings or point out areas in which further study is needed. Not all reports have recommendations.

TEXT HEADINGS

Headings are important because they allow the reader to see how a report is organized. Headings can be one of the following types:

Centered on a line by itself. Leave two blank lines above and one below the heading, which should be all capitals or initial caps.

Flush left on a line by itself. Leave two blank lines above and one below the heading, which should be all capitals or initial caps.

A *paragraph heading* begins a paragraph and is followed by text on the same line. Leave one blank line above the heading, which can be bold or underlined and should be followed by a period. Begin the text two spaces after the period.

Before selecting a subheading style, decide how many levels of subheadings are needed. Headings should be limited to a maximum of three levels.

If one head level is used, it should be flush left.

If two head levels are used, one should be flush left and the other a paragraph heading *or* one should be centered and the other flush left.

If three head levels are used, one should be centered, one flush left, and one a paragraph heading.

Formatting Suggestions

❑ Use either upper- and lowercase or all capitals. The choice is determined by the length of the majority of headings; long headings are more difficult to read in all caps. When using upper- and lowercase, use lowercase for "the," "a," "to," "of," "with," "for," "by."

❑ The report title should be bigger and/or bolder than the strongest subheading. If the number of weights and sizes are limited, dry transfer headings can be stripped in using typefaces not available on the personal computer.

❑ A heading can be one size larger in the same weight as the text.

TABLES

Tables are used to present statistical data to explain written text. All tables present data in vertical columns and horizontal rows. (See Figure 18-7.)

Formatting Suggestions

❑ Estimate the width of the table by counting the characters and blank spaces of the longest item and add two or three characters for space between columns.

❑ Maintain equal space between columns.

❑ Leave at least half an inch of white space above and below the table.

Table 1
Annual Salary Ranges by Title
(rounded to the nearest dollar)

Title	Quoted Salary Range	Average Salary Range
Administrative Assistant	$12,000–60,000	$25,555–27,605
Administrative Secretary	42,000–50,000	25,183–29,109
Executive Secretary	14,000–45,000	22,849–28,069
Secretary	8,320–48,000	21,116–24,218
Secretary/Receptionist	10,400–28,000	17,643–19,647

Source: Secretarial Want Ad Survey.

Figure 18-7 A sample table.

❏ The typeface may differ from that of the report. Sans serif figures are often preferred to serif figures (see the section on Type and Printing Styles in Chapter 19 for an explanation of serif/sans serif). Times Roman and Helvetica are usually legible and narrow, which means more information can be placed in the table.

❏ Try to keep the table vertical so readers will not have to turn the page to read it. Use a double spread over two facing pages for a wide table.

❏ If the table will not fit on the same page as the text referring to the table, put the table on the page immediately following the reference in the text. If necessary, reduce the table by photocopying so it will fit on the same page as the reference to it.

❏ Use margins equal to or wider than the report's margins.

❏ Use consistent line spacing for all tables in a report, either all single spacing or double spacing. Double-spaced reports are easier to read but take up more space. If you are using a computer, experiment with different line spacing.

TABLE NUMBERS

Tables can be numbered Table 1, Table 2, Table 3, etc., in the order they are mentioned in the text and with "Table" capitalized. It is not necessary to number tables if a report has only one table, widely scattered tables, or tables that can be easily described and found.

Tables should be numbered separately from illustrations, such as Table 1, Illustration 1. However, if the report has many tables, graphs, and charts, they can all be called Exhibit and numbered in sequence.

Tables can also be placed in an appendix. Tables in an appendix are numbered separately from those in the text. For example, Table A-1 would be Table 1 in Appendix A.

Formatting Suggestions

❏ Use either all capitals or an initial capital, i.e., TABLE 1 or Table 1.

❏ The table number can be set flush left on a line by itself with the title directly below it.

❏ The table number can also be on the same line with the title, followed by a period or a dash, or sometimes both:

Table 1. Annual Salary Ranges by Title
Table 1—Annual Salary Ranges by Title
Table 1.—Annual Salary Ranges by Title

TABLE TITLES

The title of a table should be short and direct. Omit articles such as "the" and "a" and phrases such as "summary of."

Formatting Suggestions

❏ Center the title or place it flush left.

❏ Do not use punctuation after a title unless it is a full sentence.

❑ Words should be capitalized with letters in both upper- and lowercase, except for articles and short prepositions, which should be in lowercase. Titles in all caps are difficult to read and take up more space.

❑ If a title runs two lines, the lines should be similar in length, with the first slightly longer than the second. If the title is flush left, the second line may be either flush left or indented. Otherwise both lines must be centered.

❑ Triple-space after the title and before the body of the table.

❑ Use bold type for an effective table title.

SUBTITLES

A subtitle gives an explanation of the table. It may list abbreviations or explain how the data were obtained. The subtitle should apply to the entire table and not just to one or two columns. Place specific information about columns in footnotes. (See the section on Footnotes, Endnotes, and Text Notes below for additional information.)

Formatting Suggestions

❑ The subtitle may be in the same style as the title or in parentheses.

❑ Place the subtitle on a separate line below the title.

❑ The type size is usually smaller than that of the title.

COLUMN HEADINGS

Single words or concise phrases are used above all columns in a table. Two lines may be necessary to explain columns.

Formatting Suggestions

❑ Use a minimum of two spaces between column headings.

❑ Use bold type for effective column headings.

❑ A column heading spanning two or more columns is called a spanner head. The spanner head may be separated from column heads by a space, a rule, or a different typeface.

❑ Use upper- and lowercase letters.

❑ Align headings at the left of the column for easier typing. However, center the headings to allow more space between headings. It is more attractive to center the column head if it is narrower than the column text.

❑ Avoid abbreviations and symbols that may not be understood by the reader.

FIGURES

Align columns of numbers at the right:

```
4504
  23
   2
```

DOLLAR AMOUNTS

Omit decimal points and zeros when the figures are whole amounts. However, if one amount contains a cents figure, every amount requires the cents. Place the dollar sign next to the first amount. Align the dollar sign vertically with the column containing the longest figure. (See the examples below.) Do not use commas in four-digit numbers unless the numbers appear in the same column with larger numbers.

$ 20	$ 20
1000	1,000
350	35,000

DECIMALS

Align the decimal points of every figure in a column. All figures should have the same number of decimal places.

10.000
5.535
7.750

PERCENTAGES

A percent sign follows the first figure in a column of percentages. However, percent signs are not necessary if you use the word *percent* or *percentage* in the column heading:

	Percent of
Members Responding	**Members Responding**
50.2%	50.2
30.7	30.7
28.2	28.2

PARENTHESES

Parentheses around figures signify a negative amount. If some but not all of the figures include parentheses, the figures should still align on the right:

(340,400)
2,500
(50)

FRACTIONS

Align whole numbers with fractions on the right; align fractions on the left:

$5\frac{3}{4}$
11

$$2\tfrac{9}{10}$$
$$3\tfrac{15}{16}$$

DATES

Extra space may be needed to align a column of dates by the last figure:

January 5, 19___
June   12, 19___
October 2, 19___

TOTAL AMOUNTS

The total is usually shown as the last row in a table of figures. The total should be clearly labeled and easy to find. However, it may be omitted if it is obviously a total. When a percentage adds up to 100, the *total* is optional. If the percentages do not add up to 100, a total should be given with a note such as "Percentages do not add up to 100 percent because of rounding."

35
2,365
796

TOTAL 3,196

The word *total* should be indented five spaces from the left margin of the table and may be in all caps.

WORD TABLES

Word tables should be simple. Entries should be brief, with no rules. Runover lines can be flush left as shown or indented several spaces. (See Figure 18-8.)

Formatting Suggestions
❑ Set in all caps and indent.
❑ Use bold type.
❑ Set off with one blank line above or below.
❑ Do not use periods.

FOOTNOTES

Footnotes include source notes, spelling out of abbreviations in a table, and explanations of specific items in a column. They are placed immediately below the table.

Source notes are required when the table is reprinted from another source or when the table has been created using data from another reference. Source notes should be placed before any other table notes:

Table 2
Corporate Chapters

Chapter	Corporation	Location
GTE	General Telephone Co.	Westfield, Indiana
St. Vincent	St. Vincent Hospital and Health Care	Indianapolis, Indiana
Heart of Ohio	National Ins. Co.	Columbus, Ohio
Downeast	The Jackson Lab	Bar Harbor, Maine
GTE Summit City	General Telephone Co.	Fort Wayne, Indiana
Paul Revere	Paul Revere Ins. Co	Worcester, Massachusetts
SAS Institute	SAS Institute	Cary, North Carolina
WES	Waterways Exp. Station, Corps of Engineers	Vicksburg, Mississippi
Rohr-Chula Vista	Rohr Industries	Chula Vista, California
GTE Marion	General Telephone Co.	Marion, Ohio
Medical Center	Medical Center	Houston, Texas

Source: Professional Secretaries International® Annual Report, 1988–89.

Figure 18-8 A word table.

Note: Reprinted with permission from Professional Secretaries International®.

Source: "Secretarial Want Ad Survey 1990," Dartnell Corporation, Chicago, Illinois.

Raised symbols in a table refer the reader to notes. Common symbols are *, †, ‡, and §.

Formatting Suggestions
❏ Set footnote in a smaller type size than the table.
❏ Set the words *Note* or *Source* in italics.
❏ Margins of footnotes may be narrower than the margins of the table.

❏ Begin footnotes flush left or indented the way a paragraph is.

❏ Place a period at the end of each note.

CHARTS AND GRAPHS

A chart or graph shows numbers in picture form. This representation of data can often have a greater impact than a table of figures. Tables are used when readers need precise statistical details; charts and graphs are used when readers are concerned with the overall effects of statistics. But note that too much information in one diagram is confusing; it is better to have two small charts than one large chart.

The three most popular ways of presenting statistical information in graphic form are pie charts, bar charts, and line graphs.

PIE CHARTS

Pie charts are used to show budgets, sales, and costs at a particular time. They are not effective for showing trends over a period of time. And if there is a large gap between the highest and lowest figures, it is difficult to show the smallest numbers accurately. The size of a section or wedge of the pie chart is proportional to the quantity the wedge represents. (See Figure 18-9.)

Do not use more than six sections in a pie chart; it is difficult to read a pie chart with more sections. Avoid listing small slices of the pie separately; combine small slices into a category called "Other" or "Miscellaneous." Make the slices add up to an exact figure: 1, 100%, $1, or a rounded multiple of one of these.

BAR CHARTS

Bar charts are used to show information over a period of time or to make comparisons. Bar charts allow for more complex comparison of information by presenting data in multiple bars. The height of a bar is proportional to the quantity it represents. Vertical bars are used to show increases in quantities. Horizontal bars are used to show increases in distance. As on pie charts, if there is a large gap between the highest and lowest figures, it is difficult to show the smallest numbers accurately. (See Figure 18-10.)

LINE GRAPHS

A line graph is effective in illustrating trends or comparisons over a period of time. Limit the number of lines to three if they cross one another, four if they do not intersect. (See Figure 18-11.) Charts and graphs are easy to produce using computer software, especially with spreadsheet programs such as Lotus. The following information is entered into the computer:

- Title of the chart
- Subtitle (if needed)

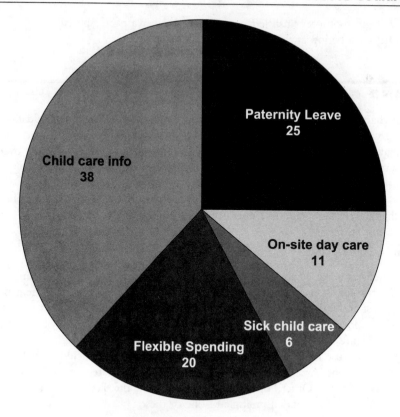

Work/Family Conflicts
% of Companies Reporting Programs
Figure 18-9 Sample pie chart.

- Heading for the x-axis (horizontal axis) and y-axis (vertical axis) if creating a bar or line chart
- Numbers for each entry in the chart or graph
- Footnotes, if needed
- Appropriate type of graph

The software then creates the graph on screen.

Not all hardware supports graphing programs. Different graphing programs require different amounts of memory. A graphics memory card must be added to the computer if it is not standard with the hardware.

Graphics can be printed using dot matrix printers, plotters, ink jet printers, and laser printers. The graphing program must support the printer. Some software limits the number of bars on a chart, the length of titles and labels, and the number of titles and labels.

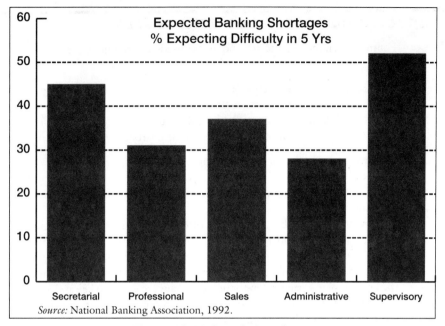

Figure 18-10 Sample bar chart.

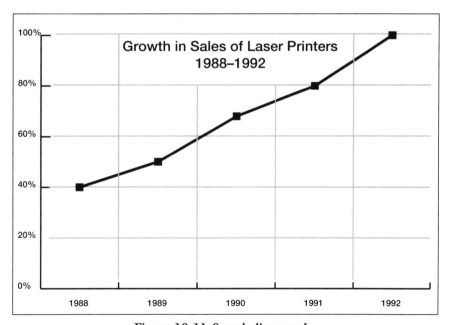

Figure 18-11 Sample line graph.

FOOTNOTES, ENDNOTES, AND TEXT NOTES

Footnotes, endnotes, and text notes are used to document the following:

- Direct quotes
- Paraphrases of written works
- Opinions of persons other than the author
- Statistical data not compiled by the writer
- Visuals such as photographs, tables, or charts not constructed by the author

Many formats exist for documenting sources used in a report or to provide information outside the main text. Footnotes are positioned at the bottom of a page, endnotes are placed at the end of a report, and text notes are notes in parentheses within the body of the material itself.

Footnotes and endnotes are now often discouraged by style manuals because of the difficulty in keying and typesetting them. Some word processing packages cannot place superior, or raised, numbers in the text. In addition, if there are many footnotes on a page, the report will look unattractive; the reader's eye must move from the body of the text to the bottom of the page. Even though endnotes are easier to key and typeset than footnotes, they still cause problems for the reader. Endnotes necessitate flipping back to the end of the report to find the reference.

Call out a footnote in the text by inserting a superior figure immediately after the information referenced in the report, preferably at the end of the sentence:

Salaries have increased 20 percent in the Bay Area.[1]

If this is impossible with the software, enclose the figure in brackets and place it at the end of a sentence or paragraph. Leave one space before the bracket and two spaces after it. If the brackets are in the middle of a sentence, leave one space before and one space after the brackets. Number the footnotes consecutively.

Formatting Footnotes

❏ Use the underscore key to draw a line 2 inches long located one line below the text to separate footnotes from the text.

❏ Leave a blank line between the underscored line and the footnote.

❏ Use a type size two sizes smaller than that of the text, if possible.

❏ Use either superior or on-the-line figures. Numbers on the line are easier to type.

❏ Single-space the footnotes; double-space between footnotes.

❏ Indent the first line of each footnote five spaces or place it flush left.

❏ Include footnotes on the same page as the superior figure.

Formatting Endnotes

❏ Place endnotes after appendices. If there are no appendices, the endnotes follow the body of the report.

❏ Center the heading "Notes" 2 inches from the top of the page (line 13).

❏ Begin typing the first endnote three spaces below the heading.

Pay Equity

Childcare workers are paid less than plumbers; physiotherapists are paid less than brewery workers; experienced secretaries are paid less than delivery truck drivers (Barbara Carlson, *Working Report,* Universal Publishers, New York, 1992, p. 85). These statistics seem shocking but they are true. They attest to the widespread pay inequities between female- and male-dominated professions.

Figure 18-12 Text notes in a report.

❏ Type the number on the line, instead of using superior figures.
❏ Single-space endnotes; double-space between endnotes.
❏ Indent the first line of each endnote five spaces or place it flush left.
❏ Use the same margins as in the report.
❏ Number the pages as part of the report.

Formatting Text Notes
❏ Text notes immediately follow the information given in the report.
❏ If there are only a few references in the report, all bibliographic data can be placed in parentheses. (See Figure 18-12.)
❏ When there are numerous references in the body of the report, give the name of the author and the page number of the text in parentheses immediately after the information presented in the report. List the sources in full at the end of the report.

REFERENCE NOTES, REFERENCE LIST, AND BIBLIOGRAPHY

Several different styles may be used for citing sources in footnotes, endnotes, or text notes. Footnotes are placed at the bottom of the page on which the citation appears. Endnotes are compiled at the end of the chapter or report, listed in the order in which they appear in the text. Text notes are given in parentheses in the body of the text. The style shown below is for business reference notes. (Academic style differs slightly in that the place of publication precedes the publisher and date, with a colon after the place.)

Book with one author:

1. Carolyn J. Mullins, *The Complete Writing Guide to Preparing Reports, Proposals, Memos, Etc.,* Aaron Publishing Co., Englewood Cliffs, NJ, 1980.

Two or more books by the same author:

2. Carolyn J. Mullins, *The Complete Writing Guide to Preparing Reports, Proposals, Memos, Etc.,* Aaron Publishing Co., Englewood Cliffs, NJ, 1980.

3.———, *Report Writing,* Cooper Press, New York, 1991, p. 54.

Book with two authors:

4. Mark Louis and Margaret Emke, *Successful Writing,* Cooper Press, New York, 1991.

Book with three or more authors:

5. Milton Hoover and others, *Report References for the 1990's,* P.J. Thomas Co., Boston, 1990.

Book title with edition number:

(the edition number is given when the book is not in its first edition):

6. Harry Shadle, *Economics of Business,* 3rd ed., Iowa State University Press, Ames, 1985.

Book with corporate author:

7. Professional Secretaries International®, *How to Get Your Article Published in* The Secretary, Kansas City, MO, 1992.

Article in a magazine or professional journal:

8. William Smith, "Accessories Improve User Comfort," *The Secretary,* 50:8, October 1990, p. 31.

9. Ron Zemke, "The Ups and Downs of Downsizing," *Training,* 27:11, November 1990, p. 27.

Article in a magazine or professional journal with no author cited:

10. "Green Ballots vs. Greenbacks," *Time,* 136:22, November 19, 1990, p. 44.

Article in a newspaper:

11. Sabin Russell, "Dow Advances 36 Points in Strong Session," *San Francisco Chronicle,* December 13, 1990, C1.

Technical paper presented at a conference:

12. Diane B. Hartman and Lorraine F. Colletti, "Secretarial Stress: The Hidden and Controlling Factor," Professional Secretaries International Convention, Salt Lake City, UT, July 25, 1990.

Speech or conversation:

13. Bernard F. White, U.S. Department of Labor, Washington, DC, speaking to the 59th annual American Vocational Association Conference, Cincinnati, OH, December 5, 1990.

A bibliography lists all the references relevant to the report, while a reference list gives just the ones cited. In a reference list, an author's first name precedes the last name; in a bibliography, the name of the initial author is reversed, with the last name appearing first. The works are numbered in a reference list but unnumbered in a bibliography. Works appear in a reference list in the same sequence that the information they contain appears in the report, while in a bibliography they are listed alphabetically by author. Reference lists and bibliographies are usually punctuated and capitalized in the same way. And both are positioned at the end of the report before attachments.

Formatting Suggestions:
- Place the title 2 inches from the top of the page (line 13).
- Use the same margins as in the report.
- Begin each reference at the left margin.
- Indent the second line five spaces.
- Single-space each reference; double-space between references (in typed matter only).
- References without authors are alphabetized by title.

Here is a sample bibliography:

"Green Ballots vs. Greenbacks," *Time*, 136:22, November 19, 1990, p. 44.

Hartman, Diane B. and Lorraine F. Colletti, "Secretarial Stress: The Hidden and Controlling Factor," Professional Secretaries International Convention, Salt Lake City, UT, July 25, 1990.

Hoover, Milton and others, *Report References for the 1990's.* P.J. Thomas Co., Boston, 1990.

Louis, Mark and Margaret Emke, *Successful Writing*, Cooper Press, New York, 1991.

Mullins, Carolyn J., *The Complete Writing Guide to Preparing Reports, Proposals, Memos, Etc.,* Aaron Publishing Co., Englewood Cliffs, NJ, 1980.

————, *Report Writing*, Cooper Press, New York, 1991.

Professional Secretaries International, *How to Get Your Article Published in The Secretary*, Kansas City, MO, 1992.

Russell, Sabin, "Dow Advances 36 Points in Strong Session," *San Francisco Chronicle*, December 13, 1990, C1.

Shadle, Harry, *Economics of Business*, 3rd ed., Iowa State University Press, Ames, 1985.

Smith, William, "Accessories Improve User Comfort," *The Secretary*, 50:8, October 1990, p. 31.

White, Bernard F., U.S. Department of Labor, Washington, DC, speaking to the 59th annual American Vocational Association Conference, Cincinnati, OH, December 5, 1990.

Zemke, Ron, "The Ups and Downs of Downsizing," *Training*, 27:11, November 1990, p. 27.

GLOSSARY

A glossary is an alphabetical listing of specialized vocabulary and definitions. A glossary is necessary if the readers will be unfamiliar with the terms used in the report.

Formatting Suggestions
❑ Type the heading "Glossary" centered 2 inches from the top of the page (line 13).
❑ Leave two blank lines after the heading.
❑ Use one of the following styles: (1) Two columns—put the terms in alphabetical order in the left column and definitions in the right. (2) Hanging indentation—begin each term at the left margin, followed by a colon, then give the definition; indent the second line five spaces from the left margin. (3) Paragraph style—indent each term five spaces from the left margin, followed by a colon, then give the definition; the second line is flush with the left margin.
❑ Terms may be in bold.
❑ Use periods at the end of definitions if they are written as sentences.

APPENDICES

Appendices include the supporting material for the report. Items in an appendix may be questionnaires, statistics, detailed test results, descriptions of data, or cost comparisons. Appendices appear in the order referred to in the report. Each appendix is assigned a letter; e.g., Appendix A, Appendix B, etc.

Formatting Suggestions
• Type the heading "Appendix A" centered 2 inches from the top of the page (line 13).
• Leave two blank lines after the heading.

CHAPTER 19

OFFICE PUBLISHING

Office publications have four functions:

- To capture attention
- To focus interest
- To create a desire
- To motivate to action

Each step of the publishing process, from writing copy to choosing paper, should contribute to one of these functions.

There are two methods of creating newsletters, brochures, and flyers. One method is to decide on content for a publication and use specialists such as graphic artists and typographers to decide layout, suggest graphics and paper, and determine type size. Another method, which is becoming increasingly popular because of advances in technology, is to use computers and software to create and design publications.

TYPESETTING VERSUS DESKTOP PUBLISHING

In conventional publishing, after the design and editing of a document are completed, it is given to a typesetter. The designer specifies the typeface (including italics and bold), type size, line spacing, and line length. Any artwork is usually done by the designer or an artist. Once the layout is completed, the originator must proof the copy and approve it for printing.

Desktop publishing (DTP) involves using the computer to create both text and graphics for a camera-ready publication, that is, one ready to be photographed and printed. Because of the capabilities of the software, changes are easy to make. Output is usually done on a laser printer.

In-house DTP eliminates the need to hire outside graphic artists and typesetters to produce publications and offers the following advantages:

- It speeds up production because it is no longer necessary to accommodate the schedules of specialists.
- It saves money after the initial equipment purchase because some or all of the work is completed in-house.
- It makes it easier to make changes and corrections.
- It offers more internal control over the design and production schedule.
- It provides greater security for confidential or sensitive documents.
- It allows a business to have more professional-looking everyday documents.

Whether a typesetter is used or not, the printing process remains the same. Small jobs can be printed out and then reproduced on a copy machine, with larger publications completed by a professional printer.

Understanding the intricacies of DTP means learning new software as well as designing layout and comprehending printing terms and vocabulary. Many firms designate employees or departments for these needs.

DESKTOP PUBLISHING HARDWARE

Existing computer hardware in an office may not be sophisticated enough for quality in-house DTP. Listed below are suggestions for hardware selection. (See also Chapter 7, Office Equipment.)

COMPUTER

A hard disk with at least 40 megabytes of storage space is necessary. Networks (a system of interconnected computer terminals) are ideal for sharing files with other people who are involved in the production process. Here are a few hints to bear in mind when selecting a computer:

❏ The Macintosh was designed with the concepts of DTP in mind.

❏ IBMs and compatibles are capable of high-quality work if the software and the peripherals (extra hardware) are selected properly. For example, the monitor, whether monochrome, gray-scale, or color, should provide high resolution.

❏ Larger screens (up to 19 inches) that can display an entire page or even two pages make editing easier.

PRINTER

Both dot matrix and laser printers are capable of producing DTP. Here are some hints to bear in mind when choosing a printer:

❏ Laser printers are preferable to dot matrix printers because their print is similar to that of conventional typesetting. Laser printers are also more flexible and easier to use.

❏ The two major families of laser printers are PostScript and LaserJet-type. Both types of printers are compatible with a Macintosh or IBM/IBM compatible. The principal difference between the two is the flexibility with which fonts (print characters) are handled. PostScript allows laser printers to change (or scale) the size of fonts at will, but scalable fonts are now available on newer LaserJet-type printers as well.

❏ Less expensive laser printers offer limited typefaces in only a few sizes and may not be able to do graphics well. They also print more slowly.

OPTIONAL HARDWARE

A *scanner* is not necessary for DTP applications but allows bringing images into the computer for manipulation. For example, it can reduce an image, such as a company logo, into a grid of dots that is then stored in the computer and can later be reproduced in a document. Available in a variety of sizes, ranging from hand-held to the size of a small copy machine, scanners require special software to use the files scanned into the computer.

A *mouse* is not necessary but is usually faster than using only keystrokes.

DESKTOP PUBLISHING SOFTWARE

DTP software includes the following types of software: word processing, page layout, and graphics software.

WORD PROCESSING SOFTWARE

Any word processing software that saves words as a text-only file in ASCII can be used. This includes most major word processing software packages.

Less complicated publications or an occasional newsletter or brochure can be done with word processing software alone, as long as the software has capabilities for graphics, line drawings, type size selections, and columns.

More sophisticated publications are created with word processing software in conjunction with page layout software (see next section).

PAGE LAYOUT SOFTWARE

Page layout software was specifically designed for DTP and will lay out pages, insert text and graphics into the pages, and allow precise changes to the layout. There are two types of page layout software. One type of program allows the merging of text created from a word processing program with pictures on the screen from a graphics program in a layout chosen by the operator. The other type allows the creation and editing of text and brings in graphics on the screen from its program or from a graphics program in a layout chosen by the operator. The second kind is generally easier to use because it is possible to write text to the correct length, eliminating the problem of merging text and discovering it will not fit into the allotted space.

The page layout program displays pages on the screen so the shape and size of columns, graphics, and text can be viewed before printing. The pages should look on the screen the way they will look in print (this is called WYSIWYG—What You See Is What You Get). WYSIWYG allows the user to see on the screen the artwork, lines, and the size and style of type.

GRAPHICS SOFTWARE

Artwork can be added to a publication either by using the traditional method of having the paste-up artist or printer insert it into designated spaces left in the layout or by using graphics software. Graphics software enables you to create and edit electronic artwork. It can be one of the following general types:

Draw and paint programs: Draw programs are used for drawing straight lines, 45- and 90-degree angles, and boxes. The items can be moved, duplicated, enlarged, or reduced on the screen with no distortion. Paint programs allow "painting" on the screen with simulated brushes (usually controlled by a mouse). Many paint programs allow letters and numbers to be mixed with the graphics. Type can be rotated or stretched for special effects.

Clip art files: Electronic clip art is a collection of digitized designs stored on disk and available for use in printed publications. Some programs combine text and clip art and others can be used with paint, draw, word processing, or page layout programs. Many DTP software packages come with their own clip art.

Chart and graph programs: These programs automatically produce pie charts, bar charts, and line graphs from data.

TYPE AND PRINTING STYLES

Various typefaces, or shapes of type, and sizes of characters are used in publishing. Different typefaces can greatly affect the appearance and legibility of a document and help deliver the appropriate message. A typesetter will have hundreds of typefaces from which to choose, but the DTP selection is more limited.

TYPEFACE

Different typefaces produce appearances that convey characteristics such as high-tech, plain, conservative, feminine, masculine, Oriental, or classic. Companies use different typefaces to reflect a style and corporate identity. Table 19-1 lists some specific typefaces that convey certain images.

The major distinction between typefaces is the presence or absence of serifs. **Serifs** are the small curves added to the ends of strokes; **sans serif** typefaces lack these small curves. Here are two different typefaces, one with serifs and one sans serif:

Desktop Publishing   (serif)
Desktop Publishing   (sans serif)

Table 19-1 Typeface Characteristics

Image	Typeface
Classic	Baskerville, Caslon, Garamond, Goudy Old Style
Clean, modern	Century Schoolbook, Bodoni
Ultramodern	Futura
Conservative	Franklin, Rockwell, Clarendon, Italienne, Egyptian, Italia, Memphis, Prestige Elite
Mainstream	Baskerville, Caslon, Times Roman, Souvenir, Cooper

Table 19-2 Common Typefaces

Serif	Sans Serif
Times Roman*	Helvetica*
Bookman	Optima
Palatino	Avant Garde
New Century (also called Century or Century Schoolbook)	Futura

*Most common typefaces

Most of the differences among typefaces are in the lowercase letters. The one letter that most often differs from typeface to typeface is the lowercase *g*. Listed below is the letter *g* in a variety of typefaces:

g   Garamond
g   Times Roman
g   Bookman
g   Gothic

Table 19-2 lists some common serif and sans serif typefaces.

Research has shown that sans serif is harder to read than serif type. Sans serif is also difficult to read in boldface or italics. Sans serif type is recommended mainly for headings and headlines.

Table 19-3 lists the recommended typefaces for various sorts of publications.

Here are a few miscellaneous but important facts about typefaces to bear in mind:

❏ Typefaces with different names can be identical because although a typeface *itself* cannot be copyrighted, the typeface *name* can be.

❏ Typefaces with geographic names (Venice, New York, Geneva) may cause problems when brought into page layout software. The characters are wide, with wider spacing between letters, and they look less attractive when printed.

❏ Times Roman and Helvetica are usually standard on DTP systems; others can be added through cartridges or purchased on disk and downloaded or copied onto the hard disk.

Table 19-3 Typefaces for Different Publications

Publication	Typeface
Advertising	Sans serif (e.g., Helvetica)
Books	Serif (e.g., Garamond, Souvenir, Optima)
Technical books	Sans serif
Charts	Sans serif (e.g., Helvetica, Avant Garde)
Documents (lengthy)	Serif
Magazines	Serif
Newsletters	Serif (e.g., Times Roman, Bookman, Trump, Palatino)
Reports	Sans serif
Signs	Sans serif
Tables	Sans serif (e.g., Helvetica, Avant Garde)

TYPE SIZE

The size of type is measured in picas and points. The pica and point system dates back to the time when all type was produced in metal or wood. A *pica* is one-sixth of an inch. Each pica is divided into 12 **points**. A point is $\frac{1}{72}$ of an inch. The size of type is called the **point size**, and is approximately equal to the distance from the top of an h to the bottom of a q.

$$1 \text{ inch } = 6 \text{ picas}$$
$$1 \text{ pica } = 12 \text{ points}$$
$$72 \text{ points } = 1 \text{ inch}$$

Twelve-point type, for example, is type that measures 12 points from the top to the bottom of the letters. DTP software programs provide measurements in fractions of points and sometimes in centimeters and millimeters. The range of type sizes available depends on the printer used and the fonts available.

Table 19-4 shows examples of Times Roman and Helvetica in different point sizes. Notice that Helvetica tends to look larger than Times Roman, although they are the same point size. For a document with a lot of text, the characters per line make a difference in the number of pages; i.e., the more characters on a line of text, the shorter the document. Listed below are some common uses of common type sizes:

Brochure to fit in No. 10 envelope	14–36 point
Copyright notice or other fine print	6 point
Formal announcements and invitations	10, 12, or 14 point
Newsletter body	10 or 12 point
Text	10 or 12 point
Overhead transparency	18 point or larger

Table 19-4 Different Point Sizes of Two Typefaces

Times Roman (serif)	*Helvetica (sans serif)*
This is 7 point.	This is 7 point.
This is 10 point.	This is 10 point.
This is 12 point.	This is 12 point.
This is 18 point.	This is 18 point.
This is 42 point.	This is 42 point.

Table 19-5 Weights of Helvetica Type

This is an example of Helvetica typeface in light weight.
This is an example of Helvetica typeface in bold weight.
This is an example of Helvetica typeface in italic.

> **Hint:** For the subtitle, use a larger point size than for the text, and use an even larger size for the main title (14 points or larger). If 10-point type seems too large, use a lighter weight type (see next section).

TYPE STYLE

Each typeface usually has a series of different **weights**, or letter thicknesses. A typesetter has typefaces with a wide range of weights and widths. Most computerized typefaces should have at least a bold weight and an italic. The advantage of having more weights is that they can be used together in a document for variety with a consistent appearance. For example, if 10-point type seems too large, use a lighter weight type. Tables 19-5 and 19-6 show different weights of Helvetica and the uses of different styles.

Other type styles include outline, expanded or extended, oblique (slanted), and back-slanted.

FONTS

A **font** is a particular style and size of a typeface. It is also called a **type family**. A font includes capitals, lowercase, small caps, punctuation marks, and mathematical symbols. Below is a font of Times Roman:

Table 19-6 Uses of Different Type Styles

Style	Use
Bold	Main titles and subtitles; used to draw attention to the most important thing first. Avoid setting large blocks of text in bold because it is difficult to read.
Italics	Quotations, names of books and magazines, emphasized words. Avoid setting large blocks of text in italics because it is difficult to read.
Capital letters	Only used if a few individual words need emphasis. A long title in capitals may take up too much space or be difficult to read.
Underlining	Avoid (left over from the days of typewriters); use italics or bold for emphasis.

ABCDEFGHIJKLMNOPQRSTUVWXYZ
abcdefghijklmnopqrstuvwxyz

A computerized font file instructs the printer on the typeface, style, and size of type to be used. Fonts are available in the following three forms:

- Internal (resident): built into the printer.
- "Soft" (disk-based): available on disks and loaded into the printer's memory.
- Font cartridge: can be plugged into the printer; consumes little of the printer's memory.

LEADING

Leading is the distance between lines of type; it is often called line spacing. Line spacing does not alter the size of the typeface or lengthen the line; it merely moves the lines farther apart. Short lines (e.g., 45 characters on a line) need less space between them than long lines (e.g., 80 characters on a line). DTP software usually has a 2-point leading default, which is acceptable for most publications.

Extra leading for bold type increases legibility and may be needed to lighten its color or weight. Sans serif type might also need extra leading to help the reader's eye drop to the next line of text. Below are two sample pieces of text with different leading:

A type set on its own body size without
additional line feed is said to be
"set solid."

A 12-point type with 3 points of extra space
is called "12 on 15 pt" or $\frac{12}{15}$ pt.
Printers refer to this as 3-point leading.

Suggestions for Using Typefaces

Here are some suggestions to guide you in making type choices:

1. Use no more than two typefaces (a headline face and a body copy face) in a document. The two typefaces should be different enough to be distinguishable from one another. Often the best mix is a serif typeface with a sans serif one.

2. Choose the most readable typeface. Ornate typefaces are difficult to read, as this example shows:

Holiday Greetings

Type should be determined by the audience. Young or older readers need larger text type so it can be read easily, while busy executives need type that can be scanned quickly. Avoid using a script typeface, which looks like handwriting, for more than a few lines of copy, because it is tiring to the eye.

3. Determine the reading distance before determining the type size. Posters, for example, take a larger type size than a booklet.

4. Lengthen the line or reduce the type size to save space rather than changing the typeface.

5. Type may be either right-justified (even along the right margin) or ragged right (uneven at the right margin). Justified text is associated with typeset copy; however, some people feel justified text is harder to read than ragged right. If text is ragged right, paragraphs should have one line of space between them and not be indented. If the text is justified, paragraphs should have one line space between them and be indented.

FORMAT

A well-designed publication has its information arranged in a consistent format on the page. The format includes page size, number of columns of type, and the dimensions of each column.

Grids

A grid (or style sheet) is a skeleton of how the finished printed pages will be set up. The grid shows the top, bottom, and side margins; number of columns; and size of paper.

The complexity of the grid depends on the kind of layout needed. For example, a single column of text that is the width of a full page needs a simple grid showing just margins.

A publication with more than one column and graphics requires a grid showing vertical columns, margins, and horizontal lines. The horizontal lines are useful when graphics are included, since the graphics usually have to be reduced to fit into the grid.

Once the basic layout for a publication has been designed, it can be saved as a template or shell and used for subsequent publications. Templates eliminate the need to create the layout over again for publications produced more than once.

COLUMN WIDTH

The width of the column depends upon the purpose of the publication. Below are suggested uses for different numbers and widths of columns.

ONE COLUMN

Used for commercial newsletters and pamphlets, this is the easiest and most economical format and can be done on a typewriter. Since a line should contain no more than 65 characters, only 10-pitch, equal-spaced pica type is appropriate; smaller type sizes have too many characters per line. Wide margins leave room for three-hole punching in order to fit the material into a ring binder. This format is used for commercial newsletters and pamphlets.

Suggested Margins and Type Size

Paper size	$8\frac{1}{2}$ **by 11 inches**
Top/side margins	$1\frac{1}{4}$ inches
Bottom margin	$1\frac{3}{8}$ inches
Line width	6 inches
Type size	10 pitch or 12 point

ONE COLUMN WITH LARGE SIDE MARGIN

One column can be made more interesting if the column is narrower; extra space is put in the inside margin (left or right, according to the page spread) or consistently in the left margin. The narrow margin can include graphics, small diagrams, illustrations, margin notes, or side headings. If margin notes are used, they are set in a smaller type size than the text. This format is frequently used for reports.

Suggested Margins and Type Size

Paper size	$8\frac{1}{2}$ **by 11 inches**
Top margin	$\frac{5}{8}$ inch
Left margin	$3\frac{1}{2}$ inches
Right margin	1 inch
Bottom margin	$1\frac{1}{4}$ inches
Line width	$3\frac{1}{2}$ inches
Type size for body	10 pitch or 12 point

TWO COLUMNS

A two-column width provides flexibility, results in comfortable reading, and is easy to produce. It can, however, be dull. It is frequently used for newsletters and is, in fact, good for most publications.

Suggested Margins and Type Size

Paper size	$8\frac{1}{2}$ **by 11 inches**
Top/side margin	$\frac{3}{4}$ inch
Bottom margin	$\frac{7}{8}$ inch
Alley	$\frac{5}{16}$ inch
Line width	$3\frac{5}{16}$ inch
Type size	11 point

Hint: Two columns can be produced on a typewriter or computer by typing it as one column and then cutting and pasting it to make two columns. A 10-pitch column can be 37 characters wide and then reduced to 90 percent on a copy machine.

THREE COLUMNS

A three-column format allows more design flexibility. It is best for publications that mix text with graphics and/or boxes. It is often used for newsletters.

Suggested Margins and Type Size

Paper size	$8\frac{1}{2}$ **by 11 inches**
Top/side margins	$\frac{1}{2}$ inch
Bottom margin	$\frac{5}{8}$ inch
Alley	$\frac{1}{4}$ inch
Line width	$2\frac{5}{16}$ inches
Type size	9 or 10 point

FOUR COLUMNS

This is an economical format for text with many short lines, such as indices, lists, and dictionaries. Note that the type needs to be small.

Suggested Margins and Type Size

Paper size	$8\frac{1}{2}$ **by 11 inches**
Top margin	$\frac{5}{8}$ inch
Bottom margin	$1\frac{1}{4}$ inches
Left margin	$\frac{1}{2}$ inch
Right margin	$\frac{11}{16}$ inch
Alley	$\frac{3}{16}$ inch

Line width $1\frac{11}{16}$ inches
Type size   9 point

FIVE OR SIX COLUMNS

Called tabloid size, this format is prepared in four $8\frac{1}{2}$-by-11-inch segments that are then pasted together. It provides more space for photographs, increases layout flexibility, and allows for larger headlines. Most pages can hold two or more stories. It is used by virtually all newspapers.

Suggested Margins and Type Size (5 columns)
Paper size   **11 by 17 inches**
Top margin $\frac{5}{8}$ inch
Bottom margin $1\frac{1}{4}$ inches
Left margin $\frac{3}{4}$ inch
Right margin $\frac{3}{4}$ inch
Alley $\frac{3}{16}$ inch
Line width   5 columns of $1\frac{3}{4}$ inches
Type size   9 point or smaller

Suggested Margins and Type Size (6 Columns)
Paper size   **11 by 17 inches**
Top margin $\frac{1}{2}$ inch
Bottom margin   1 inch
Left margin $\frac{1}{2}$ inch
Right margin $\frac{9}{16}$ inch
Alley $\frac{3}{16}$ inch
Line width $1\frac{1}{2}$ inches
Type size   9 point

GRAPHICS AND ILLUSTRATIONS

A graphic or illustration in a publication enhances the text and makes it more interesting. Graphics and illustrations can include original drawings, photographs, charts, and graphs.

ORIGINAL DRAWINGS

Original drawings can be done using paint or draw programs on computer or by hand. They should correlate with items to be emphasized in the text. Cartoons can be added for humor but should not be overused. The drawing should be of the same quality as the publication.

CLIP ART

Clip art is art done by professional artists and is copyright-free. It is typically arranged by topic or by themes, such as holidays. It may look slightly mechanical or out of date, so custom touches are often added. Sometimes it may be difficult to find art that illustrates the text. Also, be sure to avoid sources of discrimination or stereotypes when selecting clip art.

When selecting a program, find out which companies supply images in the subject areas desired (e.g., business, travel, health). Then ask for sample drawings to make certain the artwork meets your standards. Some clip art companies will create special artwork or convert logos into clip art files. And note that drawings from a computer printer look better if they are reduced to 90 percent on a copy machine.

It is very important to be aware that most drawings in newspapers, magazines, and other commercial publications are copyrighted; they are *not* clip art. Check with the publisher before reproducing.

CHARTS AND DIAGRAMS

Charts and diagrams not only provide visual interest but also supply information in a smaller amount of space than would be used by a verbal explanation. Diagrams should be kept simple and not used if they require a great deal of explanatory information.

PHOTOGRAPHS

Photographs add credibility, but they need to be reproduced by some form of halftone process. They may have to be cropped (reduced in size) to fit a space, or background might have to be removed from the picture. All these add to the printing cost.

Use a 35-mm camera with black-and-white film if taking photos for an office publication. When photographing outdoors, try to keep the sky out since it detracts from the picture. Avoid having more than five people in a picture; ideally, there should be no more than three.

Regarding the layout of photographs, note that pictures should go above type or the type may not be read. All photographs should have a caption. And heads in a photo should be at least the size of a dime.

DESIGN GRAPHICS

Rules are lines for borders or boxes. They can be done by computer or by hand, but they must be perfect. They are used to separate categories of information (e.g., numbers and words), to draw attention to information, or to decorate. They are best used sparingly.

Screen tints are shadings or fill patterns that look like light versions of the ink. They are useful in highlighting blocks of type, such as a table of contents, and in helping organize data in calendars. They can be added by a commercial printer.

Reverses consist of printing the background rather than the image (e.g., white words on a black background). They are hard to read and are best used for display type in calendars or nameplates. They can be added by a commercial printer.

SPECIAL CONCERNS ABOUT USING GRAPHICS AND ILLUSTRATIONS

Before adding any graphics or illustrations to a publication, ask yourself the following questions:

❏ Are words adequate or are graphics needed to bring attention to the message?
❏ Will graphics help explain part of a text?
❏ Is there a place, person, or event frequently referred to in the text whose illustration would aid the audience's understanding?
❏ Is there a step-by-step process that could be illustrated?
❏ Is there a mood or style that could be captured by graphics?

The following suggestions should be kept in mind when using graphics and illustrations:

❏ Use them only if they add to the message.
❏ Mix them with text instead of isolating them at the beginning or end of a page.
❏ Avoid complicated graphics—keep them simple.
❏ Place the graphic or illustration on or near the same page as the text that it depicts.
❏ Unless they are purely decorative, illustrations should be accompanied by captions. Captions should be in a smaller type size than the text; if they are in the same type size as the text, they should be in bold, italic, or a different typeface (preferably sans serif).
❏ Include a source line (reference) for an illustration if appropriate.
❏ Distort a normal image to bring a layout "to life."
❏ Use illustrations that are in different sizes and shapes to add interest. At least one visual on a page should be substantially larger than others to attract reader interest. Readers usually see visuals first and move from print to visuals while reading.

DESIGNING PUBLICATIONS

Publications that best accomplish their goals are ones that have both their content and their audience clearly identified. Whether designing a brochure, advertisement, or newsletter, it is important to ask and answer the following questions:

❏ What is the goal? To persuade? impress? explain? boost morale? If goals are high, a higher-quality publication may be necessary. Quality is determined by the design, paper, and photography.
❏ Who is the audience? Employees? Association members? Investors?
❏ What are the budget restraints?
❏ How will it be distributed? Mailed in an envelope? Sent as a self-mailer? Inserted in other publications? If it will be a self-mailer, leave part of the back page for the return address and a mailing label. Make certain to dummy the back page before printing, so the newsletter does not appear to be upside-down when opened.

❑ Is art needed? Not all publications need art. If costs are limited, clip art or scanned art can be used.

Whether a brochure, newsletter, or advertisement is being created, the following steps are suggested:

❑ Make a rough layout using pen and paper before using the computer. Drafting ideas on paper helps visualize and formulate objectives as well as accounting for the design limitations of the publication.
❑ Select the typeface. (See the section on *Typeface* earlier in this chapter.)
❑ Determine type size for the body copy, headings, and other text blocks.
❑ Decide whether to use right-justified or ragged right text.
❑ Determine what graphics will be used.
❑ Avoid bias based on gender, race, age, ethnic background, physical ability, or sexual preference.
❑ Check for correct spelling, grammar, punctuation, inconsistencies, and inaccuracies.
❑ Decide on color. A study by *Advertising News Review* found the greatest legibility is given by black type on a yellow background. Green on white ranks second, with blue on white third. The worst combination for legibility is red ink on green paper. Color, however, should be used sparingly. Ordinary text should not be printed in color; rather, color should be used for nonverbal elements, such as boxes or rules.

DESIGNING A BROCHURE

Brochures created for customers and/or the public are intended to present a positive image of the company. The rules for designing a brochure are fairly simple:

❑ Writing should be clear and concise.
❑ The typeface should be easy to read.
❑ The title will be more prominent if it is set in a sans serif typeface.
❑ Since either the front or back will be seen first, benefits should be listed in both places.
❑ Contemporary colors should be used. Good colors are off-white, light yellow, buff, goldenrod yellow, pink, and very light tan. Avoid green (unless it is bright teal or turquoise)—it is too restful to elicit action.
❑ Shading is frequently used to draw attention to layout elements.
❑ Price information and graphics, if appropriate, should be included to allow the reader to see what is being described. If price information changes frequently, include that information as an extra sheet. Always position benefits before the price.
❑ The company logo should be in a prominent position, usually on the cover, to promote the name. If the logo is purely graphic, the name should be repeated close to the logo.
❑ Company name, address, and fax and phone numbers should be included.
❑ Bullet points can be used with hanging indentations.
❑ Photographs should be contemporary. Use action shots, and crop unnecessary background to eliminate distractions.
❑ Leave sufficient white space.

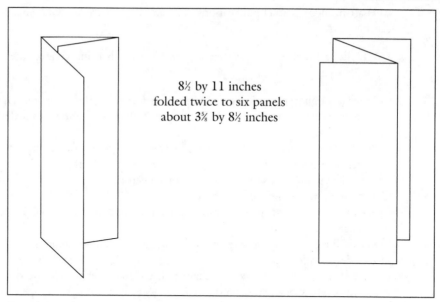

8½ by 11 inches
folded twice to six panels
about 3⅝ by 8½ inches

Figure 19-1 Two types of folds.

When creating a brochure, keep in mind how the document is to be folded. The type of fold chosen should be one that can be handled by the printer's machine. (Figure 19-1 shows two suggestions for folds.)

Any folded brochure must be designed carefully so that there is no artwork or copy on the folds. A brochure using either of the folds shown in Figure 19-1 can be used as self-mailers or inserted in a No. 10 business envelope. These brochures can also be included with a one-page letter and still be mailed at the one-ounce postal rate. Envelopes may not be available to fit odd folds.

> **Hint:** The tear-off registration portion of a brochure should not include important information on the other side.

DESIGNING AN ADVERTISEMENT

Because there are so many ways to lay out information for an advertisement, there are no typical page layouts and few rules. Simple one-page advertisements are usually on $8\frac{1}{2}$-by-11-inch paper.

The design of a poster is different from the design of a magazine advertisement. The poster must use attention-getting visuals with little text. The visuals for a magazine advertisement do not need to be so striking, since the advertisement will be seen up close and will probably contain more text than a poster.

The following are suggestions for designing advertisements:

❏ The design should immediately get the reader's attention, either with a headline or an image. Visuals should reinforce the message in the copy.

❏ Avoid unnecessary words. Either get right to the point or lead up to the point in a way that captures the reader's interest.

❏ Do not use too many images or large-type headlines.

❏ Avoid a typeface that is hard to read.

❏ Use the company logo consistently for continuity.

❏ Use rules, not underlining, for a coupon response advertisement. And make certain there is enough space for the coupon to be filled out legibly.

❏ Use plenty of white space.

❏ Use thin side borders to make a wide ad appear taller.

❏ Center headlines.

❏ Make certain that information is accurate. It is illegal to give false or misleading information in an advertisement.

DESIGNING A NEWSLETTER

Newsletters are designed to provide information to readers on a regular basis. Most are four or eight pages long on $8\frac{1}{2}$-by-11-inch paper. It is important to understand the audience well in order to write and design a successful newsletter. Listed below are some suggestions:

Know the audience. If the publication has reluctant readers, use design techniques such as large type combined with extra white space.

Design a nameplate (the top of the front page). The nameplate is also called the flag. The nameplate should include the name and subtitle of the newsletter and the publication date. The inclusion of the following elements is optional: logo, illustration, photo, issue number, slogan, publisher, editor.

Include a masthead (the area with business information). The masthead should have the same content and stay in the same location (typically the second page) from one issue to the next. The masthead includes the name and address of the sponsoring organization and the editor's name. The inclusion of the following elements is optional: frequency of publication, subscription costs, names of key officers and contributors, copyright notation, and International Standard Serial Number (ISSN) (used by librarians to catalog publications). Newsletters mailed second class must display either an ISSN or post office identification number in the nameplate, masthead, or return address.

Determine the content. A table of contents on the front cover draws attention to articles in the newsletter. Some content suggestions for a company newsletter are as follows:

- Job-related information
- Personnel policies/practices
- Effect of external events on job
- News of departments/divisions
- Organization stand on current issues
- Stories about other employees
- Personal news (births, birthdays, etc.)

- Training/professional development
- Technical information

Compose headlines before writing articles to help focus on what the article will say. The headline must:

- Convey the point of the article
- Be from the reader's point of view
- Relate to the story
- Be in the present tense with an action verb and subject
- Be specific.

Do not capitalize every word in a headline—only the first word and proper nouns.

Determine the writing style. The writing style should be consistent with company or association image. Newsletter articles are usually less formal than magazines, books, and reports. Use natural conversational tone, with concentration on "you, yours."

Choose the number of columns. (Refer to the section on Format earlier in this chapter for suggestions.) Also look at newsletters produced by others for ideas and inspiration. And bear the following format hints in mind:

❑ Most readers look at headlines, photos, and captions first while skimming.

❑ The inside pages are seen together, so the layout should be tied together with design graphics. Headlines can be set across a whole page, for example.

❑ Once the basic format is determined for a newsletter, keep it for succeeding issues. Consistency makes content easier to find and lets the designer concentrate on content for each issue.

❑ More than 90 percent of newsletters in the United States are $8\frac{1}{2}$ by 11 inches. If the publication is four pages, print on an 11-by-17 sheet folded once to become $8\frac{1}{2}$ by 11. An eight-page publication is made with two 11-by-17 sheets or one 17-by-22 sheet folded and trimmed.

❑ Bottom margins are always slightly larger than top and side margins to make it appear that copy is centered on the page.

❑ Run main stories over two columns in a three-column newsletter to gain impact.

❑ The newsletter title, page number, and date are often repeated across the top of every page. Page numbers may also be printed at the bottom of a page.

❑ Author identification can be placed at the beginning or end of an article. An author's background can be summarized at the end of an article.

Select typeface and size, bearing the following points in mind:

❑ Stay with just a few typefaces and sizes. Serif type is easier to read for long sections of type. Sans serif type can be used for headlines or captions, as long as it is compatible with the typeface used for the body.

❑ Make the most important headlines large and place them near the top of the page.

❑ Choose a thin typeface, such as Times Roman or News Gothic, for narrow columns.

Decide on graphics. Refer to the section on Graphics and Illustrations earlier in this chapter, and follow these suggestions:

- Graphics should contribute to a specific objective.
- Use rules and screen tints to organize information that is not text or in captions.

Do not crowd the page with text and/or graphics—leave plenty of white space (blank space between text and graphics). The average length of sentences should be about 15 words; paragraphs should be three to four sentences and no longer than seven lines long.

Decide whether text will be right-justified or ragged right.

Design calendars carefully. The calendar should appear in the same place in each issue and should not have important items that may be clipped out on its reverse side. When properly designed, a calendar serves as an advertising tool. Include the location and date for each listed activity. Categorize by location, activity, or date based on the readership. The design should make it easy for readers to find what they want.

Use trivia facts, boxed quotes, or clip art for filler if the text does not end at the bottom of the page.

Divide long articles and place them on more than one page.

Choose color. Most newsletters are printed in black with a second color used sparingly.

PRINTING METHODS

Printed output can be produced either with a laser printer or with phototypesetting equipment. A phototypesetter gives sharper resolution, about 1200 or more dots per inch, while most laser printers have a resolution of 300 dots per inch. (The higher the number of dots per inch printed, the higher the resolution.)

A way to improve legibility when using a laser printer is to set type larger than the size at which it will be reproduced and then reduce it with a copy machine. Reducing digital type makes the copy more dense.

Obtain quotes from printers to get the best price.

Publications produced on a computer can be stored on disk and printed at a typesetting service bureau that has a professional quality printer, such as a Linotronic or Burmisetter. Some bureaus are self-service and charge by the hour for computer rental time. Other bureaus charge for each finished page. Before sending a large project to a typesetting service bureau, send small samples to several and see which one is best. Be aware that many bureaus accept files by modem.

PREPARING TO PRINT

Before you print through a service bureau, the printer should be consulted about resolution, lines per inch, and whether to print on paper or film. The following steps should be taken before sending work to a bureau:

1. Take carefully proofread hard copy (laser-printed) to the service bureau. (If the publication is sent by modem, send a fax as confirmation.)

2. Find out what file format the bureau prefers (e.g., PostScript).

3. Deliver a list of fonts with the publication. Ask ahead of time how the service bureau wants the fonts set up.

4. Ask whether the version of software they are using is compatible with the software you used to create the file.

5. Bring the original graphics file if the document was created with a page layout program.

6. Proofread the copy again once it has been printed.

METHODS OF PRINTING

The choice of a printing or copying method depends on the following factors:

- Number of copies
- Budget
- Deadline
- Print quality

The two main ways to print multiple copies of office publications are by photocopying and offset printing. Printing by office copier is quick and convenient. Lines and large areas of black can be copied adequately, but fine details or photographs do not reproduce. This method is not recommended for more than 100 copies.

Offset printing involves making photographs or film of the camera-ready copy. A plate is made from the photographic film; separate plates are made for each color. Note that once the film is made, it is extremely expensive to make corrections. This method results in much better quality than printing by copier. *Quick printers* are good for short runs needed quickly. *Commercial printers* are used for longer runs and more complicated jobs.

PAPER

Paper costs can represent half the cost of the printing and influence the quality of a publication. Printers usually make suggestions on weight and type of paper because these decisions can be very technical. Common paper weights and type include 80-pound uncoated, 28-pound bond, and 60-pound offset.

BINDING

Binding contributes to the overall impression created by a publication. There are binding methods that are mechanical and others that do not require equipment. Table 19-7 describes binding systems that can be used in the office without sending the material to a printer.

Printers and binders offer a wide range of binding options. The type of binding should

Table 19-7 Binding Systems

Equipment Needed	Binding Method	Number of Sheets
No equipment	Two-pocket portfolios	15
	Prong-style report covers	100
	Punchless	125
	Slide lock	30
Paper punch	Two-piece plastic and pressboard report covers	600
	Vinyl ring binders:	
	$\frac{1}{2}$ inch	100
	1 inch	200
	$1\frac{1}{2}$ inches	325
	2 inches	500
	3 inches	600

Hint: Custom binders are available for camera-ready artwork. View binders with plastic overlay on the front, back, and/or spine can help you customize binders quickly and economically.

Stapler	Stapled report cover	15
Plastic ring punch-and-bind machine	Either manual or with an electric motor; binds on side or top.	12–425 (depending on equipment)
Adhesive tape machine	Uses adhesive tape to bind punched reports to special report covers designed for the machine.	Short reports
Thermal binding system	Uses a heat-sealing process to adhere pages to a one-piece, preglued spine and cover.	40–600

Hint: Thermal binding systems are used with DTP to improve the appearance of sales presentations, reports, and other important documents.

be decided on before the material is printed so that the margins are appropriate. Word processing and page layout programs can be used to adjust margins appropriately.

Hint: Since printers usually subcontract binding work, it may be less expensive to contact a binder initially.

DESKTOP PUBLISHING GLOSSARY

Printers and graphic artists use certain terms that may be unfamiliar. Listed below are some definitions.

ALLEY: Space between two columns of typeset material.
BOXED COPY: Text with horizontal and vertical lines (or rules) around it.

CAMERA-READY: Of a quality appropriate for final copy and ready to be printed or photographed.

CLIP ART: Art designed by professional artists that is copyright-free and commercially available. The art may be printed on paper or stored on a data disk for a DTP program.

CROPPING: Cutting an illustration to fit a given area or to remove unwanted background along the edges.

DESKTOP PUBLISHING: The process of designing and producing a publication with a computer.

DOT MATRIX PRINTER: A printer that uses a printhead with tiny pins to form a dot pattern for text or pictures.

DTP: An abbreviation for DESKTOP PUBLISHING.

FLAG: See NAMEPLATE.

FONT: A typeface in a particular style and size. Some DTP software programs use this term in place of TYPEFACE.

GRID: A skeleton of the finished printed page showing vertical columns, margins, and the space between horizontal lines.

HALFTONE PROCESS: A photograph broken up into fine dots for reproduction.

LASER PRINTER: A computer printer that uses a laser beam to form images on paper, a page at a time.

LAYOUT: The arrangement of text and images on a page.

LEADING: The distance between type lines, measured in points from the baseline of one line of type to the baseline of the next line. Also called *line spacing*.

MASTHEAD: The information in a newsletter that includes the business information, such as name and address of sponsoring organization.

MOUSE: A hand-controlled input device that gives commands to the cursor or icon on the screen.

NAMEPLATE: The top of the front page that includes the name and subtitle of the newsletter and publication date. Also called *flag*.

NETWORK: A system of interconnected computer systems and terminals.

PAGE LAYOUT PROGRAM: DTP program that allows placement of text and pictures on the screen before printing.

POINT: Unit of type measurement. One point is approximately equal to $\frac{1}{72}$ of an inch.

RAGGED RIGHT: The uneven alignment of text along the right margin.

READABILITY: Relative ease with which a printed page can be read.

RIGHT-JUSTIFIED: The even alignment of text along the right margin.

RULES: Lines of various thickness and pattern used to divide and box text on a page.

SANS SERIF: Characters of a typeface without SERIFS.

SCANNER: Hardware that reduces an image into a grid of dots that can be stored in the computer.

SERIFS: The short lines terminating the main strokes of certain letters in a typeface.

TEMPLATE: A page grid that has been created as a guide and can be used repeatedly for similar documents.

TYPE STYLE: An assortment of styles of a typeface, such as italic and bold.

TYPEFACE: An assortment of characters of one particular kind of type. Some DTP software programs use the word FONT instead.

TYPESETTING: The preparation of characters in a printed typeface created by a traditional metal type or by the photocomposition process.

WHITE SPACE: The blank space between text and graphics on a page.

PROOFREADING AND EDITING

Printed office documents should be written correctly and formatted attractively. Office professionals with high-level proofreading and editing skills can take pride in meeting professional standards. Reference books, dictionaries, and English grammar and usage manuals are essential sources for answering proofreading and editing questions.

Proofreading and editing are separate but integrated skills; both require concentration on the details involved in producing error-free documents. **Proofreading** entails checking copy for errors in spelling, punctuation, capitalization, word division, statistical data, and format. It takes place at two stages—first while editing the material and again after printing the final document.

Editing is a process to ensure that the content of a document is accurate, clear, and complete; that the material is organized logically and free of grammatical errors; and that the writing style is appropriate for the purpose. Editing should be completed before the final copy is printed to avoid the cost of revising or rewriting.

HOW TO PROOFREAD DOCUMENTS

Whether proofreading copy on a computer screen or on printed copy, it is easy to miss errors on your first review of the material. The efficient proofreader makes separate checks for format, mechanical accuracy, and statistical data.

Both you and the writer should be able to interpret and use proofreaders' marks. Table 20-1 shows the standard marks proofreaders use to indicate changes on printed matter.

Table 20-1 Proofreaders' Marks

Explanation	Notation in Margin	Example
Add space	#	our tuition‸plan
Align vertically	‖	‖A. Software ‖ B. Hardware
Capitalize	(caps)	Mary harrington
Center copy	] [	]CHAPTER I [
Close up space	⌒	a recent let ter
Delete	℘	proofreading℘
Double space	(ds)	to work. Thank you for
Insert	∧	two requests‸merit *have*
Insert apostrophe	⩔	company's payroll
Insert colon	⊙	Include the following items℘
Insert comma	⋀	your prompt‸helpful response
Insert hyphen	=/	well/equipped
Insert parentheses	(/)	to obtain ten(10)
Insert period	⊙	We have her check⊙
Insert quotes	℣/⩔	She said, I will increase sales.
Insert semicolon	⨀	She spoke we listened.
Let it stand	(stet)	arrive today at 5 p.m.
Move down	⊔	⊔Table 12-2
Move left	⊏	⊏proofreader can use
Move material	↰	Last month's sales
Move right	⊐	⊐ facsimile services
Move up	⊓	⊓ SECTION 2
New paragraph	¶	¶ We will attend
No paragraph	no¶	no¶ Next fall
Single space	(ss)	Please return the office supplies.

Table 20-1 *(con't)*

Explanation	Notation in Margin	Example
Spell out	⟨sp⟩	Jan. 19
Transpose	⟨tr⟩	the last payment
Underline	——	The word their
Use boldface	⟨bf⟩	The task of editing
Use italic typeface	⟨ital⟩	a bona fide transaction
Use lowercase	lc	My recent Request
Verify data	⟨?⟩	The 10 a.m. meeting ?

FORMAT

An attractive-looking document can affect a reader's impressions of a company. Do the following when checking the overall appearance of a document:

❏ Scan all pages to be sure headings and subheadings as well as the spacing between these headings are consistent. Check the paragraph indentations for consistency.
❏ Check that page numbers are consecutive and in the same location on each page.
❏ Make sure the copy is free of smudges and messy corrections.
❏ Check that the top, bottom, and side margins are in proportion to each other. Bound reports require a wider left margin than unbound reports. (See Chapter 18, Reports.)
❏ Follow the company style manual if there is one. However, take the initiative to recommend companywide adoption of new formats if a document's appearance can be improved or productivity increased with the recommended changes.

MECHANICAL ACCURACY

Producing quality documents requires precise and careful attention to details. The following points should be helpful:

❏ Learn basic spelling and word division rules in order to avoid repeated checking of reference sources. But be sure to check the dictionary or a reference manual if in doubt.
❏ Be aware that errors often occur in (1) items that are enumerated; (2) long words (syllables are often omitted); (3) words at the margins or at the bottom of a page; (4) words with double letters; (5) proper names; (6) headings, subheadings, and titles; (7) word endings, such as *-tion, -ed,* or *-s;* (8) sentences with beginning and closing marks of punctuation, such as quotes and parentheses; (9) words or phrases printed in all caps; and (10) words that are similar, such as *than* for *that* or *now* for *not.*
❏ Check carefully for transposed letters, figures, or words.
❏ Compare the inside address of a letter with the original source, and then check the inside address with the address on the envelope to be sure they agree. Check that all enclosures

are included and all copy notations are identified. Be sure that mailing instructions have been noted.

❑ Avoid excessive word division at ends of lines, especially several lines in succession.

Statistical Data

Errors in figures suggest carelessness and cause embarrassment for a company. Here are some suggestions for ways to avoid errors in monetary amounts, Social Security numbers, tabulations, etc.:

❑ Count the items in a series or in a tabulation on the original copy; then compare this count to the number of items on the final copy.

❑ Verify the accuracy of the arithmetical functions on both the original and the printed copy. Take the extra time to verify extensions and all totals.

❑ Verify the accuracy of all numbers by checking them twice. Check for transposed numbers. Check the decimal alignment within tabulations. Be sure the number of zeros is correct.

HOW TO EDIT DOCUMENTS

Productivity increases when a minimal number of printed revisions of a document are necessary. If the writer and the office professional work as a team, the editing process should be smooth. If the writer is inexperienced or careless, an office professional who has an excellent grasp of basic grammar, an understanding of the content of the material, and an appreciation for appropriate writing style can be invaluable. Be aware, however, that some writers do not appreciate having their work changed.

Language Usage

Well-written communications reflect a company's competence and reliability. Try to insure that the principles of grammar are consistently followed.

❑ Review the rules of grammar by taking refresher classes at a local college, by reviewing English grammar books at the public library, or by using an up-to-date handbook for office professionals.

❑ Use a thesaurus to avoid repetition or overuse of a word, but be sure that the substitution does not change the meaning of the sentence.

❑ Check for parallel structure; e.g., that all items in a list begin with a verb.

❑ Check that all sentences are complete.

❑ Be aware of language usage problems in areas such as (1) noun/verb agreement; (2) homonyms; (3) word usage, such as *less* versus *fewer* or *that* versus *which;* (4) dangling participles and split infinitives; (5) pronouns/antecedents; and (6) active/passive voice.

❑ Use the services offered by grammar hotlines. Faculty members and graduate students at many universities and colleges answer questions from callers about spelling, punctuation, capitalization, number style, and grammar. These services are usually free.

Hint: A free copy of the *Grammar Hotline Directory* is available each January from Tidewater Community College Writing Center, 1700 College Crescent, Virginia Beach, VA 23456. To receive a copy of the directory, send the college a stamped, self-addressed No. 10 envelope.

CONTENT

A well-written communication contains complete information and follows a logical thought pattern. Suggestions to achieve this clarity include the following:

❏ Be sure the document answers the who, what, when, where, why, and how questions.
❏ Identify the purpose of the document succinctly and directly.
❏ Begin new paragraphs when introducing new ideas.
❏ Make sure all dates are correct by checking them against the office schedule; make sure the days of the week mentioned match the dates given.
❏ Eliminate vague statements that lack precision or completeness. Be sure the intent of the document is clear.
❏ Eliminate excess verbiage.

STYLE

An appropriate writing style stimulates a reader's interest in the message. To attain this goal, try to do the following:

❏ Present information in a logical format, with a smooth flow from sentence to sentence and from paragraph to paragraph.
❏ Strive for an *average* sentence length of 16 to 20 words. If successive sentences are very short, a communication may seem curt. If sentences are too long, they may be difficult to follow.
❏ Use a writing style that is appropriate for the reader. Evaluate the situation to determine whether the tone of the letter should be formal or informal.
❏ Use words that clarify rather than confuse. Avoid unfamiliar words.
❏ Eliminate archaic, trendy, or slang expressions.

PROOFREADING BY YOURSELF

Teaming up with a coworker is the best way to proofread lengthy documents or statistical information. One person reads aloud to a second person who checks the copy. However, since a coworker is not always available, the following suggestions are for proofreading alone.

❏ Place a 3- by 5-inch card below the line you are proofreading on your final copy and your finger below the line on the original copy. This forces you to slow down your proofreading rate as you move from line to line.

❏ Read the copy character by character and then reread it for content. Finally, scan the entire document for format consistency.

   Hint: Read the material from right to left rather than the usual direction of left to right. This forces you to read each word.

❏ Count lines to compare the number of printed lines with the number of lines on the original copy.

❏ Listen to machine-dictated material a second time while proofreading the printed copy.

PROOFREADING COPY ONSCREEN

Proofreading onscreen immediately after putting the information into a computer is more productive than bringing it back onscreen later. The more editing you can do onscreen, the less time it will take to review the final printed copy. The following suggestions should prove helpful for onscreen proofreading:

❏ Strive for "first printing, final copy." Revising always takes time.

❏ Use the spell checker as a routine check for obvious errors. (Update the dictionary in the program to include terms or acronyms unique to your specific company or area.)

❏ Use a plastic ruler to remain on the correct line when proofreading onscreen, or move the cursor from line to line as you proofread. If possible, ask someone else to proof the screen as you slowly read aloud from the original copy.

❏ Divide the document into convenient viewing sections for proofreading; for example, paragraph by paragraph or 10 to 12 lines at a time.

❏ Check a revised document carefully. Words are often omitted or rekeyed, or a new paragraph is inserted without deleting the old. Or a paragraph can be moved without deleting it at its original position. Review the copy that comes immediately before and after the revisions as well.

❏ Always proofread the final printing.

SPECIAL CONCERNS ABOUT PROOFREADING AND EDITING

A current reference manual, dictionary, thesaurus, and word division dictionary are invaluable aids. To insure uniformity in style and English usage, recommend that everyone in your company use the same reference books.

   Even though your word processing software includes a hyphenation feature, check line endings for undesirable word breaks. Avoid unnecessary blank space at the end of a line.

   If space does not permit an addition or revision on a page, use a separate sheet of paper on which each insertion is identified, as A, B, or C, and correlate these letters with the appropriately identified locations for the insertions on the document.

   Never rely solely on your memory; always verify pertinent facts, such as dates, figures, and times. Errors in dates often occur at the beginning of a new year.

Prepare a style sheet that outlines the format, shows correct spellings of proper names, and lists words that cause spelling or hyphenation difficulties. Style sheets are also valuable to keep on file for future use with similar documents.

It is often advisable to put the copy aside for a while and come back to it later with a fresh eye to proofread the final copy.

USING SOFTWARE TO PROOFREAD

Software programs that identify misspellings and incorrect grammar and analyze writing style are not substitutes for good proofreading and editing skills, but they can be very useful.

ELECTRONIC DICTIONARIES AND THESAURUSES

An electronic dictionary, like a traditional dictionary, contains word definitions, syllabification, inflected forms, and parts of speech labels. It does not usually include pronunciation. An electronic thesaurus offers numerous synonyms for words. The following questions can help determine the effectiveness of dictionary and thesaurus software:

❑ Do the dictionary and thesaurus interact with each other? (This feature is a process known as cross-popping.)

❑ How many entries are included in the dictionary or thesaurus?

❑ Once loaded, can you call up these references while working on a document?

❑ Is the software compatible with the word processing program you are using as well as other programs?

❑ Does the electronic software support spreadsheet and database programs?

❑ Are customized versions available for specialized areas, such as law, medicine, and engineering? Are foreign-language versions available?

❑ Is the software based on a dictionary or thesaurus that is in print?

SPELLING, GRAMMAR, AND STYLE CHECKERS

Many word processing packages have their own built-in spelling checkers; a few also include grammar-check and style-check features. Separate software devoted only to spell checking usually has a larger vocabulary and a greater capability for adding terms unique to a company or industry than a word processing package has.

Grammar and style checkers identify certain types of writing deficiencies by using rule-based expert system techniques. On this basis, the checkers can only offer tips for improvement; specific corrective actions are still the proofreader's responsibility. Different grammar/style checkers often produce different results and recommendations, so it is imperative that the user be competent in the use of the language.

Hint: Software will not identify all errors and may indicate that some words or sentences are wrong when they are actually correct. Do not accept suggested corrections without question.

The following checklist illustrates the many decisions facing potential users of software for checking spelling, grammar, and writing style:

Does the software support your word processing package? Is the memory capacity of your hardware sufficient to accommodate the software?

Is the program easy to use? Is the documentation easy to understand? Is the cost reasonable?

Does the software check spelling as well as grammar and style?

Does the software allow the options of checking single words, blocks of text, whole documents, words as they are typed, or words in background windows?

Is the software capable of checking foreign-language documents?

Does the critique indicate excessive use of jargon? negative terms? difficult words? clichés? abstractions? Is there a critique of sentence structure? Does the software recognize such differences as *form* for *from*? Is a summary of the criticisms for the entire document available?

Does the software check the following language usage areas?

- Punctuation, including periods, commas, semicolons, quotes, apostrophes, question marks, and exclamation points
- Subject/verb agreement
- Passive voice
- Awkward phrasing
- Sentence structure
- Plurals
- Possessives
- Double negatives
- Long-sequence prepositional phrases
- Long-sequence noun modifiers
- Article usage
- Superlative versus comparative usage, e.g., *best* versus *better*
- Split infinitives
- Number agreement
- Pronoun usage
- Capitalization

When errors are identified, is corrective action suggested? Are the suggested corrective comments inserted directly into the document? Does one single command remove all the comments on a document?

When errors are identified, are there comments explaining the rules? Are you able to change rules? Can you add rules? For example, can you add a rule to correct an overuse of the words "There are" to begin a sentence and recommend an alternative construction?

Can rules be turned off if you wish to ignore some of them while writing? When can this be done—before beginning the check or after the program has used a rule to identify an error? If a company has its own guidelines regarding style, it will want to obtain software that allows changes or additions to the rules.

Does the software automatically suggest replacements for errors and misspelled words? Does the software perform a second evaluation of a sentence after it has been rewritten? (The second attempt may be worse than the first one.)

Does the software automatically recheck words whose spelling has been corrected? If not, the copy must go through the checking routine again, which is time-consuming.

How difficult is it to rework a sentence with problems? Is it easy to move backward in the document?

Is a readability grade-level analysis available? How many formulas or indices are available for this readability level? (A readability level indicates the number of years of education the reader needs to understand the document.) Index levels vary from program to program.

Is the average number of words per sentence and syllables per word as well as the number of sentences per paragraph shown? Is it possible to change a default setting; for example, the number of words in a sentence?

Can the software be customized? Are you able to select the kind of writing you plan to do—for example, fiction, reference, proposal, general business, or technical?

GROUP WRITING TOOLS

Group writing software allows several authors to make changes and annotate text without destroying the original copy. Different typefaces or colors show the changes made and enable reviewers to evaluate these changes. It is possible to display the original copy and the edited copy with the changes highlighted on a split screen.

Reviewers may add comments to a document, but the right to make final alterations belongs to the author. The number of reviewers and the number of versions that can be retained vary with the software. Comments can be initialed and the date stamped. Some group writing software can even accommodate proofreading marks.

SPECIAL CONCERNS ABOUT USING SOFTWARE

❏ Since most software for checking spelling and language usage cannot differentiate between such homonyms as *there* and *their* and *you're* and *your,* a document must still be proofread very carefully.

❏ If the software keeps the original file intact and places the comments in an output file, rename and save the marked-up document.

❏ Grammar checkers and style checkers do not "know" the definitions of words and do not understand that the exercise of literary license is often acceptable. *You* are the expert, and you have the opportunity to make the final decisions.

CHAPTER 21

ORAL COMMUNICATIONS

The ability to communicate orally is essential in today's office. All office professionals must be able to listen actively to people inside and outside the company and respond with accurate information to questions and requests. Good communication rests on a positive attitude that recognizes the needs of others.

RECEPTIONIST TECHNIQUES

Because the receptionist is often the first contact visitors have with a company, it is vital that the receptionist create a positive impression. Larger offices usually have a reception area with a trained receptionist; in smaller offices, a secretary handles these responsibilities.

WAITING AREA

Any waiting area for visitors, no matter what the size, must be clean and comfortable. The following suggestions help make waiting more pleasant.

❏ Include current magazines with subjects that appeal to both men and women, a daily newspaper, an annual report, and/or company brochures.
❏ Make coffee and tea available or indicate their location.
❏ Have a place for coats with enough hooks or coat hangers.
❏ Do not allow visitors to wait in private offices unless permission has been given.
❏ Have a separate area for children to play in if they are frequent visitors. Even if children visit infrequently, have a few children's books and toys available.

GREETING VISITORS

All visitors should be treated as important guests, with courtesy and respect. You should stop what you are doing, smile, and greet the visitor. Below are some tips for making the visitor feel welcome.

❏ Greet the visitor with "good morning" or "good afternoon." It is not necessary to rise or shake hands, unless the caller extends his or her hand first. If you are on the telephone, acknowledge the visitor with a nod and smile.

❏ Greet people by name. Use *Mr., Ms.,* or a professional title and the visitor's last name, unless you are on a first-name basis with the visitor. Refer to your supervisor by title and last name.

> **Hint:** Take a business card if offered and file it. If necessary, write the visitor's name phonetically on the card to avoid mispronunciations. Brief written notes will also help you remember the caller.

❏ Avoid initiating conversations; however, respond to visitors who wish to talk. Talk about company business in generalities and avoid controversial subjects. In answering direct business questions, it is always acceptable to say, "I'm sorry, I don't know."

❏ Follow company policy in allowing unscheduled visitors to see your supervisor. Find out the reason for the visit. If the person refuses to state the reason for the visit, it may be necessary to say something like the following: "I'm sorry, but I'm unable to make an appointment without telling Ms. Garcia the purpose of your visit." When in doubt, ask your supervisor.

❏ Stop unknown people from going beyond the reception area. Know company policy for handling sales representatives and solicitors. Be familiar with what to do in the case of emergencies or dealing with suspicious characters.

❏ Keep a list of employees who speak other languages in case a visitor does not speak English.

KEEPING A RECORD OF VISITORS

Some offices keep a register of visitors for security reasons or to help prepare client billing. The register should include the date, time, name and company, purpose of visit, and other information necessary for record keeping. Smaller offices typically use the appointment notations in a calendar for keeping information.

INTRODUCING VISITORS

The caller should be escorted to the office door. If the supervisor's door is closed, knock before entering.

Proper etiquette requires introducing the visitor first. If the visitor is a lower-ranking company employee, introduce the supervisor first; for example, "Mr. Supervisor, I would like you to meet Mr. McLean, who is in the Graphic Arts Department." For frequent visitors say, "Ms. Manager can see you now; please go right in." (For additional information, see Chapter 6, Business Ethics and Etiquette.)

DELAYED APPOINTMENTS

No matter how carefully scheduling is done, appointments may be delayed. If the supervisor is running later than scheduled, explain the delay to the visitor. If possible, try to give the approximate length of the delay so the visitor can decide whether to wait or reschedule the appointment. If possible, call the visitor ahead of time to notify him or her of and explain any delays. If a visitor's meeting is taking longer than scheduled, call and remind the manager about the next appointment or take a reminder note in.

TELEPHONE PROCEDURES

The telephone should be used properly by everyone in a firm, including executives, managers, customer representatives, receptionists, and secretaries. What is said over the telephone and how it is said helps or hurts a company's image. Proper use of the telephone establishes a positive impression that the company's employees are friendly, efficient, and helpful.

TELEPHONE COURTESY

Telephone etiquette is vital to creating a courteous and pleasant company image. Below are general suggestions for telephone usage:

❏ Speak directly into the telephone, holding the mouthpiece about an inch and a half from your lips. Do not eat, chew gum, or smoke cigarettes while on the telephone.
❏ Keep background sounds, such as a radio, low.
❏ Avoid talking on the telephone and talking with a coworker at the same time. The telephone receiver will transmit sound even though the mouthpiece is covered.
❏ Use a pleasant, professional tone of voice. Convey through your voice that you are confident, reliable, and capable. Avoid slang, "yeah," and "OK," as well as technical words a caller may not understand.
❏ Be cheerful and positive.
❏ Vary your pitch. Keep your pitch just above your best note to open a phone conversation. Use a lower pitch when emphasizing words. Lower your voice and pitch when making telephone calls in an open room.
❏ Speak loud enough to be heard.
❏ Enunciate clearly. Use words to identify letters in spelling names and places.

A as in Able	E as in Edward
B as in Boy	F as in Frank
C as in Charles	G as in George
D as in Dog	H as in Henry

I as in India	R as in Robert
J as in John	S as in Sugar
K as in King	T as in Thomas
L as in Lincoln	U as in Uniform
M as in Mary	V as in Victor
N as in November	W as in William
O as in Ocean	X as in X-ray
P as in Peter	Y as in Young
Q as in Queen	Z as in Zero

❑ Use careful pronunciation.

❑ Talk slowly enough to be understood. Talk at about the same pace as the caller.

❑ Address people by their names and titles.

❑ Use courteous phrases such as "thank you," "please," and "you're welcome."

❑ Respond verbally with "yes" and "I see" when someone else is talking so they will know you are still there and listening.

❑ Handle as many calls as possible yourself without asking for a supervisor's assistance.

❑ End the phone call pleasantly and professionally, preferably using the caller's name; for example, "It's been nice talking with you, Ms. Fortino."

❑ Let the caller hang up first. Hang up gently and securely.

❑ Return calls promptly.

❑ Do not worry about your regional or foreign accent unless others have a difficult time understanding you.

❑ Follow through with promises.

ANSWERING INCOMING CALLS

It is important that a secretary and supervisor communicate daily in order to handle incoming calls effectively. The following suggestions help a supervisor and secretary keep each other informed. (For additional suggestions about time management, see Chapter 3.)

❑ Meet the first thing in the morning to go over the schedule and prepare for the day.

❑ If your supervisor is working under a deadline, find out if anyone else might handle his or her calls or visitors.

❑ Find out whose calls are expected in order to help screen calls.

❑ Know ahead of time names of people whose calls should be transferred, no matter what the situation. Be aware that not every call from an important person is urgent.

Phones should be answered according to company policy, if there is one, and in such a way that a caller never has to guess whether it is the right number. Below are some suggested ways to answer phones:

Answering for the company:
"Good morning, Professional Secretaries International."
"Professional Secretaries International, Maria speaking."

Answering for a department:
"Sales, Maria Carlson speaking."
"Publications, Ms. Goodman. May I help you?"
Answering another person's phone:
"Dr. Fenner's office, James speaking."
Answering your own phone:
"Purchasing, Glenn Cushner speaking."

Here are some hints regarding proper phone use:

❏ Say "good morning" or "good afternoon" first to greet the caller in a friendly way.
❏ Giving your name enables the caller to address you in the conversation.
❏ If you are going to be away from your desk, ask someone to answer your phone or forward it to another phone, voice mail, or an answering machine.

The following suggestions help make a positive impression on incoming callers:

❏ Answer immediately, preferably on the first ring but before the third ring.
❏ Be prepared. If you are right-handed, place the telephone on your left so the right hand is available to take notes. Reverse the position if you are left-handed. And always have the following available: pen or pencil, message pad, watch or clock for noting the time, company extension numbers, and telephone books.
❏ Determine who is calling if that information is not volunteered by the caller; for example, "May I ask who's calling, please?" or "May I tell Mr. Manager who's calling?"
❏ Verify the pronunciation of the caller's name.
❏ Be discreet. Avoid disclosing personal information; for example, "He's not in yet"; "She's still at lunch"; "He usually doesn't work on Thursday afternoons—that's his day for golf." Step outside the office if a coworker or host takes an important call while you are there. If they motion you to stay seated, read any materials you may have brought to their office or look out the window. Discretion, however, does not include dishonesty. A secretary should never be expected to lie for colleagues or supervisors; it is unethical.
❏ Determine which calls are urgent and decide on the appropriate person to handle it. If a call is urgent, it may be necessary to interrupt a meeting or conference discreetly with a note indicating who is waiting on the phone.
❏ Thank the caller for calling before transferring to the desired destination. (See the heading *Transferring Calls* below for additional information.)

ANSWERING SIMULTANEOUS INCOMING CALLS

In order to answer a phone by the third ring, it may be necessary to interrupt one conversation to answer another line. When several incoming calls occur at once, use the following technique:

1. Put the caller on hold. (See the heading *Holding Calls* below.)
2. Answer the next call.
3. Complete the second call only if it can be handled quickly.
4. Return to the original call promptly.

HOLDING CALLS

Being put on hold irritates many callers. Anyone using a telephone needs to be sensitive to this and do everything possible to be polite and attentive. The following suggestions help promote goodwill even if a caller is put on hold.

❑ Ask permission to put the caller on hold. For example, say "May I put you on hold?" or "Is it convenient to hold or would you prefer to call back?"; avoid "I have to put you on hold" or "Can I put you on hold?" Always wait for a response.

❑ Check back every 30 to 40 seconds while the person is on hold. Thank them for holding and ask if they wish to continue holding. Avoid keeping callers on hold for more than a minute or two unless that is their preference.

❑ Inform the caller if the wait is longer than you anticipated; for example: "Thank you for holding, Mr. Customer. Ms. Manager is still on the other line. Do you want to continue holding or would you prefer to have her call you back?"

TRANSFERRING CALLS

Know how the transfer procedure works on your telephone system to avoid losing a caller during the transfer process. Remember to give the caller enough information to call back in case the transfer process does not work. When transferring calls, the following procedures are helpful:

❑ Transfer calls only if you are unable to help the caller.

❑ Ask permission to transfer calls.

❑ If you do not know where to transfer a call, put the caller on hold and ask coworkers for assistance.

❑ Give the name and complete telephone number to the caller in case the call is disconnected during the transfer process. For example: "Mr. Customer, I think the Service Department is better able to answer your question than I am. If you don't mind, I'm transferring you to Mr. Howe's office. His number is 483-3002 in case you need to call again."

❑ Suggest having the call returned instead of transferred if the caller complains about having been transferred several times.

❑ Give the called party any helpful information. For example, "Carol Sekor of North Bay Construction is holding; she has a question about last month's invoice."

CUTTING SHORT A CALL

Sometimes it is necessary to terminate a call. It takes skill to end a call with enough tact that the caller feels good about the conversation. The following suggestions are useful for cutting short a call:

❑ Give a short, sincere explanation for getting off the telephone; for example, "I'm sorry to cut this short, but I have a visitor waiting to see me" or "Excuse me, but I have a call on the other line."

❏ Make plans to get back with the caller if necessary; for example, "We have a staff meeting in five minutes; may I call you back?" or "Excuse me, but I'm trying to get a letter ready for overnight delivery; may I call you back?"

TAKING MESSAGES

Taking accurate messages is vital when answering the telephone for others. By some estimates, 90 percent of messages contain incorrect information, with errors ranging from name and phone number to reason for calling.

To avoid taking messages or having someone place a call back, try to help the caller yourself; for example: "Ms. Wong is out of the office. I expect her back after 3:00. I'm her administrative assistant and work very closely with her. May I help you?

If it is necessary to take a message, keep these points in mind.

❏ Use a form. In fact, fill out a form even if the caller indicates they will call back.
❏ Include both the time and date.
❏ Write legibly.
❏ Verify the caller's name, company name, and phone number by repeating back the information.
❏ Include as much information as possible to help the caller return the call. Attach to the message slip any material (e.g., files, invoices) that may be helpful in answering the call.
❏ Deliver the message promptly.

SCREENING CALLS

The purpose of screening calls is to decide whether to transfer a call or take a message. Screening must not offend the caller. The following suggestions are helpful when screening calls.

❏ Avoid giving the impression that calls are being screened. Avoid asking the caller's name *first* and *then* saying the manager is unavailable. Instead, immediately state that the manager is unavailable and ask if the call can be returned, in the process finding out who is calling. If it happens to be someone the manager wishes to talk with, the call can be transferred or the following statement can be made, "May I put you on hold while I see if I can interrupt her?"
❏ Use judgment in determining whether the supervisor needs to talk to every important person (including relatives or higher-ranking people) immediately. It may be necessary to say, "Mr. Nunes is in a staff meeting. Do you want me to interrupt him?"
❏ Transfer a call if it is an emergency.

PLACING OUTGOING CALLS

All businesses make outgoing calls. The manner of handling outgoing calls is just as important as prompt, courteous service for incoming calls. Before placing an outgoing call, you must have a reason for calling and know what you want to accomplish. This takes planning even before picking up the telephone receiver. Use the following guidelines in placing outgoing calls:

❏ Know the name of the person you want to reach and how to pronounce it. Check the pronunciation with others if you are unsure.

❏ Verify the phone number before calling. Keep frequently called numbers in an address book. Calling Information for a number often costs money.

❏ If you reach a wrong number, do not just hang up; say, "I'm sorry; I must have dialed the wrong number." If the wrong number is long distance, immediately call the operator to receive credit on the phone bill.

❏ Plan outgoing calls in advance. Have all materials available and make an outline or rough script (but sound natural when talking).

❏ Group outgoing calls one after another to save time—but leave some time between each call in case someone is trying to reach you.

❏ Avoid the hours of noon to 2:00 p.m. and any other times you know to be inconvenient. Take different time zones into consideration.

❏ Identify yourself immediately; for example, "This is Colleen Peppard of Hargrave and Johnson."

❏ Ask if it is convenient to talk. If it is not convenient, make an appointment to call back; for example: "Can you talk for a minute? I have three items to discuss about the conference next week."

❏ Avoid calling people at home unless they request that you do so.

❏ Insist on calling back if the connection is faulty.

HANDLING COMPLAINTS AND ANGRY CALLERS

Resolving complaints is important to the success of any business. You want to do all you can to retain the customer or client. Angry people may use abusive language, exaggeration, sarcasm, or personal attacks. While you cannot control the angry person, you can control your reaction to the situation.

Here are suggestions for handling complaints and angry callers:

❏ Listen to the complaint. Avoid interrupting until the entire complaint has been stated, getting emotionally involved, reacting to a personal attack, and allowing yourself to get angry.

❏ To angry callers focusing on their anger or on personal attacks, say, "It would really help if we could keep the conversation on the problem."

❏ If the caller is angry, pause before you respond and respond politely. If the caller is extremely angry, ask if you can call back. If the caller refuses, ask if you may have some time to collect needed information. This additional time may allow the caller to calm down. Putting angry people on hold may upset them more. Instead, put the phone on the desk. Express regret with a statement such as, "I'm sorry for your inconvenience."

❏ Find a way to agree with their circumstances. Say something like, "I understand what you are going through; I'd be upset too if it had happened to me."

❑ Ask open-ended questions that allow people to further explain the problem; for example, "You feel the last shipment . . . ?" (Allow the other person to finish the sentence.)

❑ Suggest three or four alternatives for handling the problem that (1) you are able to do and (2) you have the authority to do. Do *not* say, "Company policy says we can't." A statement like this says you do not make decisions, and the caller may demand to talk to a supervisor. An example of giving alternatives is saying, "I cannot give you your money back, but you can pick out another product of equal value or have credit toward another purchase."

❑ Follow up in a week to make certain the problem is resolved. Ask if there is anything else that would be of assistance.

ARRANGING A CONFERENCE CALL

A conference call is a telephone call involving three or more people. Many computerized phones have a conference call feature that allows the office professional to set up a call from the office telephone.

If the phone system does not have conference call capability, operator assistance is necessary. In the front of most phone directories is information on how to set up a conference call. Charges are added for the number of places connected, distance, and length of conference. If possible, give the operator advance notice of the call.

The steps for setting up the conference call are:

1. Check with the participants on their availability. Do not forget time zone differences.

2. Set the time of the conference call. Either notify the participants by telephone or in writing of the time according to their time zone.

3. Fax or mail an agenda ahead of time. This information helps participants gather materials and be better prepared for the call.

If operator assistance is necessary, dial 0 for the operator and explain that you wish to make a conference call. Give the operator the names and phone numbers of those taking part in the call and the time of the day of the call.

VOICE MAIL SYSTEMS

A voice mail system is a computerized answering machine. Messages are sent, retrieved, and saved on computer. When replayed, the person's voice sounds like it does on an answering machine.

Voice mail has the following features:

- It answers and routes large numbers of incoming calls at once.
- It provides important information, such as office hours or numbers to call for more information.
- It allows direct dialing from different locations to retrieve messages.
- It forwards calls to other locations, such as to home or a hotel.

- It allows callers to leave detailed messages in their own voices.
- It reduces the length of a phone call because communication is one-way.
- It allows people in different time zones to stay in touch 24 hours a day.
- It can send the same message to many people at preprogrammed phone numbers.

The message on the voice mail system should take into consideration the following factors:

❑ Rotary phones cannot access extensions or use the keypad for codes like touch-tone phones can.

❑ Some people prefer to talk with people instead of machines. Voice mail should make that option available.

❑ Avoid catching callers in an "endless loop" of pressing buttons so that they are not able to reach their intended party or get their questions answered.

For example, when you call Professional Secretaries International, you are connected to a recorded voice that says: "Thank you for calling Professional Secretaries International. If you know your party's extension, you may dial it now. If you are calling from a rotary telephone, please hold. If you are calling from a touch-tone telephone, please dial 0 for assistance. Thank you."

GIVING AND TAKING MACHINE DICTATION

One way to increase productivity is to dictate correspondence into a machine for later typing or word processing. Dictators can often speak at least five times faster than they write.

The following are suggestions for giving dictation:

❑ Prioritize and organize material. A written outline is helpful. Have reference materials or files handy.

❑ Identify yourself.

❑ Indicate the type of dictation (letter, memo, report).

❑ Give the approximate length and format of correspondence. If the machine has a counter, keep a list of the numbers at the start and end of a document.

❑ Indicate the type of stationery, number of copies, and enclosures.

❑ Speak at an even rate and enunciate clearly.

❑ Spell anything that could be misunderstood.

❑ Mention special punctuation marks.

❑ Indicate the beginning of a new paragraph.

❑ Press the pause key or button (or on/off switch) if it is necessary to stop and think.

❑ When using cassettes, mark the outside of each cassette with the date and other identification. Also, do not erase tapes until the dictation is transcribed.

Transcribing a dictated document takes special skill. You must listen attentively and interpret words correctly and accurately. The following are suggestions for transcribing dictation:

❏ Know the equipment by reading the manual.

❏ Have all supplies ready, such as letterhead, envelopes, and plain paper.

❏ Place reference materials and dictionaries on or near the workstation.

❏ Listen to instructions that may contain information on the order in which to transcribe the items.

❏ Transcribe confidential dictation when few interruptions are likely to occur. Do not leave transcription on the desk where others can read it when you are not around.

❏ Listen to as much material as you can remember at one time to avoid rewinding and listening to the same material twice. Try to keep keying constantly.

❏ Listen for pauses to indicate punctuation or the end of a sentence.

❏ Think about the content while transcribing in order to detect any inconsistencies or information that does not make sense.

❏ Be alert for words that sound alike but have different meanings.

❏ Proofread carefully. Use the dictionary or spell-checker software packages to check for errors. Read the document on the screen before printing to make certain it makes sense.

❏ Submit priority or rush items as soon as they are completed.

CHAPTER 22

ELECTRONIC COMMUNICATIONS

Electronic communications and telecommunications allow data to be electronically transferred from one point within an information system to another. In today's office, computers and other equipment can now be linked together to expedite the exchange of information within a business and between organizations. Telecommunications technology is quickly changing the way businesses operate.

Computer networks can be set up to distribute information within a department or an office, through a local area network (LAN), or between different locations through a wide area network (WAN). Databases provide computers with an organized means of storing large amounts of information. Public databases are available that make information available to users for a fee. Finally, teleconferencing is a way for people to meet together through electronic means without having to travel great distances.

COMPUTER NETWORKS

A computer network ties different functions together electronically, allowing for improved communication and greater sharing of information among individuals, departments, other offices or satellite offices, and other locations. Networking can also reduce equipment costs because it allows several PC users to share expensive peripheral equipment, such as laser printers and high-capacity disk drives.

The administration and management of a network is usually handled by a computer professional. Any problems arising in a network usually happen because of technical and programming issues. However, it is helpful for office professionals to understand the function of networking equipment and the terms used to describe it.

LOCAL AREA NETWORKS

A local area network (LAN) is used to distribute information in an office through different terminals, called **nodes**, that are connected to a central information depository, called a **server**. The server manages the flow of information betweeen computers hooked together on the LAN, somewhat like a traffic cop who manages the flow of traffic. The server also enables users to share peripheral equipment, disk drives, and data files.

The server is connected to each terminal or node in the network by some kind of cable (twisted-pair, coaxial, or fiber-optic). The cable is connected to a controller card in each computer terminal. The controller card interprets the messages going to and from the network. Recently, wireless LANs have been developed that use a radio frequency or infrared light to transmit information, eliminating the need for cables.

The configuration, or **topology**, of a LAN is the way each unit fits together and communicates with the network. There are three basic configurations: the star, the bus, and the token ring.

Star configuration: Every computer in the network is connected to the server, which is the heart of the star configuration. Each user can communicate with every other user by passing information through the central server. It is the easiest configuration to install.

Bus configuration: Each terminal is connected by cable to the next in the network. Information flows over the wire to all the connected computers. Each terminal acts as a "bus stop" along the wire, but each reads only its own messages.

Token ring configuration: All the network's computers are wired together in a closed circle. An electrical signal, called the **token**, is passed around the ring or network. The signal contains information that is collected and distributed around the network. Users specify where on the ring they want their data or message to go. Although this seems to be the most reliable configuration, the software is complex and has a greater chance of losing or garbling data.

ELECTRONIC MAIL

A major application of computer networks is electronic mail, or E-mail. E-mail is the sending and receiving of messages in electronic form between computers in a network. Messages can be stored, saved, and edited. They can also be forwarded to another user or users, and copies of a message can be sent to other users. A user can also reply to a message. (See section on Electronic Mail Delivery Systems in Chapter 16.)

TIME-SHARING SYSTEMS

Time-sharing systems permit an organization to allocate the cost per user. Each user has a low-cost terminal that is supported by a central computer, usually a mainframe, shared with multiple users. The terminals and peripheral devices are tied together by the communications network. These systems can be used for word processing. A variety of packaged

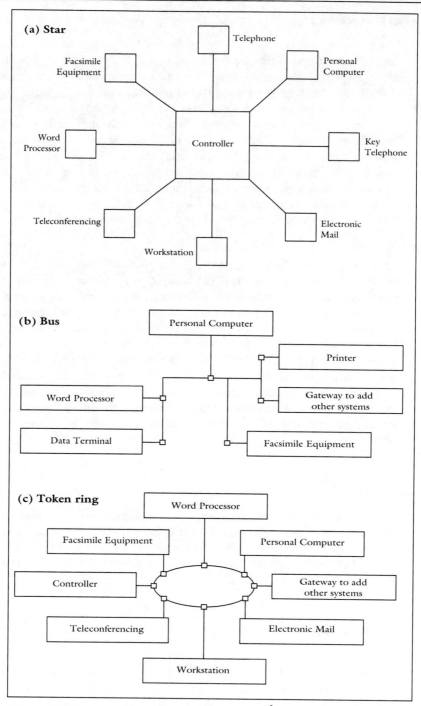

Figure 22-1 Star, bus, and token ring networks. *(Courtesy of Frederick R. Feldman of the Feldman Group Inc.)*

programs allow the development of management systems, and several programming languages exist for the development of other specialized applications.

MODEMS AND OTHER INTERFACE DEVICES

Computers operate using *digitally* encoded electronic signals (see section on The Computer in Chapter 7). On the other hand, telephone lines transmit *analog* electronic signals. In order for a computer to transmit and receive information over a telephone line, a **modem** is needed at each end. Modem stands for "modulator-demodulator." A modem translates (or "modulates") digital signals into analog signals for transmission over a phone line. At the other end, another modem converts the analog signals back into digital form for the receiving computer. A modem is sometimes also called a **data set**.

This integration of phone lines and computer systems allows information to be transmitted by voice or as data. Electronic typewriters and terminals equipped with modems can communicate as easily as humans can by making a phone call.

There are various other kinds of interface devices that allow communication between different types of equipment. They include the following:

Port extenders: These devices turn a machine's single communications outlet, or "port," into two or three channels, allowing the machine to interface with more than one device at a time.

Protocol converters: These are also known as "black boxes." They are programmed to convert or translate from the codes and modes, or protocols, of one type of equipment to the protocols of another, and vice versa.

Media converters: These allow files stored on floppy disk by one program, such as a word processor, or on one brand of computer to be converted to a different program, such as another word processing or a composition program, or to a file compatible with a different brand of computer.

The type of phone system used in the office is important when considering modems and other devices. Currently most office phone systems are PBX systems. These are telephone facilities within an office or office building that connect to the public phone network. (PBX stands for Private Branch eXchange.)

However, an international effort to set communications standards has resulted in the Integrated Services Digital Network (ISDN). When fully operational, ISDN will let users make complex connections among different telecommunications resources. ISDN will allow the exchange of data, text, voice, graphics, and video over one line. Currently, several different lines must be used. When upgrading a telephone system, a company or office should choose a system that can be upgraded to the ISDN standards in order to meet future requirements.

ELECTRONIC COMMUNICATIONS THROUGH DATABASES

A database provides computers with a means of storing information. It is a large and continuously updated file on a particular subject or subjects.

Databases can be used for various applications. They are limited only by the user's imagination and needs. Small and large companies use databases to maintain inventories or process orders. Banks use databases to maintain checking and savings accounts. The government uses databases to track income taxes owed by citizens. Databases can be private or public.

PRIVATE DATABASES

A private database is one developed specifically for a company or organization that is not available to the general public. An example of a private database would be the customer list for XYZ Company. This database would contain information on customers, their orders, their addresses, etc. It would be used by management and office professionals.

Private databases are generally determined by the computer sophistication of a company. It is important to understand that a well-organized database can quickly help employees analyze, compute, and report what might otherwise take months to do manually. It could be the responsibility of the office professional to help establish a database or work with the management information system personnel to use and further develop the database.

PUBLIC DATABASES

Information utilities have capitalized on the explosion in the need for information. An information utility is any organization that will let an individual use its information (or someone else's), usually for a fee. The information utility may use one database or several and offer many services. An individual can search and retrieve information on a variety of topics from airline information, to news and sports, to stock quotes. Different utilities specialize in different types of information.

To reach these information utilities, an individual typically either calls directly or calls through Telenet, Tymnet, or Uninet (three services that save long-distance phone charges). When connected with the utility, a person logs on, using a password and account number. Prices for these utilities range from a few dollars to several hundred dollars per hour. Some have sign-up charges, monthly minimums, subscriptions, consulting fees, and other fees associated with their use. A thorough understanding of these fees is necessary to avoid possible billing problems.

Information utilities are an outgrowth of several different technologies. They combine communications technologies (information delivered by phone lines, cable, or television), space technology (satellites), and computer technology (software and computer programming used to assemble large amounts of information or databases and retrieve them).

Information utilities offer various kinds of service, including transaction-based, communication-based, and information-based. Transaction-based services include shopping services, computerized classifieds, theater ticket sales, plane reservations, and at-home banking. It is essentially shopping by computer. Within the office, the service that would probably be utilized most is the one for making plane reservations.

Communication-based services include E-mail (see above), computerized bulletin boards, and on-line conferences. E-mail is a service that is used to send a message to anyone also using the system. A message is sent to a person's electronic mailbox. The next time that person goes to read his or her mail, the message will be there. CompuServe, for example, provides an electronic mailbox service for its subscribers.

Computerized bulletin boards function like real bulletin boards. A message is "posted" in the system and can be read. Usually bulletin boards are devoted to one subject or group of people, such as all users of IBM personal computers or individuals with the same hobby. Most are small and independent, operated by clubs, computer stores, or even by individuals. To use them, a modem, telephone, and computer are needed. Merely dial an access number and log on to the system. To "log on" simply means that an individual has electronically connected into the system—in this case, the bulletin board.

On-line conferences or forums are written conversations between two or more people. Such conferences can be a club or professional group "meeting" in different locations by computer.

Information-based services are really electronic libraries. They contain everything from bibliographic research services to stock market quotes to electronic newspapers. This service is particularly useful for doing research reports. Reference information is available in abstract and/or full-text form.

Using on-line databases requires some special knowledge and involves certain considerations. Professionals are available in many companies to search on-line databases for the necessary information. However, if the responsibility is the office professional's, several tips are offered here:

❏ Don't be intimidated. The more you use a database service, the easier it gets.

❏ Take a course. Many database services offer training sessions.

❏ Check the bulletin board. On-line bulletin boards and communications services can be used for learning more about database searches.

❏ Be prepared. Know what you are looking for before going on-line.

❏ Remember that every database is unique and may require special search techniques.

❏ When searching through full text, first look at headlines and first paragraphs. Then focus on those that seem most promising.

❏ If possible, make global searches of all databases that may be of interest.

❏ Every database is priced differently. Try the less expensive ones first.

❏ Download the documents you want and read them later to reduce on-line time. Save them on disk instead of printing.

❏ If your research needs are varied or infrequent it may make sense to pay a professional to do the searching.

INFORMATION UTILITIES

Just as there are different services offered, there are also different kinds of information utilities. Each uses different technology. They are (1) teletext, (2) videotext, and (3) interactive databases.

TELETEXT

This is an information utility that sends its information by television. Teletext is a generic term that applies to several different specific systems. One of those systems is used by PBS, NBC, ABC, and CBS in their closed-caption system for the hearing impaired.

Each "page" contains one screen of information and is sent along with the regular television transmission. The system puts the teletext information into the black bars that show up between normal television picture frames.

To use teletext, a special adaptor is required. The pages include a table of contents with the page numbers. When the page number is entered into the adaptor, that page shows up on the television screen.

Teletext has limitations, however. It is strictly one-way communication. It takes about 1 second to transmit 4 pages. If 100 pages are being transmitted, it takes about 25 seconds to broadcast. If information from a particular page is needed quickly, the wait may be irritating.

VIDEOTEXT

This is an information utility that puts information into a computer (text or graphics or both), transmits that information, and displays that information on a modified television set (in the form of pages). Using videotext is much the same as using teletext. An individual sits in front of the television with an adaptor, punches in the numbers of the pages wanted, and the pages show up on the screen. With this system, connection is directly to a computer. The television functions like a computer terminal. The system is asked directly what is wanted, and it will respond.

INTERACTIVE DATABASES

These services are available on-line (i.e., connected by personal computer terminal to the service's mainframe computer) or off-line. The latter type is available through CD-ROM disks. The on-line type of system uses time-sharing (technology that allows many people to use the same computer at the same time). An interactive process allows a command to be entered to find all information dealing with a specific topic. It is not necessary to look through menus—the system tells what stories or information fit the description. From that listing, a selection can be made of the ones to review. The computer then pulls those articles from the database.

A new technology is the use of CD-ROM (compact optical disks) for providing interactive information. Instead of connecting on-line using the computer terminal, the subscriber is sent a CD-ROM disk that can be accessed by a special drive attached to the personal computer. Many on-line databases, such as Educational Resource Information Clearinghouse (ERIC), are now available on CD-ROM. The advantage of CD-ROM is that it saves telephone costs. The disadvantage is that information is not always up to the minute.

APPLICATIONS OF ELECTRONIC COMMUNICATIONS

Communication systems can be used to hold informal or formal meetings, ranging from 2 people to 25,000. In each case, technology can play a vital part in relaying information.

One form of meeting is through teleconferencing. With the rising costs in travel, the increased demands on executives' time, and the global emphasis in business, teleconferencing allows people at different locations to hear and see one another without leaving their offices. Teleconferences can be broken into three general categories: audiographic, audio, and video. Although these methods differ in the technologies used, they have several things in common:

- They use a telecommunications channel and station equipment.
- They link people at multiple locations.
- They are interactive, providing two-way communications.
- They are dynamic, allowing the active participation of users.

AUDIOGRAPHIC TELECONFERENCES

Audiographic teleconferences transmit words, numbers, or graphics. Such teleconferences include the following:

Desktop computer conferences: Individuals use computer terminals and telephone lines to access a host computer in order to communicate with one another. Participants do not have to be gathered at telephones or in conference rooms at the same time. They can input their comments to the computer at their convenience, as long as the comments are given prior to the deadline established by the conference manager. The advantage of a computer conference is that all participants can review and comment on any material filed in the host computer on their own schedules, in their offices.

Slow-scan video: A camera scans an image from top to bottom for transmission over a phone line to a receiving monitor. It is best used for transmission of documents such as blueprints and schematics.

Freeze-frame video: Freeze-frame or slow-scan television adds visuals to an audio teleconference. Graphics are placed in front of a standard closed-circuit TV camera. The camera is connected to a scan converter that changes the picture into a still image that is then sent over a telephone line or other link.

Faxes: Faxing involves the transmission of an exact copy of something over communications lines.

Electronic blackboard: Similar to a classroom blackboard, this device sends graphics over an ordinary telephone line. Meeting participants write on the board, and the writing appears on a monitor (screen) in the other locations.

Electronic mail (E-mail): This is a message system for sending information from one person to others. E-mail systems are usually programs on computer networks.

AUDIO TELECONFERENCES

Audio teleconferences involve the transmission of sound only. A conference call uses a telephone to connect a number of people in a joint call at a designated time. A speakerphone is used to allow a person to take notes, walk around the room, or consult files during the conference call.

VIDEO TELECONFERENCES

Video teleconferencing allows several groups to meet via television cameras. They can view one another as well as see information presented through visual aids. Each room is equipped with cameras and other video and sound equipment so that pictures and voices will be clear.

USING ELECTRONIC EQUIPMENT IN THE MEETING ROOM

The workplace is shifting from one-person, one-task operations to group interactions and meetings. As a result, technology is being used more and more to bring people together. Meetings now include sophisticated electronic equipment. Video conferencing is becoming the affordable alternative to project reports, planning sessions, sales training, product development meetings, and financial reviews.

There are a number of organizations that specialize in teleconferencing, ranging from consultants to a complete system. The use of outside sources depends on the degree of involvement expected of office professionals as well as their knowledge of the equipment. Users of such equipment should expect to be trained by professionals. Training includes control panel operations (the "buttons" used to operate the equipment), graphics capabilities, seating arrangements, room scheduling, and troubleshooting.

As an office professional, you may be expected to prepare the visuals to be used during the meeting. Try to keep them simple, bold, colorful, accurate, and informative. Always make them easy to read by mixing upper- and lowercase letters and justifying the left margin. The following guidelines will help to make your visuals readable:

- Minimize the complexity and use one idea per visual.
- Do not be wordy.
- Keep the length of the text short, about six or seven lines per visual.
- Do not crowd the visual with more than one illustration.
- Use words with few syllables, two or three at most.
- Keep the letters large and bold so they can be read in the back of the meeting room.
- Keep the number of type sizes per page limited to a maximum of three.
- A maximum of four colors per visual is recommended.

Several table shapes have been developed for teleconferencing. They include the following:

- Canoe-shaped—an oval table with participants seated side by side along one side.
- Keystone—a solid "V" shaped table, with users sitting along both outside edges facing one another.
- Curved—a table bent in a crescent shape, with users seated on the long edge of the curve.

The canoe and curved formats have the advantage of placing every person the same distance from both cameras and video monitors.

General guidelines for watching a video on a monitor are as follows:

❑ People should be seated about 10 feet from a 19-inch image and about 9 feet from a 27-inch screen.

❑ Minimum viewing distance from a standard monitor is two to four times the width of the image. For color monitors, however, viewers must be at least six feet from the image.

❑ Maximum viewing distance from a monitor is estimated to be between 12 and 14 times the image width.

❑ Seat placement within 45 degrees of the center of the screen is acceptable.

❑ A screen should be angled 5 degrees below a viewer's straight vertical line of sight for the best results.

❑ Seats should directly face a monitor.

PART V

GRAMMAR AND PUNCTUATION REVIEW

CHAPTER 23

GRAMMAR

Office professionals must understand the basic rules of English grammar in order to communicate ideas clearly and effectively. The importance of good written or oral communication skills cannot be overemphasized. Words or groups of words belong to classifications known as parts of speech. The eight parts of speech are adjectives, adverbs, conjunctions, interjections, nouns, prepositions, pronouns, and verbs. The use of the word or word group in a sentence determines its classification.

ADJECTIVES

Adjectives clarify sentences by describing nouns (persons, places, or things) and pronouns. They add additional information to these nouns and pronouns, or they show comparisons between and among items. Adjectives may be words, phrases, or clauses. They answer these questions.

What kind?	We found an *old* newspaper.
How many?	The *six* reviews were favorable.
How much?	He received *some* money from his employer.
Whose?	She received *her* paycheck last Friday.
Which one?	*That* computer is too expensive.

Adjectives may appear in several places in sentences. They may precede the nouns they describe; they may immediately follow the nouns they describe or explain; they may begin sentences; or they may follow linking verbs. (See below, Verbs—Linking Verbs.)

Betty is an *excellent* typist.

The employees, *exhausted and weary*, worked extra hours.

Exhausted and weary, the employees worked extra hours.

She was *furious.*

Adjectives may limit or describe. Descriptive adjectives indicate the qualities or types of persons, places, or things involved. More than one adjective can describe a noun or pronoun.

Organized, competent office professionals are in great demand.

Descriptive adjectives may be common or proper. Proper adjectives are derived from proper nouns; they are usually capitalized. When proper adjectives have taken on a specialized meaning, do not capitalize them.

I hope this will not be a *dull* meeting.

The *English* language is used in many countries.

Our company specializes in building *china* cabinets.

Other adjectives limit the meaning of a noun by showing either possession, number, or identity. These adjectives may be definite or general.

His report is well organized.

We ordered *two* computers for the office.

This assignment is challenging.

ARTICLES AS ADJECTIVES

The words *a, an,* and *the* are articles. Articles always modify nouns, and they are of two types—definite and indefinite.

The is a definite article. It designates a definite person or thing. *The* may be used with singular or plural nouns.

The overhead projector will be needed for my presentation.

Do you have *the* reports for our meeting?

A and *an* are indefinite articles. They are used when no specific person or thing needs to be described. They are used only with singular nouns. Always determine the use of *a* or *an* on the basis of the initial sound; do *not* rely on the initial letter.

I have developed *a* plan I would like to review with you.

My flight leaves in less than *an* hour.

❑ Use *a* before a word with a consonant sound.

a desk
a human

❏ Use *an* before a word with a silent *h*.

> *an* hour
> *an* honor

❏ Use *an* before a word beginning with a vowel (a, e, i, o, u) sound.

> *an* event
> *an* image
> *an* undercover agent

❏ Use *a* before a word with a long *u* sound.

> *a* unit
> *a* university

❏ Use *a* before a word beginning with an *o* that sounds like *w*.

> *a* one-way ticket

❏ Do not use *a* or *an* after *kind of, type of, sort of.*

> What kind of format shall we use?

❏ Place the article before the first adjective when two or more adjectives modify one noun.

> *The* tall brown building is the oldest building in the city.

❏ Use an article before *each* noun when two persons, places, or things are represented. Do not repeat the article when only one person, place, or thing is involved.

> *The* president and *the* chairman of the board hosted the reception. (Two people hosted the reception.)
> *The* president and chairman of the board hosted the reception. (One person hosted the reception.)
> We ordered *a* crab and *a* shrimp salad. (Two salads are involved—one is crab, and the other is shrimp.)
> We ordered *a* crab and shrimp salad. (One salad has both crab and shrimp in it.)

NUMERICAL ADJECTIVES

Numerical adjectives are ordinal numbers (e.g., *seventh* day) or cardinal numbers (e.g., *one* day). Ordinal numbers appear before cardinal numbers.

> My *first ten* days of vacation were relaxing.

DEMONSTRATIVE ADJECTIVES

Demonstrative pronouns may also be used as *demonstrative adjectives.* (See below, Pronouns—Demonstrative Pronouns.) *This* and *that* are singular forms and describe singular nouns. *These* and *those* are plural forms and describe plural nouns. The word *them* is never used as an adjective.

> *That* report is the one you requested.
> *Those* reports must be in our clients' offices by 4 p.m.

This and *these* describe objects that are near; *that* and *those* describe objects that are farther away.

> *These* figures are current; *those* other figures are out of date.

❏ Do not use *this here* or *that here.*

> This statement is inaccurate.

❏ Use the singular forms of the nouns *kind, sort,* and *type* with the adjectives *this* and *that.* Use a singular verb with this construction.

> *This kind* of paper *is* best for our printer.

❏ Use the plural forms of the nouns *kind, sort,* and *type* with the adjectives *these* and *those.* Use a plural verb with this construction.

> *These kinds* of disks *are* expensive.
> *Those data are* inaccurate.

POSSESSIVE ADJECTIVES

When possessive nouns and possessive pronouns function as adjectives, they are referred to as *possessive adjectives.* Possessive pronouns include *my, his, her, its, our, their, whose,* and *your.*

> *My* supervisor visited *our* plant in Detroit.
> *Allen's* work is confidential.

COMPARATIVE ADJECTIVES

Most adjectives can indicate degrees of comparison. The first degree is the *base* and shows no comparison unless it makes a comparison that shows equality; it is the *simple,* or *positive,* form. The second degree is the *comparative* form; it allows two persons or things to be compared. The third degree is the *superlative* degree; it compares more than two persons or things. The superlative degree also emphasizes a description of a person, place, or thing.

> My salary is *satisfactory.* (positive)
> My salary is *as high as* Jane's. (positive)

Our budget figures are *higher* this year than they were last year. (comparative)
Jane is the *most organized* employee in our department. (superlative)
You are the *greatest!* (superlative)

❏ For a one-syllable adjective, add *r* or *er* to the base word to form the comparative. Add *st* or *est* to the base word to form the superlative.

Positive	Comparative	Superlative
cheap	cheaper	cheapest
fast	faster	fastest
fine	finer	finest
long	longer	longest
wise	wiser	wisest

❏ For a one-syllable adjective ending with one consonant and preceded by one vowel, double the final consonant before adding *er* to form the comparative or *est* to form the superlative.

Positive	Comparative	Superlative
big	bigger	biggest
sad	sadder	saddest

❏ For a one- or two-syllable adjective ending in *y* and preceded by a consonant, change the *y* to *i* and add *er* to form the comparative or *est* to form the superlative.

Positive	Comparative	Superlative
happy	happier	happiest
lonely	lonelier	loneliest
lovely	lovelier	loveliest

❏ For other adjectives of two or more syllables, use *more* for the comparative degree and *most* for the superlative degree.

Positive	Comparative	Superlative
acceptable	more acceptable	most acceptable
active	more active	most active
capable	more capable	most capable
difficult	more difficult	most difficult
often	more often	most often

❏ When indicating a negative comparison, use *less* for the comparative degree and *least* for the superlative degree.

Shirley is *less* efficient than Karen.
Connie is the *least* efficient of any of the workers.

❏ When using the comparative degree, do not use both an *er* ending and *more*. Do not use both an *est* ending and *most* when using the superlative degree.
❏ For irregular adjectives, the words change in the comparative and superlative degrees.

Positive	Comparative	Superlative
bad	worse	worst
far	farther/further	farthest/furthest
good	better	best
ill	worse	worst
late	later/latter	latest/last
little	littler/less/lesser	littlest/least
many	more	most
much	more	most
well	better	best

❑ For a comparison involving both positive and comparative degrees, use *as* after the positive adjective and *than* after the comparative adjective.

Heather is *as competent as* but *less sociable than* Veronica.
(Incorrect: Heather is as competent but less sociable than Veronica.)

❑ When using the adjectives *superior, preferable,* or *inferior,* do not use *than;* use the word *to* after any of these three adjectives. These words do not have a comparative or superlative degree.

The accommodations at Benton Inn are *superior to* those at Roseburg Inn.

❑ When comparing one person or object with several others of the same group, use *other* or *else* and the comparative degree followed by *than.* Since an item cannot be compared with itself, the words *other* or *else* exclude the subject from the rest of the group. Do not use *other* or *else* with the superlative degree.

This meeting lasted longer than *any other* meeting we have attended.
(Incorrect: This meeting lasted longer than any meeting we have attended.)

ABSOLUTE ADJECTIVES

Absolute adjectives are not comparable (complete is complete) and do not require the comparative or superlative degrees. Most absolute adjectives require such words as *nearly, more nearly,* or *most nearly* to show a movement in the direction of a degree of comparison.

The file drawer is *full.*
Our final product was *perfect.*
The last set of graphics was *more nearly perfect* than the first set.

A list of absolute adjectives follows:

circular	dead	ideal
complete	eternal	immaculate
conclusive	final	impossible
correct	full	infinite

perfect	spotless	unanimous
perpendicular	square	unique
real	supreme	whole

INDEPENDENT ADJECTIVES

Independent adjectives (coordinate adjectives) are two or more adjectives modifying the same noun. The adjectives may or may not require a comma. Reverse the two adjectives or insert the word *and* between the adjectives to determine whether or not the adjectives are interdependent. If both tests can be performed without changing the meaning of the sentence, place a comma between the two adjectives. (See Chapter 24, Punctuation.)

She maintains a *steady, accurate* pace in her daily tasks.

COMPOUND ADJECTIVES

Compound adjectives consist of two or more words that appear before nouns or after linking verbs. Many compound adjectives have hyphens. The following general rules apply to the formation of compound adjectives. Check a current dictionary to determine the proper form for compound adjectives.

❑ Use a hyphen between the words when these words act as one modifier and precede the noun. In most cases, do not hyphenate these words when they follow verbs.

Repairs are necessary on my *two-year-old* car.

I reserved a room at a *first-class* hotel for my supervisor.

I prefer to fly *first class.*

❑ Use a hyphen when *well* is linked with another word and when the joined words appear before a noun. Do not use a hyphen when the combination is used elsewhere in the sentence.

Mrs. Robertson is a *well-known* speaker.

Mrs. Robertson is *well known* in the advertising field.

❑ Always use a hyphen when *self* is linked to another word.

The candidate appeared *self-confident* at the interview.

Beth is an example of someone with high *self-esteem.*

❑ Do not use a hyphen to link an adverb ending with *ly* to an adjective that follows.

It was a *fairly* pleasant day for our open-house mixer.

❑ Use a hyphen to link a number to a noun.

Your *four-page* analysis was routed to the sales representatives.

❏ Use a hyphen with an implied modifier.

All the *one-* and *two-story* condominiums have been purchased.

❏ Use a hyphen when a fraction functions as an adjective. Do not use a hyphen in a fraction that is a noun.

Two thirds of those present were opposed to the proposal.

A *two-thirds* vote is necessary to pass this bill.

❏ Use hyphens in numerical compound adjectives when the numbers 21 to 99 are written in words.

The view from my office on the *twenty-fifth* floor is superb.

❏ Use the singular form for a measurement in a hyphenated adjective that appears before a noun.

A courier service delivered the *50-pound* box of supplies.

INTERROGATIVE ADJECTIVES

Pronouns such as *who, what, which,* and *whose* may also be used as *interrogative adjectives.* (See below, Pronouns—Interrogative Pronouns.)

What skills do you think will be in great demand in ten years?

She asked *what* skills would be in great demand in ten years.

ADJECTIVE PHRASES

Adjective phrases modify nouns or pronouns and clarify the sentence. Prepositions connect the adjective phrases to a part of the sentence. (See Prepositions, below, for an extensive list.) Place an adjective phrase immediately after the noun it explains.

The temporary worker *from the local agency* will be leaving tomorrow.

ADJECTIVE CLAUSES

An adjective clause modifies a noun or pronoun. Adjective clauses begin with such words as *that, where, which,* and *who.* (See Chapter 24, Punctuation.) Place adjective clauses immediately after the nouns they describe. If adjective clauses are separated from the items modified, they are called misplaced modifiers. A misplaced modifier makes a sentence difficult to understand.

The records *that were requested* were on microfiche.

The candidates *who were interviewed* yesterday were well qualified.

The secretary *who was just hired* is a very organized worker.
(Incorrect: The secretary is a very organized worker who was just hired.)

❏ Use commas to show that the adjective clause is not necessary for the meaning of the sentence.

Mrs. Lister, *who is my supervisor,* is planning a business trip next week.

❏ Never use commas around an adjective clause that begins with *that.*

The company *that was selected for the award* has been in business for 20 years.

ADVERBS

Adverbs modify active verbs, adjectives, and other adverbs. They provide answers to the questions "how," "where," "when," "how often," and "to what extent." Adverbs may be words, phrases, or clauses.

When: She always completed her reports *promptly.*

Where: She is sitting *outside.*

How: We wrap every package *neatly.*

How often: She *seldom* arrives late for meetings.

To what extent: The client was *very* interested.

ADVERBS INDICATING "HOW"

Most adverbs answering the question "how" are formed by adding *ly* to an adjective.

safe	safely
slow	slowly
sincere	sincerely

Several exceptions occur in such words as *due, true,* and *whole.* Drop the *e* in these words before adding *ly.*

due	duly
true	truly
whole	wholly

Other exceptions include adjectives already ending in *ly,* such as *friendly, ugly, lonely,* and *lovely.*

ADVERBS INDICATING "WHEN" AND "HOW OFTEN"

early	now	then
finally	often	today
formerly	seldom	tomorrow
frequently	soon	yesterday

We telephoned the client *yesterday*.
The applicant *finally* arrived.

ADVERBS INDICATING "WHERE"

away	outside
here	there
inside	

Put the boxes *outside* my door.

ADVERBS INDICATING "TO WHAT EXTENT"

merely	rather	too
quite	really	very

We were *rather* disappointed with the survey response rate.

One-word adverbs must appear next to the adjectives or adverbs they describe. This is not true for adverbs that modify verbs; they may appear in different locations within the sentence.

I was *quite* anxious about the results of my job interview.
She reviews our work *frequently*.

CONJUNCTIVE ADVERBS

Conjunctive adverbs connect two independent clauses. Use a semicolon before the conjunctive adverb in the sentence. (See below, Conjunctions—Conjunctive Adverbs.) The list that follows consists of frequently used conjunctive adverbs.

accordingly	for example	in fact
additionally	for instance	in the meantime
also	furthermore	likewise
besides	however	meanwhile
consequently	in addition	moreover

nevertheless	so	therefore
on the contrary	still	thus
on the other hand	that is	yet
otherwise	then	

She received the promotion; *therefore,* she had to train another person to fill her position.

COMPARATIVE ADVERBS

Adverbs have three forms: positive, comparative, and superlative. The *positive* degree is the base form and shows no comparison unless it makes a comparison that shows equality. The *comparative* degree indicates a comparison about the way two persons or things act. The word *than* appears before the second item being compared. The *superlative* degree indicates a comparison about the way more than two persons or things act.

She proofreads her work *carefully.* (positive)
She proofreads *as carefully as* Tim. (positive)

We are responding to our customers' needs *more quickly* than usual. (comparative)
I plan to take my vacation *earlier* this year than I did last year. (comparative)

The second proposal is prepared *most logically* of all the reports. (superlative)
David arrived the *earliest.* (superlative)

❏ For most adverbs use *more* to indicate the comparative degree and *most* to indicate the superlative degree. A few adverbs indicate comparison by adding *er* to the base word for the comparative degree and *est* to the base word for the superlative degree.

Positive	Comparative	Superlative
early	earlier	earliest
efficiently	more efficiently	most efficiently
hard	harder	hardest
intelligently	more intelligently	most intelligently
often	more often	most often
sincerely	more sincerely	most sincerely
slow/slowly	slower/more slowly	slowest/most slowly
soon	sooner	soonest

❏ If the second item in a comparison is a group, class, or other body and the first item is a member of that group, use the word *other* in front of the second comparison item.

Allan arrived earlier than the *other* volunteers.

❏ For a comparison involving both positive and comparative degrees, use *as* after the positive adverb form and *than* after the comparative adverb form.

Shirley speaks *as clearly as* and *more forcibly than* Ursula speaks.

❑ Do not add *er* and *est* to adverbs ending in *ful*.

Positive	Comparative	Superlative
careful	more careful	most careful
wonderful	more wonderful	most wonderful

Some adverbs are irregular and do not form degrees of comparison in the usual way.

Positive	Comparative	Superlative
badly	worse	worst
far	farther/further	farthest/furthest
little	less	least
much	more	most
well	better	best

Mary speaks *well* before large audiences.

My supervisor writes *better* than most other supervisors.

ADVERBIAL PHRASES

Adverbial phrases may modify all elements of a sentence except the nouns or nounlike elements. They may appear in several locations in a sentence. Adverbial phrases use prepositions as their introductory words. (See Prepositions, below, for an extensive list.)

ADVERBIAL CLAUSES

Adverbial clauses are dependent clauses that modify all elements of a sentence except the nouns or nounlike elements. Adverbial clauses appear as introductions to independent clauses, or they appear after the independent clauses. Subordinate conjunctions introduce adverbial clauses. (See below, Conjunctions—Subordinate Conjunctions.)

CONJUNCTIONS

Conjunctions are connecting words. They connect words, phrases, and clauses. Conjunctions do not have objects. There are four types of conjunctions: coordinate conjunctions, conjunctive adverbs, correlative conjunctions, and subordinate conjunctions.

COORDINATE CONJUNCTIONS

Coordinate conjunctions join words, phrases, and clauses that are grammatically *equal* in importance. The most common coordinate conjunctions are *and, but, or,* and *nor.* Other coordinate conjunctions include *yet, so,* and *for.*

Mr. Randall *and* Mr. Benaldi are flying to Chicago *and* to Dallas.

Check our supplies inventory, *but* do not order additional items until next week.

I did not receive the notice of the meeting, *nor* did I hear about the planned agenda.

CORRELATIVE CONJUNCTIONS

Correlative conjunctions join words, phrases, and clauses that are grammatically *equal* in importance. They must appear in pairs. These pairs include *both/and, not only/but also, either/or, neither/nor, not/but,* and *whether/or.*

Correlative conjunctions must appear as close as possible to the words they join. The sentence elements following the correlative conjunctions must be parallel in form.

She organizes *not only* her work *but also* her time.
(Incorrect: She not only organizes her work but also her time.)

At the end of the hour, he had completed *neither* the application blank *nor* the information sheet.
(Incorrect: At the end of the hour, he had neither completed the application blank nor the information sheet.)

Either Mary *or* I will attend the meeting.

CONJUNCTIVE ADVERBS

Conjunctive adverbs connect *equal* sentence parts; they link two independent clauses. Since their function is to stress the linkage between these clauses, they are often referred to as transitional expressions. Semicolons usually separate the two independent clauses. (For a list of conjunctive adverbs, see above, Adverbs—Conjunctive Adverbs.)

The semicolon separates the second independent clause from the first one. If the conjunctive adverb is an interruption in the second clause, commas are necessary to set the conjunctive adverb off from the rest of the sentence.

She completes her work on time; *however,* she neglects to proofread her final copy.
She completes her work on time; she neglects, *however,* to proofread her final copy.

SUBORDINATE CONJUNCTIONS

Subordinate conjunctions link dependent clauses to independent clauses (*dissimilar* grammatical elements of a sentence). Dependent clauses (subordinate clauses) depend on the main clause for meaning. They are not complete thoughts, and they cannot stand alone. One clause is usually less important grammatically than the other one.

A subordinate conjunction introduces the dependent clause used as an adverb; it often limits the meaning of the clause. Adverbial clauses may modify any element of a sentence except the noun or nounlike elements. They answer the questions "how," "where," "when," "how often," and "to what extent."

Although I attended the meeting, I did not participate in the discussion.

You should review the draft material *before you begin to edit it.*

The supervisor promoted Sam *because he could do the work.*

When we needed temporary help, we hired Janice.

❑ Use a comma after a dependent clause that appears at the beginning of a sentence. (See Chapter 24, Punctuation.)

Unless we hear from you, we will expect to receive a check within five days.

❑ Do not use a comma when the dependent clause appears after the main clause.

The workshop was canceled *since there were only two people present.*

There are many subordinate conjunctions. The following list contains those most frequently used.

after	inasmuch as	whenever
although	otherwise	where
as	provided	whereas
as if	since	wherever
as soon as	so that	whether
as though	that	which
because	then	while
before	though	who
for	unless	whom
if	until	why
in order that	when	

INTERJECTIONS

Interjections express strong emotions about things that have been said or done. Exclamation marks usually follow the words or the sentences or both the word and the sentence. Commas may also follow interjections within sentences.

Interjections show excitement, disapproval, disagreement, pain, joy, or support. They appear frequently in advertisements. Some common interjections follow:

Boy!	Hooray!	Ouch!
Good!	Impossible!	Wonderful!
Gosh!	Of course!	Wow!
Great!	Oh!	Yes!
Ha!	Oh no!	

Great! Your presentation was the best!

NOUNS

Nouns are the names of persons, places, or things. A sentence may have more than one noun.

COMMON NOUNS AND PROPER NOUNS

Nouns that identify specific persons, places, or things are *proper nouns*. All other nouns are *common nouns*. Proper nouns must be capitalized. A noun may consist of two or more words that form a unit.

Common Nouns	Proper Nouns
bank	The First National Bank
book	*Megatrends 2000*
brother-in-law	Robert
city	Redwood City
girl	Mary
lake	Lake Superior
month	January

CONCRETE AND ABSTRACT NOUNS

Concrete nouns are objects that can be seen, touched, smelled, heard, or tasted. *Abstract nouns* indicate qualities, concepts, ideas, or conditions. They are nonspecific terms that do not have to be sensed physically.

Abstract Noun	Concrete Noun
communication	computer
freedom	flower
initiative	peach
motivation	secretary
stress	table

COLLECTIVE NOUNS

Collective nouns are common nouns that refer to groups of people or objects. Collective nouns may be singular or plural depending on their meaning in the sentence. (See below, Sentence Structure—Subject-Predicate Agreement.)

class	department	staff
committee	group	team
council	majority	
crowd	management	

PLURAL NOUNS AND SINGULAR NOUNS

A noun is *singular* when it names one person, place, or thing. A noun is *plural* when it identifies two or more items. Most singular nouns form their plural form by adding *s* or *es*. Some nouns are referred to as *irregular nouns* and form their plurals according to specific guidelines.

Singular Noun	Plural Noun
attorney	attorneys
brush	brushes
city	cities
girl	girls
glass	glasses
man	men
son-in-law	sons-in-law
typist	typists

POSSESSIVE NOUNS

A *possessive noun* shows ownership, or it indicates a relationship to another noun. To form the possessive, first decide whether the noun is singular or plural. Use an *apostrophe and s* ('s) to write the possessive form of singular nouns *(company's)*. Add only an *apostrophe* to write the possessive form of plural nouns ending in *s (companies')*. Add an *apostrophe and s* to form the possessive of plural nouns that do not end in *s (women's)*.

USES OF NOUNS

Nouns assume different roles and positions in sentences. The functions of nouns are summarized in the examples and explanations below.

NOUNS USED AS SINGULAR SUBJECTS

When a noun is the subject of a sentence, it identifies who or what the sentence is about. In most sentences the subject appears before the verb. A singular subject requires a singular verb.

The *car* is in the office parking lot.

NOUNS USED AS COMPOUND SUBJECTS

A compound subject includes two or more persons, places, or things and indicates who or what the sentence is about. A compound subject usually requires a plural verb.

Honesty and integrity are admirable traits.

NOUNS USED AS DIRECT OBJECTS

A direct object is a noun that usually follows a verb in a sentence. It receives the action of the verb or verb form. The direct object may be singular or plural; the verb or verb form is not changed by the form of the direct object.

Jane obtained the *position.*

Robert owns five *suits.*

NOUNS USED AS INDIRECT OBJECTS

Some verbs, such as *buy, sell, ask, give, send,* and *take,* take an indirect object as well as a direct object. An indirect object usually appears directly after a verb and before a direct object. The indirect object identifies the receiver of the action of the verb.

The sales manager sent the *customer* a refund.

The supervisor gave the *committee* a report.

NOUNS USED AS OBJECTS OF PREPOSITIONS

When a noun is connected to the rest of a sentence by a preposition (e.g., *by, from, to, on, for*), it becomes the object of that preposition. A prepositional phrase consists of the preposition, the object of the preposition, and its modifiers. (See below, Prepositions.) Prepositional phrases occur at various points in a sentence.

The supervisor offered a promotion to *Linda.*

In three *weeks* we expect additional money for the *project.*

NOUNS USED AS APPOSITIVES

An appositive is a word or group of words that explains or renames the noun that it immediately follows. (See Chapter 24, Punctuation.)

Ronald Meyer, our *personnel manager,* introduced two new employees.

NOUNS USED IN DIRECT ADDRESS

A noun used in direct address identifies an individual by name. Such usage draws attention to this individual or gives a statement a personal touch. The noun or nouns are set off by commas. (See Chapter 24, Punctuation.)

Ben, will you please check these figures again.

NOUNS USED AS ADJECTIVES

Nouns used as adjectives appear as modifiers in sentences. The first noun modifies the second noun; the two nouns form a unit.

The *fax* machine was not working.

NOUNS USED AS SUBJECT COMPLEMENTS

Complement nouns (predicate nouns) follow linking verbs such as *am, are, is, was, were, seem,* and *become.* They name the subject again or define the subject more clearly. (See below, Verbs—Linking Verbs.)

Bill is our union *representative.*

It was *Mary.*

PREPOSITIONS

Prepositions link the nouns or pronouns that they take as objects to other words in the sentence. Prepositions always introduce prepositional phrases. Prepositional phrases provide a way to include additional information about nouns, pronouns, or verbs. Prepositional phrases consist of the preposition, the object of the preposition, and the modifiers. Prepositional phrases cannot stand alone.

I received a birthday gift *from my coworkers.*

Prepositional phrases may be used as adjectives or as adverbs. Prepositional phrases used as adjective phrases usually modify nouns or pronouns. They follow nouns, or they appear after linking verbs.

The candidate *with the best resume* was hired.

Her proposal is *among those being considered.*

Prepositional phrases used as adverbial phrases provide answers to "when," "where," "how,", "how often," and "to what extent" questions. They may appear in several locations within sentences—after intransitive verbs, after direct objects of transitive verbs, or at the beginning of sentences.

By May we will have corrected the problem.

The president's office is located *around the corner.*

Some frequently used prepositions are listed here:

about	across	against
above	after	along

among	for	regarding
around	from	round
as	in	since
at	inside	through
before	into	throughout
behind	like	to
below	near	toward
beneath	of	under
beside	off	underneath
besides	on	until
between	onto	up
beyond	opposite	upon
by	outside	with
concerning	out	within
down	over	without
during	past	
except	per	

PHRASAL PREPOSITIONS

Phrasal prepositions or compound prepositions may also link nouns or pronouns to clauses. Use a one-word preposition instead of a compound preposition where possible. Some frequently used combinations of words include the following:

according to	except for	in regard to (not *regards*)
along with	from between	in spite of
apart from	in accordance with	in support of
as for	in case of	instead of
as to	in addition to	next to
as well as	in connection with	on account of
aside from	in consideration of	on behalf of
because of	in contrast with	to the extent of
contrary to	in place of	together with
due to	in reference to	with reference to

USING PREPOSITIONS WITH VERBS

Certain preposition and verb combinations convey distinctive meanings. No rules apply; the combinations have developed through general usage. The following list indicates these idiomatic usages.

accompanied *by* (a person)
accompanied *with* (an item)

abide *by* (a set of terms or decision)

account *for* (give an explanation for something)

abstain *from* (an act)

agree *on/upon* (terms; plan of action)
agree *with* (a person; something)
agree *to* (conditions)
agree *in* (principle)

angry *with* (a person)
angry *about* (a situation)

argue *about* (something)
argue *with* (someone)

arrive *at* (certain time; goal; specific location)
arrive *in* (general location)
arrive *by* (means of transportation)

blame *for* (not *on*)

compare *with* (preferred to *to*)

complementary *to* (not *with*)

comply *with* or compliance *with* (not *to*)

concur *in* (an opinion)
concur *with* (a person)

conform *to* (preferred to *with*)

contract *to* (do something)
contract *with* (someone)

contrasts *with* (when used as verb)
in contrast *to* (when used as a noun)

convenient *to* (a person, place, or thing)
convenient *for* (a purpose)

dates *from* (not *back to*)

deal *in* (business transactions)
deal *with* (behavior; person)

differ *with/on/about* (person; opinion)
differ *from* (dissimilar items)

different *from* (preferred to *than*)

disagree *with* (a person)
disagree *on* (a topic or thing)

disgusted *with* (a person)
disgusted *at* (a thing)
disgusted *by* (behavior)

enter *in* or *on* (record; list)
enter *into* (an agreement; place)

expert *at* (not *in*)

identical *with* (something)
identical *to* (someone)

in accordance *with* (not *to*)

independent *of* (not *from*)

initiate *into* (not *in*)

inquire *of* (ask a person)
inquire *about/after* (a person's welfare)
inquire *into* (investigate something)

insight *into* (not *in*)

interfere *with* (hinder action)
interfere *in* (meddle in others' affairs)

into (motion from outside to inside)

live *in* (a location)
live *on* (subsist on something)
live *at* (a specific address)
live *by* (means of making a living)

offended *at* (an action)
offended *with* (a person)

part *from* (separate from one another—persons or things)
part *with* (give up something)

payment *for* (an item)
payment *of* (a fee or bill)

plan *to* (creates infinitive)
plan *on* (followed by a gerund)

profit *by* (make the most of)
profit *from* (make money)

respond *with* (a reaction)
respond *to* (a procedure)

responsible *for* (an action)
responsible *to* (another person)

retroactive *to* (not *from*)

similar *to* (not *with*)

speak/talk *to* (someone; audience)
speak/talk/discuss/chat *with* (an individual or a small group)
speak *at* (a place)
speak *of* (something)

try *to* (not *and*)

walk *toward* (or *towards*)

PRONOUNS

Pronouns are noun substitutes. They may appear in sentences as subjects, objects, or modifiers. Using pronouns eliminates repeating the nouns each time they are called for. However, pronouns must agree with their antecedents in person, gender, and number.

The *office assistants* took *their* breaks before 10:30 a.m.

We submitted a *proposal*, but we did not get *it* to the office in time.

PERSONAL PRONOUNS

Personal pronouns designate persons or things. References are in terms of person, number, gender, and case. Personal pronouns indicate a person speaking (first person), a person spoken to (second person), and a person or thing being spoken about (third person).

I checked the calculations before *I* submitted them. (first person)

You must send *your* registration material to the corporate office. (second person)

The blue car is *hers*. (third person)

Singular personal pronouns designate one person or thing. *Plural* personal pronouns refer to more than one person or thing.

I plan to audit *their* books tomorrow.

The *gender* of personal pronouns is referred to as masculine (he, his, him), feminine (she, her, hers), and neuter (it).

She enjoys *her* work.

Personal pronouns also have three cases: nominative, possessive, and objective.

NOMINATIVE CASE

The following pronouns are nominative case pronouns:

	Singular	**Plural**
First Person	I	we
Second Person	you	you
Third Person	he, she, it	they

Nominative case pronouns may be used as subjects, as appositives of subjects, or as subject complements. *Subject complements* are words in predicates that define, describe, or identify the subjects.

You must be in the client's office by 3 p.m. (subject)

Two students, Jane and *I,* received A's. (appositive of subject)

It is *I.* (subject complement) (See below, Verbs—Linking Verbs.)

OBJECTIVE CASE

The following pronouns are objective case pronouns:

	Singular	**Plural**
First Person	me	us
Second Person	you	you
Third Person	him, her, it	them

Objective case pronouns may be used as direct objects of verbs, indirect objects of verbs, objects of prepositions, subjects of infinitives, or objects of infinitives.

We hired *her.* (direct object)

I gave *her* a receipt. (indirect object)

Betty faxed the materials *to you.* (object of preposition)

Employees wanted *them* to make decisions. (subject of infinitive)

We plan to contact *her* tomorrow. (object of infinitive)

POSSESSIVE CASE

The following pronouns are possessive case pronouns:

	Singular	**Plural**
First Person	my, mine	our, ours
Second Person	your, yours	your, yours
Third Person	his, her/hers, its	their, theirs

Possessive case pronouns are used to indicate ownership. The pronouns do not have to appear directly before the nouns. No apostrophes are necessary. When gerunds are used as nouns, the pronouns preceding the gerunds are possessive pronouns.

Please send the check to *my* home address. *His* insurance premium increased.

The decision to work for *our* firm is *hers* to make.

I appreciate *your* writing about *my* overdue bill.

RELATIVE PRONOUNS

Relative pronouns join dependent clauses to antecedents. Relative pronouns include *that, who, whom, whoever, whomever, whose, which, what,* and *whatever.*

That restricts the meaning of a sentence. The phrase that it introduces is not set off from the rest of the sentence by commas. This pronoun refers to things or places.

Please give Jane the letter *that* arrived this morning.

Which usually introduces nonrestrictive (nonessential) clauses. This pronoun refers to things.

The brown file cabinet, *which* has been here for nearly 20 years, contains important legal correspondence.

What is often used instead of *that which* or *those which.* This pronoun refers to places and things.

The red folder is *what* I want.

What appeared to be risky turned out to be quite safe.

Who and its related forms refer to people.

The interviewee *who* typed 75 words a minute is Jenny O'Grady.

He was a supervisor *whom* I admired.

Please hire *whomever* you need to get the job completed.

He was a supervisor *whose* management skills were outstanding.

DEMONSTRATIVE PRONOUNS

Demonstrative pronouns designate the specific persons, places, or things to which they refer. The singular forms of demonstrative pronouns are *this* and *that;* the plural forms are *these* and *those.* When demonstrative pronouns are used as adjectives, they are referred to as demonstrative adjectives.

These are the correct answers. (demonstrative pronoun)

These answers are correct. (demonstrative adjective)

INDEFINITE PRONOUNS

Indefinite pronouns do *not* designate specific persons or things; they are not modifiers. When some of these words are used as modifiers, they become adjectives. (See above, Adjectives.)

Everyone arrived early. (indefinite pronoun)

Several employees decided to attend the reception. (adjective)

The following indefinite pronouns are singular and require singular personal pronouns and singular verbs.

another	everybody	one
anybody	everyone	some one
anyone	everything	somebody
anything	neither	something
each	no one	someone
each one	nobody	
either	nothing	

Nothing is gained by rushing through a project.

Everybody is needed to assist us with this emergency.

The following indefinite pronouns are plural and require plural pronouns and plural verbs.

both	others
few	several
many	

Few have indicated acceptance.

Several were disappointed with *their* test results.

The following indefinite pronouns are either singular or plural. Sentence usage determines the form.

all	other
any	some
more	such
none	

All are planning vacations.

All was lost in the fire last week.

INTERROGATIVE PRONOUNS

Interrogative pronouns are used to ask questions. Interrogative pronouns include *who, whom, whose, which,* and *what.* When any of these words appear before a noun, they are interrogative adjectives.

Who is used as a subject or as a subject complement. It is the nominative case form.

Who received the award?

Whom is the object of a preposition or of a verb. It is the objective case form.

With *whom* do you wish to speak?

Whose shows ownership. It is the possessive case form.

Whose is it?

Whose keys were left on the desk?

Which differentiates one thing or person from another. It may be used as a subject or object; its form is the same in the nominative and objective cases.

Which of the two jobs do you prefer?

Choose *which* looks best to you.

What may be used as a subject or an object; its form is the same in the nominative and objective cases. The word refers to things.

What is the most feasible solution?

You said *what?*

REFLEXIVE PRONOUNS

Reflexive pronouns are formed by adding *self* or *selves* to the appropriate personal pronouns. Words such as *myself, ourselves, yourself, yourselves, herself, himself, itself,* and *themselves* are reflexive pronouns. Reflexive pronouns are used to show that the subject and object are the same person. They also are used to emphasize a preceding noun or pronoun.

She made *herself* a list of frequently misspelled words.

The policy increase *itself* was not sufficient.

RECIPROCAL PRONOUNS

Reciprocal pronouns show a relationship to another person. *Each other* and *one another* are the reciprocal pronouns. *Each other* has a reference to two persons or things and *one another* has a reference to three or more persons or things.

In small offices employees know *one another.*

The two chief executive officers already knew *each other.*

VERBS

Complete sentences must include at least one subject and at least one verb. Verbs are the strongest parts of speech; they show action—physical or mental. They indicate what the subject is doing. Verbs also signify a link between the subject and the condition, description, or identity of the subject. Verbs may consist of one word or several words.

Verbs are divided into the following groups: transitive, intransitive, linking, and helping.

TRANSITIVE VERBS

Transitive verbs are action verbs that relay the action from subjects to direct objects. Transitive verbs always require objects. In addition to direct objects, transitive verbs may also have indirect objects. If the objects are pronouns, they must always be in the objective case.

We *completed* the conference arrangements.

My supervisor *gave* me a challenging project.

INTRANSITIVE VERBS

Intransitive verbs are action verbs that do not require direct objects. The subject and verb accomplish their purpose without an object. Intransitive verbs do not direct action toward someone or something else.

Our products *have improved*.

Kayla *proofreads* carefully.

Some verbs may be either transitive or intransitive.

She *types* reports.

She *types* well.

LINKING VERBS

Linking verbs link complements (nouns, pronouns, adjectives) to the subjects they are describing or identifying. The words following these verbs provide meaning to the sentences, but these words are not the recipients of the actions. The two categories of linking verbs are those representing the state of being and those expressing the senses or the condition of the subject. When pronouns are used as complements, they are in the nominative case.

Linking verbs that represent the state of being include *am, is, are, was, were, be, being,* and *been.* When these forms of *to be* verbs are used alone, they join the subject to nouns, pronouns, or adjectives.

Kay *is* the newest employee.

The data *were* accurate.

It is *she.*

Linking verbs also include the sense verbs such as *feel, taste, smell, look, touch,* and *sound.* The verbs *seem* and *appear* are also linking verbs; they express the condition of the subject. These forms of linking verbs join the subject to an adjective. They can be identified by substituting *is* or the appropriate *to be* form for the verb. If the original meaning of the sentence is not changed, the verb is a linking verb.

Our lunch *tasted* good.

That job *appears* difficult.

HELPING VERBS

Helping (auxiliary) verbs help to clarify the meanings of the principal (main) verbs. They are necessary to form verb tenses. More than one helping verb may be involved with the same principal verb. Helping verbs may also serve as main verbs.

The company *is planning* a merger.

I *may approach* John about the problem.

I *might have read* the article.

Julie *does* all the bookkeeping for our firm.

The principal helping verbs include the following:

am	had	ought
are	has	shall
can	have	should
could	is	was
do	may	were
does	might	will
did	must	would

VOICE OF VERBS

The voice of verbs designates the emphasis placed on either the person performing the action or the receiver of the action. Voice is *active* or *passive.*

ACTIVE VOICE

The active voice indicates that the subject of a transitive verb is *performing* the action. The active voice is more assertive than the passive voice. Its use makes it very clear who is doing the acting.

The typist *prepared* the copies.

Bendix Corporation *employs* seasonal workers.

PASSIVE VOICE

The passive voice shows that a subject of a transitive verb is *receiving* the action. The passive voice always involves the appropriate past participle form of a verb and one or more helping verbs. When it is not appropriate to identify or it is not necessary to know the person who performed the action, the passive voice works well.

Several proofreading mistakes *were made* in this report.
(Explanation: At times it might be more tactful to refrain from identifying the person or persons who made the mistakes.)

The work *was completed* when we arrived this morning.
(Explanation: The completion of the work is more important than who completed it.)

Mood

Mood indicates the type of action intended by the verb. The three moods are indicative, imperative, and subjunctive.

INDICATIVE MOOD

Most verbs are in the indicative mood. It is used to state facts or ask questions.

We *plan to hire* five new employees.
Will our company *hire* additional employees?

IMPERATIVE MOOD

The imperative mood is used to make courteous requests or to give commands or instructions. The subject is always "you," which may be omitted.

Will *you* please *take* this report to John.

Take this report to John.

SUBJUNCTIVE MOOD

The subjunctive mood is not used frequently. However, it does appear in formal documents such as resolutions or minutes. The subjunctive verb form *were* is used for *was* when making a statement that expresses an unlikely situation or doubt. Words such as *if, unless, wish,* and *as if* introduce these statements. The subjunctive form *be* is used in *that* clauses following verbs that demand or suggest.

It was moved and seconded that the meeting *be adjourned.*

If I were the supervisor, I would terminate Lawrence.

The chairperson specified that everyone *be given* copies of the report before the meeting.

VERB FORMS

Verbs have three principal forms: the present tense, the past tense, and the past participle. Verbs may change their forms with the tense used, the mood, and the voice. Verbs are either regular or irregular.

REGULAR VERBS

Most verbs are regular. The following rules apply for forming the past tense and past participles of regular verbs.

❏ Add *ed* (or *d* when verbs already end in *e*) to most verbs.

Present	Past	Past Participle
assist	assisted	assisted
raise	raised	raised
complete	completed	completed
work	worked	worked

❏ Change the *y* to *i* and add *ed* to verbs that end with a *y* preceded by a consonant.

Present	Past	Past Participle
study	studied	studied
try	tried	tried

❏ Double the last consonant before adding *ed* to a one-syllable verb that ends with a single consonant preceded by a single vowel.

Present	Past	Past Participle
rob	robbed	robbed
drop	dropped	dropped
hum	hummed	hummed

❑ Double the last consonant before adding *ed* to a verb of two syllables that ends with a single consonant preceded by a single vowel and that is accented on the last syllable.

Present	Past	Past Participle
occur	occurred	occurred
prefer	preferred	preferred

IRREGULAR VERBS

Some verbs do not form their past tenses or past participles by adding *d* or *ed*. Irregular verbs often change spelling when forming past tense forms and past participles. Below is a list of past tenses and past participles of frequently used irregular verbs:

Present	Past	Past Participle
arise	arose	arisen
awake	awoke/awaked	awaked/awoken
be (am/is/are)	was/were	been
bear	bore	borne
become	became	become
begin	began	begun
bite	bit	bitten
blow	blew	blown
break	broke	broken
bring	brought	brought
broadcast	broadcast	broadcast
build	built	built
burst	burst/bursted	burst/bursted
buy	bought	bought
catch	caught	caught
choose	chosen	chosen
come	came	come
dive	dived/dove	dove
do	did	done
draw	drew	drawn
drink	drank	drunk
drive	drove	driven
eat	ate	eaten
fall	fell	fallen
fight	fought	fought
fly	flew	flown
forbid	forbade	forbidden
forget	forgot	forgotten
forgive	forgave	forgiven
freeze	froze	frozen

get	got	got/gotten
give	gave	given
go	went	gone
grow	grew	grown
hang (suspend)	hung	hung
hang (death)	hanged	hanged
have	had	had
hide	hid	hidden
hurt	hurt	hurt
keep	kept	kept
know	knew	known
lay	laid	laid
lead	led	led
leave	left	left
lend	lent	lent
lie	lay	lain
mistake	mistook	mistaken
pay	paid	paid
read	read	read
rid	rid	rid
ride	rode	ridden
ring	rang	rung
rise	rose	risen
run	ran	run
say	said	said
see	saw	seen
set	set	set
sew	sewed	sewn
shake	shook	shaken
shine	shone	shone
show	showed	showed/shown
shrink	shrank	shrunk
sing	sang	sung
sink	sank/sunk	sunk
sit	sat	sat
speak	spoke	spoken
spend	spent	spent
spring	sprang/sprung	sprung
stand	stood	stood
steal	stole	stolen
strike	struck	struck
string	strung	strung
strive	strove	strived/striven
swear	swore	sworn
swell	swelled	swelled/swollen

swim	swam	swum
swing	swung	swung
take	took	taken
teach	taught	taught
tear	tore	torn
think	thought	thought
throw	threw	thrown
wake	waked/woke	waked/woken
write	wrote	written
wear	wore	worn
win	won	won

VERB TENSE

Verb tense involves the concept of time expressed by a verb. Most verbs change form to show these differences in time. The six verb tenses include the present, past, and future tenses (primary tenses) and the present perfect, past perfect, and future perfect tenses (perfect tenses). A progressive form is also used and is sometimes included as a tense.

PRESENT TENSE

The present tense indicates the action is taking place now, or it indicates the action occurs regularly.

She *has* a meeting at 9 a.m.

This report *explains* your concerns.

Jane *works* five days a week.

❑ When the subject is a singular noun, or when the subject is the personal pronoun *he*, *she*, or *it*, add *s* to a present tense verb. When the verb ends in *o*, add *es*. When the verb ends in *s*, *x*, *sh*, *ss*, or *ch*, add *es*.

John *signs* my timecard.
My supervisor *does* the bank reconciliations.
She always *finishes* her correspondence tasks as soon as possible.

❑ Always add *s* to present tense verbs when the pronouns *each*, *every*, *any*, or *one* are used. These pronouns are singular. (See above, Pronouns.)

Each error *causes* unnecessary consequences.

❑ Do not add *s* to a present tense verb when the subject is plural.

The supervisors *manage* the office.

Women *work* for economical reasons.

PAST TENSE

The past tense indicates the action has occurred. The past tense form does not depend on the number or person for its formation. The past participle is not necessarily the same as the past tense form. (See Verb Forms—Irregular Verbs.)

Mary *asked* me to help her last evening.

I *went* to the cafeteria for lunch.

FUTURE TENSE

The future tense indicates an action that will occur in the future. To form the future tense of most verbs, include *will* before the present form of the verb. (Most business writers now use *will* in their business communications; some prefer to use *shall* consistently with the first person and sometimes with the second and third person to emphasize that a policy or instruction must be followed.) The verb form does not change with a plural or singular subject or with the person.

They *will arrive* on Flight 16.

The passenger *will arrive* on Flight 16.

She *will arrive* on Flight 16.

PRESENT PERFECT TENSE

The present perfect tense indicates that an action has taken place in the past and has continued to take place *into* the present. It also indicates that an action has taken place in the past and that it has continued to occur *to* the present time. The words *has* or *have* appear before the past participle.

Our customers *have appreciated* our prompt service.

She *has evaluated* my work to determine my strengths and weaknesses.

I *have requested* those files three times this month.

PAST PERFECT TENSE

The use of the past perfect tense indicates an action that had been completed in the past before another action in the past had occurred. The word *had* appears before the past participle.

Jack *had worked* at the company for three years before the plant closed.

I contacted my attorney only after I *had notified* the insurance company of my accident.

FUTURE PERFECT TENSE

The use of the future perfect tense indicates an action that will be completed in the future before another future event will have taken place. The words *will have* appear before the past participle.

Jane *will have completed* three management courses by the end of the year.

She *will have typed* the report and *collated* the pages before our meeting on Friday.

PROGRESSIVE FORMS

The progressive forms emphasize ongoing action or action in progress. To form the progressive forms, add a helping verb *(am, is, are, was, were)* to the present participle of a verb.

I *am reading* your evaluation of the workshop.

He *was leaving* the office when his supervisor called.

We *will be attending* classes regularly.

VERBALS

Verbals are verb forms used as adjectives, nouns, or adverbs; they are not used as verbs. The three kinds of verbals are *gerunds, infinitives,* and *participles.*

GERUNDS

Gerunds are forms of verbs that end in *ing.* They are always used as nouns in sentences. Gerunds may function as subjects, objects of verbs, complement nouns, objects of prepositions, or appositives. Nouns or pronouns modifying gerunds always assume their possessive forms.

Reading is his major leisure activity. (subject)

John enjoys *reading.* (direct object)

His major leisure activity is *reading* a good book. (subject complement)

He relaxes by *reading.* (object of a preposition)

My major leisure activity, *reading,* is relaxing for me. (appositive)

❏ Avoid dangling introductory gerund phrases. The answer to the question "Who?" must follow the introductory gerund phrase. It must appear *immediately* after the phrase.

After making several calls, I could not locate a computer repair person.
(Incorrect: After making several calls, no computer repair person could be located.)

❏ Omit *the* and *of* in gerund phrases.

In replenishing the petty cash fund, the bookkeeper located two inaccurate transactions.

(Incorrect: In the replenishing of the petty cash fund, the bookkeeper located two inaccurate transactions.

INFINITIVES

Infinitives are verbs with the word *to* before them; for example, *to file*. The *to* may be expressed or implied.

My supervisor wants *to see* you as soon as possible.

She watched him *demonstrate* the new telephone system.

Infinitives have two main tenses—present and perfect. The present tense is used in most situations. The perfect tense indicates that an action has been completed before the action indicated by the main verb.

I helped *to obtain* funding for our annual charity event.

I regret *to have inconvenienced* you yesterday.

Infinitives can be used as nouns, adjectives, or adverbs.

To remain in good health is her goal. (noun)

I needed more experience *to obtain* the job. (adjective)

He is *too nice* to do such a thing. (adverb)

❏ Avoid split infinitives. A *split infinitive* means that a word or words have been placed between *to* and the verb. A split infinitive is acceptable, though, if otherwise the wording of the sentence is awkward or its meaning is unclear. Rewording the sentence, however, may be more effective.

To complete the work properly, you need extra help.
(Incorrect: To properly complete the work, you need extra help.)

❏ Avoid dangling introductory infinitive phrases. The answer to the question "Who?" must follow the introductory phrase. It must appear immediately after the phrase.

To inform our clients of several immediate price changes, we mailed them flyers.
(Incorrect: To inform our clients of several immediate price changes, flyers were mailed.)

PARTICIPLES

Participles are verbals that function as adjectives; they can modify nouns or pronouns. Participial phrases are either restrictive (essential) or nonrestrictive (nonessential). (See Chapter 24, Punctuation.) There are three participle tenses—present, past, and perfect.

Present	**Past**	**Perfect**
working	worked	having worked
going	gone	having gone

PRESENT PARTICIPLE

Present participles end in *ing*.

The *growing* demand for our products means additional jobs.

The woman *answering* the telephone is Mrs. Crandall.

PAST PARTICIPLE

Past participles end in *ed* for regular verbs. Irregular verbs are formed in other ways. (See above, Irregular Verbs.)

The *completed* copies were ready for the meeting.

Answered correctly, the telephone is a powerful communication device.

The idea *presented* by Mr. DeWitt pleased the board of directors.

PERFECT PARTICIPLE

Perfect participles consist of the past participle preceded by the word *having*.

Having built a reputation for service, we have to work hard to maintain it.

Having answered the telephone correctly, Mrs. Crandall proceeded to answer the caller's questions.

❑ Place participial phrases close to the nouns they modify. Avoid dangling participles.

Surveying the employees, I identified numerous employee complaints.
(Incorrect: Surveying the employees, numerous complaints were identified.)

SENTENCE STRUCTURE

Effective written communication begins with the sentence. A sentence must be complete yet concise.

TYPES OF SENTENCES

Sentences fall into four general groups—declarative, imperative, interrogative, and exclamatory.

DECLARATIVE

A declarative sentence states facts or opinions; it ends with a period.

The procedures manual is ready for distribution.

IMPERATIVE

An imperative sentence requests or demands action; it ends with a period. Some imperative sentences sound like questions. These sentences do not require a response in words; they suggest or require an action by someone.

Come to our telecommunications seminar next week.

Will you please call Bob Jennings.

INTERROGATIVE

An interrogative sentence asks a question; it ends with a question mark.

Are you going to attend the CPS seminar next month?

EXCLAMATORY

An exclamatory sentence shows emotion; it ends with an exclamation point. Business writers do not use the exclamatory sentence frequently.

What a great job that was!

SENTENCE ELEMENTS

A sentence consists of words or word groups. Every sentence must have a subject and a predicate.

SUBJECT

The subject identifies "who" or "what" the sentence is about. If a subject is being described or modified, the subject and the modifiers become the complete subject.

California is a large state.

I supervise two employees.

Our branch office in California will be closing in April.

PREDICATE

The predicate indicates something about the subject. The verb is the most important part of speech in the predicate. If a verb has an object, an indirect object, or modifiers, these become part of the predicate.

We *enjoyed the luncheon.*

The company *is expanding its operation.*

DIRECT OBJECT

The direct object usually follows a verb in a sentence. The subject acts on an item through the verb. The direct object answers the questions "what?" or "who?" to an action verb.

She accepted the *award.*

INDIRECT OBJECT

The indirect object precedes the direct object. A sentence may have a direct object and an indirect object. An indirect object indicates *to whom* or *for whom* or *to which* or *for which* the action of the verb is being performed.

We wrote *them* a check.

Please offer *him* a refund for the returned merchandise.

COMPLEMENTS

Complements name or describe the subject. They appear in the predicate. Complements that follow linking verbs are predicate nouns or predicate adjectives; these are often called subject complements. The complements complete the meaning intended by the verbs.

He is *a personnel manager.*

This is *she.*

My supervisor called the discussion *a disaster.*

MODIFIERS

Modifiers describe or limit other parts of speech.

Three companies have requested *our sales* brochures.

Your statement is a *very positive* testimonial for *our* service.

Everyone agreed the *new* project would be *an exciting challenge.*

WORD GROUPS

Word groups involve phrases and clauses. These word groups assume various roles in sentences.

PHRASES

Phrases are word groups without subjects and verbs, but the phrases themselves can be used as nouns, adjectives, or adverbs.

She enters data *at an incredibly fast speed.*
(adverb)

Supervising office professionals is challenging.
(noun)

CLAUSES

Clauses are word groups that include both subjects and predicates. *Independent clauses can* be complete sentences—they can stand alone. *Dependent* (subordinate) *clauses* cannot stand alone as sentences. They depend on the independent clauses to which they are joined for their meanings. Subordinate conjunctions link the dependent clause or clauses to the independent clause or clauses.

We missed our deadline.
(independent)

Because we missed our deadline, the report was incomplete. (dependent)

SENTENCE LENGTH

Sentence length varies; it depends on the type of sentence. The types of sentences include the simple sentence, compound sentence, complex sentence, and compound-complex sentence.

SIMPLE SENTENCE

A simple sentence is a complete thought with a subject and a verb. The subject or verb may be singular or compound (more than one). The sentence can stand by itself.

Beth types.

A computer improves office efficiency.

A computer and a fax machine improve office efficiency.

COMPOUND SENTENCE

A compound sentence involves two or more independent clauses linked by a coordinate conjunction. Each independent clause can stand alone. (See above, Conjunctions—Coordinate Conjunctions.) (See Chapter 24, Punctuation.)

A computer improves office efficiency, but it requires a skilled operator.

COMPLEX SENTENCE

A complex sentence involves an independent clause or clauses and one or more dependent clauses. The independent clause is a simple sentence with a single or compound subject and a single or compound verb. The dependent clause depends on the independent clause. Subordinate conjunctions link the two clauses.

When Dr. Sforza returns from the meeting, I will give her your message.

Carmen, who is one of our best office assistants, planned a surprise retirement party for her supervisor.

COMPOUND-COMPLEX SENTENCE

A compound-complex sentence contains a dependent clause linked to two or more independent clauses. Subordinating conjunctions connect dependent clauses to independent clauses.

Please let me know if my flight arrangements have been confirmed; if they have, contact the hotel to make a reservation.

SENTENCE ERRORS

SENTENCE FRAGMENT

When phrases or dependent clauses are treated as if they were independent clauses and are followed by periods, sentence fragments result.

A job that includes several steps and is usually billed as one procedure may be billed separately.
(Incorrect: A job that includes several steps and is usually billed as one procedure.)

RUN-ON SENTENCE

When two independent clauses run back to back without a punctuation mark separating them, they form a run-on sentence.

> Thank you for your order. We will process it within three days.
> or
> Thank you for your order; we will process it within three days.
> (Incorrect: Thank you for your order we will process it within three days.)

COMMA SPLICE

A comma splice is a punctuation error that results when two complete sentences are joined with a comma. The statements could be made into two sentences; they could be separated by a semicolon; or they could be separated by a comma and a conjunction.

> I arrived late at the office this morning. My supervisor arrived late also.
> or
> I arrived late at the office this morning; my supervisor arrived late also.
> or
> I arrived late at the office this morning, and my supervisor arrived late also. (Incorrect: I arrived late at the office this morning, my supervisor arrived late also.)

SUBJECT-PREDICATE AGREEMENT

The subject and predicate in a sentence must agree in number.

❑ Use a singular predicate with a singular subject. Use a plural predicate with a plural subject.

> *She works* in the marketing division.

> Three sales *representatives work* in the Wheeling branch office.

❑ Use a plural predicate when two or more subjects are separated by *and*.

> Good executive *secretaries and* administrative *assistants are* always in demand.

❑ Use a plural or singular predicate when two or more subjects are separated by *or* or *nor*. The predicate must agree with the subject closest to it.

> Neither the *desk nor* the filing *cabinets have been delivered.*

> The other *secretaries or Jane has* to solve the problem.

❑ Use a singular predicate with such words as *each, everybody,* and *nobody*.

> *Each* of the office workers *is* eligible.

❑ Disregard word groups such as *together with, as well as,* or *in addition to* when determining singular or plural predicate forms.

Mr. Nakaguki, together with several of his associates, *is arriving* on Flight 18.

❏ Use a singular predicate with a collective noun if the group acts as a group.

The *Safety Committee suggests* additional lighting in the south and east corridors.

❏ Use a plural predicate if *each* member of a group does the same thing but does it independently of the others in the group.

The *staff are surveying* office professionals to determine areas that need improvement.

❏ Use both the plural and singular predicate forms in a sentence if the subjects require separate forms.

The *catalogs were mailed,* but *one was returned* because the addressee was unknown.

❏ Use a plural predicate when the subject is *a number.* Use a singular predicate when the subject is *the number.*

A number of secretaries *are going to lunch.*

The number of work-related accidents *has decreased.*

❏ Use a singular predicate with periods of time or sums of money expressed as total units.

Five dollars is the amount I plan to donate for Sylvia's gift.

Fifteen years with one company *is* a good record.

PARALLELISM

Elements in a sentence that function similarly should be in the same grammatical form; for example, *ing* words matching *ing* words.

My supervisor prepared the final bid proposal; Shane Tomlinson verified the supporting data.
(Incorrect: My supervisor prepared the final bid proposal; the supporting data were verified by Shane Tomlinson.)

She listed these job tasks on her resume:
• Organized statistical data for grant proposals
• Arranged appointment schedules for seven council members
• Coordinated travel arrangements for all company personnel
(Incorrect:
She listed these job tasks on her resume:
• Organizes statistical data for grant proposals
• Arranged appointment schedules for council members
• Responsible for travel arrangements for all company personnel)

DANGLING MODIFIERS

When introductory verbal phrases do not modify specific words, they are known as dangling modifiers. To avoid dangling modifiers, place the word being modified *immediately* after the verbal phrase.

Having accepted the extra job responsibilities, I found that my workload had increased.
(Incorrect: Having accepted the extra job responsibilities, my workload increased.)

After waiting for two hours, I learned the flight was canceled.
(Incorrect: After waiting for two hours, the flight was canceled.)

MISPLACED MODIFIERS

When modifiers such as words, phrases, or clauses become separated from the words that they modify, they are referred to as misplaced. This often creates sentences that are unclear or improbable. Place the modifiers as close as possible to the words they modify.

Only the secretary was asked to attend the meeting.
The secretary was *only* asked to attend the meeting.
The secretary was asked to attend the meeting *only*.
(Explanation: Each of the sentences may be correct; the meaning determines which is appropriate.)

At the meeting the speaker told us about getting the CPS certification.
(Incorrect: The speaker told us about getting the CPS certification at the meeting.)

As we interviewed the candidates from the personnel agency, we found several that we liked.
(Incorrect: We interviewed several candidates from the personnel agency that we liked.)

❏ Check the meaning of the subject to determine whether it is singular or plural. Some words end in *s* but are not plural.

The *news* of the pending merger *is* surprising.

CHAPTER 24

PUNCTUATION

Using punctuation correctly is a basic skill in written communication. External punctuation appears at the end of a sentence. It includes periods, question marks, and exclamation points. Internal punctuation marks a break in the written material. It includes apostrophes, asterisks, braces, brackets, colons, commas, dashes, diagonals, ellipsis, hyphens, parentheses, quotations, and semicolons.

EXCLAMATION POINT

GENERAL RULES

❑ Do not overuse the exclamation point in business documents.
❑ Do not use a period *and* an exclamation point at the end of a sentence.
❑ Space twice after an exclamation point at the end of a sentence in typed material.
❑ Never use double or triple exclamation points for emphasis.
❑ In sentences that end with a quotation, place the exclamation point outside the quotation marks.
❑ When the complete sentence is a quotation or a parenthetical exclamation, place the exclamation mark inside the quotation marks or the final parenthesis.

END OF SENTENCE

❑ Use an exclamation point at the end of a sentence, clause, phrase, or word to show strong emotions such as enthusiasm, disbelief, excitement, or authority. It is often used in advertising copy for emphasis.

Congratulations! You got the job!
Bargains for the entire family!

WITHIN A SENTENCE

❑ Use an exclamation point immediately following an exclamation within a sentence. Place parentheses around the exclamation. Do not space after an exclamation point if quotes or a parenthesis follow.

I spent the day at Pacific Bell (what a fantastic building!) where I visited every department.

PERIOD

GENERAL RULES

❑ Leave two spaces after a period at the end of a sentence in typed matter.
❑ Leave a space after an abbreviation within a sentence, but do not leave a space within an abbreviation; for example, a.m.
❑ Do not leave a space before or after a decimal point.
❑ Leave a space after the period that follows an initial.
❑ Do not use a second period when an abbreviation with a period ends a sentence.
❑ Place a period within the final quotation marks.
❑ In a sentence that ends with an abbreviation and that requires a question mark or exclamation point, place the punctuation mark *after* the period that ends the abbreviation. Do not leave a space between that period and the final question mark or exclamation point.

ABBREVIATIONS

❑ Periods are used after most abbreviations.

Mr.
e.g.
Co.

❑ Omit periods in abbreviations that represent governmental agencies, businesses known by their initials, radio and television stations, military service areas, and organizations or clubs. Omit periods in two-letter state postal abbreviations.

NATO
CBS
NJ
IBM
NAACP

DECIMAL POINTS

❑ Use a period to separate dollars and cents.

$5.25

❑ Use a period to separate whole numbers from decimal fractions.

8.25 feet
12.75 percent

END OF SENTENCE

❑ Use a period to mark the end of a declarative sentence.

I will order the supplies on Monday.
Our last meeting was productive.

❑ Use a period at the end of a command. (A gentle command is a reminder rather than a forceful order.)

Please respond to our request for payment by June 30.

❑ Use a period at the end of a courteous request. The answer implies that an action will be taken or disregarded; it does not require a "yes" or "no" response.

Would you please contact Sheryl tomorrow.

❑ Use a period at the end of an indirect question.

My supervisor wanted to know if I could work until 6 p.m. this evening.

ENUMERATIONS

❑ Do not use a period after letters or numbers enclosed in parentheses within a sentence.

The secretary's administrative tasks are (a) supervising staff, (b) preparing budget reports, and (c) organizing conferences.

❑ Use a period at the end of each line that contains a complete sentence in enumerations, whether or not the lead-in sentence ends with a colon. Do not place a period at the end of an incomplete sentence.

The following guidelines will assist you:
1. Use two-letter state abbreviations for all the addresses.
2. Type the address in all capital letters.

Hint: It is also acceptable to use periods at the end of every line without distinguishing between complete or incomplete sentences. Periods are also sometimes used only at the end of the last enumerated item; in this case, commas or semicolons are used with the other items. Although such variations are permissible, it is still important to be consistent.

INITIALS

❏ Use a period after an initial in a person's name. Leave spaces between initials.

Mary A. Randall
C. D. Bryan

PARAGRAPH HEADINGS

❏ Use a period at the end of a paragraph heading. The heading may begin at the left margin or it may be indented from the left margin. Capitalize only the first letter of a paragraph heading.

Travel funds. Travel funds include letters of credit, traveler's checks, and company credit cards.

QUESTION MARK

GENERAL RULES

❏ Space twice after a question mark at the end of a sentence.
❏ Use only one mark of punctuation at the end of a sentence. If the sentence ends with a period for an abbreviation, add the question mark after the period.
❏ Space once after a question mark that comes within a series of short statements.
❏ Do not space before or after a question mark within parentheses.
❏ Do not space after a question mark that is followed directly with another mark of punctuation.

END OF SENTENCE

❏ Use a question mark at the end of a direct question that requires an answer.

When is the next meeting scheduled?

❏ Use a question mark at the end of a rhetorical sentence for which no answer is expected.

How can we possibly complete that work by tomorrow?

❏ Place a period rather than a question mark after an indirect question.

My supervisor asked when we would be ready to send the newsletter to the printer.

❑ Place a question mark at the end of a sentence that has a direct question appended to it. Separate the question with a comma, dash, or colon.

You've already informed the Traffic Department about the delay, haven't you?

❑ Use a period at the end of a sentence that is considered a courteous request. The answer does not require a "yes" or "no" response but implies an action will be taken or not taken.

May we call you next week with our final figures.

❑ When a sentence includes a question that is in quotes or parentheses, place the question mark inside the quotes or parentheses. Place the question mark outside the quotation marks or the parentheses if the entire sentence, not just the quoted material or the material within the parentheses, is a question.

Mary asked, "When are vacation schedules due?"
Who suggested, "Use the funds for the charity drive"?

❑ Use a question mark at the end of a question that implies a longer and more complete question.

We had only one question. Why?

❑ Use a question mark at the end of a statement that sounds like it should be a question.

In spite of all the evidence on hazards to one's health, he still continues to smoke?

QUESTIONS WITHIN QUESTIONS

❑ Use only one question mark at the end of a question that includes another question. Place the question mark inside the quotes.

Why do you always ask, "How will we ever make our deliveries on schedule?"

QUESTIONS WITHIN SENTENCES

❑ Place a question mark at the end of each of a series of short questions within a sentence. Do not capitalize the first word in each question unless it is a proper noun or a complete sentence. Space once after a question mark that appears within a sentence.

Are you familiar with accounting software? word processing? database? spreadsheet?

❑ Express doubt or uncertainty with a question mark enclosed in parentheses at the point the uncertainty occurs.

Last June (?) she presented the initial plan for our consideration.

Hint: Be careful when using a question mark to indicate doubt. Do not use it in a sarcastic manner or to question an individual's integrity.

APOSTROPHE

GENERAL RULES

❏ The apostrophe is used to indicate possessives, plurals, and the omission of letters in contractions or shortened words.

The CPAs' offices were located on First Avenue.

Do you know when they're planning the meeting?

If you enjoy steaks and seafood, I recommend the Surf 'n' Turf restaurant.

PLURALS OF SINGLE LETTERS

❏ Use the apostrophe and "s" to form the plurals of lowercase letters.

We had difficulty differentiating between her t's and f's.

❏ Add an apostrophe and "s" to form the plurals of the capital letters A, I, M, and U. Do not use the apostrophe and "s" to form the plurals of other capital letters.

Use M's to avoid confusion with Ms.
We have added all the Fs and Gs in our database mailing list.

POSSESSIVES

❏ Use the apostrophe to indicate the possessive case of nouns and indefinite pronouns.

Our company's profits increased this year.

SINGLE QUOTATION MARKS

❏ Use an apostrophe as a single quotation mark when double quotation marks have already been used in a sentence.

Mr. Rothman said, "The last 'Municipal Investments' should be sent to our client's office."

SYMBOLS

❏ Use the apostrophe to indicate feet or minutes in such documents as technical tables, order forms, or invoices.

26′ 3″   26 feet 3 inches
12′ 2″   12 minutes 2 seconds

YEARS

❏ Use an apostrophe for numbers that have been omitted in expressing years.

The company showed its first profit in '89.

❏ Do not use an apostrophe to indicate an omission in figures that represent a span of years. Use a hyphen between the years.

She served as president during 1980–87.

ASTERISK

GENERAL RULES

❏ Use an asterisk to indicate material being referenced and to note the reference itself. Leave one space after the asterisk.

The 1991 figures* show a marked increase in payroll costs.

❏ Place the asterisk before a dash or a closing parenthesis.

Mr. Decker called (he wanted the last cost figures for the Dobson account*) so I gave him your message.

❏ Place the asterisk after a comma, semicolon, colon, or period.

When you have finished with the Kirchener report,* please return it to the Sales Division.

FOOTNOTES

❏ Use an asterisk within the copy to indicate that a footnote reference or explanation appears below. Asterisks are often used in tables or diagrams. Limit the number of footnotes to three per page. Two asterisks represent a second footnote on a page; three asterisks represent the third.

923   4,563   2,100*

❏ Do not leave a space after the asterisk in a footnote reference.

*Figures represent 1991 data; data for 1992 were not available at the time of publication.

OMISSIONS

❑ Use three asterisks to show the omission of an unprintable word. Leave one space before the three asterisks. Do not space between them. If the omission is at the end of the sentence, place the ending mark of punctuation after the asterisks. Do not leave a space between the last asterisk and the ending mark of punctuation.

The union representative became disgruntled after hours of nonproductive talks and called the chief negotiator a ***.

BRACE

GENERAL RULES

❑ Use a brace to show that items belong to the same group. Braces may be used in pairs or singly.

❑ Use the brace character found on most computer keyboards. It is the same size as the parenthesis. To make the brace fit the material, stack the braces until they reach the height necessary to enclose the material.

❑ Use a brace to join several items or to group figures or letters in tables and graphic displays.

$$\left. \begin{array}{l} \{ A = 5 \} \\ \{ B = 10 \} \\ \{ C = 25 \} \end{array} \right. \text{Grade Distribution}$$

❑ Use the brace in legal documents.

$$\left. \begin{array}{l} Tom\ Smith \\ Defendant \end{array} \right\}$$

BRACKETS

GENERAL RULES

❑ Use brackets to enclose figures, words, phrases, or sentences that must be set apart from the rest of the sentence. Brackets are always used in pairs.

❑ Leave one space *before* an opening bracket and one space *after* a closing bracket. Do not leave a space after the closing bracket if another mark of punctuation follows it.

According to company policy [Section 4, Item 21], smoking is not allowed in the public areas.

EDITORIAL COMMENTS

❑ Use brackets to set off an explanation or an editorial comment inserted in quoted material. This explanation or editorial comment is not part of the original text.

The consensus is that this multimedia production [Images and Sounds] is the best on the market today.

Completion of the forms is not only time-consuming but *formidable.* [Emphasis added by reviewer.]

❑ Use brackets to correct errors in quoted material.

The last time a delegation of foreign guests visited our city was April 1990. [1991—Ed.]

❑ Use brackets to indicate references or publication dates of articles that were printed previously. These comments are often found in letters to the editor or follow-up articles. Place the period outside the closing bracket when the statement within the brackets is not a complete sentence.

B. J. Mathison is obviously well informed about his subject ["Corporate Strategies," September 1992].

ERRORS

❑ Use brackets to indicate that a grammatical error, a misspelled word, or a factual error is quoted *exactly* as it was submitted. The item in question is followed by the Latin word "sic" enclosed in brackets. The word "sic" means *thus* or *so* and indicates the original text was quoted verbatim.

The customer wrote, "The product I purchased from you last week is all ready [sic] saving my company money."

PARENTHETICAL REMARKS WITHIN PARENTHESES

❑ Substitute brackets for parentheses if a statement is already enclosed within parentheses. Enclose the shorter parenthetical remark in brackets. Use the parentheses for the larger parenthetical statement.

(See Chapter III [Microcomputer Software] for additional references.)

My supervisor's suggestion (to submit budget proposals by February 1 [see minutes of the Finance Committee of November]) was finally approved.

VERBATIM TRANSCRIPT

❏ Use brackets to indicate comments or actions observed when a verbatim transcription of a speech or testimony is made.

We are pleased to honor Marilyn Raye for her 35 years of outstanding work for this company. [Standing ovation.]

COLON

GENERAL RULES

❏ Use a colon to introduce the material that follows, such as a list, enumeration, or quotation.
❏ In typed matter, leave two spaces after a colon, but do not space before it.

Please remember one thing: you need medical insurance.

The office assistant ordered the following supplies (rush request): 12 reams of beige paper, 2 printer replacement ribbons, and 2 boxes of calculator ribbons.

EXPLANATORY SENTENCES

❏ Separate two independent clauses with a colon to show that the first clause will be restated or explained by the material that follows the colon. Do not capitalize the word that follows the colon if the second clause explains or repeats the first clause.

We have only one alternative: operating expenses must be decreased substantially.

❏ Do not use a colon between two independent clauses when a connective word or words join the two independent clauses together; instead, use a semicolon.

I have only one alternative to present; namely, our operating costs must be decreased substantially.

❏ Do not use a colon between two independent clauses when the second clause shows a relationship to the first clause or develops the first clause further. Use a semicolon.

I have only one alternative to present; perhaps you have some additional ideas.

LISTINGS

❏ Use a colon to introduce a list of items or examples. Common expressions used in these introductions are "the following," "as follows," and "these." Capitalize the first word on each line of a list that follows a colon. Do not capitalize the word that follows a colon if the words following do not make a complete sentence. If the first word that follows a colon is a proper noun or adjective or the pronoun "I," capitalize it.

The following topics were discussed:
Time management
Problem solving
Motivation

These were the topics discussed: time management, problem solving, and motivation.

❏ Do not use a colon if a sentence with an expression such as "the following," "as follows," and "these" is separated from the listing by another sentence. Use a period after each sentence.

Participants will find the following topics helpful. They have been selected from evaluations of previous workshops.
Time management
Problem solving
Motivation

❏ Do not use a colon if an expression such as "the following," "as follows," or "these" is used at the beginning of a sentence and a considerable number of words separate the expression from the listing. Use a period before beginning the listing.

The following procedures were adopted by members of the Policies and Procedures Committee and presented to the president for approval.
1. Requests for tuition reimbursement must be presented in writing to the employee's supervisor one month before the course begins.
2. Arrangements for released time to attend classes must be made with the employee's supervisor.

❏ Do not use a colon if the listing appears after a verb. Do not separate a verb from its object.

Our nominations are Jane Worth, president; Tom Calloway, vice president; and Heather Turner, secretary-treasurer.

❏ Do not use a colon if the listing follows a preposition. Do not separate a preposition from its object.

Our telephone training session consists of hardware introduction, tips for effective use, and sources of assistance.

LONG QUOTATIONS

❏ Use a colon to introduce a long statement or quotation. Capitalize the first word in a quotation that comes after the colon. Capitalize the first word in each of the remaining sentences in the quotation.

John Barton stated: "We have had a long period of low growth. This means we must review our reinvestment plans and reallocate our capital."

❑ Quotations of four or more typewritten lines following a colon are not enclosed in quotation marks. They are typed as separate paragraphs indented from the left and right margins.

PARTS OF LETTERS

❑ Use a colon after a salutation in a business letter with mixed punctuation. (Mixed punctuation is a formatting style that includes marks of punctuation after the salutation and the complimentary close.)

> Dear Ms. Wong:
> Ladies and Gentlemen:

❑ Separate the writer's initials from the typist's with a colon.

> JMM:tm

PUBLICATIONS

❑ Use a colon to separate the place of the publication from the name of the publisher in academic bibliographies and footnotes. (See Chapter 18, Reports.)

> New York: Random House, 1992.

❑ Use a colon to separate the volume number from the page number in bibliographies and footnotes.

> 15:125–130

❑ Separate literary titles and subtitles with a colon.

> *Business English: A Practical Approach*

RATIOS

❑ Use a colon to show ratios or proportions. The colon can be read as the word "to." Do not space before or after the colon.

> During that accounting period, the profit and loss sharing ratio was 3:2.

TIME

❑ Separate hours and minutes with a colon.

> His plane will arrive at 3:30 p.m.

COMMA

GENERAL RULES

❏ A comma can help to differentiate between the writer's central thought and any material that interrupts or explains it. It is also used to set off words, dates, numbers, and locations from the rest of the sentence.

There is, however, a difference of $10,985 between the two days' deposits.

❏ The comma always appears inside quotation marks. (See section on Quotation Marks, below.)

If any business knows the meaning of the saying "Time is money," it is a financial institution.

❏ Omit the comma before ellipses. (See section on Ellipses, below.)

She reported, "We must have temporary help in sales, accounts receivable, accounts payable . . . by the end of this month."

❏ Place a comma outside brackets or parentheses. (See sections on Brackets and Parentheses.)

After we reviewed the dress code policy (Regulation 33.4), we voted to change it.

ADDRESSES

❏ Use a comma to divide parts of addresses or geographical locations. Do not use a comma between the state or two-letter state abbreviation and ZIP Code. Place a comma after a ZIP Code when it appears with an address within a sentence.

We mailed all materials to 220 Williams Road, Casper, Wyoming 70062.

We mailed all materials to 220 Williams Road, Casper, Wyoming 70062, last week.

ADJECTIVES

❏ Use a comma to separate two or more adjacent adjectives that independently modify a noun. If the word "and" can replace the comma, the comma is necessary. Do not use a comma between the adjectives if another conjunction already separates them.

Betty is a competent, enthusiastic supervisor.

Betty is a competent and enthusiastic supervisor.

Hint: Adjectives that refer to number, color, size, age, or geographical location are usually not separated by commas from the nouns they modify.

❏ Do not use a comma between the last adjective and the noun.

We'd like to plan a unique, exciting, dynamic presentation.

APPOSITIVES

❑ Use commas to set off appositives or appositive phrases. An appositive identifies or describes the noun or pronoun it follows. If the appositive is not needed to identify the noun or pronoun previously used, use a comma to enclose the appositive.

Mrs. Keoto, a member of the Policies Committee, shared preliminary plans for the revisions of policies and procedures.

❑ Do not use a comma to set off appositives or appositive phrases if the appositive is necessary to identify the noun or pronoun it follows. (This type of restrictive appositive answers the key question: Which one?)

The book *Investing in Stocks in Today's Market* is being reordered. *(The appositive indicates which book is being reordered.)*

I talked with my instructor Basilia Melendez to obtain additional practice materials. *(The appositive indicates which instructor is involved.)*

❑ Do not use a comma to set off one-word appositives.

We managers need to respond to our employees' concerns as soon as possible.

BUSINESS LETTERS

❑ Use a comma after the salutation in a personal letter. In business letters, use a colon.

Dear Rebecca, (personal)
Dear Rebecca: (business)

❑ Use a comma after the complimentary close in a business or personal letter. Capitalize only the first word in a closing.

Sincerely yours,

COMPANY NAMES

❑ Use commas to set off such words as "Inc." and "Ltd." when they are used in company names. When the words "Inc." and "Ltd." appear within the sentence, place a comma before and after them.

Random House, Inc., is located in New York City.

❑ Do not use a comma as part of a company's formal name if the company does not include it. Check the letterhead to verify a company's preference.

We made the last loan payment to B. D. Harris Inc. last month.

Compound Sentences

❏ Use a comma (if there are no other commas in the sentence) to separate two independent clauses of a compound sentence connected by the conjunctions "and," "but," "nor," "for," "or," "so," and "yet." Use a comma only when the material on both sides of the conjunction can stand alone; each side must contain a subject and a predicate.

I started the project five weeks ago, but I have had difficulty finishing it. (*Both phrases separated by the conjunction can stand alone.*)

I started the project five weeks ago but have had difficulty finishing it. (*Only the phrase preceding the conjunction can stand alone.*)

❏ Use a comma when the subject "you" is understood in an imperative sentence with two independent clauses. An imperative statement contains a command.

Read the document by Wednesday, and forward your comments with the document to Bill.

❏ Do not use a comma to separate two independent clauses when the dependent clause that begins the sentence applies equally to both independent clauses.

After you finish talking with the applicant, set a date for the first interview and ask him to complete the application form. (*"After you finish talking" refers to the verbs* "ask" *and* "set.")

Contrasting Expressions

❏ Use a comma to set off a contrasting expression from the rest of the sentence. These expressions are often preceded by such words as "not," "yet," or "never."

She improved her typing speed, yet her spelling is still poor.

Dates

❏ Use commas to separate days of the week, calendar dates, and the year. When only the month and the year are used, the commas are optional.

We will meet on Tuesday, May 14, 1992, to make preliminary plans for our national conference.

We will meet in May, 1992, to make preliminary plans for our national conference.

or

We will meet in May 1992 to make preliminary plans for our national conference.

❏ Do not use commas to enclose any form of a date that stands alone.

He contacted me on March 16 to ask for an extension on his loan.

Our last contract was prepared in 1988 by Rodney Dunlop.

DIRECT ADDRESS

❑ Use a comma to set off words of direct address that introduce or conclude a sentence.

Tom, your report at today's presentation was outstanding.

❑ Use commas to set off parenthetical forms of direct address.

You understand, Jon, that promotions depend on job performance.

GEOGRAPHIC LOCATIONS

❑ Use commas to set off geographical locations, such as the name of a city and state or city and country, from the rest of the sentence.

Our branch offices are located in Orlando, Florida, and Knoxville, Tennessee.
He worked in Berlin, Germany, for two years.

INTRODUCTORY EXPRESSIONS

❑ Use a comma after an introductory dependent clause to separate it from the independent clause that follows. Dependent clauses have subjects and verbs but do not convey the entire thought intended by the writer. Some of the words used to introduce dependent clauses are:

after	however	until
although	if	when
as	inasmuch as	whenever
as soon as	in case	whereas
because	provided	wherever
before	since	whether
even though	though	while
following	unless	

Although the details have not been fully developed, we expect to have an outstanding conference this fall.

❑ Do not use a comma to set off the dependent clause if it appears after the central thought or independent clause and is essential for the meaning of a sentence.

You can work at home if you have a computer and a modem.

❑ Use a comma to set off an introductory prepositional phrase from the rest of the sentence. If the phrase is short (five or fewer words), the comma may be omitted. However, if the comma is necessary for clarity, include it. A prepositional phrase is made up of a preposition and an object. The prepositions that follow are often used to begin introductory prepositional phrases.

about	between	off
above	by	on
after	down	over
among	during	to
around	except	under
at	from	until
before	in	up
below	into	upon
beside	of	with

At the beginning of a new job, I always worry about my performance.

❏ Use a comma to set off an introductory prepositional phrase of any length when it contains a verb form.

After I started the audit, I knew I would need all the bank reconciliations for the past year.

❏ Do not use a comma after an introductory prepositional phrase if the words in the sentence are not in their normal order.

After the congratulatory remarks came the biggest surprise of my life.

❏ Use a comma to set off an introductory infinitive phrase from the rest of the sentence. An infinitive phrase is made up of a verb preceded by "to." Do not use a comma when the phrase becomes the subject of the sentence.

To understand the computer software, I need to take a course at company headquarters.

To understand the computer software would have required a course at company headquarters.

❏ Use a comma to set off an introductory participial phrase. A participial phrase is a verb form used as an adjective.

Pleased with the results, they encouraged us to continue our experiments.

❏ Use a comma after introductory words that are not essential to the meaning of the sentence. These words are often transitional expressions and may function as connectors. Many of these words can also be used paranthetically within a sentence. Some of these words include:

accordingly	after all	anyway
according to	all things considered	as a matter of fact
actually	also	as a result

as a rule	in fact	on the other hand
at any rate	in general	remember
besides	in my opinion	second
by the way	in other words	so
consequently	in short	still
even so	in the meantime	that is
finally	meanwhile	then
first	namely	therefore
for example	naturally	too
fortunately	nevertheless	under the circumstances
frankly	no	without a doubt
however	no doubt	yes
incidentally	obviously	yet
in effect	of course	

Under the circumstances, we will allow you an extra week to send us your payment.

Yes, I agree that Shane's proposal is the best one for the project.

❏ Use a comma to set off an interjection from the rest of the sentence.

Oh, what will we do now?

❏ Use a comma after the introductory phrase even if the phrase follows another type of introduction. Ignore the first set of introductory words.

My supervisor indicated that on March 5 he would be issuing new safety regulations.

My supervisor indicated that to draw our attention to the importance of safety, he would be issuing new safety regulations.

NAMES

❏ Use a comma to separate a surname from the first and middle names when the name is transposed.

Young, Kim A.

Randall, Donald A., Jr.

❏ Use commas to set off "Jr." from an individual's name.

Donald Crowell, Jr., visited plants in Hong Kong and Tokyo.

❏ Do not use commas to set off Roman numeral suffixes.

John Saunders III is arriving today.

NONRESTRICTIVE AND RESTRICTIVE CLAUSES

❏ Use commas to set off a nonrestrictive clause or phrase. A nonrestrictive clause or phrase is not essential to the central thought. Do not use a comma to set off restrictive phrases and clauses. Restrictive (essential) phrases and clauses cannot be separated from the rest of a sentence without changing the meaning of the sentence.

Jill Rosen, the one with computer experience, is the best candidate for the managerial position. (nonrestrictive)

An individual with computer experience is the best candidate for the managerial position. (restrictive)

❏ Use commas to set off nonrestrictive adjective clauses from the rest of the sentence. Adjective clauses begin with such words as "who," "which," "whose," "of which," or "that." Nonrestrictive adjective clauses are frequently introduced by "which;" restrictive relative clauses by "that." The word "who" can introduce either restrictive or nonrestrictive clauses.

The books that are shelved in the conference room are available for the employees.

At our last meeting, which was held in the board room, we nominated five people to become members of company committees.

❏ Use commas to set off nonrestrictive adverbial clauses. If the adverbial clause is restrictive (essential), do not use a comma. Adverbial restrictive clauses provide answers to the questions "when," "how," and "why."

My supervisor accepted my resignation, although he seemed reluctant to do so.

Please complete the application by May 1 so that we may schedule you for an interview the following week.

NUMBERS

❏ Use a comma to separate a number with more than three digits.

We had 1,500 responses to our survey.

❏ Use a comma to separate unrelated numbers when both of them require figures.

On April 1, 127 entries for our grand prize drawing had already been submitted.

❏ Do not use commas to separate digits in years; policy, account, or serial numbers; page numbers; or telephone numbers.

You will find that Policy Nos. 928643 and 929958 have been canceled.

Omissions

❏ Use a comma to indicate the omission of words understood by the parallel construction of the preceding statement.

Yolanda is organizing the computer files; Marie, the manual.

Parenthetical Expressions

❏ Use commas to set off parenthetical words and phrases. Parenthetical expressions are words, phrases, or clauses that are not essential to the meaning of a sentence. If omitted, they would not alter the basic meaning or affect the grammar of the sentence. Parenthetical expressions are used for emphasis or to express the writer's thoughts about the statement. They may interrupt the sentence or act as transitional expressions. Transitional expressions help relate the present idea to a previous one. (See section above on *Introductory Expressions.*)

Most people, for example, know they need a will.

Sales are available, however, if you know where to look for them.

❏ Do not use commas to set off parenthetical expressions if the thought is not interrupted by them.

We were indeed fortunate to have your field manager spend an extra day with us.

❏ Do not use a comma to separate "too" from the remainder of the sentence when it is the last word in a sentence or clause. Use a comma to separate "too" from the rest of the sentence when it appears within the sentence.

Are you working on Saturday too?

You, too, need a vacation this summer.

❏ Do not use a comma to set off the word "too" from the rest of the sentence when it means *an excessive amount.*

There were too many people in the room.

Professional Degrees

❏ Unless restricted by customs of a particular organization, use commas to set off professional titles from an individual's name.

Kayla Williams, Ph.D., will be speaking at the next meeting of the Personnel Network Association.

Janice Van Doyle CPS is the administrative assistant to the president.

QUOTATIONS

❑ Use commas to set off quotations from the rest of the sentence.

"If you fax this report," the supervisor said, "it will reach our client today."

REPEATED WORDS

❑ Use a comma between words that are repeated.

Everyone needs quiet time, quiet time without interruptions of any kind.

SERIES

❑ Use a comma to separate a series of three or more words, phrases, or clauses. The final comma before the conjunction is important; its omission can affect the meaning of the sentence.

We may need to send money to close a business transaction, to cover general expenses, or to assist our agents when they are away from home.

❑ Do not use a comma to separate items in a series if the items are already connected by a conjunction.

We plan to hire receptionists and data-entry clerks and secretaries.

❑ Do not use a comma to separate two related items that are considered a single unit within a series.

The lunch menu consists of an appetizer, a main course, salad, bread and butter, various beverages, and dessert.

❑ Use commas to set off the abbreviation "etc." (The abbreviation "etc." means *and so forth.*)

Mileage coupons, discounts, package deals, etc., can be used to lower travel costs.

❑ Write the name of an organization with multiple elements the same way the organization writes it. Some firms omit the comma before the "and"; others do not use a comma before the ampersand (&). Use the official letterhead to determine the company's preference.

Walker, Schroeder, Davis and Broehmer
or
Walker, Schroeder, Davis, and Broehmer

TIME ZONES

❏ Use commas to set off a time zone from the clock time.

When it is 2 p.m., PST, it is 5 p.m., EST.

DASH

GENERAL RULES

❏ Use a dash as a substitute for a comma, semicolon, colon, or parentheses only when there is an abrupt break in the sentence or a need to emphasize an item. Do not use it as a principal mark of punctuation. Never substitute it for the correct punctuation because you are unsure about which mark to use.

❏ Dashes are always used in pairs within a sentence; do not substitute a comma for the second dash.

❏ Be sure the sentence would make sense even if the phrase within the dashes was omitted.

❏ In typewritten copy, two unspaced hyphens indicate a dash. The dash appears as one solid line in copy set by a professional printer.

I think—no, I am positive—that I called the printer on Tuesday.

❏ Omit marks of punctuation before the opening dash.

On January 5—the same day the company was founded—we announced our merger with Allied Chemicals International.

❏ Do not begin a new line with a dash. If it is necessary to break a sentence onto two lines, the dash should appear at the end of the line.

When office politics interfere with your work, ask yourself what you can do to avoid—or prevent—the problem.

❏ When the parenthetical phrase comes at the end of the sentence, do not use a closing dash. Use the normal closing mark of punctuation instead.

We announced our merger with Allied Chemicals on January 5—the anniversary of the company's founding.

❏ When the parenthetical phrase occurs within a sentence, precede the closing dash with the appropriate end mark of punctuation—question mark, period (in abbreviations), or exclamation point. If a complete sentence is enclosed in dashes, do not capitalize the first word unless it is a proper noun or adjective or the first word of a full-sentence quotation.

When Mr. Simpson comes in on Friday—do we have Sue's calculations yet?—I'll have the figures ready for him.

INTERRUPTION OF THOUGHT

❏ Use dashes to indicate a change of direction or an interruption of thought in a sentence.

Our recent shipment—I don't have the purchase order number right now—arrived in unsatisfactory condition.

❏ Use dashes to separate a nonessential remark from the rest of the sentence.

Her ability to communicate—she had many leadership qualities as well—was the major reason for her success.

❏ Use a dash to separate an afterthought from the rest of the sentence.

If Mr. Simpson can come in on Friday, I'll have the figures ready for him—we'll still need Sue's calculations.

❏ If a question or exclamation breaks off abruptly before it is completed, use a dash followed by a question mark or an exclamation mark. If the sentence is a statement, use a dash alone followed by two spaces.

Do you want to tell him or—?

I thought— Well, that won't be possible today.

OMISSIONS

❏ Use a dash to replace part of an offensive word.

Where the h— is he?

QUOTATION SOURCES

❏ Use a dash before an author's name or a source of information that follows a quote. Place the dash before the name or source.

We must go forward . . . but we cannot kill the past in doing so, for the past is part of our identity and without our identity we are nothing.
                                                                    —Carlos Fuentes

SPECIAL EMPHASIS

❏ Use a dash to emphasize a related or parallel point.

That's our final offer—now we'd like to hear yours.

❏ Use a dash after a statement to append additional information.

The schedule of accounts receivable—the list showing credit customers and their balances—is useful for large or small businesses.

❑ Use a dash after a single word for special emphasis.

Communication—that is the key to success.

❑ Use dashes when it is important to repeat a statement or remind a reader of a fact.

Our meeting will be in Room C12—not the conference room—at 2 p.m. today.

SUBSTITUTION FOR OTHER PUNCTUATION MARKS

❑ Use dashes to set off an appositive when commas might result in confusion with the commas within the appositive phrase.

Three traits—listening, following directions, and demonstrating initiative—are crucial to the success of the office professional.

❑ Use a dash when the appositive appears at the end of the sentence rather than adjacent to the expression it amplifies.

Two companies offered me similar salaries and working conditions—AHT and Braun's.

❑ Place a dash before a statement that summarizes several thoughts, attributes, ideas, or concerns.

Access to high-technology resources, skilled workers, and reputable educational institutions—these are the reasons we are relocating to Austin.

❑ Substitute a dash for a semicolon to separate two closely related sentences when greater emphasis is intended.

Mary spent a week preparing the graphics—there were so many errors I had to do them all over again.

❑ Substitute dashes for parentheses when greater emphasis is desired. Dashes and parentheses are sometimes used interchangeably.

Please confer with Tina Young—the lead member of the project group—whenever you need additional information.

DIAGONAL

GENERAL RULES

❏ Use a diagonal to indicate that either one or the other item may be used. It is also used to separate numbers or to indicate the shortened form of a word.
❏ Do not space before or after the diagonal.

ABBREVIATED FORMS

❏ Use a diagonal for commonly used shortened forms.

c/o Sales Division
A/P ledgers

CHOICE

❏ Use a diagonal between words to show that either one is acceptable.

A professional must meet his/her deadlines.
Please call and/or write.

NUMBERS

❏ Use a diagonal between two numbers to indicate a fraction.

3/4 page

❏ Use a diagonal to separate the numbers in the shortened form of a date.

8/5/93

ELLIPSES

GENERAL RULES

❏ Use ellipses to indicate omissions in quoted material to draw attention to specific points, or after an unfinished statement.
❏ Use three periods to designate an ellipsis. Type ellipses with spaces before, after, and between each period. Omit other punctuation before and after ellipses.

The author recommends: "Organize your job search . . . and make each contact count."

DISPLAY

❑ Use ellipses to draw attention to certain points. Ellipses are particularly effective in advertising.

Read *The Secretary* magazine for up-to-date reviews of
. . . technology
. . . office techniques
. . . business methods

QUOTED MATERIAL

❑ If an omission in quoted material occurs at the end of a sentence that normally requires a period, use four periods. Leave a space between the period (end mark of punctuation) and the first period of the ellipses. Leave two spaces between the last period of the ellipses and the next sentence.

"Education is an opportunity. . . .   Every learning experience provides a chal-lenge."

HYPHENS

GENERAL RULES

❑ Hyphens are used in compounds and numbers and to indicate syllabification. You may need to consult a dictionary to determine current usage. Practices vary, and changes occur as words become more commonly used.
❑ Do not leave a space before or after a hyphen that appears within a word or number.

CLARITY

❑ Use a hyphen to avoid confusion in the pronunciation or meaning of a word.

recover from the flu *but* re-cover a sofa
a chicken coop *but* an agricultural co-op

COMPOUND ADJECTIVES

❑ Use a hyphen to connect a compound modifier that appears before the noun it modifies. Do not hyphenate the compound modifier when it appears after the noun it modifies.

A well-known speaker was invited.
The speaker is well known.

❏ Do not hyphenate a compound modifier that includes an adverb ending in "ly."

newly minted coins
heavily edited copy

❏ Use a hyphen to show that two words are used as a unit to describe a noun.

the two-letter state abbreviation
an out-of-print brochure

❏ Use a hyphen to identify words or figures appearing in a series that modify the same noun.

one-, two-, or three-page reports

❏ Do not use a hyphen with compound adjectives that have become commonly used.

Social Security number
high school athlete

COMPOUND NOUNS

❏ Use a hyphen to form a compound noun that consists of two or more words and indicates that the two have been combined into one unit.

AFL-CIO
secretary-treasurer

❏ Use a hyphen to form a compound noun that consists of two or more words containing other parts of speech.

free-for-all
editor-in-chief

❏ Do not use a hyphen to form a compound noun that consists of chemical terms, military rank, or certain governmental positions.

sodium chloride
sergeant at arms
attorney general

NUMBERS

❏ Use a hyphen to join compound numbers 21-99 when they must be spelled out.

thirty-three
one hundred fifty-nine dollars

❏ Use a hyphen to separate the numerator from the denominator of a fraction that is written out and used as an adjective. Do not use a hyphen to indicate a fraction if either the numerator or denominator already has a hyphen in it.

a two-thirds majority
one thirty-second of an inch

PREFIXES AND SUFFIXES

❏ Use a hyphen to join a prefix or suffix to the main word in the compound.

all-points bulletin
co-chair
president-elect

❏ Always use a hyphen to join the prefixes "self" "ex," and "quasi" to the main word.

ex-husband
self-evaluation
quasi-legal

RANGES OF LETTERS AND NUMBERS

❏ Use a hyphen to designate a range of letters, numbers, or dates.

Policy Numbers 52-80 were not renewed.
The last names all began with the letters A-F

SINGLE LETTERS

❏ Use a hyphen to join a single letter to the main word.

U-turn
X-rated

SPELLING

❏ Use a hyphen when spelling out a word or a name.

c-o-n-v-e-n-i-e-n-t

SYLLABIFICATION

❏ Use a hyphen to divide a word into syllables.

of-fice
pro-fes-sion-al
man-u-al

❏ Use a hyphen when dividing a word at the end of a line to show that it is to be completed on the next line.

PARENTHESES

GENERAL RULES

❑ Use parentheses to indicate an interruption in a sentence consisting of nonessential material that does not contribute to the central thought. Using parentheses is less abrupt than using dashes. Parentheses are also used to refer a reader to another location.

❑ Use parentheses sparingly. When too many appear in the same text, they lose their effectiveness. Single words, phrases, or entire sentences may be placed within parentheses.

❑ Use a question mark or exclamation point with the material within parentheses if the mark of punctuation at the end of the sentence is different from the one required in parentheses.

The property on Barnes Avenue (are you aware of its location?) was sold yesterday.

ABBREVIATIONS

❑ Use parentheses to define an abbreviation.

The CPS (Certified Professional Secretary) exam will be held next week.

DIRECTIONS

❑ Use parentheses to enclose directions.

Please mail this contract this afternoon. (Send it certified with return receipt requested.)

EXPLANATIONS

❑ Use parentheses to enclose an explanatory word or phrase that is not part of the sentence.

We saw the announcement in *The Marshfield* (Wisconsin) *News Herald*.

The terms are 2/10, n/60, which gives you ten days (until June 12) to take advantage of the discount.

FOOTNOTES

❑ In footnotes, parentheses may be used to set off the city of publication, the publisher, and the date.

*Studs Terkel, *Great Divide* (New York: Pantheon, 1988), p. 115.

LISTINGS

❏ Use parentheses around numbers or letters to designate listed items. Always use a letter if numbers already identify the main paragraph. Do not capitalize incomplete statements following a colon unless the word that follows is a proper noun or adjective.

New employees were assigned the following tasks: (1) checking supplies, (2) taking inventory, and (3) updating files.

NUMBERS

❏ Use parentheses to designate numbers that represent the same amount that is written in words. Some business or legal documents require this format.

The policy will be in effect in thirty (30) days.
We agreed to sell the company for four million dollars ($4,000,000.00).

PARENTHETICAL REMARKS

❏ Use parentheses to designate parenthetical remarks. A dash can also be used. Dashes and parentheses are often interchangeable.

Microcomputers (often referred to as PCs) are indispensable in offices.

REFERENCES

❏ Use parentheses to indicate a reference that is not part of the main sentence. When the material within parentheses is a complete sentence, capitalize the first word within the parentheses. Place a period before the closing parenthesis if the material represents a complete sentence. When the material within parentheses is an incomplete sentence, do not capitalize the first word. Place the period outside the closing parenthesis if it is not a complete sentence.

The statistics proved our original theory. (See Figure 12.)

TIME PERIODS

❏ Use parentheses to enclose time periods.

The crisis in the Persian Gulf (1990–1991) was stressful for many families.

QUOTATION MARKS

GENERAL RULES

❏ Use quotation marks to emphasize words or statements, to identify titles, and to indicate the use of another person's words.

❏ Use quotation marks in pairs before and after a word, phrase, sentence, or paragraph.

"We analyzed the figures for you," said Mr. Madsen.

❏ Place a question mark or an exclamation point inside the closing quotation marks when it applies to the quoted material only.

"Would you like to be a part of the project team?" asked the supervisor.

❏ Place a question mark or exclamation outside the closing quotation marks when the entire sentence is a question or exclamation.

Which of you asked, "Where is the latest copy of the company newsletter"?

❏ Semicolons and colons always appear outside the closing quotation marks. Commas and periods appear inside.

There are several reasons why Nancy was selected as "Employee of the Month": she is helpful, courteous, and friendly.
"Sheryl," said Jon, "please stop by my office."

DIRECT QUOTES

❏ Enclose short direct quotes within quotation marks. Use a comma to separate the quotation from the source of the quotation. Capitalize the first word of the quoted material. If the quotation is broken up by intervening text, do not capitalize the second part of the quotation.

"When you finish with the budget," said Mrs. Roberts, "show me the new figures."

❏ Use quotation marks around words, sentences, or paragraphs that are quoted verbatim from the original source.

In yesterday's paper, the mayor said, "Water conservation is the responsibility of every citizen in this city."

❏ Do not use quotation marks to enclose indirect quotations.

The supervisor asked how many had completed the survey.

but

The supervisor asked, "How many of you have completed the survey?"

EMPHASIS

❏ Use quotation marks to emphasize a word or phrase that is itself being discussed. The words may also be underscored. An underscore is an indication to the printer that the underscored material should be placed in italics.

The words "there" and "their" are often confused.

❏ Use quotation marks to enclose words that are used for special effect.

Every office should have a "gofer."

❏ Use quotation marks or italics to define terms. Use quotation marks for the term to be defined; use the underscore for the definition itself.

A "gofer" is a *person who goes for things.*

❏ Use quotation marks to identify words or phrases that suggest a different style from the context.

"Garbage in, garbage out" refers to the inaccurate entering of data on a computer.

INSTRUCTIONS

❏ Use quotation marks to draw attention to directions or special instructions. Capitalize the first letters of such directions or instructions. Some of the words used to introduce these directions or instructions are "marked," "signed," "entitled," "headed," and "labeled."

The package was marked "Special Delivery."

PUBLICATIONS

❏ Use quotation marks to enclose titles of minor works such as newspaper and magazine articles, speeches, unpublished dissertations, essays, stories, poems, and chapters of books. The books or periodicals in which they appear are underscored.

An article entitled "Automated System Speeds Billing Procedures" appeared in a recent issue of *Modern Office Technology.*

SPECIFIC NAMES

❏ Use quotation marks to enclose names of radio or television programs within a series.

"Dead Letter" is my favorite episode in the series *Murder, She Wrote.*

❏ Use quotation marks to enclose titles of paintings, drawings, photographs, and sculptures.

Leonardo's "Mona Lisa" is one of the most famous paintings in the world.

❑ Use quotation marks to enclose titles of short musical compositions and songs.

He sang the "Figaro" aria from *The Barber of Seville.*

❑ Use quotation marks or underscores to enclose names of ships or airplanes.

Please make reservations for me on the "Queen Mary."

SYMBOLS

❑ Use quotation marks to indicate inches or seconds in tables or technical material. Place the period outside the quotation marks.

The original diagram was only 3″ × 6″.

SEMICOLON

GENERAL RULES

❑ A semicolon is stronger than a comma, but it is not as strong as a period.
❑ Leave one space after a semicolon.
❑ The semicolon always appears outside quotation marks, parentheses, or brackets.

CLOSELY RELATED SENTENCES

❑ Use a semicolon to separate closely related independent clauses that are not joined by a conjunction.

The copier was not working; it needed extensive repairs.

EXPLANATORY STATEMENTS

❑ Use a semicolon to precede an abbreviation or word that introduces an explanatory or summarizing statement.

She has excellent time management skills; e.g., she updates her "to do" list every evening before leaving work.

SERIES

❑ Use a semicolon to separate long or potentially confusing items in a series.

The officers of our Legal Secretaries Association are: Kathy Sadler, president; Bonnie Luke, vice president; Shelby Moran, secretary; and Donna Burns, treasurer.

TRANSITIONAL EXPRESSIONS

❑ Use a semicolon to separate independent clauses of a compound sentence when the second clause begins with such words as "accordingly," "consequently," "furthermore," "in fact," "however," "moreover," "nevertheless," "therefore," and "yet." Place the comma after the connecting word.

Several staff members are out sick this week; therefore, the work must be delayed.

WITH COMMAS

❑ Use a semicolon rather than a comma to separate independent clauses of a compound sentence when one of the clauses already has a comma.

If you find a suitable fax machine, notify the accounts payable manager; but do not pay for it until she has assigned a purchase order number.

UNDERSCORE

GENERAL RULES

❑ Use the underscore sparingly for emphasis. Do not overuse it.
❑ Use an underscore to substitute for italics. If words and punctuation are underscored, the printer will set them in italics.
❑ Use a solid line to indicate an underscore. Include commas, periods, colons, and semicolons in the underscore only if they are intrinsic to the underscored material.

FILMS AND PROGRAMS

❑ Use an underscore to designate titles of videotapes, television and radio series, or films. Use quotation marks to designate individual titles of television or radio programs within the series.

Did you watch 60 Minutes last week?

PUBLICATIONS

❑ Use an underscore to designate books, magazines, pamphlets, newspapers, and long musical works. Titles may also be typed in all capital letters; no underscore is necessary when the title appears in all caps.

We subscribe to The Secretary magazine every year.

SPECIAL EMPHASIS

❑ Use an underscore to identify words or figures used as words or figures. Quotation marks may also be used.

The word <u>parallel</u> appears on most lists of frequently misspelled words.

My name is spelled with a second <u>n.</u>

❑ Use an underscore to emphasize examples or words being defined.

Successful employees are <u>enthusiastic</u>—not uncooperative.

SPECIFIC NAMES

❑ Use an underscore to designate the names of ships, airplanes, or trains. Quotation marks can also be used.

Howard Hughes built an experimental aircraft known as the <u>Spruce Goose</u>.

INDEX

ABOUT PROFESSIONAL SECRETARIES INTERNATIONAL®

Founded in 1942, Professional Secretaries International® (PSI®) is the nation's leading professional secretarial organization with more than 40,000 active members. Representing all office professionals, PSI is dedicated to improving the quality of work life within the office environment by providing opportunities for educational, personal, and professional growth.

PSI certifies secretaries with the Certified Professional Secretary® (CPS®) rating and has recently established the Office Proficiency Assessment and Certification™ (OPAC™) program. Discounts on educational products, professional seminars, and conferences are offered. *The Secretary*®, PSI's official magazine, alerts secretaries to new ideas, office products and services, and new technology applications for implementation on the job.

Professional Secretaries Week®, originated by PSI in 1952, is observed annually the last full week in April.

For more information, write or call:

Professional Secretaries International
10502 NW Ambassador Drive
P.O. Box 20404
Kansas City, MO 64195-0404
(816) 891-6600
Fax (816) 891-9118